# INNOVATIONS IN PLAY THERAPY

# INNOVATIONS IN PLAY THERAPY

## Issues, Process, and Special Populations

*edited by*

## Garry L. Landreth

Published by
Brunner-Routledge
29 West 35th Street
New York, NY 10001

| UK | BRUNNER-ROUTLEDGE |
|---|---|
| | *A member of the Taylor & Francis Group* |
| | 27 Church Road |
| | Hove |
| | E. Sussex, BN3 2FA |
| | Tel: +44 (0) 1273 207411 |
| | Fax: +44 (0) 1273 205612 |

**INNOVATIONS IN PLAY THERAPY: Issues, Process, and Special Populations**

4 5 6 7 8 9 0


A CIP catalog record for this book is available from the British Library.

⊗      The paper in this publication meets the requirements of the ANSI Standard
        Z39.48-1984 (Permanence of Paper)

**Library of Congress Cataloging-in-Publication Data**

Available from the publisher


ISBN: 1-56032-881-9 (paper)

# Contents

## II. CLINICAL INNOVATIONS IN PLAY
## AS A DIAGNOSTIC TOOL

## III. INNOVATIVE PROCEDURES IN PLAY THERAPY

## IV. PLAY THERAPY WITH SPECIAL POPULATIONS

# About the Editor

**Garry L. Landreth, Ed.D., LPC, RPT-S.**, internationally known for his writings and work in promoting the development of play therapy, is a Regents Professor in the Counselor Education Department at the University of North Texas. He is the founder and director of the Center for Play Therapy, the largest play therapy training program in the world, and has conducted workshops focusing on play therapy throughout the United States and in Canada, Europe, China, South Afirca, and South Korea.

Dr. Landreth's more than 100 publications and videos include three books on group counseling and seven books on play therapy. His award winning book *Play Therapy: The Art of the Relationship* has been translated into Chinese, Russian, and Korean. Dr. Landreth is a licensed professional counselor, licensed psychologist, founding member of the Board of Directors of the Association for Play Therapy, and a registered play therapy supervisor. He has been the recipient of numous professional honors and awards, and he is a frequent featured speaker at national and state conferences.

## Contributors

**Meredith K. Ater, M. Ed.**, is a Child Therapist for Family Service Inc. in Fort Worth, Texas.

**Patricia A. Chuck, M. Ed.**, is a Child Therapist for Focus on Youth in Cincinnati, Ohio.

**Jodi Crane, M.A.**, is Assistant Professor of Counseling in the Department of Human Services for Lindsey Wilson College in Columbia, Kentucky.

**Kay Draper, Ph.D., LPC.**, is Assistant Professor in the Department of Counseling and Psychological Services at Georgia State University in Atlanta, Georgia.

**Geraldine J. Glover, Ph.D., LPCC, RPT-S.**, is a private practice Play Therapist in Santa Fe, New Mexico and Adjunct Professor at the College of Santa Fe in Santa Fe, New Mexico.

**Tina Edling Harris, M.Ed.**, is a counselor at Bradfield Elementary School in Garland, Texas.

**Pat Ledyard Haynes, M.Ed.**, is an Academic Mentor for the Education and Health Science Department at the University of Arkansas in Fayetteville, Arkansas.

**Shirley Hendricks, Ed.D.**, is a Professor Emeritus in the Department of Counseling at Southwest Missouri State University in Springfield, Missouri.

**Linda E. Homeyer, Ph.D., LPC, RPT-S.**, is an Assistant Professor in the Department of Educational Administration and Psychological Services at Southwest Texas State University in San Marcos, Texas.

**Shaunda Peterson Johnson, M.Ed., LPC, RPT.**, is a Treatment Specialist for the Arrow Project in Porter, Texas.

**Elizabeth Murphy Jones, Ph.D.**, is a private practice Play Therapist in Fort Worth, Texas and Adjunct Professor at the University of North Texas in Denton, Texas.

**Nancy Pittard Jones, Ed.S., RPT.**, is a School Counselor for the Gwinnett County Schools in Tucker, Georgia.

**Shu-Chen Kao, Ph.D.** is an Assistant Professor in the Department of Guidance and Counseling at the National Chang-Hua University of Education in Chang-Hua, Taiwan.

**Jeffrey W. Klein, M.Ed., LPC**, is a therapist for the Austin-Travis County MHMR Partial Hospital Program in Austin, Texas.

**Ashley Tyndall-Lind, Ph.D., LPC-S, RPT-S, NCC.**, is the Director of Clinical and Professional Services at the Genesis Women's Shelter in Dallas, Texas and Adjunct Professor at the University of North Texas in Denton, Texas.

**Wynne Mittledorf, M.Ed., LPC.**, is Care Manager at Magellan Behavioral Health in Dallas, Texas.

**Brenda Niel, M.Ed., RPT.**, is a private practice play therapist in Chattanooga, Tennessee.

**Lessie Perry, Ph.D., LPC, RPT-S.**, is a private practice play therapist in Denton, Texas and Adjunct Professor at the University of North Texas in Denton, Texas.

**Phyllis Post, Ph.D., LPC, NCC, NCSC.**, is a Professor in the Department of Counseling, Special Education, and Child Development at the University of North Carolina at Charlotte in Charlotte, North Carolina.

**Daniel S. Sweeney, Ph.D., LPC, MFCC, RPT-S.**, is an Assistant Professor in the Counseling Department at George Fox University in Portland, Oregon.

**Ross J. Tatum, M.D.**, is a Child Psychiatrist in private practice in Fort Worth, Texas.

**Pamela Webb, M.Ed., LPC, LMFT.**, is a Special Education Counselor for the Austin Independent School District in Austin, Texas.

**JoAnna White, Ed.D., LPC, RPT-S.**, is a Professor in the Department of Counseling and Psychological Services at Georgia State University in Atlanta, Georgia.

# Preface

Although there are many other play therapy texts, the topics and issues dealt with in this text are unique. The objective is to bring together essential information related to important issues, dynamics of the process, and special populations in play therapy. The specific dimensions of play that contribute to the therapeutic process of play therapy are explained and cultural issues which need to be considered in working with different populations of children are discussed with some suggested modifications in the typical play therapy approach. Play therapists are seeing increasing numbers of children who have been placed on various medications. Therefore, a chapter is included to help play therapists to become more conversant with psychopharmacological issues related to children.

Play therapists are constantly confronted with legal and ethical issues beginning with the arrangements necessary to initiate therapy with a child. An initial concern, also, involves issues related to working with parents and how to utilize parents in the helping process. Therefore, these dimensions are presented in an overview format to help the play therapist focus on essential considerations.

The difficult dimension of diagnosis is made clear through specific descriptions of how the play therapist can use play behaviors to diagnose physical abuse, sexual abuse, and emotional maladjustment in children. Common play themes of abused children are presented to help the play therapist identify such problems and a new scale for determining sexual abuse is described. In the play therapy process, it is essential that play therapists recognize and understand common patterns of play, types of play behaviors, and typical themes that emerge during play therapy with abused children.

This book is unique in exploring the process and accompanying research results for conducting short-term, intensive group play therapy and focuses on play therapy with special populations of aggressive acting-out children, autistic children, chronically ill children, traumatized children, selective mute children, adults with dissociative identity disorder child alters, and the elderly. The book also describes an innovative approach to becoming a traveling play therapist.

Although this book provides an emphasis on play therapy with special populations, the relationship with the child is the foundational basis for therapeutic change in all play therapy experiences. The relationship with the child always takes precedent over the use of techniques or structuring of the child's play. The essence of change for the child lies in the significance and impact of the relationship as experienced by the child in the developing encounter with the play therapist who understands and accepts the child as a unique person worthy of respect. Nothing of therapeutic significance occurs outside the perceived importance of the relationship to the child.

When given the opportunity within the safety of a caring relationship, children will provide direction for their own growth. It is within the context of this philosophy that this book was written. The issues, diagnostic procedures, and process of play therapy with special populations of children and adults are based on an unwavering belief in the profound healing capacity of the relationship as supported by a multitude of research studies. It is hoped that the information in this book will help play therapists to understand the special needs of children and thus to feel more secure in their relationships with children.

PART *I*

# SPECIAL CONSIDERATIONS
# FOR THE ROLE
# OF THE PLAY THERAPIST

# 1

# Facilitative Dimensions of Play in the Play Therapy Process

## GARRY L. LANDRETH

There are over 4,000 languages communicated throughout the world (Comrie, 1987), and although play is not listed anywhere as one of these languages, it should be. Children from all parts of the world use play to express themselves. Their efforts to communicate are facilitated by the use of toys as their words and play as their language. During play, children can express what they want to express in any way they wish. Verbal words are sometimes used in addition to the child's play, but are not necessary for the child's communication to be complete. Free play interaction serves as the child's vocabulary and thus can be viewed as a limitless language of self-expression because of the unlimited subtle nuances possible in play and the absence of specific rules of meaning found in verbal communication.

Play is the singular central activity of childhood, occurring at all times and in all places. Seldom do children sit down and talk to each other for very long periods of time without doing anything active. Children do not need to be taught how to play, nor must they be made to play. Play is spontaneous, enjoyable, voluntary, and non-goal directed. In order to make children's play more acceptable, some adults have invented a meaning for play by defining it as work. The attitude is that children must be accomplishing something or working toward some important goal acceptable to adults—that play can only be important if it somehow fits what adults consider important in their world. It is regrettable that play has been identified by many writers as children's work. Just as childhood has intrinsic value and is not merely preparation for adulthood, so too, play has intrinsic value and is not dependent on what may follow for importance. In contrast to work, which is goal focused and directed toward accomplishment or completion of a task by accommodating to the demands of the immediate environment, play is intrinsically complete, does not depend on external reward, and assimilates the world to match the individual's concepts as in the case of a child pretending a block of wood is an airplane (Landreth, 1991).

## DEFINITION OF PLAY

Play is an integral part of childhood, a unique medium that facilitates the development of expressive language, communication skills, emotional development, social skills, decision-making skills, and cognitive development in children. Play is also a medium for exploration and discovery of interpersonal relationships, experimentation with adult roles, and understanding of one's own feelings. Play is the most complete form of self-expression developed by the human organism.

Play is a complex multidimensional series of behaviors that change significantly as children grow and develop, and we have yet to fully describe what play is and what it is not. Play is often easier to recognize and observe than it is to define. A problem that arises when attempting to derive an acceptable definition is that there is no single set of behaviors that includes the many types of play.

Erikson (1977) defined play as a situation in which the ego can deal with experiences by creating model situations and that can also master reality by experimenting and planning. Moustakas (1981) described play as "a form of letting go, merging freely into experience, immersing oneself totally in the moment so that there is not distinction between self and object or self and other. Energy, life, spirit, surprise, fusion, awakening, renewal, are all qualities of play. . . . it is free flowing-form, opening and expanding in unexpected and unpredictable ways" (p. 20).

Coleman and Skeen (1985) defined play as free of space, time, and role limitations; self-directed and spontaneous; and involving internal rewards of self-expression and self-discovery of one's capabilities. Following the suggestions of various authors, play can be defined as an activity that is intrinsically motivating, bringing pleasure and gratification simply for the joy of doing it. The play activity is voluntarily chosen, and an activity in which the child asks, "What can I do with this object?" (Ellis, 1984; Guerney, 1984; Tegano, Sawyers, & Moran, 1989).

## SIGNIFICANCE OF PLAY IN SELF-EXPRESSION

White (1960) maintained that play may be fun, but it is also a serious business in childhood. During play, children build up confidence in dealing with their environment. Bruner (1986) believed play gives children their first and most crucial opportunity to have the courage to think, to talk, and to be themselves. According to Amster (1982), play is an activity children comprehend and in which they are comfortable—their method of communication, and their means of testing, partly incorporating and mastering external realities. Since play provides a nonthreatening environment and a flexible atmosphere, creative thoughts are encouraged as children explore and experiment with a variety of solutions to different problems (Tegano et al., 1989). Play allows this process to proceed on a scale controllable by the child. It is through the process of play that children can consider new possibilities not possible in reality, thus greatly expanding the expression of self.

Through play, children find out what the world is like, try on different roles, and cope with conflicting emotions (Papalia & Olds, 1986). The urge to play is universal, and when thwarted, can hamper the joyful path of development and self-discovery that is the calling of every child (Bettelheim, 1987a). Only through engaging in the process of play can children express and use the totality of their personality. Thus, children extend the person they are, the self, into the creative expression of play. As children develop an appreciation for their play, they begin to discover and accept themselves. Frank (1952) enumerated the ways in which play facilitates these discoveries: children express emotions in play, they express their thoughts in play, they rehearse behaviors in play, they exert their will in play, they move through developmental stages with play, and they learn with play. Everything the child is, does, and becomes may at one time or another be demonstrated through play.

Play provides healing for hurts and sadness, breaks down tension, and releases pent-up urges toward self-expression. The activity of play is one of the most important ways in which children learn that their feelings can be safely expressed without reprisal or rejection from others (Cass, 1973). Since play is a spontaneous and safe environment, it allows children to express strong emotions and to learn to cope with anxieties and conflicts. During play, children feel free to act out inner feelings of fear, anger, or loss that might otherwise become overwhelming (Segal & Segal, 1989). Erikson (1977) believed that through this process of self-expression in play, children resolve conflicts by reconstructing them in symbolic play. Maslow (1968) observed that though children do not plan or set out to grow, growth takes place, and children express outwardly through play what has taken place and is taking place inwardly.

## FOSTERING A SENSE OF CONTROL

There are many experiences in childhood in which children feel they have little or no control. Play is children's way of working out accompanying feelings of anxiety and fear and reestablishing some sense of balance and control in their lives. A child in the hospital might play out the events of that experience with the use of dolls. In doing so, the child gains a sense of control over the hospital procedures and is freed from thinking that the event is taking place as a punishment. When children have experienced a traumatic event, they will play it out in an effort to gain understanding (Erikson, 1963). Curry and Arnaud (1984) described an experience in which a preschool teacher had fainted in front of her class and eventually died from a terminal disease. After a few weeks of disorganized play in the classroom, the children got caught up in hospital play, which continued until their anxiety was alleviated. This self-expression through play is not only freeing to children but allows them to express new parts of themselves.

Play is an environment children can control. It is this sense or feeling of control, rather than actual control, which is essential to emotional development and positive mental health. Children may experience environments at home or at school that are overly structured and controlling, interactions in which they experience being controlled by others, but in unstructured free play, the child is the master, the boss, the person in control, the one who decides what to play, how to play, and the outcome. The story, happening, or activity can be what the child wants it to be. In the safety of play, the child can confront monsters, fantasy characters, and frightening experiences with real people and be in charge of the outcome.

Through the process of expressing themselves in play, children can learn perseverance, the pleasure of choosing a project alone, self-direction, self-responsibility, and that they, along with their choices, are accepted. In addition, the opportunities to engage in problem solving are limitless. Children also develop the self-discipline necessary to engage in a sustained effort, and the resulting satisfaction is a tremendous boost in building positive self-esteem.

Through peer interactions involved in play, real social problems are presented to children that they are fully capable of working through and solving (Rogers & Ross, 1986). Social development, therefore, is impacted since play facilitates the learning of negotiating, compromising, and the taking of turns (Greenburg, 1989). The development of these cooperative skills thus becomes a quality of the child's positive self-expression in play with others.

## STAGES IN THE PLAY THERAPY PROCESS

Although children engage in play activities largely for the sake of pure enjoyment, and are seldom aware of the functional elements of play, there are times when play is experienced at a conscious level. Initially, in play, children often express what they have observed adults doing. They play out familiar roles and scenes depicting home routines and the roles played by adults in those routines. At other times, it is obviously clear that a child is quite aware of what he is expressing in play as in the case of seven-year-old Scott, who grabbed Bobo (the bop bag) around the neck in a hammer lock and yelled, "I'm gonna show you what I did to Roger on the playground today!"

Children's emotions are often diffused and undifferentiated and not directly related to reality, since they have lost contact with the people and situations that originally aroused the feelings of frustration, anger, fear, or guilt. Moustakas (1982) has described five stages through which emotionally disturbed children progress in their play as they move toward self-expression and self-awareness in the therapeutic process of play therapy. Initially, diffuse negative feelings are expressed everywhere in the child's play as in the case of a child who cannot tolerate any kind of mess and is overly concerned with cleanliness and neatness. Sometimes the reaction may be diffuse hostility expressed toward the room, toys, or therapist. There may also be accompanying high levels of anxiety as in the case of a child who just stands in the middle of the playroom unable to initiate any activity. Following these initial expressions, during the second stage the child usually expresses ambivalent feelings that are generally anxious or hostile. Moustakas (1982, p. 225) describes a child who picked up the puppets one by one, banged each puppet on the table with exclamations of disgust, threw each puppet on the floor, and said, "I don't like any of them, but I like this one," as she picked up the mouse puppet. She then quickly added, "I don't like this one either," as she squeezed the mouse's head.

The third stage is characterized by more focused, direct negative feelings expressed toward parents, siblings, and other persons in the child's life. These feelings or attitudes are often evident in the child's symbolic play as in the case of a child who acted out strong negative reactions toward her parents and new sibling by lining up the mother, father, and baby family doll figures, and then announced, "They're robbers, and I'm going to shoot them," which she did, one at a time.

In the fourth stage, ambivalent feelings are expressed again in the child's play. In this stage, however, ambivalence is a mixture of positive and negative feelings and attitudes expressed toward parents, siblings, and other persons in the child's life. Five-year-old Kathy feeds the baby doll as she rocks the doll and sings to it. Then she takes a nail from a can and says, "I'm going to stick this down her throat so she can't cry so much." Six-year-old David hits and kicks the bop bag with great vigor and expenditure of energy, yelling, "I'm gonna beat you up. Nobody likes you!" Later he gets the doctor kit, doctors the bop bag, and says, "I'll bet that makes you feel better now."

The expression of these feelings in a relationship with an adult who is both accepting and understanding frees the child to move to the final stage of expression of self through play that is characterized by clear, distinct, separate, and usually realistic, positive and negative attitudes, with positive attitudes predominating in the child's play. Moustakas (1982) concluded that the child's clear and distinct expression of feelings through play reveals that the child has achieved insight and an understanding of reality; thus, self is being expressed fully through the facilitative dimensions of play. The stages in this emotional process and the changes in feeling tones evident in the play process are not always distinctly identifiable and do not always occur in a step-by-step process. Likewise, the stages in the process often overlap at many points.

Axline (1982) described a similar process of stages or patterns of self-expression through play by noting that as play therapy sessions progress, many of the children's feelings and attitudes are expressed symbolically, toy to toy, toy to invisible person, child to imaginary person, child as a real person, and child to the object of his feelings. Axline observed that at the conclusion of play therapy, children take responsibility for their own feelings and express themselves honestly and openly in their play. Thus, through the process of expressing self through play, children bring their feelings to the surface of awareness and either learn to control them or discard them. That children express their self-awareness through play certainly seems to be fully evident in the descriptions of Moustakas (1982) and Axline (1982).

In an accepting and safe environment such as that afforded the child in play therapy, each child's complex uniqueness is expressed more freely and thus more completely. As this uniqueness of self is accepted by the play therapist, the child internalizes that acceptance and begins to accept and appreciate his own uniqueness, thus beginning the process of self-knowledge. This self-knowledge is then expressed through the facilitative process of play.

## SYMBOLIC EXPRESSION IN PLAY

Fantasy play has been described as functioning as an inner resource to help children adapt to environmental demands (Newman & Newman, 1978) and as providing children with an opportunity to assimilate novel experiences into familiar schema (Piaget, 1962). Symbolic play provides a safe or controlled way for children to express emotions, since the emotion itself or the target of the emotion is disguised through the symbolism. It would seem, then, that symbolic play is a way to integrate solving problems and expressing emotions. According to Bettelheim (1987b), what a child chooses to play is motivated by inner processes even when the child engages in play partly to fill empty moments. When children encounter an insurmountable problem, they play it out in symbolic ways that they may not understand because they are reacting to inner processes whose origin may be buried deep in the unconscious.

By acting out a frightening or traumatic experience or situation symbolically, and by returning to that happening again and again through play—perhaps changing or reversing the outcome in the play activity—the child moves toward an inner resolution and is better able to cope with or adjust to the problem in what is sometimes referred to as *real life*—that is, those experiences outside play. As Frank (1982) has pointed out, the child learns to face terrifying objects with increasing self-confidence as he plays out relations to the adult world, and in the process "the child accepts the not-me world of actuality, by learning to relate himself to that world through various modes of activity and response, which he develops as his idiomatic way of putting order and meaning into the actual world and dealing with those meanings as his way of stabilizing and equalizing the flux of experiences" (p. 27).

Children communicate their unconscious feelings through play and utilize available toys and materials as symbols to express the feelings of which they may not be aware at that time. Children are unaware consciously that they are coming to terms with their feelings about wetting and soiling as they pour and dribble water or squeeze moist clay. They are unaware that during this kind of play process and expression of self, they are working through their anger toward their parents (Cass, 1973). Children can unconsciously express their hatred as they tellingly tear apart the doll they are holding (Caplan & Caplan, 1973).

The use of symbols by children enables them to transfer interests and fantasies as well as anxieties and guilt to objects other than people (Ginott, 1982). Play is their symbolic language of self-expression and allows them to "enjoy forbidden pleasures in acceptable substitute ways" (Ginott, 1982, p. 151). Through play, children can distance themselves from traumatic events and experiences with adults by the use of symbolic materials (Mann & McDermott, 1983). Play allows children to work through emotions to their conclusion in an environment the children control. Thus, children are safe from the intensity of their own emotional expressions. It could be said that in the expression of self through play, children are safe from themselves. They are not overwhelmed by their own actions because the act takes place in fantasy.

That children unconsciously express happenings, experiences, concerns, and problems in their play can readily be seen in the following cases. Six-year-old Brenda had to wear a catheter as a result of complications following surgery. She experienced considerable difficulty in trying to empty the bag appropriately and make the necessary connections to put it back in place. The connections were always leaking, and that caused her a great deal of frustration and embarrassment. In her play, she repeatedly acted out a story using a doll house and depicting a problem with a leaky sink or some related plumbing problem. With great exasperation, she would call a plumber to come and fix the plumbing. She stopped acting out these scenes when she learned to attach the catheter bag correctly.

Eight-year-old Jacob played out a scene involving horses, a corral, and barn. He pretended to put a bridle on the horse and commented, "It doesn't hurt his mouth." Then he took the horse to the barn and said, "When the horse kicks the stall, a light comes on over here in the house where the man stays who takes care of the horses so he will know the horse needs help." The significance of this play becomes evident when it is discovered that Jacob received electrical stimulation twice a week to strengthen the muscles in his jaws as a part of his speech therapy program. Small electrodes are placed inside his mouth, and the procedure is generally painless, but sometimes the muscles get tense from the stimulation, and Jacob can let the therapist know he is experiencing some discomfort by pressing a button to make a light come on.

Amster (1982) described a clinical case in which a child who was encopretic played out his problem by using building blocks to create a house without a bathroom and then later constructed an ornate bathroom outside the house.

Klein (1982) described the case of Peter, a seven-year-old boy who was neurotic. He was unable to play freely, could not tolerate frustration, was timid, sometimes aggressive, overbearing, and ambivalent toward family members.

After sleeping with his parents when he was still eighteen-months-old, and having observed their sexual intercourse, he became difficult to manage and demonstrated regressive behavior. In play therapy sessions, Peter repeatedly returned to play scenes of bumping the toy horses together and then would put them to sleep. Although Peter experienced emotions of jealousy, aggressiveness, and anxiety, he did not have a conscious knowledge of these feelings and their association with people in his life. He acted out his aggression by pretending that the horses were dead and by throwing them about the room.

## THERAPEUTIC VALUE OF PLAY

Play is to children what verbalization is to adults. Given the opportunity, children will play out their feelings and needs in a manner or process of expression similar to that for adults. The dynamics of expression and vehicle for communication are different for children, but the expressions—fear, satisfaction, anger, happiness, frustration, contentment—are similar to those expressed by adults. Children may have considerable difficulty in trying to say what they feel or how they have been affected by what they have experienced. But in the presence of a caring, sensitive, and empathetic adult, they will show what they feel through the toys and material that they choose, what they do with and to the materials, and the story acted out (Landreth, 1991).

It is through play that children engage in the process of organizing their experiences, their personal world. This attempt to gain control is described by Frank (1982):

> The child in his play relates himself to his accumulating past by continually reorienting himself to the present through play. He rehearses his past experiences, assimilating them into new perceptions and patterns of relating. . . . In this way the child is continually discovering himself anew, revising his image of himself as he can and must, with each alteration in his relations with the world. Likewise, in his play the child attempts to resolve his problems and conflicts, manipulating play materials and often adult materials as he tries to work through or play out his perplexities and confusions. (p. 24)

The process described here is one of play facilitating a child's self-expression through a continuous and dynamic process of here-and-now focus. Axline (1969) viewed this process as one in which the child plays out feelings, thus bringing them to the surface, getting them out in the open, facing them, and either learning to control them or abandon them. It would seem, then, that play allows children to express themselves in a way that reduces tension and anxiety and thus allows them to gain control of their lives. Hartup and Smothergill (1967) wrote: "It has been said in play the child 'reduces tensions,' 'masters anxiety,' 'generalizes responses,' or manifests a polarity of 'pure assimilation'" (p. 96). As children relive their own experiences in imaginative play, they are able to solve problems or overcome specific fears, and ultimately are responsible for easing their own pain (Weissbourd, 1986).

## HOW TO READ PLAY SYMBOLS

Since toys are like words to children in their efforts to communicate their experiences and their world, and play is children's natural language of expression, the importance of understanding the possible meanings in children's play seems obvious. Frank (1982) pointed out that in observing children's play, we must recognize equivalent stimuli. "Learning to live in a symbolic world of meanings and symbols involves the capacity to accept equivalents (surrogates) of widely varying dimensions and divergence from the actual world and cultural norms, but having equivalent meaning for the individual" (p. 26). He suggests that it may be useful to think of play as a figurative language, recognizing that the child's play reveals equivalents of almost all our familiar figures of speech, metaphor, analogy, hyperbole, synecdoche, onomatopoeia, and so forth.

Understanding the meaning in children's play is at best a difficult process, and Amster (1982) insisted that the play activity of children "must be recognized always as a complex distorted assortment of the child's conscious and unconscious expressions" (p. 42). Equally as important is the observer's knowledge of child development and how children of a given age typically play. Only then can the observer decide if there is some unique meaning in the child's play. In assessing play behavior the observer, then, is constantly comparing what an individual child is doing, saying, and feeling to what is normal for that child's age, level of development, and environment. These comparisons can then provide some clues to what the unique meaning may be.

Emotional experiences and happenings that are important or have in some way significantly impacted children will often show up as repeated behavior in their play. A theme is the recurrence of certain events or topics in the child's play, either within a play experience, such as during a play therapy session, or across several play experiences or sessions. A key point here is the recurrence of the play after some lapse of time or an intervening period of play in which the theme is not played out. For example, four-year-old Shawn's twenty-minute play with a rubber snake would not be considered a theme even though that is considered to be an unusually long time for a child that age to engage in such play. Although the play may be significant, the expression must occur more than once or twice to be considered a theme.

When Shawn came to the playroom for his second session and again played out the same scene of the rubber snake crawling around the dollhouse, sticking its head into each window and door, and then slowly and deliberately crawling around the top of the dollhouse, the therapist suspected a theme. This suspicion was confirmed when Shawn repeated the same play in the third session. It was at this point that the therapist learned that Shawn's home had been burglarized twice just a few weeks before his first play therapy session.

The theme may not always be readily recognizable because what is being played, the activity, or the toys being played with may be different each time, but the theme of the play or the underlying meaning of the play is the same. This was the case with Paul in his play sessions. A theme of reluctance to leave the security of home was evident in the scenes he played out involving an airplane trip in which he announced, "They're going on a trip to New York," loaded the doll family into the airplane, and then promptly announced, "They're back!" without the people ever having flown away from the dollhouse. A second scene involved a family auto trip in which Paul stayed very close to the dollhouse and never went out into the room with the car. A third scene consisted of his announcing, "They're going to move," loading all the dollhouse furniture and fixtures into the truck and then quickly announcing, "They decided to live here again," and unloading and replacing the furniture in the dollhouse. Paul experienced a tremendous fear of abandonment. Such repeated play behaviors can indicate emotional issues the child is playing out. When the theme is no longer observable, that can be an indication that the child has been able to move on emotionally to something else (Landreth, 1991).

Caplan and Caplan (1983) have concluded that there are some patterns of play that have fairly universal meaning and may indicate the type of problems that underlie a child's disturbance. They suggested that children who tend to be meticulously clean and avoid dirty or messy play, who arrange toys in only neat patterns, and whose drawings often require the use of a ruler, may indicate a rigidity that is seriously limiting their personal development. Also, children who either keep up a constant chatter or play silently for long periods of time may be hiding their feelings. Constant regression to earlier levels of maturity and compulsion to use materials such as sand and water, which may have cleansing symbolism, may signify unresolved conflict.

Waelder (1976) stated that children repeat in their play everything that has strongly affected them in their daily life. He gave examples of children who have been sexually abused repeatedly "washing" themselves with sand, covering their genital area with sand while playing in the sand box, burying or otherwise hiding objects from view. Allen and Berry (1987) indicated that a child will show his or her own emotional turmoil and chaos in chaotic sand play, where the sand and unrelated toys are tossed in a heap. The use of squares, rectangles, and circles may indicate completion and wholeness. Battles and wars, powerful figures like robots and monsters who all end up killed, are indicative of destructive impulses. Symbols are forms that have significance by virtue of the fact that they mean something (Reifel & Greenfield, 1982), and children often identify dolls with people in their lives. Therefore, when children make dolls do what they do to one another, children may be showing exactly how they feel toward those people and how they think those people feel toward them and each other (Caplan & Caplan, 1973).

Inferring meaning in the use of certain toys or interpreting children's play can be quite easily accomplished depending on the interpreter's theoretical assumptions. However, Anna Freud (1928/1927) cautioned that the therapist has no right to impute a symbolic meaning to every one of a child's actions. This view is reiterated by Vinturella and James (1987), who encourage the therapist to avoid adhering to a fixed interpretation of symbols. They believed that a symbol can have several meanings, and its subjective meaning for the child should be respected. For example, a snake could represent danger, wisdom, fascination, or simply the child's latest object of interest. Irwin (1983) proposed that the data obtained by interpreting play should be used in "the same way other projective data are used—as impressions to be verified, refuted, or altered in the course of ongoing work" (p. 161). Moustakas (1973) pointed out that objects have varied meanings to different children. Blocks, sand, clay, or other unstructured objects may symbolize a multitude of things such as parents, siblings, a painful experience, as well as feelings of hate, love, or hostility in the imagination of a child. According to Klein (1949/1931), many distinct and different associations are brought by a child to the individual parts of his or her play as evidenced by the fact that a doll may represent either the mother or the child.

It seems obvious that caution should be exercised in interpreting symbolism in children's play. As Ginott (1982) pointed out, banging two blocks together may represent spanking, or intercourse, or may merely be a test of the therapist's tolerance for noise. However, when a father doll is placed on top of a mother doll with accompanying movements, the possibility of misinterpretation is less likely. As can be seen in these examples, the play materials chosen by the child may be equally useful as a means of expression for the child, but the adult's understanding of the child's expression may be limited by the child's choice of play materials. Therefore, proper selection of toys and materials for children's self-expression in any setting is crucial.

## TOYS FOR FACILITATING SELF-EXPRESSION

Careful selection of toys and materials is essential in providing children with opportunities for self-expression through their play. The type of toy a child uses can determine the type and extent of play exhibited, and thus the degree of self-expression. Toys with only one use can limit or inhibit self-expression. Unstructured toys can be used by children in many ways to express themselves. Toys and play materials become an extension of the child's self, just as words are an extension of the adult's self. Therefore, words and play behaviors are idiomatic expressions unique to each child.

Neumann (1971) stated that ambiguity and diversity of materials tends to foster creative play in which the child can ascribe the identity and function to the object. Ambiguous materials tend to facilitate reflective, transforming responses, whereas realistic and elaborate materials facilitate stereotyped exploration. Rubin and Howe (1985) concluded from their review of the literature on children's toys and the types of play associated with them, that for younger children realistic toys tend to be more conducive to facilitating pretend play than are abstract toys. The opposite reaction was noted with older children.

Toys and materials can determine or structure the kind and degree of expression by the child and his interaction with the adult. Some toys and materials, by the very nature of their construction and design, are prone to elicit certain kinds of behaviors more than others and to some extent structure the behavior of the child. The bop bag is a good example. As it stands there in the middle of the floor, everything about it seems to say, "Hit me" and so children are more likely to push, shove, or hit the bop bag than to pretend it is a sick friend and nurse it back to health. Some materials should be provided that are nondescript and facilitate the child's creative and symbolic expression. Blocks can become cars, trains, airplanes, fences, houses, and so forth.

Toys and materials that facilitate self-expression of children can be grouped into three broad categories (Landreth 1991).

1. *Real-life Toys.* A doll family, doll house, puppets, and nondescript figures (e.g., Gumby) can represent family members in the child's life and thus provide for the direct expression of feelings. Anger, fear, sibling rivalry, crises, and family conflicts can be directly expressed as the child acts out scenes with the human figures. Puppets and doll family figures allow children to distance themselves from what is expressed. Attributing feelings to such toys is often easier for children than expressing the same feelings directly. A car, truck, boat, and cash register are especially important for the resistive, anxious, shy, or withdrawn child because they can be played with in noncommittal ways without revealing any feelings. When children are ready, they will choose play media that will help them express their feelings more fully and openly. The cash register provides for a quick feeling of control as the child manipulates the keys and calls out numbers. The car or truck gives an excuse for moving about and exploring the room and can also be used to act out real-life happenings.

2. *Acting-out—Aggressive-release Toys.* Children often have intense pent-up emotions for which they do not have verbal labels to describe or express. Structured toys and materials such as the bop bag, toy soldiers, alligator puppet, guns, and rubber knife can be used to express anger, hostility, and frustration. Aggressive children seem to experience the permission to release aggressive feelings in the accepting environment of a playroom as satisfying, and are able to move on to more self-enhancing positive feelings. Driving nails into a softwood log or pounding on a Peg-Board releases feelings, and at the same time facilitates the focusing of attention and energy in a manner that increases concentration.

   Ginott (1961) suggested including animal toys that depict wild animals because some children find it difficult to express aggressive feelings even against human figure dolls. These children, for example, will not shoot a father doll but will shoot a lion that may represent the father. Some children will express their hostility through the alligator puppet by biting, chewing, and crunching. Clay is an example of a material that fits into two categories: creative and aggressive. It can be pounded, smashed, rolled out with great vigor, and torn apart with intensity. Clay can also be used by the child to create figures for play.

3. *Toys for Creative Expression and Emotional Release.* Sand and water are probably the most popular unstructured play media for children, and are excellent for expressing feelings. Children can use sand to express their aggression by manipulating it and burying dolls and other items in it. Water allows children to act out those times when they need to regress. Sand, water, and clay are reversible play materials that allow children to change the identity of the object. When the scene being played out becomes too frightening or intense, the child can make the play material turn into something else. Blocks can be houses, they can be thrown, they can be stacked and kicked down allowing the child to explore what it feels like to be constructive and destructive. As with water and sand, the child can experience a feeling of satisfaction, because there is no correct way to play with blocks. Easel paints afford the child an opportunity to be creative, to be messy, to pretend bathroom scenes and smear, to express feelings.

Millar (1968) reported that the kind and number of available toys make a difference in the manner and kind of children's play. When fewer toys are available, children make more social contact with each other, tend to display undesirable behaviors, and increase play with sand and dirt. When many toys are accessible, social contacts are lessened and individual exploration and construction increases.

## CASE ILLUSTRATIONS: WHAT PLAY REVEALS

The following excerpt is from seven-year-old Brian's fifth play therapy session. A brief family background is described at the end of the excerpt to allow the reader to form his or her own opinion as to the possible meaning of the play. At the beginning of each session, Brian checked the playroom carefully to make sure everything was there.

Brian: (*walks over to the shelf and gets the doctor kit*) I'll probably play doctor today.

Therapist: You decided that is something you might like to do.

Brian: Yeah. I never did it before, but I'll try.

Therapist: Hmmm. You seem to like to do all these things you didn't do before.

Brian: (*sits down on the floor and opens the medical kit*) There's a lot of neat stuff in here!

Therapist: You really like all of that.

Brian: Watch this. (*takes the syringe out and pretends to give himself an injection very quickly*).

Therapist: You did that one real fast.

Brian: I'm always good.

Therapist: You're good at a lot of things.

Brian: I'm good at everything.

Therapist: Uhmmm.

Brian: I'll try to umm, do something here on your wrist. (*goes over to therapist and puts the blood pressure instrument on her wrist*) Check you.

Therapist: You want to see how I am.

Brian: Here. Wait. (*works the blood pressure instrument*) Pretty low.

Therapist: Pretty low, huh? Doesn't sound like it's very good.

Brian: Me, either. (*puts the blood pressure toy back in the kit*). Just because I'm playing doctor doesn't mean that it's real.

Therapist: Oh, so even though it seems like it's low, it doesn't mean I'm really sick.

Brian: That's right, because I'm just playing doctor. (*gets the stethoscope out of the kit and goes over to the therapist and listens to her heart*) Looks like doctors use this thing. Nothin' to it!

Therapist: Nothing to it. Just as easy as can be.

Brian: Yeah . . . kind of (*gets the syringe from the kit again*) Here's that thing. A shot! (*goes over and gives the therapist an injection*) Right here. (*shows her the needle*) Look at all this! (*gives her another injection*)

Therapist: So . . . just like that . . . with one hand.

Brian: Yeah, I can do anything with one hand. (*puts the syringe back into the kit*)

*Comments:* Brian's family life was chaotic. His father was an alcoholic, he was abused at home, he had few friends, and his academic progress in school was unsatisfactory. Several features of this play excerpt seem to stand out: Brian's reference to being good at everything, his need to point out that what he was playing was not real, and his pretending to doctor the play therapist. Brian seems to be expressing his need to be important and successful. Taking care of the play therapist seems to be an important issue for Brian, and he makes sure she knows he does not intend any ill will. Checking the room at the beginning of each session seems to be an expression of his need for order and predictability in this relationship, unlike the chaos at home and the unpredictability of an alcoholic father. The need to be good at everything is sometimes characteristic of children who grow up in alcoholic families.

Paul is six years old. The following excerpt is from his second play therapy session. In the first session, Paul cooked poison, fed it to Batman (bop bag punching toy), and killed him. The reason for referral is described at the end of this excerpt.

Paul: (*going to sandbox*) He's going to find something he likes someday, ain't he? Do you have another truck? Now stay tuned for Batman (*runs over to bop bag, punches bop bag fiercely nine times in face, wrestles him and pushes him down*). He's down for a little while. I'm gonna put him on this chair (*puts Batman bop bag on a chair*). I'm gonna shoot him. I got these many guns. I'm gonna shoot at him (*picks up guns and small plastic TV*). Oooo! This can be a different TV.

Therapist: Uh huh.

Paul: (*puts TV in the dollhouse*) I guess that's Daddy's TV.

Therapist: So he's going to have a special one.

Paul: Yeah (*picks up rifle that shoots ping pong balls*). Hey, where's those round balls? (*picks up ping pong ball*) I'm gonna shoot him (*Batman*) for good, ain't I? Ain't I?

Therapist: So you know just what you're going to do. You've got it planned.

Paul: Look! Ready for Batman? Batman's gonna be in big trouble, ain't he? (*shoots*) I got him down, didn't I?

Therapist: You got him the first shot.

Paul: I'm gonna kill him more (*aims, shoots and misses*). Hmmm, better try another gun (*tries dart pistol*). There's another. I got it (*shoots to side of bop bag*). I missed him, didn't I?

Therapist: It went right past him.

Paul: (*shoots again to side of bop bag*) It's a hard shot, aint't it?

Therapist: It's hard to hit it from way over there.

Paul: (*shoots again and misses*) I missed him a bunch, didn't I? (*picks up the darts*) When I get him, guess what I'm gonna do? I'm gonna tie him up and kill him. I'm gonna cut him up.

Therapist: You're really going to kill him.

Paul: (*shoots and misses, then shoots bop bag again*) Got him! (*runs over, puts bop bag on the floor, head under a chair so that bop bag is horizontal*) Supposed to be dead for a little while. You know what I'm gonna do to Batman? Ahhh. (*gets rubber knife and cuts the middle of bop bag, then goes to kitchen and looks through the dishes*) You know what I'm gonna do?

Therapist: You've got something planned now.

Paul: I'm not gonna poison him. (*He cooked poison last session and fed it to Batman.*) You know what I am going to do this time? Na. I'm not going to. I'm gonna kill him again. I'm gonna poison him. That's what I was gonna do. Let's see (*picks up hand gun, walks over to Batman, aims gun right next to Batman's face and shoots*). Ha. Ha. (*goes to sandbox, stands in the middle and fills bucket with sand*) Guess what I'm gonna do?

Therapist: You can tell me what you're going to do.

Paul: Well, I'm gonna put Batman in this (*drops bucket, starts sweeping in the sandbox and outside the sandbox*). Sweep the blood off. Ha. Ha. Sweep the blood. Batman's gonna be really dead this time 'cuz I'll really kill him.

Therapist:   This time you'll make sure you kill him.

Paul: You're right. This time I'm going to make sure you're gonna get killed.

Therapist: Oh, I'm going to get it too.

Paul: I know. You're Robin.

Therapist: You're going to kill both of us.

Paul: Bet you're right. Hope I don't miss ya (*with lilt to voice and big grin*).

Therapist: I'm not for shooting (*aims way over therapist's head and shoots wall*). I know you would like to shoot me. You can shoot Batman (*again shoots over therapist's head—it is obvious he does not intend to shoot the therapist*).

Paul: Ohhh. I missed you (*shoots again*). Ahhhhh, gosh (*begins to play with phone*). You know who I'm gonna call? Mmm ammm (*gets other phone and dials*). Yeah, Batman's dead. Hum hum okay (*leaves phone and goes across room*). Hey, I'm gonna make a little song to wake Batman up, ain't I? (*plays xylophone and looks expectantly at Batman*) He's almost woke up (*walks over to Batman*). Chop his neck off, ain't I? (*hits Batman*) Now he's dead. Now I'm going to play with Dad again. Mr. old Dad (*plays in dollhouse and with the scooter truck*). Here's his new truck. That's gonna work better. He bought a new television, didn't he?

Therapist: So now they have two televisions.

(*later in the session*)

Paul: Oh my God, look! They're having a tornado in this area by their home. They better hurry home, right?

Therapist: Tornadoes are dangerous.

Paul: I know. It can blow houses down. One of them's, one of them's in the graveyard. That's the girl (*buries doll in sand—therapist can't see doll being buried*).

Therapist: So the girl got left in the graveyard.

Paul: Uh uh, she's buried.

Therapist: Oh, she's buried in the graveyard.

Paul: She does not want . . . she does not want the tornado to get her.

Therapist: So the tornado can't get her there.

Paul: The tornado's passed. Oooh. Look what happened! (*knocks over toys near the dollhouse*) God!

Therapist: The tornado wrecked some things.

Paul: Yeah, some but it didn't wreck this (*points to scooter truck*). All the kids have to get in the house fast, lay down and rest.

Therapist: So they're hoping they'll be safe in the house.

Paul: And she told her to get in and rest too, while Daddy got the pickup truck over (*pulls truck over*). Ah, oh. The tornado's out. Guess what? Daddy's gonna be surprised. Guess what? Stay tuned for Batman!

Therapist: Now it's time for Batman again.

Paul: (*goes over to Batman and attempts to put handcuffs on himself*) Uh, oh, they caught me, didn't they?

Therapist: You got caught by somebody.

Paul: The police (*continues trying to handcuff his hands behind his back*).

Therapist: Oh, the police caught you. Hmm.

Paul: For killing Batman.

Therapist: So you killed Batman, and then the policeman caught you.

Paul: Yeah. Batman is alive now. Ouch. No wonder I can't put these on when I have my hands behind my back. Here (*brings handcuffs to therapist for aid; therapist fastens them behind his back*). OK, I'm in jail.

Therapist: So the policeman handcuffed you and took you to jail.

Paul: I know. First he has to do something. He can't kill nobody. The police surrounded him, and he has to put this (*knife*) back.

Therapist: So they fixed him up so he can't kill anyone.

Paul: Yeah. They have to put the knife back. The Batman's alive. Better get him up (*stands Batman up*).

Therapist: So he's okay now.

Paul: But first wait (*moves Batman around*). There. Uh oh, I'm out of jail now. Help me (*tries to take handcuffs off*). Ouch, ouch (*handcuffs pinch his wrists*).

Therapist: Sometimes those things pinch.

Paul: Yeah (*takes handcuffs off*).

Therapist: But you got them off.

Paul: Guess what? I'm the police now. I'm going to get to be a police, didn't I?

Therapist: So now you're going to be the one with the handcuffs.

Paul: I'm the police now. I'm Batman and I'll bring you in jail, okay?

Therapist: You can pretend that someone is doing that and I'll watch.

Paul: Okay. That Mr. Policeman is having trouble, ain't he? (*tries to hook hand-cuffs together*)

Therapist: Looks like he's having a hard time getting those on there just right.

Paul: Oh no, he got it. Now he don't have trouble.

Therapist: You figured it out.

Paul: Uh huh, I found the way (hooks handcuffs on pocket).

Therapist: Hmmm. You found a way to do it.

*Comments:* Paul's grandfather, to whom he felt very close, died when Paul was four years old. Paul missed his grandfather a great deal and grieved over the loss. During the two years following his grandfather's death, Paul focused so much on his grandfather's death that he developed a fear of death, often made references to death, and pretended to talk to his grandfather. At one point, Paul refused to drink water for two months because he overheard a neighbor remark that the water in their town tasted bad. Paul interpreted bad to mean it would kill you. Paul began to act out his anger, and as a first grade student had been sent to the principal's office several times for hitting other children. When Paul started play therapy, he was watching an average of six hours of television per day. During his play therapy sessions, he made frequent references to television. Paul's great ambivalence about death can readily be seen in this episode as he killed Batman and then made a song to wake Batman up. Death is unexpected and so are tornadoes. Paul played out a dramatic scene of a girl being buried in the graveyard but made no references to her being dead. Later, Paul gets punished for killing Batman, but then Batman is suddenly alive again and no one can get killed because the weapons are taken away. It seems quite clear that Paul is expressing his fears and trying to come to terms with the permanency of death. That is the essence of the power of play, the opportunity to express even the deepest and most threatening fears or problems within the safety of play, which protects the child from his expressions because he is separated from that which he plays out.

## REFERENCES

Allen J., & Berry, P. (1987). Sand play. *Elementary School Guidance and Counseling, 21,* 300–306.

Amster, F. (1982). Differential uses of play in treatment of young children. In G. Landreth (Ed.), *Play therapy: Dynamics of the process of counseling with children* (pp. 33–42). Springfield, IL: Charles C. Thomas.

Axline, V. (1969). *Play therapy.* New York: Ballantine.

Axline, V. (1982). Nondirective play therapy procedures and results. In G. Landreth (Ed.), *Play therapy: Dynamics of the process of counseling with children* (pp. 120–129). Springfield, IL: Charles C. Thomas.

Bettelheim, B. (1987a). *A good enough parent.* New York: Vintage.

Bettelheim, B. (1987b). The importance of play. *The Atlantic Monthly, 259,* 35–46.

Bruner, J. (1986). Play, thought, and language.

*Prospects: Quarterly Review of Education,* 16, 77–83.

Caplan, F., & Caplan, T. (1973). *The power of play.* New York: Anchor.

Caplan, F., & Caplan T. (1983). *The early childhood years.* New York: Grosset & Dunlap.

Cass, J. (1973). *Helping children grow through play.* New York: Schocken.

Coleman, M., & Skeen, P. (1985). Play, games, and sports: Their use and misuse. *Childhood Education, 61,* 192-198.

Comrie, B. (1987). *The world's major languages.* New York: Oxford University Press.

Curry, N., & Arnaud, S. (1984). Play in developmental preschool settings. In T. Yawkey & A. Pellegrini (Eds.), *Child's play: Developmental and applied* (pp. 273–290). Hillsdale, NJ: Lawrence Erlbaum Associates.

Ellis, M. (1984). Play, novelty, and stimulus seeking. In T. Yawkey & A. Pellegrini (Eds.), *Child's play: Developmental and applied* (pp. 203–218). Hillsdale, NJ: Lawrence Erlbaum Associates.

Erikson, E. (1963). *Childhood and society.* New York: Norton

Erikson, E. (1977). *Toys and reason.* New York: Norton.

Frank, L. (1952). *The fundamental needs of the child.* New York: National Association for Mental Health.

Frank, L. (1982). Play in personality development. In G. Landreth (Ed.), *Play therapy: Dynamics of the process of counseling with children* (pp. 19–31). Springfield, IL: Charles C. Thomas.

Freud, A. (1928). *Introduction to the technic of child analysis.* (L. Clark, Trans.). New York: Nervous and Mental Disease Publishing Company. (Original work published 1927)

Ginott, H. (1961). *Group psychotherapy with children: The theory and practice of play therapy.* New York: McGraw-Hill.

Ginott, H. (1982). A rationale for selecting toys in play therapy. In G. Landreth (Ed.), *Play therapy: Dynamics of the process of counseling with children* (pp. 145–152). Springfield, IL: Charles C. Thomas.

Greenburg, P. (1989). Learning self-esteem and self-discipline through play. *Young Children,* 45, 28–31.

Guerney, L. (1984). Play in developmental preschool settings. In T. Yawkey & A. Pellegrini (Eds.), *Child's play: Developmental and applied* (pp. 273–290). Hillsdale, NJ: Lawrence Erlbaum.

Hartup, W., & Smothergill, N. (1967). *The young child.* Washington, DC: The National Association for the Education of Young Children.

Irwin, E. (1983). The diagnostic and therapeutic use of pretend play. In C. Schaefer & K. O'Connor (Eds.), *Handbook of play therapy* (pp. 148–166). New York: John Wiley & Sons.

Klein, M. (1949). *The psycho-analysis of children* (3rd ed.) (A. Strachey, Trans.). London: Hogarth Press. (Original work published 1931)

Klein, M. (1982). The Psychoanalytic technique. In G. Landreth (Ed.), *Play therapy: Dynamics of the process of counseling with children* (pp. 74–91). Springfield, IL: Charles C. Thomas.

Landreth, G. (1991). *Play therapy: The art of the relationship.* Muncie, IN: Accelerated Development.

Mann, E., & McDermott, J. (1983). Play therapy for victims of child abuse and neglect. In C. Schaefer & K. O'Connor (Eds.), *Handbook of play therapy* (pp. 283–306). New York: John Wiley & Sons.

Maslow, A. (1968). *Toward a psychology of being.* New York: D. Van Nostrand.

Millar, S. (1968). *The psychology of play.* Baltimore: Penguin Books.

Moustakas, C. (1973). *Children in play therapy.* New York: Jason Aronson.

Moustakas, C. (1981). *Rhythms, rituals and relationships.* Detroit, MI: Center for Humanistic Studies.

Moustakas, C. (1982). Emotional adjustment and the play therapy process. In G. Landreth (Ed.), *Play therapy: Dynamics of the process of counseling with children* (pp. 217–230). Springfield, IL: Charles C. Thomas.

Neumann, E. (1971). *The elements of play.* New York: MSS Information Corp.

Newman, B., & Newman, P. (1978). *Infancy and childhood.* New York: John Wiley & Sons.

Papalia, D., & Olds, S. (1986). *Human development.* New York: McGraw-Hill.

Piaget, J. (1962). *Play, dreams and imitation in childhood.* New York: Norton.

Reifel, S., & Greenfield, P. (1982). Structural development in a symbolic medium: The representational use of block constructions. In

G. Forman (Ed.), *Action and thought from sensorimotor schemes to symbolic operations* (pp. 203–233). New York: Academic Press.

Rogers, D., & Ross, D. (1986). Encouraging positive social interaction among young children. *Young Children, 41,* 12–17.

Rubin, K., & Howe, N. (1985). Toys and play behaviors: an overview. *Topics in Early Childhood Special Education, 5,* 1–10.

Segal, J., & Segal, Z. (1989). Child's play. *Parents' Magazine, 64,* 126.

Tegano, D., Sawyers, J., & Moran, J. (1989). Problem finding and solving in play: The teacher's role. *Childhood Education, 66,* 92–97.

Vinturella, L., & James R. (1987). Sand play: A therapeutic medium with children. *Elementary School Guidance and Counseling, 21,* 229–238.

Waelder, R. (1976). Psychoanalytic theory of play. In C. Schaefer (Ed.), *The therapeutic use of child's play* (pp. 79–93). New York: Jason Aronson.

Weissbourd, B. (1986). The importance of play. *Parents' magazine, 61,* 142.

White, R. (1960). Competence and the psychosexual stages of development. In M. Jones (Ed.), *Nebraska symposium on motivation* (pp. 97–141). Lincoln, NE: University of Nebraska.

# 2

# Essential Personality Characteristics of Effective Play Therapists

## TINA EDLING HARRIS
## GARRY L. LANDRETH

*P*lay, the purposeful activity of childhood, has long been considered a child's natural method of expression and has received much attention from child therapists over the years. Many authors have sought to determine the essential elements of this unique form of therapy.

Although the theoretical orientations of play therapists may vary, there is consistent agreement as to the significance of the relationship between the child and the therapist (Axline, 1969; Ginott, 1994; Landreth, 1993; Moustakas et al., 1956; Smith & Herman, 1994). In play therapy, the relationship is the key to growth and the success or failure of the therapeutic encounter hinges on the therapist and the developing relationship (Axline, 1969; Landreth, 1991,1993; Moustakas et al., 1956). The play therapist sets the climate in the playroom by his or her manner, attitudes, and beliefs about the child, about self, and about the nature of life and living (Hyde, 1971). The most significant resource the therapist brings to the relationship is the dimension of self; the therapist is more important than anything the therapist knows how to do (Landreth, 1991). Therefore, the personality characteristics and interpersonal skills of the play therapist are critical.

According to Axline (1969), the personality qualities of the play therapist may be summarized by saying that the therapist must be a person who "can and will accept the word and the spirit" of eight basic principles that guide all therapeutic contacts with children (Axline, 1969, p. 65). It seems appropriate, therefore, to consider the personality characteristics of effective play therapists in light of each of these eight principles that Landreth (1991) revised and expanded.

## FIRST PRINCIPLE: THE THERAPIST IS GENUINELY INTERESTED IN THE CHILD AND DEVELOPS A WARM, CARING RELATIONSHIP

Warmth, respect, and acceptance must be integral parts of the play therapist's personality (Axline, 1969; Landreth, 1991,1993; Waterland, 1970). In play therapy, the therapist assumes the role of a benevolent, accepting, supportive observer who takes a neutral stance with respect to a child's behavior. The play therapist should be emotionally mature, stable, and skilled (Axline, 1969). The play therapist is kind, warm, and friendly to the child (Axline, 1969; Bow, 1988; Landreth, 1991) with a sense of humor that relaxes the child, puts the child at ease, and encourages the child to share his or her inner world (Axline, 1969). The effective play therapist appreciates the world of the child, attempts to understand that world on the basis of the child's own expressions, and has a genuine liking for children. The play therapist is sensitive to children, and is sincerely interested in helping them (Axline, 1969; Bow, 1988; Landreth, 1991; Moustakas & Schalock, 1955). The therapist is able to demonstrate understanding of the child's developmental level along with accurate perception of the child's feelings and thoughts (Axline, 1969; Landreth, 1993; Smith & Herman, 1994; Tanner & Mathis, 1995). The therapist respects the child as a growing, changing, and lovable person, different from all other people (Axline, 1969; Hyde, 1971; Landreth, 1991; Smith, 1977). Although the therapist may say little, the child is acutely aware of voice tone, gestures, postural signals, and facial expressions (Moustakas et al., 1956). Therefore, therapist self-awareness is essential. It is imperative for the therapist's manner to be honest and genuine (Axline, 1969; Hyde, 1971; Landreth, 1991; Moustakas et al., 1956).

The ability to warmly accept a child is predicated on the therapist's ability to accept and understand herself. The effective play therapist, therefore, is engaged in a continuing process of self-discovery. The therapist possesses insight into her or his own motivations and is able to accept personal limitations without feeling threatened (Landreth, 1991). The therapist needs to be real and genuine (Axline, 1969; Landreth, 1991) and does not try to fit into a stereotyped role of what a play therapist should be or hide behind a false front (Landreth, 1991; Smith, 1977).

One dimension that is considered essential to effective therapy is referred to as "being present" or "being there." Being fully present means that the therapist is actively interacting with the child. "Being there" has to do with listening to what the child verbalizes and observing what the child conveys through activity (Axline, 1969; Landreth, 1991; Moustakas et al., 1956; Tanner & Mathis, 1995). For the play therapist, this means being aware of and being congruent with what is being experienced internally. "Being there" requires far more than the therapist's physical presence alone, and it is what sets the play therapist apart from other adults in the child's world (Axline, 1969; Landreth, 1991).

## SECOND PRINCIPLE: THE THERAPIST EXPERIENCES UNQUALIFIED ACCEPTANCE OF THE CHILD AND DOES NOT WISH THAT THE CHILD WERE DIFFERENT IN SOME WAY

The play therapist demonstrates respect by maintaining a warm, steady, and friendly relationship with the child (Axline, 1969). The therapist stays neutral, accepting the child exactly as the child is. The therapist avoids judging or evaluating the child's behavior, either positively or negatively, reacts to the child with interest, and demonstrates acceptance of the child by encouraging the child to express feelings fully (Axline, 1969; Hyde, 1971; Landreth, 1991).

In working with children, the therapist conveys acceptance through patience, flexibility, and creativity. The play therapist needs to be able to adjust and adapt to the unexpected (Axline, 1969; Bow, 1988; Landreth, 1991). The therapist welcomes the child's choice to play or not to play, to talk or not to talk. The child does not need to change or behave in any particular way to receive the therapist's acceptance, and the therapist resists imposing any conforming behavior on the child. The therapist may have goals or ideas, but does not have expectations regarding the child. The therapist knows that expectations can easily be disappointed, and that disappointment may be conveyed to the child. Instead, the therapist endeavors to meet the child where the child is at the moment, and moves with the child (Axline, 1969; Landreth, 1991,

## THIRD PRINCIPLE: THE THERAPIST CREATES A FEELING OF SAFETY AND PERMISSIVENESS IN THE RELATIONSHIP SO THAT THE CHILD FEELS FREE TO EXPLORE AND EXPRESS SELF COMPLETELY

The play therapist is charged with creating a safe and comfortable relationship in which the child is helped to feel protected, liked, and respected (Bow, 1988). The child gains a sense of security from the predictability of the therapist and the therapeutic hour (Axline, 1969; Ginott, 1994; Landreth, 1991). It is imperative that the therapist remain steady, consistent, and honest (Axline, 1969). Compassion and empathy tend to increase a child's confidence, encouraging open expression of emotions and thoughts (Kaufman, 1994). A child will withhold comments until the child is sure that the therapist understands and can be trusted (Hyde, 1971; Landreth, 1991). A therapist who is patient, friendly, calm, self-confident, and in control provides the child with protection and emotional safety (Bow, 1988).

Ginott (1994) defined permissiveness as the total acceptance of all symbolic behavior, whether constructive or destructive. While aggressive or destructive behavior may have to be limited, the therapist acknowledges and accepts the child's desires to engage in such activities and provides acceptable alternatives for expressing the feelings (Axline, 1969; Ginott, 1994; Landreth, 1991; Roden, Kranz, & Lund, 1981; Smith & Herman, 1994).

The effective play therapist is accepting and creates an atmosphere of permissiveness at all times. This permissiveness is communicated by the therapist's attitude toward the child, tone of voice, and actions (Axline, 1969; Landreth, 1991). The therapist grants the child the right to choose; the child may go or stay, talk or be silent, use or not use the playroom materials. The therapist does not push or endeavor to control or change the child in any way (Axline, 1969; Landreth, 1991; Waterland, 1970).

## FOURTH PRINCIPLE: THE THERAPIST IS ALWAYS SENSITIVE TO THE CHILD'S FEELINGS AND GENTLY REFLECTS THOSE FEELINGS IN SUCH A MANNER THAT THE CHILD DEVELOPS SELF-UNDERSTANDING

Adults rarely attempt to comprehend the subjective world of children. Yet, until that private world is accepted and understood, children are not free to explore, to share their struggles, or to change (Landreth, 1991). To perceive that private world of the child, the therapist must listen intently, not only to what is being said, but also to the way it is voiced, and to what is left unsaid. The play therapist pays attention to the messages the child communicates through activity and behavior. The therapist is alert to recognize feelings the child is expressing through play or conversation and attempts to reflect these feelings accurately to the child (Axline, 1969; Landreth, 1993; Tanner & Mathis, 1995; Waterland, 1970).

The play therapist must maintain a high level of emotional connection and participation with the child in order to enter into the child's private world with sensitivity. The therapist acts as a mirror, reflecting the child's thoughts and feelings. Through this careful reflection the child can begin to understand his or her attitudes and perceptions, and, in time, change them (Axline, 1969; Hyde, 1971; Landreth, 1991; Smith, 1977; Tanner & Mathis, 1995).

The therapist works hard to understand the child's world, to recognize the child's feelings, and to allow the child to express those feelings (Axline, 1969; Hyde, 1971; Landreth, 1991; Tanner & Mathis, 1995). Sensitive understanding takes place to the degree that the therapist is able to release her or his own reality and expectations and enter with appreciation into the world of the child (Axline, 1969; Landreth, 1991; Landreth, 1993). In this regard, effective play therapists have a high tolerance for ambiguity, which allows them to enter the child's world as a follower (Landreth, 1991).

## FIFTH PRINCIPLE: THE THERAPIST BELIEVES DEEPLY IN THE CHILD'S CAPACITY TO ACT RESPONSIBLY, UNWAVERINGLY RESPECTS THE CHILD'S ABILITY TO SOLVE PERSONAL PROBLEMS, AND ALLOWS THE CHILD TO DO SO

Play therapy concentrates on the child as a growing and ever changing person. The play therapist believes that the child is constantly striving to make sense of his or her often confusing world (Smith, 1977). The therapist trusts that the child's inborn motivation is toward health, independence, and self-actualization, and believes that the child has the capacity within himself to become more mature, if given the opportunity (Axline, 1969; Hyde, 1971; Landreth, 1991, 1993). The play therapist knows that healthy children must be problem solvers and communicates an inner faith in the child's ability to work out his own problems, to recover, and to adapt (Axline, 1969; Landreth, 1991,1993; Smith, 1977; Waterland, 1970). The play therapist sees the individual as important, capable, and dependable (Axline, 1969; Landreth, 1993) and helps the child become independent by allowing the child to assume responsibility for making decisions and choices. The therapist doesn't try to make things happen or pressure the child to change. The decision to change or not to change behavior always remains with the child (Axline, 1969; Hyde, 1971; Landreth, 1991, 1993; Smith, 1977).

## SIXTH PRINCIPLE: THE THERAPIST TRUSTS THE CHILD'S INNER DIRECTION, ALLOWS THE CHILD TO LEAD IN ALL AREAS OF THE RELATIONSHIP AND RESISTS ANY URGE TO DIRECT THE CHILD'S PLAY OR CONVERSATION

The play therapist is convinced that children carry within themselves unique and exciting possibilities for growth, but this potential is only realized if growth takes place in a nurturing atmosphere. The therapist takes a "hands off" stance and allows the child to lead the way within the confines of the playroom (Axline, 1969; Hyde, 1971; Landreth, 1991, 1993; Smith, 1977). The play therapist respects the child's ability to make his own decisions (Axline, 1969; Landreth, 1991; Waterland, 1970), conveying to the child that he is regarded as worthwhile and important. The therapist doesn't attempt to direct a child's actions or conversation, and no effort is made to control or change the child. In the playroom, the child leads, the therapist follows the child's lead (Axline, 1969; Hyde, 1971; Landreth, 1991; Landreth, 1993; Smith, 1977). The therapist knows that when ideas are offered, objects are labeled in the playroom, or decisions are made, the child is deprived of the opportunity to do so for himself (Axline, 1969; Landreth, 1991; Tanner & Mathis, 1995). The therapist trusts the child to take the play therapy experience to the areas the child needs to explore. The therapist becomes a sounding board for the child's personality so the child can perceive himself as he is (Axline, 1969).

## SEVENTH PRINCIPLE: THE THERAPIST APPRECIATES THE GRADUAL NATURE OF THE THERAPEUTIC PROCESS AND DOES NOT ATTEMPT TO HURRY THE PROCESS

The therapist is careful not to rush the play therapy process. The therapist realizes that the child cannot be made to "grow faster" (Landreth, 1993) and allows the child to move at his own pace (Axline, 1969; Landreth, 1991, 1993). The therapist keeps in mind that all worthwhile change must come from within the child; and does not prod, push, or suggest (Axline, 1969). The play therapist recognizes and accepts that only when the child is ready will the child express feelings or make changes in his or her life (Axline, 1969; Landreth, 1991, 1993; Smith, 1977).

## EIGHTH PRINCIPLE: THE THERAPIST ESTABLISHES ONLY THOSE THERAPEUTIC LIMITS THAT HELP THE CHILD ACCEPT PERSONAL AND APPROPRIATE RELATIONSHIP RESPONSIBILITY

"Children need to know, deep down inside, that the people who love them will keep them safe, even when they play" (Campbell, 1993, p. 8). No child can feel safe if the child's aggressions overpower a parental figure (Smith & Herman, 1994). The wise play therapist understands that without limits there can be no therapy. The therapist knows that appropriate limits must be set because they provide the child with the security necessary for satisfactory therapy to take place (Axline, 1969; Ginott, 1994; Landreth, 1991; Smith & Herman, 1994).

The limits the therapist sets are few in number and provide a clear definition of acceptable and unacceptable behavior. These commonsense limitations protect the child, the therapist, and the playroom and are a constant reminder of the distinction between fantasy and reality. Such limits anchor the child's therapy to the world of reality. The therapist is aware that limits are conducive to developing self-discipline and hopes that the child will eventually set limits for himself (Axline, 1969; Ginott, 1994; Landreth, 1991, 1993; Smith & Herman, 1994).

When setting limits, the therapist should be firm, just, and strong (Ginott, 1994). It is critical for the therapist to maintain neutrality while sympathetically reflecting the child's feelings. The therapist does not react to the child with irritation or anger but sets limitations in an impersonal, non-punishing manner.

The counselor communicates limits decisively and seeks to convey the spirit of a non-punitive, helpful authority (Axline, 1969; Ginott, 1994; Landreth, 1991; Smith & Herman, 1994).

To be successful, the therapeutic relationship must be built upon genuine respect that both the child and the therapist have for each other. The play therapist is willing and able to set appropriate limits to preserve the necessary sense of respect and acceptance for the child. The therapist knows it is possible to be accepting of the child's feelings without permitting the child to carry those feelings into action (Axline, 1969; Hyde, 1971; Landreth, 1991; Smith, 1977). The therapist recognizes and respects the child's wish to break the limits and harmless channels are provided so that the child can express his or her feelings. The play therapist remains accepting, even when the child chooses to break a limit (Axline, 1969; Ginott, 1994; Landreth, 1991, 1993; Roden, Kranz, & Lund, 1981; Smith & Herman, 1994).

The experience of play offers the therapist the opportunity to build a therapeutic, child-centered relationship. It is this therapeutic relationship, rather than the materials or the techniques, which bring about healing and growth. Therefore, the personality characteristics and interpersonal skills of the play therapist are critically important.

## REFERENCES

Axline, V. (1969). *Play therapy*. New York: Ballantine.

Bow, J. (1988). Treating resistant children. *Child and Adolescent Social Work Journal, 5*(1), 3–15.

Campbell, C. (1993). An interview with Violet Oaklander, author of windows to our children. *Elementary School Guidance and Counseling, 28*, 52–61.

Ginott, H. (1994).*Group psychotherapy with children: The theory and practice of play therapy*. Northvale, NJ: Aronson.

Hyde, N. (1971). Play therapy: The troubled child's self-encounter. *American Journal of Nursing, 71*(7), 1366–1370.

Kaufman, B. (1994). Day by day: Playing and learning. *International Journal of Play Therapy, 3*(1), 11–21.

Landreth, G. (1991). *Play therapy: The art of the relationship*. Muncie, IN: Accelerated Development.

Landreth, G. (1993). Child-centered play therapy. *Elementary School Guidance and Counseling, 28*(1), 17–29.

Moustakas, C., & Schalock, H. (1955). An analysis of therapist-child interaction in play therapy. *Child Development, 26*(2), 143–157.

Moustakas, C., Sigel, I., & Schalock, H. (1956). An objective method for the measurement and analysis of child-adult interaction. *Child Development, 27*(2), 109–134.

Roden, B., Kranz, P., & Lund, N. (1981). Current trends in the use of limits in play therapy. *The Journal of Psychology, 107*, 191–198.

Smith, A., & Herman, J. (1994). Setting limits while enabling self-expression: Play therapy with an aggressive, controlling child. *International Journal of Play Therapy, 3*(1), 23–26.

Smith, L. (1977). An experiment with play therapy. *American Journal of Nursing, 77*(12), 1963–1965.

Tanner, Z., & Mathis, R. (1995). A child-centered typology for training novice play therapists. *International Journal of Play Therapy, 4*(2), 1–13.

Waterland, J. (1970). Actions instead of words: Play therapy for the young child. *Elementary School Guidance and Counseling, 4*(3), 180–187.

# 3

# Cultural Considerations in Play Therapy

## GERALDINE J. GLOVER

*T*he acknowledgment of the importance of culture in a person's life has a natural place in the field of counseling. Most therapists are aware of how their role in a relationship impacts cultures other than their own and work hard to accept differences as strengths. However, acceptance of differences is much more complicated than it appears. First, differences and similarities must be recognized.

Locke (1990) identified several guidelines for becoming more culturally responsive. Therapists must develop an understanding of their own cultural backgrounds, culturally-laden beliefs, values, and assumptions. They need to develop an understanding of a group's cultural makeup, both historical and contemporary, and a sense of the problems the group faces. They should learn about different cultures and their mores, yet retain the uniqueness of each child by avoiding stereotyping within cultural groups. Therapists should encourage children and their parents to be open about their cultural backgrounds. Therapists must also eliminate all personal behaviors that suggest bias or prejudice and hold high expectations for all children across all cultural groups.

In order to help prepare therapists for multicultural considerations in play therapy, this chapter will explore child-centered play therapy and the development of a culturally sensitive therapeutic relationship with both the child and the child's family. In addition, the adequate preparation of the play therapy environment is paramount for responsible multicultural play therapy.

## CHILD-CENTERED PLAY THERAPY

Strupp (1993) noted that between the choices of healing through the therapeutic relationship or emphasis on technical skills and specific therapeutic techniques, those who favor transferring therapy methods from one culture to another focus heavily on the significance of the therapeutic relationship. As a relationship-based therapy, child-centered play therapy will be presented here as an intervention for working with children who may have a different cultural background than the therapist.

Although only a minimal amount of research has been done in the area of child-centered play therapy with children of different cultures, those studies which have been conducted show promising results for its effectiveness. Trostle (1988) researched the effects of child-centered group play sessions on the social–emotional growth of bilingual Puerto Rican preschool children and found that child-centered group play facilitated the children's social, representational, and adaptive skills in group settings. In studies conducted by Glover (1996), Chau (1996), and Yuen (1997), parents reported positive results with their children after having been trained in child-centered play therapy techniques. These studies involved Native American families residing on the Flathead Reservation in northern Montana, Chinese families in the north Texas area and immigrant Chinese families in Canada. An earlier study of child-centered group therapy revealed no differential process issues or significantly different results for minority groups (Ginsberg, Stutman, & Hummel, 1978).

The intent of child-centered play therapy is to allow the child the freedom to be who the child is, thus providing the basis for a culturally sensitive relationship. The use of empathic understanding, acceptance, warmth, congruity, and behavioral limits, provide the environment in which the child is then given the opportunity to move toward adaptive behaviors. When the therapist does not have a specific structure in mind, the child is allowed to explore the issues which are most significant to that child. The child is relied upon to direct the process. Opportunities for responsible self-direction are maximized. An accepting, nonevaluative relationship allows the child to explore new ways of feeling and behaving (Dorfman, 1951). The therapist actively reflects the child's thoughts and feelings, believing that when a child's feelings are expressed, identified, and accepted, the child can accept them and then is free to deal with those feelings (Landreth, 1991). In child-centered play therapy, the therapist tries to see the child's point of reference and understand the meaning to the child without imposing beliefs or solutions on the child (Ramirez, 1999). It is exactly this accepting and respectful relationship that makes child-centered play therapy an ideal intervention for children who are of a different culture than the therapist.

## RELATIONSHIP WITH THE CHILD'S FAMILY

Because of the impossibility of knowing exactly how important certain aspects of a culture can be, a therapist is advised to become aware of the parents' or guardian's concerns and what they consider to be developmentally appropriate for their child within their culture (Glover, 1999). This knowledge can only be captured by personal research and high involvement with the adults in this child's life. It is essential to encourage these adults to educate the therapist about cultural and personal systems of language, metaphors, world views, and meanings just as it is essential for the therapist to be accepting of this new information (Westwood & Ishiyama, 1990). The therapist must recognize that families are experts in their own realm of experience and that what is functionally adaptive for one person may not be so for another (Hoare, 1991).

The therapist should be sensitive to and well-grounded in knowledge about the sociocultural world that the child comes from in order to understand and be able to integrate the cultural themes that are elicited during play therapy (Martinez & Valdez, 1992). In order to discover the aspects of a culture that may be unfamiliar to a therapist, questions can be interspersed in the intake interview and at follow-up conferences, which reveal much information that could be inadvertently taken for granted. York (1991) and Forehand and Kotchick (1996) made several suggestions for gathering useful information from parents. It is important for the therapist not to attempt to be color-blind or culture-blind with the family. Although this may seem nonjudgmental and accepting, it denies the impact of culture. Parents can be asked about their ethnic and cultural background and how they have chosen to identify themselves. Asking a family about their traditions, celebrations, religious background, and what they consider valuable can increase effectiveness with both the family and the child client.

According to Gonzalez-Mena (1998) there are two opposing goals that influence parenting styles—individualism versus connectedness. When the goal is individualism, parents tend to see a baby as connected and dependent. It is the responsibility of the parents to help the baby learn that the baby is separate and apart. This type of parent will concentrate on the development of autonomy and self-help skills such as feeding, dressing, and toileting. This parent may promote the idea of possession, an orientation toward objects, may provide choices, and encourage the expression of feelings. Independence, self-assurance, competence, and the sense of being special are all important to this parent.

Parents whose goal it is to maintain connections perceive independence as getting in the way of the close lifelong relationship to family (Gonzalez-Mena, 1998). These parents know some independence is inevitable, but want the baby to forever be connected before the baby discovers autonomy. This type of parent will focus on interdependence as the greatest value. Self-help skills such as feeding, dressing, and toileting may be delayed compared to what is typical for those children whose parents consider independence a primary goal. Rather than expression of feelings, this parent may promote a need for peace and harmony amongst family members. Humility and humbleness are encouraged and feelings of worthiness are connected to fitting in, belonging, and putting others first (Gonzalez-Mena, 1998).

York (1991) identified other aspects of raising children that may be culturally related. In addition to different age-related expectations for children to acquire self-help skills, different cultures might respond differently to crying. Children of different cultures might show different levels of attachment to adults. Gonzalez-Mena (1998) contended that if you do not thoroughly understand the culture and perhaps even the family, you cannot make judgments about the way people are raising their children and whether or not they have a healthy attachment. A child's role and responsibility in the family can also be culturally determined (York, 1991). In addition, diet and mealtime behavior, dress and hair care, discipline and child guidance methods, and the importance of gender identity and traditional sex roles are all influenced by culture. Parents of different cultures may have different ways of talking to their children and different ways of showing affection. Illness and the use of medicine or folk cures and remedies may be more common in minority families.

The greater extent to which therapists know the symbols, meanings, and messages of a child's culture, the greater will be their ability to achieve cross-cultural identification (Glover, 1999). This requires listening carefully, asking sensitive questions about those meanings, reading and studying about the culture native to the child, and recognizing that the families are experts in their own realms of experience (Hoare, 1991). The following sections examine some common values and parental expectations of African Americans, Hispanic Americans, and Native Americans. Asian Americans are dealt with in the next chapter.

## CULTURAL VALUES AND PARENTAL EXPECTATIONS

### African Americans

Values that many African American families hold dear include a strong sense of family and a positive racial identity (Forehand & Kotchick, 1996). There is a sense of great loyalty to the family, which is reinforced through community pressure that everything a person does reflects on the family (Hines, Garcia-Preto, McGoldrick, Almeida, & Weltman, 1992). No person succeeds for self alone, but for family and race. At the same time, people are respected not for their successes, but for their intrinsic worth.

The elderly are generally revered, especially women who are looked to for wisdom and support. For many African American families there is a strong reliance on religion and church structure to provide guidance (Forehand & Kotchick, 1996). And, possibly as a result of years of oppression, great value is placed on perseverance in the face of adversity. Parents have certain expectations for and ways of interacting with their children. Children can voice their opinions, but are not to argue with adults once a decision has been made (Hines et al., 1992). Strong and sometimes seemingly harsh discipline is used to help children learn acceptable behaviors. Parents are concerned that their children obey and are respectful of adults (Forehand & Kotchick, 1996).

In addition, many African American parents attempt to educate their children about the duality of their existence in American society. The goal is to live as close to the mainstream culture as possible while maintaining their African cultural identity. This education may also include developing an awareness of prejudices and how to maintain a strong self-esteem in spite of negative stereotyping and racist behavior. Some parents take the added responsibility of protecting their children from the insensitivities of others. For example, a professional African American father took his child to a pediatrician's office. The receptionist was selling pickaninny dolls (i.e, black dolls dressed in traditional slave attire). The father voiced his disapproval of this practice to the white receptionist who did not see any problem with her behavior. Being sensitive to the images to which he wanted his child to be exposed, this father chose to find a new pediatrician for his child.

The African American child may be sensitive to both verbal and nonverbal forms of communication (Hines et al., 1992). Children often prefer hands-on experiences and can be very persistent in their efforts to complete a task (Dunn et al., 1990; Griggs & Dunn, 1989). They may be considered louder in their verbal interactions than other children. If a therapist is sensitive to noise, this may be an opportunity for personal growth. It is essential that the therapist communicate genuineness, familiarity, and respect for the cultural, historical, and current sociopolitical context of the African American family (Hines et al., 1992).

## Hispanic Americans

The current United States census designation of Hispanic includes persons who refer to themselves as Chicano, Hispanic, Latino, and Mexican. Many generations of Hispanic families have inhabited the areas of California, Arizona, New Mexico, and Texas long before the establishment of those states. Other families immigrated from Mexico, Puerto Rico, Central America, South America, and Cuba. It is important that the therapist take into consideration the origins of the Hispanic family as well as the specific value system of a given family.

A primary value for many Hispanic Americans is the strength of the family (Hines et al., 1992; Westwood & Ishiyama, 1990). Strong family ties are maintained from generation to generation. This support and emotional acceptance can be healthy, nurturing, reassuring, and validating (Hines et al., 1992). Parents expect to have very close relationships with their children, especially mothers with their children. Mothers and daughters develop a reciprocal relationship in adulthood and eldest sons are often expected to become a source of financial support for older parents. Hispanic parents prefer behaviors in children that encourage family closeness, respect for parental authority, and interpersonal relatedness (Zayas & Solari, 1994).

In therapy with Hispanic children, consideration must be given to the influence of parents' stated desires about how they want their children to behave. The Hispanic child is better served, at least until more data are gathered that point to specific issues, if the therapist can view compliance in play or verbal therapy as a result of socialization for proper, respectful, and conforming behavior (Zayas & Solari, 1994).

Other aspects of therapy in relation to the Hispanic child might include the tendency for children to move about a lot and to take breaks from their play (Griggs & Dunn, 1989). It is not uncommon for psychological problems to be described in physical terms such as nerves or a stomachache. In order to be more in tune with families and children, it would be helpful for the therapist to become familiar with culturally meaningful expressions (Santiago-Rivera, 1995). Religion is often a great source of strength for many Hispanic families and the relative importance of religion should be assessed (Westwood & Ishiyama, 1990). Awareness of support systems that the family could rely on adds to the credibility of the therapist. In addition, the therapist should not be afraid to consult an Hispanic therapist for additional insight into this particular group.

## Native Americans

Native Americans display a significant amount of diversity between the over five hundred recognized tribes in the United States through their many languages and customs. Just as with other minority groups, this diversity must be acknowledged. However, when looking at this group as a whole, there are some similarities. Traditional Native American values include sharing, respect for others, independence, cooperation, and noninterference (Heinrich, Corbine, & Thomas, 1990). Elders are held in high esteem. The mind, body, spirit, and nature are considered inseparable. There is a preference for explaining natural phenomena according to the supernatural. Rituals and sacraments are of great importance and breaking with tradition results in disharmony which may be manifested in disability, disease, or distress (Lewis & Hayes, 1991). While interacting with parents it is important for the therapist to recognize the history of very difficult cross-cultural relations between tribal and nontribal peoples. Political, territorial, and cultural sovereignty continues to be highly valued by many Native Americans (Lewis & Hayes, 1991).

Time is not rigidly structured but circular, and there is never a lack of time. Many traditional Native Americans have a very present-oriented relationship with time. This can become a source of irritation for a therapist who is more comfortable with regular schedules. Even though a Native American parent may believe in and support the therapeutic relationship between their child and the therapist, if a family crisis or opportunity arises unexpectedly, a previous appointment with the therapist is likely to be disregarded in favor of the current event. Such a thing occurred when a group of Native American parents were participating in filial therapy. An Hawaiian dance troupe arrived on the reservation for a hastily scheduled performance. Parents felt this would be an excellent and entertaining opportunity for their children and chose not to attend the scheduled filial therapy meeting. Parents did not call to explain their absence. It was assumed, being a small community, that the therapist knew about this event and would most likely be attending as well.

Spiritual beliefs and practices can vary considerably between tribal peoples. Some practice more rituals than others and this can affect how they interact with the world outside of their own communities. For example, traditional Navajos have strong beliefs about death. It is taboo to discuss relatives who have passed on. Places where a dead body has been laid must be ritually cleansed with a blessing. It would be important for a therapist to know how to work with a Navajo child grieving the loss of a loved one in ways that respect this belief. Other tribal peoples who were involved with Catholic or Mormon missionaries may have converted to Christianity and practice religion in ways similar to the dominant culture. And still others may have become involved with the contemporary Native American Church.

Within the extended family, oftentimes children refer not only to their parents' siblings as auntie and uncle, but also to other significant adults. All elders may be referred to as grandmother or grandfather. If a child is being raised by extended family members, those adults acting as parents become mother and father, and cousins may be referred to as brothers and sisters, even though no legal adoption has occurred. This could become a difficulty for therapists who are accustomed to working with a nuclear family group.

Native American parents are often considered to be permissive. Because of the value placed on independence and noninterference, children are allowed abundant opportunities to make choices without coercion with the understanding that to make a decision for a child is to make the child weak (Brendtro & Brokenleg, 1993). Children are not prevented from making mistakes unless the consequences would be life-threatening. Native American parents hope that their children will learn to give unreservedly as the accumulation of property for its own sake is considered disgraceful. Children are not punished often and the form of punishment when used generally involves inductive reasoning. The consequences of the bad behaviors are put into community terms of how the behavior effects others. Embarrassment is also used to correct unacceptable behaviors (Burgess, 1980).

As with other groups, children are taught to be aware of nonverbal communication (Thomason, 1991). Long pauses and silence during play may not be unusual. The therapist may need to be aware of speaking softly. Because of the belief that time is circular, lateness and absence may be more common than with other children (Garrett, 1995). Goals for therapy may be best understood if they are short-term and oriented toward the present. Play therapy allows for both visual and oral communication.

## Other Issues

Three additional circumstances of which therapists should be aware include multiracial or children of mixed race, the level of acculturation of the child and the child's family, and English as a second language. Although not all children of mixed race have problems, a certain kind of social marginality and loneliness are descriptors of those children who have difficulty finding a group that accepts them. Children of a white and a minority parent tend to identify with the minority parent because they think that the white community will not accept them; however, an exploration of all sides of racial heritage helps children to form a positive sense of identification with ethnic and cultural roots (Herring, 1992). All children need to believe that their family, whether traditional or not, is respected and validated. Herring (1992) suggested that the therapist needs to examine the circumstances of being of mixed race as a possible influencing factor, being alert to possibilities that the child's presenting problem may shield a deeper problem of ethnic identity confusion—or not.

Acculturation is the process of becoming like the adopted culture. The level of acculturation depends on the strength of the group's support systems and their own conviction to maintain their traditions. When a group enters the dominant culture, they necessarily make adjustments in their behavior in order to fit into their new community. Garrett (1995) described four levels of acculturation. At the traditional level a person holds onto only traditional beliefs and values. At the transitional level, a person holds both traditional beliefs and values and those of the dominant culture. They may not accept all of either culture. The third level is to be bicultural. The person is accepted by the dominant culture and also knows and practices traditional ways. The fourth level of acculturation is to become assimilated. That is, to embrace only dominant cultural beliefs and values.

An example of the third level of acculturation, biculturalism, might be that of a-six-year-old Native American Salish girl who carefully wrapped her baby doll in the traditional Indian way and sang a Salish lullaby. Upon completing this first song, she immediately sang the theme song to Barney, a popular children's show character played by a purple dinosaur.

Clients whose first language is not English require special sensitivity from the therapist. If the intent is for the children to express themselves, explore their feelings, and practice new responses, it is best done in their first language. An interpreter may be necessary for the therapist to interact on a significant level. Child-centered play therapy provides ample opportunities for children to express themselves in ways other than by language such as through dramatic play, art, music, storytelling, and collage-making. The therapist can encourage the child to speak in the child's native language (words and phrases) to best illustrate feelings at the moment for ease of expression. The therapist can observe and sense what the child is trying to express while providing an opportunity for catharsis. The therapist must continually check the accuracy of interpretation of nonverbals and be ready to solicit the assistance of a well-trained bilingual interpreter (Westwood & Ishiyama, 1990).

## THE PLAY THERAPY ENVIRONMENT

Although the relationship between child and therapist is probably the single most important tool in child-centered play therapy, the environment also plays a significant part in this intervention. In play therapy, toys can be selected without cultural responsiveness assuming that any doll will do as a vehicle for children to express themselves. Alternatively, toys can specifically be considered part of the therapeutic work, such as in the inclusion of Barbies for mainstream American girls, or origami for Japanese children (Koss-Chioino & Vargas, 1992). Martinez and Valdez (1992) asserted that the play environment should contain items that convey the therapist's openness to the child's cultural background. Including such items may engender positive feelings toward the therapist and enhance the therapist's credibility, as children may perceive the therapist as being more similar to them.

It is the therapist who has control over the environment in which therapy occurs. In child-centered play therapy, a variety of culturally sensitive toys and materials should be provided from which the children choose in order to work through the issues that may be significant to them. During a play therapy session in a poorly equipped playroom, a young Hispanic boy picked up a couple of white dollhouse figures and said these are ugly. The child's play was interrupted. Since no other people figures were available, the child resumed play with the white figures, although obviously disappointed in their appearance. Sensitivity to the images available in the play room is paramount. Ideally, every playroom should be fully-equipped with a variety of materials that reflect the multitude of cultures existing in the United States. This is a noble goal, but may be unfeasible for most play therapists. The alternative is to be fully aware of the particular groups that the therapist encounters and create a playroom which reflects this diversity.

Not only should the playroom reflect this diversity, but also the waiting area or school corridors so that children, parents, and guardians feel welcome. Researchers have discovered that first impressions have been found to remain stable over time (Cantor & Mishel, 1979; Taylor, Fiske, Etcott, & Ruderman, 1978). And, as the old saying goes, you never get a second chance to make a first impression.

Derman-Sparks (1992), York (1991), and Allen, McNeill, and Schmidt (1992) all contributed suggestions for creating an environment which is culturally sensitive to the young child. A numerical balance should be maintained among different groups, making sure that people of color are not represented as a token one or two. There should be a fair balance of images of women and men, elderly people of various backgrounds, differently-abled people of various backgrounds, and diversity in family styles (e.g., two mothers or fathers, extended families, interracial and multiethnic families, differently-abled families).

For the waiting area the therapist can select artwork, prints, sculpture, and textiles by artists of various backgrounds that reflect the aesthetic environment, and the cultures of the families represented in the local community. Rather than dolls in ethnic costumes, artwork and artifacts can be displayed from existing cultures: fabric, paintings, beadwork, rugs, wall hangings, musical instruments, sculpture, windsocks, wind chimes, and photos.

Within the playroom itself, the various areas provide the opportunity to acknowledge diversity. The art area can provide colors, patterns, and textures from multiple cultures. Additional materials include origami paper for folding, rice paper for painting, and red clay for modeling. Various fabric scraps of imported cloth, leather scraps, and beads and feathers are appropriate for creating collages. It is important to provide skin-colored crayons, markers, paint, paper, and play dough in order that children can accurately portray themselves and their families.

The dramatic play area should include multiethnic dolls in contemporary clothing. Nurturing themes are often recreated in the playroom. Providing familiar materials in the kitchen area supports this activity. Items that reflect diverse cultures include tea boxes, tea tins, canned foods, cardboard food containers, plastic bottles, and plastic play food. Rice, flour, and potato bags can be stuffed with batting and sewn closed. Baskets, gourds, mesh bags, and pottery are all used as storage containers by various cultures. Different cultures use different cooking utensils such as a tortilla press, molenellos, tea ball, rolling pin, strainer, ladles, wok, steamer, food grinder, mortar and pestle, cutting board, frying pan, and kettle. The playroom can supply a variety of eating utensils such as silverware, wooden spoons, spatulas, grate, egg beaters, whisk, rice bowl, wooden bowls and plates, tin plates, plastic plates, teacups, chopsticks, a tea pot, and a coffee pot.

Traditional costumes might be useful; however, typical daily wear of various cultures is less specific in supporting dramatic play. Clothing can be provided such as dresses, skirts, jackets, and large pieces of fabric in squares, rectangles, and triangles. Fabric can be of different patterns such as batik, tie-dyed, and madras prints.

## REFERENCES

Allen, J., McNeill, E., & Schmidt, V. (1992). *Cultural awareness for children.* Menlo Park, CA: Addison-Wesley Publishing Company.

Brendtro, L. K., & Brokenleg, M. (1993). Beyond the curriculum of control. *The Journal of Emotional & Behavioral Problems, 1*(4), 5–11.

Burgess, B. J. (1980). Parenting in the Native American community. In M. D. Fantini, & R. Cárdenas (Eds.), *Parenting in a multicultural society* (pp. 63–73). New York: Longman.

Cantor, N., & Mishel, W. (1979). Prototype in person perception. *Advances in Experimental Psychology, 12,* 3–52.

Chau, I. (1996). *Filial therapy with Chinese parents.* Unpublished doctoral dissertation, University of North Texas, Denton, TX.

Derman-Sparks, L. (1992). *Anti-bias curriculum: Tools for empowering young children.* Washington, DC: National Association for the Education of Young Children.

Dorfman, E. (1951). Play therapy. In C. R. Rogers (Ed.), *Client-centered therapy: Its current practice* (pp. 235–277). Boston: Houghton Mifflin.

Dunn, R., Gemake, J., Jalali, F., Zenhausern, R., Quinn, P., & Spiridakis, J. (1990). Cross-cultural differences in learning styles of elementary-age students from four ethnic backgrounds. *Journal of Multicultural Counseling and Development, 18*(2), 68–93.

Forehand, R., & Kotchick, B. A. (1996). Cultural diversity: A wake-up call for parent training. *Behavior Therapy, 27,* 187–206.

Garrett, M. W. (1995). Between two worlds: Cultural discontinuity in the dropout of Native American youth. *The School Counselor, 42*(3), 186–195.

Ginsberg, B., Stutman, J., & Hummel, J. (1978). Notes for practice: Group filial therapy. *Social Work, 23*(2), 154–156.

Glover, G. J. (1996). *Filial therapy with Native Americans on the Flathead Reservation.* Unpublished doctoral dissertation, University of North Texas, Denton, TX.

Glover, G. J. (1999). Multicultural considerations in group play therapy. In D. Sweeney & L. Homeyer (Eds.), *Group play therapy: How to do it, how it works, whom it's best for* (pp. 278–195). San Francisco: Jossey-Bass.

Gonzalez-Mena, J. (1998). *The child in the family and the community* (2nd ed.). Upper Saddle River, NJ: Merrill.

Griggs, S. A., & Dunn, R. (1989). The learning styles of multicultural groups and counseling implications. *Journal of Multicultural Counseling and Development, 17*(4), 146–155.

Heinrich, R. K., Corbine, J. L., & Thomas, K. R. (1990). Counseling Native Americans. *Journal of Counseling and Development, 69*(2), 128–133.

Herring, R. D. (1992). Biracial children: An increasing concern for elementary and middle school counselors. *Elementary School Guidance and Counseling, 27*(2), 123–130.

Hines, P. M., Garcia-Preto, N., McGoldrick, M., Almeida, R., & Weltman, S. (1992). Intergenerational relationships across cultures: Special issue: Multicultural practice. *Families in Society: The Journal of Contemporary Human Services, 73*(6), 323–338.

Hoare, C. H. (1991). Psychosocial identity development and cultural others. *Journal of Counseling and Development, 40*(1), 45–53.

Koss-Chioino, J. D., & Vargas, L. A. (1992). Through the cultural looking glass: A model for understanding culturally responsive psychotherapies. In L. A. Vargas & J. D. Koss-Chioino (Eds.), *Working with culture: Psychotherapeutic interventions with ethnic minority children and adolescents* (pp. 1–22). San Francisco: Jossey-Bass.

Landreth, G. L. (1991). *Play therapy: The art of the relationship*. Muncie, IN: Accelerated Development, Inc.

Lewis, A. C., & Hayes, S. (1991). Multiculturalism and the school counseling curriculum. *Journal of Counseling and Development, 70*(1), 119–125.

Locke, D. (1990). Fostering the self-esteem of African American children. In E. R. Gerler, J. C. Ciechalaski, & L. D. Parker (Eds.), *Elementary school counseling in a changing world* (pp. 12–18). Alexandria, VA: The American School Counselor Association.

Martinez, K. J., & Valdez, D. M. (1992). Cultural considerations in play therapy with Hispanic children. In L. A. Vargas & J. D. Koss-Chioino (Eds.), *Working with culture: Psychotherapeutic interventions with ethnic minority children and adolescents* (pp. 85–102). San Francisco: Jossey-Bass.

Ramirez, L. M. (1999, March). A reader's response to working with Latino/a clients: Five common mistakes [On the other hand: working with diversity]. *Association for Play Therapy, Inc. Newsletter, 18*, 3–4.

Santiago-Rivera, A. L. (1995). Developing a culturally sensitive treatment modality for bilingual Spanish-speaking clients: Incorporating language and culture in counseling. *Journal of Counseling and Development, 74*(1), 12–17.

Strupp, H. H. (1993). The Vanderbilt psychotherapy studies: Synopsis. *Journal of Consulting and Clinical Psychology, 61*, 431–433.

Taylor, S., Fiske, S., Etcott, N., & Ruderman, A. (1978). The categorical and contextual basis of person memory and stereotyping. *Journal of Personality and Social Psychology, 28*, 778–793.

Thomason, T. C. (1991). Counseling Native Americans: An introduction for non-Native American counselors. *Journal of Counseling and Development, 69*(4), 321–327.

Trostle, S. L. (1988). The effects of child-centered group play sessions on social-emotional growth of three- to six-year-old bilingual Puerto Rican children. *Journal of Research in Early Childhood Education, 2*(3), 93–106.

Westwood, M. J., & Ishiyama, F. I. (1990). The communication process as a critical intervention for client change in cross-cultural counseling. *Journal of Multicultural Counseling and Development, 18*(4), 163–171.

York, S. (1991). *Roots and wings: Affirming culture in early childhood programs* (pg. 169). St. Paul, MN: Redleaf Press.

Yuen, T. (1997). *Filial therapy with immigrant Chinese parents*. Unpublished doctoral dissertation, University of North Texas, Denton, TX.

Zayas, L. H., & Solari, F. (1994). Early childhood socialization in Hispanic families: Context, culture, and practice implications. *Professional Psychology: Research and Practice, 25*(3), 200–206.

# 4

# Play Therapy with Chinese Children

## Needed Modifications

SHU-CHEN KAO
GARRY L. LANDRETH

lthough play therapy is a product of western society, the tenets of play therapy are universal since children of all cultures play and express themselves actively through their play. All individuals—child and play therapist—are, however, culturally encapsulated. Therefore, sensitivity to cultural diversity is always a prerequisite for the play therapist when working with any child. This chapter explores some cultural differences and the modification of some play therapy techniques and procedures, which may be necessary to ensure the effectiveness of play therapy with Chinese children.

There is a significant diversity in demographic profiles among Asian Americans. Over forty different Asian groups in the United States include Asian Indians, Chinese, Filipinos, Japanese, Koreans, Southeast Asians, Cambodians, Laotians, Vietnamese, Pacific Islanders, Hawaiian, Guamanians, and Samoans. Even with this diversity, there do seem to be some common themes among these groups; however, the Chinese culture is the focus of this chapter as a representative group of Asian Americans. It is not within the intended scope of this book to deal in-depth with the many specific issues related to play therapy with each of the major cultural groups. The intent of the following exploration of play therapy with Chinese children is to facilitate play therapists' awareness of the existence of similar issues in other cultures and to provide ideas for necessary adaptations.

# THE PROCESS OF PLAY THERAPY

## *With The Child*

Commenting on the race issue in young children, Axline stressed the importance of seeing things "from the inner frame of reference of the child" (1948, p. 301). Because different child behaviors are valued in the Chinese culture as compared to the American culture, play therapists should be aware of and sensitive to these cultural differences when they work with Chinese children.

As the relationship begins in the playroom, the play therapist usually tries hard to create a safe place for the child to grow. An important objective for the play therapist is to understand how the child feels. To understand how Chinese children may feel, the play therapist needs to understand that children reared in more traditional Chinese homes are taught to be cooperative and obedient, which might be viewed as a nonassertive and dependent behavior from the western society's standard. The child's concern in the playroom might be, "Will I please this adult?" Since Chinese children are prone to be cooperative and to follow the play therapist, the play therapist may need to be more patient with the Chinese child. An early evaluation of a Chinese child as dependent may be grossly incorrect.

Chinese students tend to be more quiet in the classroom. The learning mode of most Chinese children is absorbing rather than interacting. Therefore, play therapists might experience more silence and anxiety on the part of Chinese children if they expect them to be verbally active in the playroom. It is not necessarily true that more verbally active children are assuming more responsibility. However, the child may be working by listening and reorganizing what is heard and experienced into his or her system. The play therapist should keep in mind that because of their different learning mode, Chinese children are processing and learning even when they are quiet in the playroom.

Chinese children experience academic pressure even from the preschool years. Studies show that Chinese parents emphasize the value of academic achievement more than American parents (Lin & Fu, 1990). Chinese children are pushed to achieve academic success in school as well as to learn a "useful hobby." A typical life for a school-age Chinese child in his or her home country: school attendance from 8:00 A.M. to 4:00 P.M., Mondays through Fridays, and 8:00 A.M. to 12:00 A.M. on Saturdays. The child usually joins some night classes to learn "useful skills," such as piano study, computer science, a second language, math, etc. Furthermore, the child usually has a lot of school homework everyday. Helping Chinese children cope with school stress might be a common issue in the playroom. The play therapist should be sensitive to Chinese children's potential frustration and possible low self-esteem resulting from school competition. For Chinese children, failure in school competition is internalized as failure to honor their families. This focus on honoring the family is in contrast to the emphasis usually found in play therapy—helping children to like, appreciate, and accept themselves.

The criteria for determining therapeutic progress in play therapy may be different for Chinese children. According to the western perspective, therapeutic progress can be indicated through increased independence, self-control, inner-directedness, and responsibility for one's own feelings and actions (Landreth, 1991). These qualities are not highly valued by Chinese parents. In most Chinese families, children are taught to adjust to the environment rather than to overcome the environment, to obey the rules rather than to create new rules (Li & Yany, 1972). The western view of independence and self-directedness may be viewed as aggressiveness and stubbornness in the Chinese culture. The play therapist should consider these differences in parental and societal expectations when working with Chinese children. Since the development of internal control rather than external control is the natural result of most play therapy experiences, the play therapist may need to pay extra attention to the process of helping Chinese parents anticipate and accept these changes.

## With The Parent

For most Chinese families, the child–parent bonding is usually tighter, not necessarily healthier, than in the western society. Chinese parents feel a strong responsibility for their children's success and welfare. Compared to American parents, Chinese parents tend to control their children more (Lin & Fu, 1990). As a result of parental and societal pressure, Chinese children do not feel free to live their lives alone without thinking about their parents. Therefore, it may be more important to involve parents in the counseling process when working with Chinese children. The process of filial therapy would seem to be especially effective since the children would not feel as if they were keeping something hidden from their parents, as might be the case in play therapy.

Chinese are especially sensitive to the word *therapy*. It implies that the child is mentally impaired in some way, which is viewed as a shame for the family. Therefore, when working with Chinese parents, the play therapist is encouraged to be creative in choosing a nonthreatening title to describe the play therapy process in order to desensitize parents' emotional reactions. Some possible alternative terms in lieu of play therapy could be counseling with toys, emotional growth through play, developmental growth through play, or any similar title (Landreth, 1991).

During parent consultation time, Chinese parents tend to exhibit a heightened level of concern, more so than most parents, regarding the progress of their child in the play sessions, the play therapist's diagnosis of the child's problem, how to resolve the child's problem, etc. The play therapist needs to be patient in reeducating toward a healthy boundary in the parent–child relationship and in explaining the importance of confidentiality in the play therapy relationship.

Since teachers are held in high esteem in the Chinese culture, second only to parents and elders, the play therapist is encouraged to work closely with teachers to help them to be more accepting and actively supportive of positive changes Chinese children exhibit. This may be especially significant when the parent is uncooperative in the helping process.

A difficult issue that may be raised when working with Chinese parents is the giving of gifts. Gift giving is a natural and common way for Chinese to show appreciation or to build up a relationship. Chinese value the process of giving and receiving in terms of the social meaning. If the play therapist strictly adheres to the ethical standards regarding gifts, Chinese parents may feel rejected or confused. It is recommended that Chinese parents be informed during the initial parent consultation that the custom of gift giving is not necessary in this counseling relationship. If the parent should bring a gift, it is suggested that the play therapist wisely judge the gift in terms of the social meaning. The therapist must also always be sensitive to potential personal feelings of obligation when receiving gifts.

## PLAY THERAPY PROCEDURES

Modification of some basic play therapy procedures may be necessary to ensure efficiency of facilitation of the play therapy process with Chinese children.

### Limit Setting

The Chinese culture emphasizes the social aspect of the individual's behavior. Children are taught to behave themselves and to not "lose face" in front of others. Unlike most approaches to play therapy, which emphasize the development of inner control, guilt and shame are primary determents utilized in the Chinese culture to control misconduct. Chinese children are likely to experience feelings of shame in association with perceived misconduct. When the play therapist sets a limit, the child may very likely think he or she did something wrong, and experience accompanying feelings of guilt and shame. Although such feelings may arise, the importance of therapeutic limit setting (Landreth, 1991) in the play therapy relationship cannot be overemphasized. What may be necessary is a modified approach to limit setting.

Landreth (1991) recommends three steps in therapeutic limit setting. "A—Acknowledge the child's feelings, wishes, and wants. C—Communicate the limit. T—Target acceptable alternatives" (p. 223). In order to accommodate Chinese children's perceptual reality when the therapist is the focus of the child's anger, a change is suggested in the first step of this limit setting process by focusing on the child's feelings about self rather than the child's feelings toward the therapist. This shift of focus away from the child's feelings will avoid the possibility of the child personalizing the event as misconduct with resulting feelings of shame.

For example, when Robert picks up the dart gun and glares at the play therapist as he begins to load the dart gun (Landreth, 1991, p. 224), the play therapist's statements could be modified as follows:

Therapist: "Robert, I can see you are really angry at me."

Modification: It seems that shooting me will make you feel good.

Robert: "Yes! And I'm going to shoot you good!"

Therapist: "You are so angry at me, you would like to shoot me. But I'm not for shooting."

Modification: So I will know that you are very angry. But I'm not for shooting.

Robert: "You can't stop me. Nobody can!"

Therapist: "You're so powerful no one can stop you. But I'm not for shooting. You may pretend the Bobo is me (therapist points toward the Bobo) and shoot the Bobo."

Modification: You are your own master. No one can stop you. But I'm not for shooting. You can pretend the Bobo is me (therapist points toward the Bobo) and shoot the Bobo.

Although these are only slight changes in wording, the result is quite different in the Chinese culture since the focus of the response is shifted from the child's feelings about the therapist to the child's feelings about self. This shift of focus greatly decreases the possibility of the child feeling shame or guilt in the interchange.

## Returning Responsibility to the Child

Because the Chinese culture so strongly emphasizes teaching children to be cooperative and obedient, efforts to encourage children to assume more responsibility for self in the playroom may need to be approached differently. Since Chinese children are prone to be obedient, responding to a child who asks, "What color should I paint this?" with "In here that's something you can decide," may sound critical to the Chinese child since the child is likely to internalize the returning of responsibility as a sense of obedience. When this occurs, the child wants to please the adult and may feel dependent because he or she takes on the responsibility in terms of obedience and thus has a desire to please the adult.

Chinese children can be helped to take on responsibility by adding the word "try" to the above response. "In here that's something you can try to decide." The word "try" is more encouraging to Chinese children and they are less likely to feel pressured to follow the perceived expectation of the play therapist. When attempting to return responsibility to Chinese children, responses such as "Show me what you want done" are generally effective because they show the child is assuming responsibility for the action or direction. Therefore, the child learns to rely on self in a cooperative atmosphere consistent with earlier teachings.

*Showing Understanding of the Child's Feelings*

Compared to the western culture, the Chinese culture is more reserved in revealing feelings in the presence of other people. Control of feelings is viewed as maturity. This is especially true for older children. Therefore, if there is no significant emotional expression on the child's part, the play therapist will need to avoid using emotionally-revealing words which may cause the child to feel awkward or to think that he or she needs to control him/herself more in the playroom. This is not to say feelings should not be reflected, but rather that emotionally-revealing words should be carefully chosen. Furthermore, the play therapist will need to be more sensitive to the child's facial expressions and nonverbal behaviors in order to identify the child's real feelings.

## PLAY MATERIALS

The toys and materials recommended by Landreth (1991) can be used effectively with Chinese children. Some modifications, however, will be helpful in accommodating the Chinese culture and to facilitate the playing out of real-life experiences. Since Chinese school-age children experience much pressure to succeed academically, school supplies, such as a pencil, eraser, paper, and school bag, are especially needed. Books of any kind should be avoided because Chinese children are very likely to spend the entire session reading to the exclusion of interaction with available toys.

Traditional Chinese toys that are similar to the toys recommended by Landreth (1991) can be selected to promote a feeling of familiarity and comfort for the child. Traditional Chinese musical instruments can replace the xylophone and cymbals. Kitchen materials should include typical Chinese utensils and table materials. Oriental figures, puppets, and dolls can replace typical western society figures.

Some play therapy items such as a dragon may typically have a different meaning for Chinese children. In western society, a dragon is usually used by children to communicate anger, violence, destruction, or something "bad." In Chinese culture, however, a dragon represents celebration, prosperity, and happy times. Thus, a Chinese child playing with a dragon may represent a positive event. The play therapist should be sensitive to such possible differences in the meaning of children's play.

## OTHER CONCERNS WITH CHINESE CHILDREN

When working with a Chinese child, it may be helpful to know the immigrant status of the child's family. Recently immigrated children may experience a sense of loss and a feeling of being out-of-control because they did not choose to come to a new country but rather their parents chose for them. Many Chinese parents choose to go to another country because of the political situation in their home country and because they want a better life for their children. However, Chinese children may not appreciate this.

Peter's parents moved to the United States because they believed Peter would be happier in the American educational system. They sacrificed their career development in their country and transferred all of their hopes to Peter. According to his teachers, Peter had trouble controlling his behavior at school. However, Peter's mother insisted that she did not have any trouble controlling Peter's behavior at home. In the family assessment session, Peter was a compliant boy who looked timid, but during his play sessions Peter was very bossy and critical of himself. The play therapist sensed that Peter had a need to free himself from the family's control and that he experienced tremendous pressure and guilt because he knew that his parents' hopes and dreams rested on him.

Second-generation Chinese-American children have grown up in the United States, and they have many life experiences similar to those of American children. However, second-generation Chinese children often experience conflict about how to fit into the American culture without denying their Chinese culture.

John was in the first grade and was referred to play therapy because of behavioral problems in the classroom. One of his play themes in the first three sessions was in-and-out play, in which he would throw the toy soldiers out of their container one at a time. In the fourth session, he continued this activity with the added verbal comment as he threw each one out, "This one is out. This one is out. This one is out." After a few seconds of silence, he said, "Because they have different colors." Then, he quickly switched to another play activity. When the play therapist gave the five minutes warning, John went to the blackboard and tried very hard to write three Chinese words and told the play therapist, "You know, this is my Chinese name."

## SUMMARY

When working with Chinese children in play therapy, the play therapist should be familiar with cultural differences, especially in the areas of parental control and child rearing emphasis on cooperation, obedience, and academic success. The play therapist must also be sensitive to the Chinese emphasis on shame and reservation of affection.

## REFERENCES

Axline, V. (1948). Play therapy and race conflict in young children. *Journal of Abnormal and Social Psychology, 43,* 300–310.

Landreth, G. L. (1991). *Play therapy: The art of the relationship.* Muncie, IN: Accelerated Development.

Li, Y. Y., & Yany, K. S. (1972). *Symposium on the character of the Chinese.* Taipei, Taiwan: Institute of Ethnology Academia Sinica.

Lin, C. C., & Fu, V. R. (1990). A comparison of child-rearing practices among Chinese, immigrant Chinese, and Caucasian American parents. *Child Development, 61*(2), 429–433.

# 5

# What the Play Therapist Needs to Know about Medications

## DANIEL S. SWEENEY
## ROSS J. TATUM

*H*istorically, psychopharmacology has not been an area of research or concern for the play therapist. A review of the play therapy literature (Landreth, Homeyer, Bratton, & Kale, 1995) revealed an almost absolute dearth of references to play therapy and medication. Many play therapists develop treatment programs with the hope of limiting or eliminating the need for medication, rather than encourage its use. A trend of thought among play therapists appears to be that medications for children are at best probably unnecessary and at worst harmful.

With the move toward managed health care and brief therapy in the mental health field, however, insurance companies and third party payment providers are looking for the swift reduction of symptoms that pharmacological approaches might provide. This concept is clearly at odds with the goals of play therapy, which focus upon providing a child with a safe environment in which to process intrapsychic issues in their own language (play). Symptom reduction is a by-product, rather than a focus of treatment, for many child play therapists.

The authors have not attempted to address the political issues of managed health care, or the appropriate focus of child mental health treatment. This chapter will, however, address the concern that so many children are on some

From Sweeney, D., & Tatum, R., (1995). Play therapy and psychopharmacology. *International Journal of Play Therapy*, 4(2), 41–57. Adapted and reprinted with permission.

form of medication and that the play therapist must have some basic knowledge of child psychopharmacology. Additionally, it will address some medication considerations specific to the treatment modality of play therapy.

The need for play therapists to be educated about psychopharmacological issues is clear. Phillips and Landreth (1995) conducted a survey of play therapists, and found that seventy-four percent had a master's degree or below, and that sixty percent had ten years or less of experience in the field. The average play therapist (graduate degree and less than ten years of experience) has little if any training in psychopharmacology. Psychopharmacology is not included in the curriculum requirements for all accredited master's programs in counseling, psychology, and marriage and family therapy (Patterson & Magulac, 1994). While most doctoral level training programs offer pharmacology courses, many do not require them. One result of this trend is that students of psychotherapy often ignore the treatment possibilities of medications or the negative side effects that medications might have (Patterson & Magulac, 1994).

The position of the authors is that possession of even a cursory knowledge about child psychopharmacology places the play therapist in a better position to provide quality treatment. An understanding of the medical records of a referred client and adequate knowledge to assess the necessity for a psychiatric referral are imperative in treatment planning and implementation. The play therapist, in order to best meet the needs of the child client, must become knowledgeable about psychopharmacology, and must overcome issues of power, control, and "turf" through being educated and aware.

## PSYCHOPHARMACOLOGY WITH CHILDREN

The majority of research and experience in the field of psychopharmacology has been with an adult population. There is, unfortunately, scant empirical study of the efficacy and safety of psychotropic medication with children (Biederman, 1992; Bukstein, 1993; Campbell, Godfrey, & Magee, 1992; Gitlin, 1990; Green, 1991). The use of psychotropics with children has not generally been addressed by the Food and Drug Administration (FDA). FDA approval, however, is not meant to direct prescribing habits, but rather to limit pharmaceutical company advertising. An additional issue of concern is that an increasing number of nonpsychiatric physicians, including pediatricians, family doctors, and neurologists, are prescribing psychotropics for children.

Despite these, and other related concerns, the use of psychotropic medications for treating children has increased dramatically beyond the common use of stimulants for Attention Deficit Hyperactivity Disorder (ADHD) (Gadow, 1992). These include antidepressants for major depression, anxiety disorders, and ADHD; lithium for bipolar disorders; neuroleptics for psychotic disorders; and some antihypertensive agents for dyscontrol (Biederman, 1992). The discovery of new pharmacological treatments and the evaluation of psychotropic uses for nonpsychiatric drugs have led to a significant increase in the pharmacologic treatment of childhood mental health issues (Gadow, 1992).

Just as the nonmedical therapist would not argue the existence of physiological roots in the etiology of adult psychiatric disorders, so must he or she recognize this dynamic in children. Bukstein (1993) noted: "For prepubertal children, biochemical and neurophysiological correlates exist for several disorders. Research has implicated neurotransmitter dysfunction in a variety of psychopathologic behaviors and disorders" (p. 14). Whereas play therapy may address core issues of some disorders and arguably peripheral symptoms in most disorders, neurobiological contributions to childhood psychopathology must be addressed medically.

There are multiple pre-treatment and treatment considerations of which—although primarily the concern of the prescribing physician—the play therapist should be aware. First, it should be noted that several medications may be utilized for a variety of symptoms or diagnoses. Specific psychotropics may be effective for dissimilar disorders because of their influence on neurotransmitters and psychoendocrine events in the brain along common routes (Green, 1991).

Secondly, developmental issues of childhood and adolescence must be considered. Children are, from a biological standpoint, immature and growing organisms, and thus metabolize chemical agents differently than adults. Children may respond differently to psychotropic medication taken by the similarly diagnosed adult (Biederman & Steingard, 1991; Bukstein, 1993; Gadow, 1992; Green, 1991). Issues of absorption and disposition are primary concerns, and the prescribing physician may look to adjust dosage strength and frequency to achieve the maximum therapeutic effect of a medication. Blood levels may be closely monitored.

Another consideration in prescribing psychotropics to children is the absolute necessity of a complete physiologic and psychiatric assessment. Biederman and Steingard (1991) stated the primary goal of such an assessment: "Psychopharmacologic evaluation of the child should address the basic question of whether the patient has a psychiatric disorder (or disorders) that may respond to psychotropics" (p. 343). If this inquiry is answered affirmatively, a complete physical examination (sometimes including laboratory tests), psychosocial history, and baseline behavioral assessment must be conducted. The valuable contribution of the play therapist to this process will be commented upon later.

A final concern must be the consideration of alternative and/or concurrent treatment approaches in the psychiatric intervention with children. "Treatment with psychotropic drugs should always be part of a more comprehensive treatment regimen and rarely, if ever, is appropriate as the sole treatment modality for a child or adolescent (Green, 1991, p. 771). The effects of concurrent treatment interventions and environmental influences should be considered when examining the efficacy of psychopharmacology (Bukstein, 1993; Biederman & Steingard, 1991; Green, 1991).

# PHARMACOLOGIC TREATMENT OF CHILDHOOD DISORDERS

Although children are referred for psychiatric evaluation primarily to address unwanted symptoms, treatment planning generally occurs according to diagnostic category. Discussion of treatment will follow along diagnostic lines. For the sake of brevity, diagnostic definitions are not given. Table 5.1 provides a summary of the *Diagnostic and Statistical Manual of Mental Disorders*-4th ed. (DSM-IV) (American Psychiatric Association, 1994) diagnoses and psychotropic medications that may be indicated.

## Attention-Deficit Hyperactivity Disorder

The category that has been most researched in the psychopharmacological treatment of children is ADHD (Gitlin, 1990). The most commonly prescribed medications for the diagnosis of ADHD are the stimulants Ritalin [methylphenidate], Dexedrine [dextroamphetamine], Adderall [mix of amphetamine salts], and Cylert [pemoline]. Cylert is now used much less frequently due to concern over possible liver dysfunction. The manufacturer of Cylert now recommends biweekly blood tests. The antidepressants Effexor [venlafaxine] and Wellbutrin [bupropion] are also used with ADHD. Tricyclic antidepressants (Tofranil [imipramine], Pamelor [nortriptyline], and Norpramin [desipramine]) have also been used successfully. While used safely in many children, the tricyclic antidepressants are used less frequently due to cardiac events that have led to the deaths of several children. More specifically, some psychiatrists have recommended discontinuing use of desipramine with children at all. Catapres [clonidine] and Tenex [guanfacine] are frequently used to augment partial responses to stimulants. There is, however, some concern over the safety and efficacy of these medications with children.

## Affective Disorders

Although the existence of childhood depression is no longer clinically questioned, the efficacy of the commonly prescribed antidepressants in treating this disorder has been difficult to establish. However, prescribing antidepressants for children is a common practice. The medications commonly used include Effexor, Zoloft [sertraline], Paxil [paroxetine], Prozac [fluoxetine], and Celexa [citalopram]. Wellbutrin and Serzone [nefazodone] are used occasionally, and the tricyclic antidepressants are now used less frequently. Monoamine oxidase inhibitors (MAOIs) generally are not prescribed for children due to the severe dietary restrictions that are required. Sometimes lithium is used to augment a partial response to antidepressants.

For symptoms of mania, lithium and anticonvulsants, such as Depakote [valproic acid] and Tegretol [carbamazepine] have been used. Neuroleptics (also known as antipsychotics) and benzodiazepines can be used to treat the acute

TABLE 5.1. Childhood DSM-IV diagnoses and
psychotropic medications that may be indicated

| DSM-IV Diagnosis | Medications Used |
| --- | --- |
| Attention-Deficit Hyperactivity Disorder | Stimulants, Antidepressants (including Effexor, Wellbutrin, & Tricyclics), Catapres, Tenex |
| Major Depression | SSRIs, Effexor, Wellbutrin, Serzone, Remeron |
| Mania (acute and for maintenance) | Anticonvulsants, Lithium, Antipsychotics, Benzodiazepines |
| Mental Retardation (with severe aggression or self-injurious behavior | Antipsychotics, Lithium, Inderol, Trexan |
| Pervasive Developmental Disorder | Antipsychotics, Trexan |
| Conduct Disorder (with aggression) | Antipsychotics, Lithium, Anticonvulsants, Inderal |
| Anxiety Disorders | |
| Generalized Anxiety Disorder | Antidepressants, Benzodiazepines, Buspar |
| Obsessive-Compulsive Disorder | SSRIs, Clomipramine |
| Posttraumatic Stress Disorder | Antidepressants, Benzodiazepines, Buspar, Clonidine |
| Separation Anxiety Disorder | Antidepressants, Benzodiazepines |
| Panic Disorder | Antidepressants, Benzodiazepines |
| Schizophrenia | Antipsychotics |
| Intermittent Explosive Disorder | Propranolol, Lithium, Antipsychotics |
| Sleep Disorders | Some Antidepressants (Remeron, Desyrel), Benzodiazepines, Antihistamines |
| Enuresis (not due to medical disorder) | DDAVP, Tricyclic Antidepressants |
| Tourette's Syndrome | Haloperidol, Pimozide, Clonidine, Risperdal |

agitation of mania. Long term use of neuroleptics for the treatment of bipolar disorder is not recommended because of the risk of tardive dyskinesia. Tardive dyskinesia is a syndrome of involuntary movements that can result from the use of neuroleptics.

## Anxiety Disorders

The medications most often used in the treatment of anxiety problems in children are the antidepressants. Because they have a better safety profile, the newer antidepressants (e.g., SSRIs [selective serotonin reuptake inhibitors], Effexor) are used more often than the tricyclic antidepressants. Buspar [buspirone] has also been used. In addition to the antidepressants, benzodiazepines like Xanax [alprazolam] are used with children having separation anxiety disorder. Obsessive compulsive disorder has been shown to respond to medications that primarily affect the re-uptake of serotonin. These include Zoloft, Paxil, Prozac, Celexa,

Luvox [fluvoxamine], and Anafranil [clomipramine]. Generally, psychopharma-cologic treatment of post-traumatic stress disorder (PTSD) is based on the treat-ment of comorbid anxiety or mood disorders. Antidepressants are used most often. Inderal [propranolol] and Catapres have also been used. According to clinical reports, both antidepressants and benzodiazepines may be helpful in treating children with panic disorder (Popper, 1993).

## Schizophrenia

Onset of schizophrenia in prepubertal children is rare, as is psychopharmaco-logic research in this population (Gitlin, 1990). Antipsychotics are prescribed. The newer atypical antipsychotics, Risperdal [risperidone] and Zyprexa [olanzapine], are progressively being used as an initial intervention with these children. High potency neuroleptics such as Haldol [haloperidol] and Navane [thiothixene] likely cause less problems with learning (but more problems with stiffness) than low potency neuroleptics such as Mellaril [thioridazine] and Thorazine [chlorpromazine], which are more sedating (Campbell & Spencer, 1988). Clozaril [clozapine] has been used in adults showing a poor response to traditional neuroleptics, and has seen some use in adolescents. It is only used with children infrequently.

## Enuresis

In the authors' experience, the initial approach to enuresis should involve be-havioral methods or a bed alarm. After these approaches have failed, medica-tion may be quite appropriate. The antidiuretic hormone, Desmopressin (DDAVP), is administered intranasally or in pill form. Low doses of tricyclic antidepressants are also used. Relapse following discontinuation of medication is common.

## Sleep Disorders

Although sleep disorders in children are not commonly medicated, in the au-thors' experience they do respond to specific medications. Some psychiatrists use Benadryl [diphenhydramine] for brief periods for children and adolescents experiencing difficulty falling asleep. Catapres has also been used to treat the insomnia that may be associated with stimulant use. More recently, there has been increased use of Remeron [mirtazapine] and Desyrel [trazodone] for sleep difficulties. Some benzodiazepines, such as Valium [diazepam] and tricyclics, have been prescribed for night terrors and sleepwalking.

## Tourette's Syndrome

Haldol and Orap [pimozide] have been used effectively to reduce tic behaviors (Gadow, 1992). The tics may also respond to Catapres. Some of the newer antipsychotics, such as Risperdal, have shown some efficacy with tics and have a lower rate of tardive dyskinesia. Some psychiatrists will opt for the use of these new neuroleptics to avoid the potential of serious cardiovascular side effects that may be associated with clonidine.

## Other

The diagnosis of an eating disorder itself does not call for the use of pharmacotherapy. Severe anxiety, obsessive-compulsive symptoms, or psychosis that may accompany the eating disorder symptoms, may be treated with appropriate medications. Likewise, severe depression may be treated with an appropriate antidepressant. Studies with adults have noted that antidepressants can decrease the severity of binge-eating (Green, 1991).

In general, developmental disorders are treated according to specific indications. This is another area where the newer atypical antipsychotics are finding increased use. Neuroleptics, such as Haldol, and Trexan [naltrexone], an opiate antagonist, have been used with positive results in children with autism (Gadow). Again, children on neuroleptics must be monitored closely for the development of movement disorders. Comorbid symptoms associated with developmental disorders such as anxiety, depression, obsessive-compulsive behavior, and hyperactivity, may be treated accordingly.

## Aggression

Aggression, while not a diagnostic category itself, is a common complaint encountered by those working with children. The symptom of aggression cuts across many diagnostic categories. Successful intervention takes into account comorbid symptoms which can be treated such as problems with impulsivity, depression, bipolar disorder, and psychosis. In the authors' experience, antipsychotics have been effective in reducing aggressive behavior in hyperactive and conduct-disordered children, as well as children with mental retardation and autism. Because of the risks associated with these medications, they should be used long-term only after other options have failed. Lithium, Inderal, and Tegretol have also been used to treat aggression. Depakote may also be of some benefit.

# THERAPEUTIC AND SIDE EFFECTS OF PSYCHOTROPICS

In addition to a basic knowledge of psychiatric medications prescribed for childhood disorders, the play therapist should also be aware of the primary therapeutic effects and potential side effects of psychotropics.

## Antidepressants

Though there are few FDA-approved indications for the use of the newer antidepressants (SSRIs, Effexor, Serzone, Remeron, and Wellbutrin) in children, the prescribing of these medications now exceeds that of the older tricyclic antidepressants. This is primarily because of the lack of risk for severe cardiac side effects. The antidepressants may have side effects including gastrointestinal discomfort, headaches, sleep and behavioral disturbances, and weight loss or gain. Remeron is sedating and is often associated with significant weight gain. Because of these side effects, it is now occasionally used with children having the side effects of appetite and sleep difficulties due to the use of stimulants. Wellbutrin is contraindicated in persons with a history of seizures or tics, and can cause weight loss.

Enuresis and ADHD are the only established indications for the tricyclics. Tricyclics have the possible side effects of dry mouth, constipation, blurred vision, weight change, and decreased blood pressure. Treatment requires electrocardiographic monitoring, and the monitoring of blood serum levels is recommended. Tricyclics are the most lethal of the psychotropics in an overdose.

## Psychostimulants

The stimulant medications commonly used with ADHD children are very well-researched and considered safe and effective (Gitlin, 1990). Common side effects include insomnia, decreased appetite, and headache. Less frequently, they may cause agitation, enuresis, and depression. Rarely, tics and psychotic symptoms may occur.

## Antipsychotics

The neuroleptic medications are used with a variety of symptoms and disorders. These include psychosis, bipolar disorders, aggression, and tic disorders. Common side effects include dry mouth, constipation, blurred vision, sedation, stiffness, and in some cases of chronic administration, tardive dyskinesia. The newer atypical antipsychotics may lead to significant weight gain, but also are less likely to be associated with tardive dyskinesia. Cogentin [benztropine] and Benadryl are anticholinergic medications commonly used to treat stiffness caused by the neuroleptics.

## Lithium

Lithium is used in the treatment of childhood bipolar disorder, to augment the treatment of depression, with schizoaffective disorder, and with aggression. Common side effects include polyuria, polydipsia, gastrointestinal upset, tremor, nausea, diarrhea, weight gain, acne, and possible thyroid and renal effects with chronic administration. Treatment requires monitoring blood serum levels, and thyroid and kidney tests. Electrocardiogram (EKG) monitoring has also been recommended.

## Anti-anxiety

The benzodiazepines, although used sparingly with children, have been administered effectively with sleep disorders and in overanxious and avoidant children. Possible side effects are drowsiness, disinhibition, agitation, confusion, and depression.

## Other

Catapres, although indicated as a treatment for hypertension, has been used with some success for Tourette's symptoms, ADHD, and aggression. Possible side effects include sedation, hypotension, dry mouth, confusion, and depression. There have been recent concerns about the potential for clonidine to cause serious cardiac events. Tenex is similar to Catapres, but is longer-acting and less sedating. Inderal, a beta-adrenergic receptor blocker, has been administered for anxiety disorders, aggression, and self-abusive behaviors. The potential side effects are essentially similar to clonidine. Its use is contraindicated in the presence of diabetes or asthma. Depakote and Tegretol are anti-convulsant medications that have been used in bipolar disorder and aggression. Possible side effects include bone marrow suppression, dizziness, sedation, rashes, and nausea. It requires blood serum monitoring.

# FREQUENTLY ASKED QUESTIONS ABOUT MEDICATION USE

Parents of children for whom medication has been recommended often have questions about the process and about specific issues. Although the nonmedical therapist should defer to qualified psychiatric personnel on medication questions, the therapist should have a fundamental ability to respond to the following typical questions:

Q: Will my child have to take his/her ADHD medicine forever?

A: Studies vary, but it has been suggested that 66% or more of ADHD patients have symptoms that continue into young adulthood.

Q: Are stimulants addictive?

A: Stimulants are not addictive. Stimulants have been abused, but this is usually not a problem in the child population.

Q: I do not want my child "doped up" on stimulants. Will this happen?

A: As opposed to impairing the patient's sensorium, stimulants generally improve concentration and attention.

Q: Will stimulant medications stunt my child's growth?

A: It is felt that the patient's long-term height is not significantly compromised.

Q: Does my child have to take the Ritalin and Dexedrine even on weekends and during the summer?

A: If the child requires the medication in order to have a good weekend/summer, there is no reason to discontinue it. If the child's problem is mainly focusing on school work, and the child can function well medication free when school is out, it does not hurt to stop it.

Q: What about intermittently stopping other medications?

A: Because of differences in the rates of onset, metabolism, etc., most other psychotropic medications should be taken on a regular basis.

Q: Will taking medication this early in life predispose my child to substance abuse?

A: No. Protection against future substance abuse is a positive outcome of appropriate medication use.

## PLAY THERAPY CONSIDERATIONS

The play therapist who is educated about the basics of child psychopharmacology is a better advocate for his or her client, both in the playroom and in the psychiatrist's office. There are several considerations about psychopharmacological issues that may help address this dynamic.

An initial consideration is the advantage of doing play therapy with an appropriately medicated child. The concurrence of pharmacotherapy and play therapy could provide the ideal milieu for a child. If medications could give a child an increased capacity for benefiting from the play therapy and are not prescribed, the potential efficacy of the therapy is diminished. Some authors advocate that concurrent psychosocial interventions are crucial to the lasting therapeutic effects of psychoactive agents (Campbell, Godfrey, & Magee, 1992).

The psychosocial effects on the child of being placed on medication is an issue very appropriately dealt with in the play therapy setting. Taking medications, particularly over an extended period of time, may affect the child's or adolescent's self-concept. It could begin a process of chronic self-esteem difficulties. The child who is medicated may identify himself or herself as having or being a "problem," and may further identify the medication as a mechanism of control. Play therapy provides a child with an opportunity to learn self-control, to respect themselves, to make choices, and to accept themselves (Landreth, 1991). Golden (1983) noted in his play therapy work with hospitalized children that a child can restore a sense of mastery when being medically treated through the play—"The goal of the play therapist is to help the child become involved in his or her own treatment (even if only in some small way) and to help the child retain a sense of competence" (p. 226).

A related issue that children have the opportunity to process in play therapy is the possible situation where medications are being presented as a coercive form of behavioral control rather than as a therapeutic adjunct (Gitlin, 1990). Although, hopefully, this is an exceptional situation, the perceived need by parents, teachers, and therapists for an instant panacea may lead to this concern. Children in this case have not only lost a sense of power and control, but have been manipulated and intruded upon. Play therapy offers these children opportunities to process these issues. Children can begin to make sense of and bring organization to their confusing world. They can manage an unmanageable situation through the fantasy of the play. They can express the grief and anger that often result from being "controlled" in the above manner.

The valuable contribution that a play therapist might offer to the psychiatric assessment was noted previously. With the proper authorization to release information, the play therapist is in a unique position to provide both initial input and ongoing evaluation for the prescribing physician. The baseline assessment necessary to appropriately initiate pharmacotherapy is often inadequate if the psychiatrist must rely solely on parent report and observation of a child in an office. The play therapist will often have greater insight into the child's basic mental status. Providing this input is not only an ethical obligation, but is clearly in the best interests of the child client.

Another important consideration for the play therapist comes in the area of play interpretation. It is possible to misinterpret a child's play behavior if that behavior is being acted-out by an unmedicated child who is in legitimate need of psychopharmacological intervention. For example, a child's agitated shifting from one play activity to another may be an indication of personal anxiety—due to the new experience of being in the playroom, getting closer to intrapsychic issues, and so forth. It may also be that the child is an undiagnosed ADHD client who would appropriately respond to stimulant medication.

An inverse situation should also be noted. It is a legitimate possibility that a child may be psychiatrically medicated for what is viewed as biologically-based symptoms when in fact the child is behaviorally responding to an emotional trauma or inappropriate parenting. For example, a child who has been severely physically or sexually abused may respond by enacting bizarre defense mechanisms, to protect against further adult intrusion. These bizarre behaviors may be interpreted as some level of psychosis, which would appear to indicate the need for neuroleptic medication. These behaviors may well ameliorate in the play therapy room, where the safety of boundaries and the therapeutic relationship make processing of emotional pain possible.

An example of the effects of medication on play behavior is detailed in Mayes's work on play assessment of preschool hyperactive children (1991). In using a widely published observation system for hyperactivity, she noted that of "hyperactive children receiving methylphenidate [Ritalin], the number of quadrant crossings decreased significantly during free play, and the number of toy changes decreased during both free and restricted play" (Mayes, 1991, p. 251).

A final issue that the play therapist might consider is in working with the child who is uncooperative with psychiatric treatment. It is not uncommon to work with children who are noncompliant with respect to taking medications. In addition to the basic opportunity to process their possible anger, frustration, or fear in their own language, the therapist has the opportunity to utilize directive techniques if deemed appropriate. Structured doll play, art work, or the non-play technique of storytelling may be helpful in this situation.

## DISCUSSION

The play therapist has an obligation to his/her child clients to be educated on issues of child psychopharmacology. There is, additionally, an obligation to the profession at large. Biederman (1992) noted that the long-term outlook for pediatric psychopharmacology is dependent on research to balance the potential risks with the real benefits to suffering children. Play therapists must be a part of this process, which will certainly progress with or without play therapy input.

An element of this process must involve a willingness to interact and cooperate with the medical profession. Certainly, in the same way that play therapists need education on psychiatric matters, the psychiatrist needs education about the world of play therapy. As previously noted, multidisciplinary cooperation advances the best interests of the children and the profession. One therapist noted a common frustration and a compelling view of medication: "There used to be a sense of shame when you put clients on medication. It was like an admission of failure that therapy wasn't working and that you, the therapist, had to get help" (Markowitz, 1991, p. 26). The real shame would be to remain ignorant. For the sake of the children whom play therapists want to see grow in the therapeutic process, play therapists must grow as well.

## REFERENCES

American Psychiatric Association. (1994). *Diagnostic and statistical manual of mental disorders* (4th ed.). Washington, DC: American Psychiatric Association.

Biederman, J. (1992). New developments in pediatric psychopharmacology. *Journal of the Academy of Child and Adolescent Psychiatry, 31*(1), 14–15.

Biederman, J., & Steingard, R. (1991). Pediatric psychopharmacology. In A. Gelengerg, E. Bassuk & S. Schoonover (Eds.), *The practitioner's guide to psychoactive drugs* (3rd ed., pp. 341-381). New York: Plenum Medical Book Company.

Bukstein, O. G. (1993). Overview of pharma-

cological treatment. In V. Van Hasselt & M. Hersen (Eds.), *Handbook of behavior therapy and pharmacotherapy for children* (pp. 13–27), Boston: Allyn & Bacon.

Campbell, M., Godfrey, K., & Magee, H. (1992). Pharmacotherapy. In C. Walker & M. Roberts (Eds.), *Handbook of clinical child psychology* (pp. 873–902). New York: John Wiley & Sons.

Campbell, M., & Spencer, E. (1988). Psychopharmacology in child and adolescent psychiatry: A review of the past five years. *Journal of the American Academy of Child and Adolescent Psychiatry, 27,* 269–279.

Gadow, K. (1992). Pediatric psychopharmacotherapy: A review of recent research. *Journal of Child Psychology and Psychiatry and Allied Disciplines, 33*(1), 153–195.

Gitlin, M. J. (1990). *The psychotherapist's guide to psychopharmacology.* New York: The Free Press (Macmillan, Inc.).

Golden, D. B. (1983). Play therapy for hospitalized children. In C. Schaefer & K. O'Connor (Eds.), *Handbook of play therapy* (pp. 213–233). New York: John Wiley & Sons.

Green, W. H. (1991). Principles of psychopharmacotherapy and specific drug treatments. In M. Lewis (Ed.), *Child and adolescent psychiatry: A comprehensive textbook* (pp. 770–795). Baltimore: Williams & Wilkins.

Landreth, G. L. (1991). *Play therapy: The art of the relationship.* Muncie, IN: Accelerated Development, Inc.

Landreth, G., Homeyer, L., Bratton, S., & Kale, A. (1995). *The world of play therapy literature: A definitive guide to authors and subject in the field.* Denton, TX: Center for Play Therapy.

Markowitz, L. M. (1991, May-June). Better therapy through chemistry. *Family Therapy Networker,* 22–31.

Mayes, S. D. (1991). Play assessment of preschool hyperactivity. In C. Schaefer, K. Gitlin, & A. Sandgrund (Eds.), *Play diagnosis and assessment* (pp. 249–271). New York: John Wiley & Sons.

Patterson, J. E., & Magulac, M. (1994). The family therapist's guide to psychopharmacology: A graduate level course. *Journal of Marital and Family Therapy, 2*(2), 151–173.

Phillips, R., & Landreth, G. (1995). Play therapists on play therapy I: A report of methods, demographics and professional/practice issues. *International Journal of Play Therapy, 4*(1), 1–26.

Popper, C. W. (1993). Psychopharmacologic treatment of anxiety disorders in adolescents and children. *The Journal of Clinical Psychiatry, 50*(Supplement), 52–63.

# 6

# Legal and Ethical Issues in Play Therapy

## DANIEL S. SWEENEY

*T*he choice to use play therapy when working with children is borne out of the recognition that children do not communicate in the same way that adults do. To impact children psychotherapeutically involves entering their world, which is recognized in this book as the world of play and play therapy. Therapists who work with children are a special and dedicated group, focusing on a unique and dependent population.

Although the focus of treatment should always be on the child, it is important to remember that the context of play therapy is nevertheless within an adult world. In this adult world, legal and ethical responsibilities must not be forgotten. Many play therapists believe, appropriately, that they are truly "called" to do the work that they do. It becomes necessary, therefore, to preserve the continuity of this "calling" through knowledge of and adherence to basic legal and ethical standards in the field. This chapter will briefly consider these fundamental guidelines.

When working with children, it is imperative to remember that while the child may be the focus of treatment, the legal guardian is essentially the client from a legal and ethical perspective. This is simply because the presumption of the state is that minors are legally incompetent. This means that children are not considered to have the legal capacity to consent (or refuse) services, or the right to obtain and retain privilege in regard to confidential information. It is the legal guardian, which is most often the parent, who is the holder of these rights. This can make the legal and ethical aspect of counseling children occasionally ambiguous for all involved persons. Thompson and Rudolph (2000) concluded: "The rights of minors and the rights of parents to serve in a 'guiding role' can cause confusion. While adults agree on the worth and dignity of children, it must be recognized that legally, minors have fewer rights than adults because of their supposed limited experiences and cognitive abilities to make decisions" (p. 502).

While the focus of treatment in play therapy should always be the child, exclusion of the parents from the process is both impractical and unethical. In most cases, the parents are not only the significant caretakers for the child, they are legally responsible for the child.

Generally, ethical considerations for the play therapist are not based upon the modality of play therapy but rather on the ethical guidelines of licensure and professional organizations to which the therapist belongs. The licensed psychologist and professional counselor, for example, are expected to follow the standards of their respective state boards of licensure as well as the American Psychological Association (APA) and American Counseling Association (ACA) if they are members.

## CONFIDENTIALITY

In most circumstances, children need parental consent to authorize treatment. Because of this, parents have the right to information about their child's treatment from the therapist. As a result, confidentiality generally can not be promised to a minor. This may present a challenge to the therapist wanting to establish a therapeutic relationship. The play therapist can not promise her client that everything shared, whether verbally or nonverbally, will not be shared with the parents. Following some general comments about confidentiality, this dilemma will be further explored.

There is frequently some level of confusion among therapists concerning the differences between the terms *privacy, confidentiality*, and *privilege*. Stadler (1990) noted that privacy essentially means that persons have the right to choose what others may know about them; confidentiality refers to the ethical responsibility of the therapist to respect and limit access to the personal information of clients; and privilege refers to the legal responsibility of therapists to protect client confidentiality. Essentially, confidentiality is an ethical obligation that the therapist owes to the client (confidentiality, therefore, is *owned* by the client), and privileged communication is a legal concept that protects the rights of clients from having information disclosed.

For purposes of therapy, confidentiality may be defined as the client's right to have communications expressed in confidence, not to be disclosed to outside parties without implied or expressed authorization. Gladding (1995) further elucidated, noting that confidentiality is the "ethical duty to fulfill a contract or promise to clients that the information revealed during therapy will be protected from unauthorized disclosure . . . [which] becomes a legal matter as well when it is broken" (p. 336).

For minors, the parent or guardian is the legal authority and decision maker.

Only the parent or guardian can authorize treatment and can obtain information about the diagnosis, prognosis, and treatment plan. This legal authority may be restricted to the person with legal custody, although this varies according to state law. Any therapist who works with children should be aware of state and local statutes regarding parental rights.

Confidentiality with children can be challenging. Hendrix (1991) discussed these challenges, and suggested that absolute confidentiality may not be desirable nor required with child cases. He focused on the concept that confidentiality is for the benefit of the client, and that this benefit may be outweighed by other factors. Issues of mandated reporting and responsibility to parents are examples. Hendrix further noted that the situation changes when children become adolescents, a case in which the clients have an increased ability to be involved in legal decisions. He suggested that obtaining informed consent from children is advisable.

It is necessary and important that the play therapist deal with the issue of confidentiality at the beginning of the treatment process. While it is important to recognize the developmental limitations of children to understand the abstract concept of confidentiality, it is always better to have fully explained the process to all involved. Goldberg (1997) suggested a practice that may be helpful: "Along with many other practitioners who work with children and adolescents, I generally believe it is best to discuss the issue of confidentiality at the first session with the child and parents together, and to encourage the parents to respect their child's need for privacy. I always reassure them that I will inform them if there is imminent risk of harm to their child or to someone else" (p. 104).

All therapists should be aware of the basic exceptions to confidentiality. Although these may vary slightly from state to state, these exceptions include the following: disclosure of child or elder abuse; disclosure of an intent to commit harm to self or others; written authorization by the parent or guardian; a legal action brought against the therapist, which is initiated by the client; and, when ordered by a court to release information. It is crucial that play therapists be aware of the mandated reporting laws in the state in which they practice, as well as other case and statute laws that affect confidentiality in the therapy process. When releasing confidential information, the therapist should disclose the minimal amount of confidential material necessary to comply with the specific situation.

It is also important for the play therapist to keep confidentiality issues in mind in light of the increasing use of technology. Records stored on a computer should be encrypted, and preferably not stored on the computer's hard drive. If a therapist sends a computer to be repaired, with its hard drive filled with client information, confidentiality has been compromised. Electronic mail should also be encrypted, and fax machines closely monitored. Phone conversations with clients should not be made over cordless or cellular phones, as these employ airwaves which can be accessed or monitored. If parents use a nonsecure means to communicate with the therapist, it is the therapist's responsibility to make the appropriate adjustments to ensure the maintenance of confidentiality.

# INFORMED CONSENT

Based upon the principles of respect and autonomy, all clients in psychotherapy have the right and authority to consent to services. Persons who enter into therapy have the fundamental right to make decisions that affect their well-being, and therefore need to consider the potential benefits and risks of these decisions. With regard to any psychotherapeutic intervention (including play therapy), informed consent refers to the decision of clients whether to engage in treatment, what happens during the course of treatment, and what information the therapist may disclose to third parties (DeKraai, Sales, & Hall, 1998).

There are several elements of the informed consent process. One is that the therapist must disclose all relevant information about the process to the client. This involves more than the basic discussion of office policies, and may be especially important for the play therapist, as the rationale for and the process of play therapy is often unclear to parents and children. Another component of informed consent is the client's comprehension of this information. Establishment of client comprehension must be followed by a voluntary agreement to participate in therapy, free from undue influence or coercion. These issues are commented upon further below.

To satisfy the principle of informed consent, which is essentially a legal and ethical doctrine, the consent of clients must be given in a voluntary, knowledgeable, and competent state. This is where the issue becomes complex for child clients. Because of their minor status, children are not considered voluntary, knowledgeable, and competent clients. Play therapists choose to use play as a means of communicating with children because they lack the developmental skills to engage in therapy in the same manner as adult clients. The very concept of informed consent is sophisticated and abstract, and as such is counter to this basic rationale for using play therapy. Informed consent remains, however, a therapeutic imperative.

Children are rarely voluntary clients; most often, they are compelled to enter treatment by their parents. It is difficult to view children as knowledgeable clients, due to their developmental immaturity. This relates as well to the issue of competence. DeKraai, Sales, and Hall (1998) noted: "In most cases, a person is presumed competent to consent: that is he or she has the necessary cognitive capacity to give a legally valid consent to treatment" (p. 541). Children, however, lack this cognitive capacity. There is for children, therefore, a presumption of incompetence.

Since children are generally considered legally incapable of consenting to the process of play therapy, a substitute must make the decision. In most cases, this will be the parent or legal guardian. In cases where the parent is not involved, the therapist must ensure that the person providing the consent is legally able to do so. A grandparent or other relative, who is not the legal guardian, generally can not provide consent. However, since one guideline in the treatment process is to follow the best interests of the child, and since the decision maker is a substitute for the incompetent child, it might be arguable that a third party could provide the consent. It is obviously the most advisable and prudent course for the therapist to get proper legal consent.

When working with a divorce situation, it is important that the therapist be aware of the state laws concerning custody and parental rights. Some states permit either parent, regardless of who has been appointed primary custodian, to consent to treat (and review records), while others do not.

Additionally, there are exceptions to the general requirement for parental consent to treatment, which vary from state to state. These may include emergency treatment situations; the case of an emancipated minor; drug and alcohol treatment for children (generally aged 12 or older); counseling for birth control, pregnancy, or sexually transmitted diseases; and, other specific situations as outlined by statute. Appendix A displays a sample informed consent form.

## PROFESSIONAL DISCLOSURE

It is the play therapist's responsibility to provide information about her professional identity and office policies to parents, and with children when developmentally appropriate. This "professional disclosure statement," which is required by law in some states, should educate the client about several items, including such specifics as: (1) information about the orientation of the play therapist in regard to theory and technique; (2) degrees and credentials held by the therapist; (3) specific training and supervised experience relevant to the therapist's practice; (4) information about fee schedules and payment process; (5) limits to confidentiality; (6) process of working with insurance companies; and other information specific to a therapist's practice that will help ensure that the client is fully aware of the process and therapist's qualifications to be involved in that process.

Professional disclosure has an additional benefit beyond assisting in the informed consent process. Child therapists, who are already focused on developmental issues, can find a developmental benefit in creating a professional disclosure statement (Huber & Baruth, 1987). These statements help to clarify professional practices and identity, and assist the therapist to examine issues that pertain to the therapeutic relationship. Appendix B displays a sample professional disclosure statement.

## CLINICAL COMPETENCE & TRAINING

It is both clinically and ethically imperative that play therapists have adequate training and supervised experience in the field. It is an ethical mandate of most professional codes (e.g., APA, ACA, American Association of Marriage & Family Therapists (AAMFT), National Association of Social Workers (NASW)) that clinicians practice only within the boundaries of their competence. While the assessment of competence is ambiguous at best, it is nevertheless an obligation for those working with any special population to have adequate training and experience in the chosen field.

Unfortunately, there are some persons in the mental health field who are claiming to be "play therapists" with inadequate training in the field. Landreth's (1991) fundamental definition of play therapy includes the importance of being trained in the field. Most readers would agree that providing basic "adult" counseling and including toys in the session does not make the process into play therapy. If the process involves more than this, the question remains what distinguishes play therapy from other forms of treatment interventions and what qualifies a therapist to use the modality.

The International Association for Play Therapy (IAPT) has established a process for becoming a Registered Play Therapist (RPT) and a Registered Play Therapist-Supervisor (RPT-S). Although this is not licensure or certification, the "credential" of being an RPT or RPT-S does serve as evidence that a play therapist has met minimal training and supervised experience standards. The IAPT may be contacted at their web site (www.a4pt.org).

There are, unfortunately, too few training opportunities for therapists wanting to learn about play therapy. Although there are increasing numbers of individuals providing workshops in the field of play therapy, there are not nearly enough universities that offer course work and supervised experience in play therapy. One exception would be the Center for Play Therapy at the University of North Texas (www.coe.unt.edu/cpt ), which is directed by the author of this text. The Center is the largest play therapy training center in the world, offering more courses on play therapy and more play therapy rooms (with mirrors and videotape equipment) than anywhere else. It is important to be reminded that workshops, although helpful, can not be considered a replacement for the depth of training received in a graduate course.

The difficulty of finding adequate training on play therapy is an unfortunate reflection of the inadequate training in child therapy in general. Despite the continued overwhelming mental health needs for children, there also continues to be a failure of existing mental health programs to provide adequate clinical training in working with the population (Tuma, 1990). The aspiring play therapist must be intentional about seeking out quality training and qualified supervision.

Continuing education, which is a requirement for the maintenance of most mental health licenses, is particularly important for therapists choosing to work with children. This should also be an intentional process, with a focus on play therapy training that is clinical and experiential in nature.

## CUSTODY EVALUATIONS

With the high incidence of family conflict and divorce, play therapists may be called upon to conduct custody evaluations. Generally, the question at issue will be what is in the best interest of the child(ren). This is frequently a complicated issue not only for the clients involved, but also for the therapist.

A number of concerns should be addressed. The play therapist may frequently find herself in the awkward position of dealing with competing family members while still attempting to "promote the best interests of the child." There is also the question about whether the play therapist can engage in the dual roles of both therapist and evaluator for the family. It may be professionally and ethically challenging for the treating therapist to conduct an evaluation. While a therapist may indeed conduct an objective and unbiased assessment, there often remains an appearance of partiality in the legal proceedings.

The play therapist may appear in court on custody matters as either a fact or expert witness, or both. The fact witness may provide simple testimony to the court regarding a client's history, diagnosis, treatment, etc. The custody evaluator, however, is often operating in the capacity of an expert witness, providing the court with a professional opinion on issues of custody and visitation.

Most states have family law codes, which any therapist working with children should be familiar with. These codes are often lengthy and detailed, but usually understandable. Consultation with a family law attorney may be helpful.

It is most helpful if both parents can be involved in the custody evaluation process. Recognizing the value of systemic interventions, it is always appropriate to involve the entire family when possible. With evaluations, it is also important to recognize that custody is an emotionally charged issue, and that all family members will likely be under considerable stress. If the evaluator can avoid getting caught between marital conflict and parent–child conflict in the evaluation process, the best interests of the child can be appropriately evaluated and determined.

## RECORDS

The play therapist has the responsibility to maintain records that are professionally adequate, appropriately secure, and retained for a prescribed length of time. While it may be generally acknowledged that many persons in the helping professions do not care for the administrative aspect of their job, it is, nevertheless, imperative.

All therapists are responsible for the production and maintenance of records. These include, but would not be limited to: intake information, basic office forms (informed consent, office policies [billing information, cancellation fee policy, etc.], professional disclosure statement, release forms, etc.), client history, psychological tests, progress notes, treatment plan, etc. A reasonable standard for play therapists to consider in the maintenance of a client file would be if they would feel comfortable having the file subpoenaed and reviewed by a court and professional peers.

Many play therapists choose not to take notes during a play therapy session. Since the focus is on the child, it can be argued that taking notes is a distraction that detracts from fully attending to the child client(s). It is crucial, however, that adequate progress and process notes be included in the client record. Some therapists respond to this issue by videotaping their sessions (which will be discussed in further detail below), which is fine as long as it is recognized that the videotape must be considered part of the client's official record. Making notes after a play therapy session can certainly be sufficient.

Records should be secured appropriately. It is recommended that client files be stored in a locked file cabinet, behind two locked doors (the office door, and the door to the room where the records are stored). As previously noted, computer records should be encrypted. A more sound policy on computer records would be to store client information on a zip drive or writable CD-ROM, which could then be removed and locked up. If a cleaning service is employed by the therapist, they should not have access to the room where the client files are stored, if possible.

Concerning the appropriate length of time in which to keep client records, most states and professional organizations have stated minimums. Therapists should be well acquainted with these laws in the state in which they practice. A conservative recommendation would be to maintain records for ten years following termination of therapeutic services. Additionally, it is recommended that records for child clients be stored for four years beyond the age of majority. While the storing of records may be cumbersome, particularly in terms of space, it is always better to store records for too long than not long enough.

Although it may seem obvious, therapists should also have a policy for the secure disposal for confidential material. This includes the destruction of client files that have been stored for an adequate amount of time, as well as the disposal of any other confidential materials. These materials should be shredded. Computer records should not only be deleted, but the user should employ some manner of defragmentation program to erase or cover deleted space.

Finally, it is the responsibility of therapists to ensure that all persons having access to files, such as support staff, be trained in the appropriate and confidential handling of client records. Therapists are legally liable for errors (mistaken or purposeful) made by persons in their employ.

## DUAL RELATIONSHIPS AND BOUNDARY ISSUES

A detailed discussion of dual relationships is not possible in this chapter, nor is it necessary for the trained mental health professional. It does warrant brief mention, however, within the context of counseling children.

One boundary issue that is not uncommon when working with children involves the giving of gifts. Children (and parents) often give gifts for the therapist, frequently around holiday time. On the one hand, to accept a gift (particularly one that has more than nominal value) is not appropriate; but on the other, the refusal of a gift can be particularly difficult for a child to understand and accept. The acceptance of a painting made in the playroom or a handmade holiday ornament or baked goods would certainly seem reasonable (as a side note, it is a breach of confidentiality to display a child's artwork produced in therapy). The situation becomes more complicated, however, with a store-bought gift.

The therapeutic and common sense judgment of the therapist must be used in this situation. The therapist and the parents should discuss this and other boundary issues in advance, as well as the purpose for these boundaries. Other dual relationship and boundary concerns (some of which are unavoidable) include: mental health professionals working in rural areas and small communities, attending the same church or other social functions as clients, accepting a client's invitation to a special event (e.g., graduation), or physical contact with the child. Discussion of these issues with parents from the outset of therapy and consultation with other professionals can serve to assist in handling potentially difficult situations.

## VIDEOTAPING PLAY THERAPY SESSIONS

It is a common (and necessary) practice for therapists in training to videotape counseling sessions for the purpose of supervision and professional growth. It is suggested that this practice continue throughout the professional life of any play therapist. The author maintains a current policy of videotaping all play therapy sessions, with appropriate parental consent. If parents are not willing to sign this consent, children are referred to another therapist.

There are two primary reasons for this policy of videotaping. The first is to maintain a professional edge and have a practice that can and should be supervised. Supervision should not end with the completion of a training program and/or licensure. There is simply no better way in which to review play therapy skills and therapeutic progress than taping and reviewing sessions. Simply knowing that a play therapy session is being taped tends to heighten the therapist's awareness and dedication to the process.

The second reason for the author's choice to videotape play therapy sessions is for liability protection. As a male therapist who frequently works with children who have experienced physical or sexual trauma, a video record of play therapy sessions provides evidence of ethical and competent therapeutic behavior. As an example, it would not be unusual for a child who has been sexually abused to engage in sexualized play during a therapy session. Although this has not occurred for the author, it is possible that such a child could return home or to school and report: "I played sex with (therapist) today." A videotaped record of the session would circumvent the question of unprofessional behavior, and avoid the risk of damage to professional reputation and licensure.

As previously noted, it is necessary to obtain appropriate consent to videotape sessions. It is also important to remember that these tapes are a part of the therapeutic record, and should be treated appropriately. The tapes should be properly secured and a specific policy should be in place regarding the length of maintenance and erasure. If session videotapes are to be considered for use as training material, it is recommended that an additional release be signed. Appendix C displays a sample release for this type video usage.

## REFERRALS

There are several circumstances in which the therapist must make a referral. This is an important issue to consider from an ethical perspective. The play therapist must always keep the best interests of the child in mind, and the situation may call for a referral for different or adjunct services.

When there is reasonable evidence that a child's situation requires medical evaluation, the therapist must make a referral to a physician. Even if it is the judgment of the therapist that a symptom is most likely psychosomatic in origin, a referral for medical evaluation is nevertheless the appropriate course of action. If there is a need for psychiatric evaluation and medication, the referral must be made.

It is preferable to refer a child with psychiatric needs to a child psychiatrist. While this may seem obvious, it is frequently the pediatrician or family practitioner who prescribes psychiatric medication (the most common situation is the pharmacologic treatment of Attention Deficit Hyperactivity Disorder (ADHD). If possible, it is best to have children evaluated for consideration of psychotropics by child psychiatrists, who clearly have the expertise to do so.

The awareness of clinical competence has been discussed above. When a client situation is beyond the therapist's scope of expertise, it is clearly necessary to make a proper referral. The play therapist has a legal and ethical responsibility to make the referral to a competent person, and must make the referral and transfer of the client in a competent fashion. It is possible that there would be legal liability for the referring therapist if the referral source acts in a negligent or incompetent manner.

## CONCLUSION

There are several guidelines that are always helpful when dealing with legal and ethical issues. It is always helpful and frequently necessary to consult with other professionals in the field. Ongoing supervision is clearly helpful in terms of professional growth as a clinician, but also as a resource concerning ethical matters. Honest and open dialogue with clients is also an imperative from a legal and ethical perspective. Clients are always more likely to file a complaint or legal action against a professional when they feel uninformed and discounted—empathy matters! Finally, any ethical concern, including any action taken by either the therapist or the client, should be carefully documented in the client record.

This chapter has provided a brief overview of some of the common legal and ethical considerations that a play therapist should keep in mind. It is not a complete or comprehensive treatise—this is not possible. All therapists should have professional training in this important area. When it comes to the consideration of practice and ethics, there is a "reasonable professional" standard that is applied. This standard is, essentially: would a panel of the therapist's peers, with similar training and experience, consider the issue at question to be clinically and ethically appropriate? If play therapists are willing to subject their practice to this fundamental question, if they are willing to expose their work to the professional and general community in the light of day, there should never be a concern.

Therapists who work with children using the modality of play therapy do so because of a commitment to reaching children through their natural medium of communication. This process may not be well understood by parents, other therapists, and the general public. In addition to the importance of educating clients in terms of informed consent and professional disclosure, it is important that play therapists educate the wider field of mental health and the general public about the process and benefits of play therapy. Within the boundaries of time constraints and the like, play therapists promote the welfare of children by sharing the fundamental truths about the field to a wider audience. Although not specifically an ethical mandate, this should be a valued priority for play therapists.

Therapists who work with children are a special group of people who have answered a call that too few have. Simply choosing to touch the lives of children through play therapy speaks positively about a professional's ethics and values. Knowledge of and adherence to basic ethical guidelines and principles is more than a professional mandate. It is an extension of the play therapist's commitment to children.

## REFERENCES

DeKraai, M., Sales, B., & Hall, S. (1998). Informed consent, confidentiality, and duty to report laws in the conduct of child therapy. In R. Morris & T. Kratochwill (Eds.), *The practice of child therapy* (3rd ed., pp. 540–559). Boston: Allyn and Bacon.

Gladding, S. (1995). *Family therapy: History, theory and practice*. Englewood Cliffs, NJ: Prentice Hall.

Goldberg, R. (1997). Ethical dilemmas in working with children and adolescents. In D. Marsh & R. Magee (Eds.), *Ethical and legal issue is professional practice with families* (pp. 97–111). New York: John Wiley & Sons, Inc.

Hendrix, D. (1991). Ethics and intrafamily confidentiality in counseling with children. *Journal of Mental Health Counseling, 13*(3), 323–333.

Huber, C., & Baruth, L. (1987). *Ethical, legal, and professional issues in the practice of marriage and family therapy*. Columbus, OH: Merrill Publishing Co.

Landreth, G. (1991). *Play therapy: The art of the relationship*. Muncie, IN: Accelerated Development Press.

Stadler, H. (1990). Confidentiality. In B. Herlihy & L. Golden (Eds.), *Ethical standards casebook* (pp. 102–110). Alexandria, VA: American Counseling Association.

Thompson, C., & Rudolph, L. (2000). *Counseling Children* (5th ed.). Pacific Grove, CA: Brooks/Cole Publishing.

Tuma, J. M. (1990). Standards for training psychologists to provide mental health services to children and adolescents. In P. Magrab & P. Wohlford (Eds.), *Improving psychological services for children and adolescents with severe mental disorders: Clinical training in psychology* (pp. 51–65). Washington, DC: American Psychological Association.

# Sample Informed Consent for Play Therapy

Counseling clients have certain rights and responsibilities when consulting a therapist for treatment and evaluation services. This form should be carefully read and fully discussed with your therapist. My signature below affirms the following:

1. Prior to the commencement of therapy, I was given adequate information to understand the nature of counseling and the process of play therapy. This information included, but was not limited to: the professional identity and qualifications of the counselor, the professional identity and nature of the counseling practice, the potential risks and benefits of counseling, the issue of confidentiality and its limits, and alternative treatment options.
2. I agree that I have sought and consent to participate in the play therapy process with the counselor named below. This includes the development of treatment goals and a treatment plan together with the therapist. I agree to be involved in the process and regularly review the treatment progress and process.
3. I understand that I have the right to discontinue treatment and request a referral to another therapist.
4. I understand that the play therapy sessions will be videotaped, and that the videotapes will become part of the permanent client record, following all applicable legal and ethical rules of confidentiality.
5. I understand that any cancellation of an appointment must be made at least 24 hours before the time of the appointment. If I do not cancel or do not show up, I understand that I will be charged for that appointment.
6. I further understand that no guarantees have been made to me as to the results of the counseling and play therapy process.

My signature below affirms that I have read, understand, and agree with the statements above, that my questions have been sufficiently answered fully, and that I voluntarily consent to counseling and play therapy.

_____     _____
Signature of client                                                                    Date

(continued)

**Minor Client:** I affirm that I am the legal guardian of _____. My signature below affirms that I have read and understand the statements above, and that I voluntarily consent to counseling and play therapy for the child named above.

_____ _____

Signature of parent or legal guardian               Date

_____ _____

Signature of counselor                         Date

# Sample Professional Disclosure Statement

Therapist name
Business address

**Philosophy & Approach to Counseling:** _____
_____
_____
_____

    I subscribe to the Codes of Ethics of the American Counseling Association (ACA), the American Association of Marriage & Family Therapists (AAMFT), the American Psychological Association (APA).

**Education, Training, & Experience:** _____
_____
_____
_____

**Continuing Education & Supervision:** As a licensed psychotherapist, I am required to participate in ongoing continuing education. This is not only to maintain my license, but also to continue my growth as a therapist and for the benefit of my clients. In addition to continuing education, I am committed to seeking consultation and supervision in my practice as needed.

**Payment for Services:** The fee for counseling is _____ per session, payable at the beginning of each session. I will be happy to work with your insurance company as needed. Additionally, there may be recommended reading or diagnostic testing for which additional fees may be required. These will be discussed with the client prior to their use.

**Cancellation Policy:** Since the scheduling of an appointment involves the reservation of time specifically for you, please note that any cancellation must be made 24 hours in advance. Sessions that are missed without this advance cancellation will be billed at full charge.

**Referrals:** Should the client and/or I believe that a referral would be appropriate during the course of the counseling relationship, I will take the responsibility of identifying referral services and assist in making the referral. Referrals may be made for a number of reasons, including the client's or my identifying any source of conflict in the relationship, a client need that requires a greater degree of expertise or a different area of counseling specialization, or a need for medical or psychiatric attention. Referrals will be discussed openly and the transfer completed to the best of my ability.

**Professional Boundaries:** The counseling relationship is a professional relationship. It should not, therefore, become a social or business relationship at any time. This would be detrimental to the purposes of counseling and would contaminate the process. As such, I would request that my clients do not invite me to social events or solicit me for business. I will do the same. If I encounter clients outside of the counseling setting, I will not acknowledge the existence of any relationship.

**Confidentiality:** All information disclosed within sessions is confidential and may not be revealed to anyone without your written permission, except where disclosure is required by law. Disclosure may be required under the following circumstances:

1. Reporting suspected child or elder abuse;
2. Reporting imminent danger to client or others;
3. Reporting information required in court proceedings or by client's insurance company, or other relevant agencies;
4. Providing information concerning licensee case consultation or supervision; and
5. Defending claims brought by the client against licensee.

**Additional Charges:** Other financial considerations may arise in the counseling experience. At times, books will be recommended to save the client time and expense. Testing, which may assist with diagnosis and treatment planning, may also be done. I will discuss these items and the associated expense with you.

**Informed Consent:** I affirm that prior to becoming a client of _____, s(he) gave me sufficient information to understand the nature of counseling. The information included the nature of the agency, the therapist's professional identity, possible risks and benefits of counseling, nature of confidentiality, including legal and ethical limits, and alternative treatments available. My signature below affirms my informed and voluntary consent to receive counseling.

**Minor Client:** I affirm that I am the legal guardian of _____. With an understanding of the above information and conditions, I do grant permission for my child to participate in counseling.

With the understanding of the above information and conditions, I agree to participate in counseling and release the counselor from any liability.

_____      _____
Client's signature                                                              Date


_____      _____
Counselor's signature                                                         Date

# APPENDIX C

## Sample Authorization to Videotape for Educational Purposes

I give my permission for my child, _____, to participate in videotaped play therapy sessions with _____ for the purpose of creating a videotape for educational purposes. I understand that videotapes of my child's counseling sessions have value as educational tools for counselors in training at universities and professional counselors who attend professional workshops. I understand that any student or professional who sees a videotape will be reminded of rules of confidentiality that prohibit discussion of the videotape except for professional training purposes.

I also understand that the confidentiality of my child will be protected and that only my child's first name may be stated on the tape. No other identifying information will be available to those viewing the tape for educational purposes.

My signature below affirms that my child's participation in the videotaping is entirely voluntary.

I affirm that I am the legal guardian of _____, and that I understand the above conditions. I release _____ from any liability associated with the videotaping or viewing of the counseling sessions.

_____     _____
Parent's signature                                                          Date


_____     _____
Therapist's signature                                                      Date

# 7

# The Parents' Part in the Play Therapy Process

## JODI CRANE

*M*ost play therapists attempt to see one or both of the child's parents some time during the play therapy process. However, how much to involve parents in the child's experience of play therapy and what to do with the parents once they are included tends to be a confusing issue for play therapists. My experience supervising beginning play therapists and discussing this topic with more advanced play therapists leads me to believe that this confusion may be due to play therapists' tendency to prefer to work with children rather than adults and their general lack of training in working with parents specifically. The purpose of this chapter, then, is to dispel some of this confusion by providing practical information that can be utilized by any play therapist regardless of theoretical orientation.

## PARENTS' FEELINGS AND BELIEFS

Parents experience a variety of reactions when they bring their child to play therapy. Their thoughts and emotions are due to a myriad of factors including the sometimes negative social stigma associated with being in therapy, the parents' own prior experiences with therapy and their expectations of therapy, the personalities of the parents and their interaction with the child's personality, and the parents' experience of dealing with the child's problematic behavior.

For many parents, admitting that they need help for their child and/or for themselves be very difficult. They may believe they are bad parents if they have their child in therapy or think that others, including the therapist, will assume that they are not good parents or that their child is "crazy." Some parents initially feel ashamed or guilty that somehow they have failed as parents. As a result, it can be helpful to counteract these beliefs by commending the parents for bringing their child to therapy, because it shows how much they care for their child. Raising children is difficult in today's complex world and everyone can, therefore, benefit from some assistance from an unbiased outsider.

Parents may also feel confused, anxious, and worried, because they do not understand what is happening to their child. They become uncomfortable when the child's behavior is inappropriate to the child's age, occurs frequently, and becomes worse over time. They look to the therapist as an expert for guidance in addressing the behavior that brought them into therapy. For parents who see the therapist as an expert, the therapist can let them know that, as parents they are experts on their particular child, and because of this, the therapist needs their assistance in helping their child.

Some parents are so caught up in their child's problem that they can no longer see new ways to deal with the behavior. In this case, a little advice can jump-start the change process and be supportive to the parents. However, giving advice can be overdone if the parents become dependent upon the therapist and put the therapist on a pedestal without seeing the role they have played in their child's progress. Giving advice may also reinforce scapegoating of the child by focusing on the child as the problem, which may result in the parents not seeing their part in the problem. Boiling all problems down to problematic parenting can be too simplistic since many of the problems seen in play therapy are complex. In other words, a change in the child's behavior may not totally occur until, for instance, the parents address problems in their marriage, or one of the parents deals with a personal issue, or the child's teacher begins to treat the child differently.

Many parents want to know why the child has a problem or what is causing it. They believe that if one knows why, then the problem can be "fixed." This is characteristic of the medical model that is so pervasive in our society today. The "why" of a problem cannot be known because there are so many factors that influence the development and maintenance of a problem. Although parents want to know the cause of a particular behavior, they often do not want to accept their part in possibly contributing to the problem. However, in most cases the parents have had some influence on the development and maintenance of the problem. The therapist is in a precarious situation attempting to help parents see their responsibility or holding them accountable without blaming them. I attempt to do this by normalizing the situation and empathizing with the parents' feelings. For instance, I let the parents know that I can understand that they would behave the way they do given their situation but what they are doing is no longer working and therefore, something needs to change.

Some parents may feel anger toward their child and think that the child's symptoms are deliberate and within the child's control. A few of these parents cannot even be with the child very long without feeling upset. These parents feel frustrated as they often believe they have tried everything to deal with the problematic behavior and are ready to give up. Underneath this anger may be feelings of helplessness and sadness. These parents may wish to have someone take over responsibility for the child's problems and therefore, want the therapist to fix the child.

In this case as with all parents, it is important to discuss the expectations and goals for therapy. One way this can be accomplished is by asking parents how they will know when it is time to terminate therapy and how they think the therapist can help them and their child. I enlist parents' help in the therapeutic process because they know their child better than anyone else.

When parents believe they have tried everything in order to alleviate a particular behavior, they tend to become narrowly focused and blind to other possibilities. They need to try something in a different way or try something new. The therapist's job, then, is to provide parents with new alternatives and encourage them to keep trying.

Still other parents may be in denial about the seriousness of their child's behavior and play down their concerns about their child. Denial often occurs when the family has been referred by someone other than themselves, such as a teacher or the courts. These parents do not want to appear weak to others and may be defensive toward the therapist. Parents can be engaged by asking the therapist what needs to happen in order to get the referral source "off their backs." This, then, can become the goal for therapy.

Fortunately, most parents bring their child to therapy out of love and concern for the child's well-being. It is rare for a parent not to be concerned about the child's development or to only feel rejection and hatred toward the child. Even those parents who are in denial or have been referred from elsewhere have a choice as to whether or not to be involved in the therapy. Almost every parent wants to be included in the therapeutic process but many do not know how to help. Part of the play therapist's role, then, is to find ways to involve the parents.

## Therapist's Attitude

Given the parents' feelings and beliefs when they bring their child to therapy, the attitude the therapist has toward the parents can affect how therapy proceeds and whether or not the parents continue to bring the child to therapy. Overall, the therapist should convey an attitude of empathy, respect, acceptance, and hope toward the parents. These attitudes are not distinct from one another as they often overlap. It is important that the therapist not just have these attitudes, but that the parents perceive them from the therapist. The objective is to facilitate the parents' potential to learn, to explore themselves, and to grow.

The therapist should have an empathetic attitude toward the parents that is conveyed by listening fully to them and attempting to understand their point of view. The therapist understands their difficulties, needs, and emotions; encourages the parents to verbalize their feelings; and empathizes with their pain while utilizing the skill of reflecting their feelings, thoughts, and experiences. Once parents feel understood, they begin to relax and are more open to new ways of viewing their child and interacting with the child.

Respect involves taking a collaborative position with the parents by seeing them as important helpers in improving the well-being of the child. The therapist does not operate as an expert who tells parents what to do, but instead works together with parents by making suggestions, asking for their ideas, and together determining what is effective. Collaboration involves the recognition that parents are valued as important resources in helping their children.

The therapist must also be open-minded. This means that the therapist is nonjudgmental and is able to entertain alternative points of view and ways of behavior. This may be particularly important when the parents and therapist are of distinct cultures and backgrounds and hold different values. On the other hand, being open-minded does not mean that anything goes. The therapist must always follow legal and ethical guidelines when working with parents and children. For instance, the therapist would not be open to abuse of the child.

In addition, it is important that the play therapist exhibit an attitude of acceptance of parents by approaching them with the belief that they have done the best they know how with the child. The therapist does not criticize or blame them or assume that they are somehow pathological, but believes that they have the strength to improve the ways they interact with the child.

The therapist holds a positive outlook and focuses on the strengths of the parents by pointing out anything effective in their ways of parenting or in their relationship with the child. Along these lines, the therapist attempts to have the parents focus on learning new behaviors in the present, instead of focusing on what they have done wrong in the past (Guerney, Guerney, & Stover, 1972). The therapist also encourages the parents' efforts at change.

Finally, the therapist must instill hope. If the parents do not feel that the therapist believes the situation can improve, they will have little motivation to continue with therapy (Landreth, 1991). Hope is imparted through the attitudes of empathy, concern, acceptance, and respect and having a positive outlook. Hope is also seen in the humanistic belief that human beings have the ability to solve their own problems.

## INITIAL PARENT INTERVIEW

The purpose of the first session with the parents is for the therapist to evaluate the child's need for therapy and for the parent to evaluate the therapist. Helpful information about conducting a parent interview can be found in Boy and Pine (1995), Doft and Aria (1992), Kottman (1995), Landreth (1991), and O'Connor (1991). The goals of the initial interview are to (a) establish rapport, (b) obtain background information, (c) assess the situation, (d) discuss expectations for therapy, (e) set goals, and (f) explain the play therapy process.

It is important to have both parents attend the initial interview session and any other caregivers who spend a frequent amount of time with the child, such as a grandparent who lives in the home or a nanny, because these individuals play a major role in the child's development and each will have a unique understanding of the child's situation. The initial parent interview can be a time to conduct a thorough assessment in order to discover what factors are contributing to the child's problems and therefore, focus the therapy. A child-centered play therapist, on the other hand, would not be as concerned with as comprehensive an assessment since this approach is not prescriptive. However, a child-centered play therapist would gather information about the presenting concern. Landreth (1991) pointed out that during the initial session, the therapist alternates between focusing on the presenting problem and exploring the parents' feelings. He also described that the interview involves three areas: intake by information gathering, therapeutic discussing of feelings, and parental suggestion giving. In other words, the first session is not a sterile question and answer format.

The therapist uses the basic counseling skills of reflection, clarification, and summarization, as well as the therapeutic attitudes described earlier to establish a trusting relationship with the parents. Establishing a positive relationship between the therapist and parent characterized by open communication is crucial to the successful treatment of children. When obtaining information from the parents in order to better understand the child and the child's situation, the therapist should utilize appropriate, specific questions and make sure parents respond precisely and concretely. For example, if the parents say they are concerned about "attention problems," the therapist has them describe what "attention problems" means to them in such a way that you could see it in your mind like watching a videotape. This is important because many words used to describe children have been so overused that there no longer is a consensus as to what they mean. The therapist's definition and the parents' definition of a particular word or term may differ.

Several kinds of information can be obtained from the parents during the initial interview. It is important to understand the following: the presenting concern, child's background history, social development, discipline, and family history. Some of these areas may not be addressed if they do not seem relevant to the presenting problem. Parents can also be asked to describe the child's strengths. It is particularly telling when a parent cannot think of anything positive to say about the child.

Expectations for therapy is another important area to address during the parent interview. The therapist explains the importance of the parents' role in the process of therapy, the therapist's need for their help, and the significance of consistently attending sessions. Together the parents and therapist decide how the parents will be involved in the therapy whether in parent consultation, individual or marital counseling for the parents, filial therapy, family play therapy, or a combination of these. The therapist's role in the therapeutic process should also be made explicit. For instance, will the therapist provide suggestions for doing things differently with the child?

Finally, the therapist and parents should discuss the goals of therapy and come to an agreement about them. Older children may also be included in the process. Goals can be set for both the child and the parents. Goals are more likely to be attained and understood by those involved in the therapeutic process if they are worded as small, concrete behaviors in the affirmative. For instance, instead of saying, "Michael will become less aggressive," one goal could be stated, "Rather than hitting his sister, Michael will learn to tell her he is feeling upset, go in his room and calm himself down, or talk to his parents about his feelings."

## EXPLANATION OF PLAY THERAPY

Part of the initial session with the parents involves an explanation of the play therapy process. This description includes the following: (a) definition and purpose of play therapy, (b) discussion of confidentiality and sharing of information, (c) preparation of the parent and child for play therapy, (d) preparation of the parent for after the play session, and (e) discussion of artwork, clothing, and the fact that some play therapy may be messy or noisy.

### Definition and Purpose of Play Therapy

The therapist can summarize the following information when describing play therapy to parents and explaining its purpose:

> Play therapy is to children what counseling is to adults. Play is the child's natural way of communicating just as talking is the adult's natural way of communicating. In the playroom, toys are used like words and play is the child's language. Children are provided special toys in play therapy to enable them to say with the toys what they have difficulty saying with words. When children can communicate or play out how they feel to a trained play therapist who understands, they feel better because the feelings have been released. As a parent you have probably experienced the same thing when you were bothered or worried about something and told someone who really cared about you and understood; you felt better and could handle the problem. Play therapy is like that for children. They can use the dolls, puppets, paints or other toys to say what they think or how they feel. (Landreth, 1991, pp. 148–149)

After explaining the purpose of play therapy, the parents should be given the opportunity to see the playroom and the toys. The therapist should move slowly and encourage the parents to ask questions. Showing the parents the playroom helps them to better understand play therapy (Landreth, 1991; Ginott, 1982).

## Confidentiality

The therapist must explain to the parents that the play therapy sessions are confidential, but that he or she will give the parents general impressions about the session such as play themes, behavioral characteristics of the child, or concerns about the child, but will not offer specifics about what occurs in the playroom. The child needs to be able to feel that the time with the therapist is private and that the parent will not use whatever the child says or does against the child.

The issue of confidentiality can be difficult for some parents, because they feel responsible for the child, are curious about what occurs in the playroom, or are overly involved in the child's problem. I tell parents that they can trust that I will use my professional judgment in deciding what to tell them based on what is in the child and family's best interest.

Sometimes parents may wish to share something about the child with the therapist in the waiting room before the play session. The therapist should inform the parents to save their comments for a scheduled meeting time. The parents should be advised not to send notes to the therapist via the child, because the child will wonder what the notes say. The parents may be invited to call the therapist before the session if they feel there is something the therapist should know. Many parents often talk about their children to others in the presence of their children and this should be avoided.

## Preparation for Play Therapy

Preparing the child for the experience of play therapy shows respect for the child. Many parents may not adequately prepare the child, because they do not know what to say or are afraid the child will not want to attend once they inform the child he or she is going to therapy. Whatever the parents decide to tell the child, it should be done in a straightforward way that shows concern and confidence.

What the therapist suggests depends upon the therapist's theoretical orientation. Landreth (1991), a child-centered play therapist, advises parents to inform children that they will meet with the therapist in a special playroom every week where there are lots of toys. If the child wants to know why he or she is going to the playroom, the parents may say something like, "When things are hard for you at home (or at school), sometimes it helps to have a special place to play." Referring to specific child behaviors or problems can be damaging to the child. Other play therapists recommend telling the child that the parents are taking the child to a person whose job is to help children with problems like the child's.

Whether the parents should bring up "the problem" also depends on the age of the child. A very young child does not understand what problems are, but older children tend to know that their parents are upset about something that involves them. In this case, the parents can tell the child that they are *concerned* about how the child, for instance, is doing at school, getting along with his or her siblings, or feeling angry and sad a lot of the time. The difficulty with this is that the play therapy process is not entirely problem-focused and the child may be labeled as "bad." When children are brought to play therapy, they are often a scapegoat for a larger systemic problem. To counteract this difficulty, the therapist can recommend that parents tell the child that the therapist is there to help the whole family and that because of this, the therapist will be spending time with them as an entire family and time with just the parents, the siblings, and the child alone.

The therapist should also explain that if the child does not want to go to the playroom, this behavior does not reflect badly on the parents. The child may not want to attend if the entire focus of the play therapy has been presented to the child as the child being bad or having a problem. Naturally, the child may also feel scared and anxious about the new situation. The parent can be asked to accompany the therapist and the child down the hall to the playroom and then separate at the door to the playroom.

### Preparation for After the Play Session

The therapist should explain to the parents that after the play session is over they should not ask the child questions about what happened or how the child felt about the session (Landreth, 1991). When the parents refrain from asking questions, the child's privacy is ensured (Haworth, 1982) and the child feels safe and trustful (Doft & Aria, 1992). The parents can be reminded that if they were in the child's shoes they would not like to be given the third degree. When the therapist and child leave the playroom, the parents should just greet the child and go home. It is helpful to give parents exact words to say: "Hi, we can go home now" (Landreth, 1991).

Questioning the child can interfere with the progress of therapy. Parents who question their child may be concerned that the child is growing too close to the therapist or is saying negative things about the parents. The parents may also be unconsciously trying to sabotage the therapy (Ross, 1964). In addition, they may be very enmeshed in the problem, feel responsible for the child, or are curious about what happened. However, as discussed previously they must trust the therapist and the therapeutic process.

When the therapist suspects that the parents feel in competition with the therapist, this issue should be addressed directly with the parents or the therapist may prepare the parents for this possibility by discussing it in the first session. Feeling jealous of the child's relationship with the therapist can be a natural reaction for the parents.

Some children volunteer to discuss what happens in play therapy, while others are very quiet about it. It is acceptable if the child wants to talk, but the parents should allow the child to lead the conversation.

# OTHER ISSUES

The therapist should also explain to the parents what to do when the child brings home a drawing or a painting. The parents should avoid asking what the painting represents, praising it, or criticizing it. The parents instead can be told to describe what is seen in the picture. For example, "You drew a picture of two people" or "You painted a picture with green and red and purple" (Landreth, 1991).

In addition, the therapist should tell the parents to dress the child in old clothes because of the messy materials used in play therapy: sand, paint, and water. The child should not be disciplined for getting dirty in the playroom (Landreth, 1991; Haworth, 1982; Anderson & Anderson, 1984). The child must be free to express him or herself without being judged or told "no." Children are already told what to do in so many aspects of their lives.

Finally, the therapist should warn the parents that at times they may hear loud noises or crying coming from the playroom. All these behaviors are acceptable. The therapist should reassure the parents that nothing is wrong and that the therapist is always present in the playroom with the child (Ginott, 1982; Landreth, 1991).

## Methods for Ongoing Parental Involvement

After the initial session, parents can continue to be involved in the process of play therapy through parent consultation, individual counseling for one or both parents, marital therapy, family play therapy, or traditional talk family therapy. Filial therapy may be added as the play therapy process moves toward termination. The goals of parent consultation are to increase the parents' effectiveness and to facilitate the growth of the child. Consultation with the parents can lead to a change in their attitude about the child, which can enhance what the child accomplishes in play therapy (Boy & Pine, 1995). Consultation can also provide the parents with insight into the child's feelings and perceptions. In addition, working with parents can improve communication and parenting skills that enhance the parent and child relationship.

Parent consultation sessions typically begin by the therapist following up on anything that was discussed during the last session or on the phone. Then, the therapist asks the parents about what has been occurring at home. Next, the therapist talks to the parents about the child's sessions and explains areas of concern. The therapist should also report any progress the child has made and address any concerns of the parents. When providing the parents with information about the child's sessions, the therapist must assess the parents' ability to accept the information appropriately, the content of the information, the vulnerability of the child, and the safety of the parents and the child.

Consultation with parents may also involve mutual problem solving, joint planning and collaborating through sharing ideas and comparing information, and providing information and the learning of new skills as the therapist educates the parents. Educational material may include information about developmental norms, bibliotherapy, or work on specific parenting skills. Any recommendations the therapist provides should fit the child and the family. Initially, the therapist provides a large amount of direction to the parents. The therapist then gradually eases the parents into the role of being totally responsible for initiating changes in the child.

There are various views on the recommended time for parent consultation sessions. Landreth (1991) suggests that the parents should be seen first if the session is split between the parents and the child. This structure prevents the child from feeling that the parents are telling the therapist of the child's misdeeds. The therapist should be respectful of the child's privacy and help the parents to also accept it. Although it is difficult for some children to wait to go to the playroom when they first come to the therapist's office, delayed gratification may be a goal for the child. Older children can be allowed to choose who goes first.

The therapist may tend to see the parents more frequently near the beginning of therapy or during periods when much is happening in the child's life. Toward the end of therapy, the therapist may have less regular contact with the parents. Generally, play therapists tend to meet with the parents about every two or three sessions for about 15 to 20 minutes and see the child for 30 minutes of the session. I believe that most parents can benefit from more time with the therapist. I am not able to discuss as much as I would like with the parents in such a short amount of time. Therefore, I prefer to schedule around 90 minutes for a session so there is ample time to spend with both the child and the parents. Whatever amount of time is decided, it is important that the therapist and parents stick to the schedule so that time is not taken away from the child.

Working with parents can take on a more therapeutic nature in one of three ways: the parents involved in individual or marital therapy on their own, joint family sessions with the child, or engagement of the parents as therapeutic agents for the child in filial therapy. In order for the play therapist to utilize each of these modalities, the therapist must have specific training and supervision in marital, family, and filial therapy. The therapist's decision to see the parents in individual or marital therapy should be based on the therapist's ability to meet the needs of both the parents and the child and maintain appropriate boundaries. The therapist and parents must be clear about what the therapist's role is with the parents and with the child and any limits to confidentiality.

When the child's problems seem to stem from difficulty within the marriage, parent consultation sessions may be used to help the couple with communication and cooperation. However, Kottman (1995) advised that if the marital problems are severe, the therapist should refer the parents to another therapist.

Sometimes parents may have personal problems that interfere with their ability to interact appropriately with their child. In this case, if the problems are mild, the therapist may wish to do personal counseling with one of the parents by meeting with the parent at a time other than the child's scheduled session. If the play therapist works in a clinic with other therapists, one therapist can meet with the parents for individual or marital therapy while another does play therapy with the child. Landreth (1991), however, prefers that parents have parent training, because parents may make changes in their personal therapy but still interact with their children in less than helpful ways. Yet, he points out that parents can benefit from both personal therapy and parent training.

The therapist may hold a conjoint session between the parents and the child for several reasons. In family sessions, both the parents and the child are changing at the same time and therefore, a new equilibrium is reached. As a result, the parents are less likely to prevent the child's changes from becoming permanent. Family sessions also allow the therapist to observe the family members' interactions and assess how the child's symptoms are influenced by and influence the family system. These sessions can help therapists better understand how interactions between family members and the family's interactions with systems outside the family (e.g., schools) can foster and sustain children's problems. Family sessions allow additional beneficial ways to intervene in the child's social context. Interventions can be geared to the family's patterns of communication, expression of affect, family members' roles, problem solving, and conflict resolution (Malone, 1979).

Conjoint sessions can also help reduce the jealousy some parents may feel toward the therapist. In addition, during the family session the therapist can support a child who needs more independence or show the parents that the child has progressed in therapy. Family sessions are particularly helpful when there is a crisis within the family or termination is drawing closer (Krall, 1989).

One way of conducting a family session is to involve the parents in a conjoint play therapy session with the child. Axline (1967) described how seeing the parents and child together in the playroom gave her the opportunity to learn about their relationship. It is important that the therapist explain the parents' roles in a conjoint play session. They should be active participators instead of observers but should not direct the session. Directing the session may inhibit the child's play. Russo (1982) explained that he structures conjoint play sessions by first having the parents observe the child and the therapist. Next, the parents join the session in a three-way interaction with the therapist and the child. Eventually, the therapist refrains from interacting and instead observes the parents and the child. Afterwards, the therapist discusses the session with the parents.

Family play therapy combines play therapy techniques with family systems therapy and can be used for both assessment and treatment of family dynamics. Observation of parents and children playing together allows the therapist to observe the parent–child relationship in the here and now, the parents' tolerance of the child's messes, the way the parents control or are controlled by the child, and the way they cope with the child's needs. Family play therapy includes the process of intervention by facilitating an atmosphere of trust, the creative generation of solutions, and the enhancement of communication and interaction. Play also disrupts interaction patterns that maintain the symptomatic behavior and balances the adult work ethic by freeing family members to relax (Eaker, 1986). In addition, play allows family members to try out new roles and behaviors and express painful feelings.

Family play sessions may involve time for the more verbal members of the family to process feelings, thoughts, behaviors, and patterns of the play or activity. During this time, the young children continue to play and listen to what is said or the therapist may meet with just the parents. Eaker (1986) advised that initial sessions involve free play and latter sessions use structured play to focus on the presenting problem. A variety of family play techniques have been reported in the literature (c.f. Busby & Lufkin, 1992; Carey, 1991; Dare & Lindsey, 1979; Gardner, 1971; Gil, 1994; Irwin & Malloy, 1975; O'Brien & Loudon, 1985; Orgun, 1973; Ross, 1977; Rubin & Magnussen, 1974; Schachter, 1978; Simon, 1972; Villeneuve, 1979; Wolfe & Collins-Wolfe, 1983).

Filial therapy is a method of integrating child and family therapy often used by play therapists. It involves training parents to implement child-centered play therapy skills and procedures to use in play sessions with their children. The goal is to enhance the parent–child relationship (Guerney & Guerney, 1987). Filial therapy was first developed by Bernard and Louise Guerney in the 1960s (Guerney, 1964). Since then, Landreth (1991) has developed a ten week model of filial therapy combining didactic instruction, role playing, and supervision of play sessions in a supportive group setting. The supervision is oriented toward intrapsychic and interpersonal issues. The children benefit intrapsychically from the play sessions while the parents are helped through the filial group sessions.

From the initial session with the parents, I assess what factors seem to be contributing to the child's problems. I then make recommendations to the parents and together we decide how they should be included. I also involve older children in this planning process. However, I realize that as one person I cannot satisfy every family member's needs. Therefore, I have found it helpful to collaborate with other therapists. For instance, I experienced great success when I did counseling and filial therapy with a single mother while another therapist saw her daughter in play therapy. In another scenario, I did marital therapy with a couple and held family sessions with the entire family. Another therapist saw one of the children individually.

Including parents in the play therapy process can be exciting since both the parents and the children benefit. Involving parents does require extra effort, but the positive results make it all worthwhile.

## REFERENCES

Anderson, R. M., & Anderson, F. B. (1984, December). What you need to know when your child attends play therapy. *Association for Play Therapy Newsletter, 3,* 3–5.

Axline, V. M. (1967). *Play therapy* (Rev. ed.).

New York: Ballantine Books.

Boy, A. V., & Pine, G. J. (1995). *Child-centered counseling and psychotherapy*. Springfield, IL: Thomas.

Busby, D. M., & Lufkin, A. C. (1992). Tigers

are something else: A case for family play. *Contemporary Family Therapy, 14,* 437–453.

Carey, L. (1991). Family sandplay therapy. *Arts in Psychotherapy, 18,* 231–239.

Dare, C., & Lindsey, C. (1979). Children in family therapy. *Journal of Family Therapy, 1,* 253–269.

Doft, N., & Aria, B. (1992). *When your child needs help: A parent's guide to therapy for children.* New York: Harmony Books.

Eaker, B. (1986). Unlocking the family secret in family play therapy. *Child and Adolescent Social Work, 3,* 235–253.

Gardner, R. (1971). *Therapeutic communication with children: The mutual storytelling technique.* Northvale, NJ: Jason Aronson.

Gil, E. (1994). *Play in family therapy.* New York: Guilford.

Ginott, H. G. (1982). Play therapy: The initial session. In G. L. Landreth (Ed.), *Play therapy: Dynamics of the process of counseling with children* (pp. 201–216). Springfield, IL: Thomas.

Guerney, B. (1964). Filial therapy: Description and rationale. *Journal of Consulting Psychology, 28,* 304–310.

Guerney, L., & Guerney, B. (1987). Integrating child and family therapy. *Psychotherapy, 24,* 609–614.

Guerney, B. G., Guerney, L. F., & Stover, L. (1972). Facilitative therapist attitudes in training parents as psychotherapeutic agents. *The Family Coordinator, 21*(3), 275–278.

Haworth, M. (1982). Explaining play therapy to parents. In G. L. Landreth (Ed.), *Play therapy: Dynamics of the process of counseling with children* (pp. 233–234). Springfield, IL: Thomas.

Irwin, E. C., & Malloy, E. S. (1975). Family puppet interview. *Family Process, 14,* 179–191.

Kottman, T. (1995). *Partners in play: An Adlerian approach to play therapy.* Alexandria, VA: American Counseling Association.

Krall, V. (1989). *A play therapy primer: Therapeutic approaches to children with emotional problems.* New York: Human Sciences Press.

Landreth, G. L. (1991). *Play therapy: The art of the relationship.* Muncie, IN: Accelerated Development Press.

Malone, C. (1979). Child psychiatry and family therapy: An overview. *Journal of the American Academy of Child Psychiatry, 18,* 4–21.

O'Brien, A., & Loudon, P. (1985). Redressing the balance—involving children in family therapy. *Journal of Family Therapy, 7,* 81–98.

O'Connor, K. (1991). *The play therapy primer: An integration of theories and techniques.* New York: John Wiley & Sons.

Orgun, I. N. (1973). Playroom setting for diagnostic family interviews. *American Journal of Psychiatry, 130,* 540–542.

Ross, A. O. (1964). Confidentiality in child guidance treatment. In M. Haworth (Ed.), *Child psychotherapy: Practice and theory* (pp. 80–87). New York: Basic Books.

Ross, P. T. (1977). A diagnostic technique for assessment of parent–child and family interaction patterns: The family puppet technique. *Family Therapy, 4,* 129–142.

Rubin, J., & Magnussen, M. A. (1974). A family art evaluation. *Family Process, 13,* 185–200.

Russo, S. (1982). Behavioral play therapy with children. In G. L. Landreth (Ed.), *Play therapy: Dynamics of the process of counseling with children* (pp. 137–142). Springfield, IL: Thomas.

Schachter, R. S. (1978, July). Kinetic psychotherapy in the treatment of families. *The Family Coordinator,* 283–288.

Simon, R. M. (1972). Sculpting the family. *Family Process, 6,* 37–55.

Villeneuve, C. (1979). The specific participation of the child in family therapy. *Journal of the American Academy of Child Psychiatry, 18,* 44–53.

Wolfe, L. A., & Collins-Wolfe, J. A. (1983). Action techniques for therapy with families with young children. *Family Relations, 32,* 81–87.

# PART *II*

## CLINICAL INNOVATIONS
## IN PLAY
## AS A DIAGNOSTIC TOOL

# 8

# Play Therapy Behaviors of Physically Abused Children

JOANNA WHITE
KAY DRAPER
NANCY PITTARD JONES

*T*his chapter describes common play themes and behaviors of children who have been physically abused. Case illustrations are provided to enhance understanding of each category of behavior. All cases describe children in a public, elementary school, and the play therapists are school counselors and a registered play therapist/supervisor who worked at the school one day a week. In addition, special considerations in the assessment and treatment of physically abused children are addressed along with a separate section on children who witness domestic violence and are indirect recipients of physical abuse.

## INTRODUCTION

Physical abuse is the "infliction by other than accidental means of physical harm upon the body of a child," and signs may include "extensive bruises/patterns; burns/patterns; lacerations, welts or abrasions; or injuries inconsistent with information offered" (American School Counselor Association, 1993, p. 10–11). An all too common occurrence in the lives of children, physical abuse injures not only the body of a child, but the psyche as well.

Physical abuse is a societal concern that should alarm everyone because the repercussions of physical abuse are likely to be felt in some way by all individuals. While the statistics on child physical abuse are shocking and disheartening to those who care about children, they are important to summarize in order to gain perspective on the magnitude of the problem of child abuse. In the United States in 1997, nearly three children died every day from physical abuse or neglect. In 1998, more than 3.19 million children were reported to child protective service agencies as alleged victims of child maltreatment. Each year as a result of abuse, an estimated 18,000 children are permanently disabled. While neglect accounts for the largest percentage of substantiated cases of child abuse (54%), physical abuse accounts for the next largest percentage of all proven cases (22%) (Georgia Council on Child Abuse, 1999).

The numbers, although startling, do not tell the whole story. The following excerpt is a true account of a child's internal processes as he endured the ongoing abuse of his mother. The author, who recounted his torturous childhood in a courageous book, remembers:

> I'm late. I've got to finish the dishes on time, otherwise no breakfast; and since I didn't have dinner last night, I have to make sure I get something to eat. Mother's running around yelling at my brothers. I can hear her stomping down the hallway toward the kitchen. I dip my hands back into the scalding rinse water. It's too late. She catches me with my hands out of the water. SMACK! Mother hits me in the face and I topple to the floor. I know better than to stand there and take the hit. I learned the hard way that she takes that as an act of defiance, which means more hits, or worst of all, no food. I regain my posture and dodge her looks, as she screams into my ears . . . another blow pushes my head against the tile countertop. (Pelzer, 1995, p. 3–4)

Physical abuse has profound effects on children. Gil (1991) outlined many of the consequences of physical abuse for children. First, biological consequences can be tragic. Head injuries can result in permanent neurological damage that may manifest as mental retardation, cerebral palsy, learning disabilities, and sensory deficits. Likewise, damage sustained to other parts of the body can result in, for example, chronic pain, permanent limps or diminished use of limbs, and scarring to the point of disfigurement. Studies have found that developmental delay is common among abused children as compared to non-abused children (Howard, 1986). Deficits in gross motor development, speech, and language are prevalent (Martin & Rodeheffer as cited in Gil, 1991).

In addition to physical consequences there are emotional, behavioral, and social consequences. Low self-esteem, impaired social skills, learning problems in school, and an "impaired capacity to enjoy life" are among the consequences described by Gil (1991, p. 8). Physical abuse has a significant, negative impact on children's self-esteem. Childs and Timberlake (1995,) explained, "because shame goes hand in hand with doubt, abused/neglected children develop a pervasive feeling that they can never accomplish anything and increasingly blame themselves for their parents' actions" (p. 291). One study (Oates, Forrest, & Peacock, 1985) examining the effects of physical abuse on children's self-esteem found significant differences between abused and non-abused children.

Abused children saw themselves as having significantly fewer friends and reported playing with their friends less often than non-abused children. In addition, abused children were not as ambitious or hopeful about their desired future occupation than non-abused children and scored significantly lower on the *Piers–Harris Self-Concept Scale.*

Researchers have found that physically abused children have more difficulties with friendships and social skills than non-abused children do. It appears that when early environments are "rejecting and unresponsive, children become mistrusting, are negative and rejecting of others, and reason in defensive and impoverished ways about social situations" (Parker & Herrera, 1996, p. 1025). An examination of friendship dyads (Parker & Herrera, 1996) indicates that while there are some similarities among the dyads containing an abused child and dyads of two non-abused friends, there are also significant differences between the two. Abused children and their friends demonstrated less overall intimacy than non-abused children and their friends. Also, dyads containing an abused child were more conflictual, especially during game-playing activities, than dyads without abused children. In another study, children who were socially withdrawn and maltreated (including physically abused) were compared to socially withdrawn, non-abused children in terms of their social play behaviors. The maltreated children were found to be significantly more isolated and less interactive in their peer play than the non-abused children were, even though both groups of children had been identified as socially withdrawn (Fantuzzo, Sutton-Smith, Atkins, Meyers, Stevenson, Coolahan, Weiss, and Manz, 1996).

Not only do physically abused children have difficulties with social relationships, they may also exhibit learning difficulties for a variety of reasons. The most obvious of these reasons is the impairment of academic functioning resulting from insults to the child's neurological status. That is, if brain damage has occurred as a consequence of abuse, then it can be expected that learning will be compromised to some extent. Learning problems may also result from a student's difficulty with paying attention at school. If a child is preoccupied with the misery of what is happening to them at home, they have little mental energy to devote to school tasks.

Another possible cause of learning problems is the developmental delay that children who are physically abused may display. It follows that if a child is lagging in his or her development, whether cognitive, social, or emotional, the child will have difficulty keeping up in the classroom. Last, the behavioral problems exhibited by many children who are physically abused may interfere with learning. When a child misbehaves frequently in the classroom, both the behavior and the time the teacher spends trying to redirect the child's behavior detracts from time that could be spent learning.

Psychiatric symptoms and disorders have been identified as occurring frequently among children who have experienced physical abuse. Some of the more common resulting disorders include depression, anxiety disorders, especially post-traumatic stress (PTSD), oppositional defiant disorder, and enuresis and/or encopresis. Bizarre behaviors may also be present, which can indicate emotional disturbances that lead to special education services in the school setting. At times professionals may mistakenly attribute these unusual behaviors to an organic origin when in fact they are coping behaviors of the physically abused child.

Related to the emotional consequences of physical abuse already described, disturbances in attachment are likely to result from physical abuse by a caregiver. If an adult who is supposed to be the object of primary attachment for a child is the one inflicting abuse, this situation is obviously confusing for the child and disruptive to the developmental process of achieving a secure primary attachment figure. Such a major insult to the developmental needs of a young child can unfortunately lead to lifelong consequences for the human being who had his or her basic needs thwarted at such an early age (Mills & Allan, 1992).

The major indicator of significant attachment problems in childhood is disturbed and developmentally inappropriate social relatedness as evidenced by either (a) persistent failure to initiate or respond to social interactions, or (b) diffuse attachments. In the first situation, the child is often very inhibited, hypervigilant, or notably ambivalent in his or her responses (may approach, avoid, resist comforting, or be extremely watchful with caregivers). In comparison, children displaying diffuse attachments are indiscriminately social and display an inability to select attachment figures appropriately. These children may be excessively familiar with complete strangers or not be at all selective about the figures to which they attach (American Psychiatric Association, 1994). Garbarino (1999) makes a strong case for the relationship between an insecure attachment between parent and child, and abuse and neglect by the parent.

Furthermore, longitudinal studies have shown that early caretaking experiences of children affect subsequent relationship patterns. Children whose parents aggressed toward them display aggressive tendencies as they mature. In addition, if these children later become parents, their relationships with their children, in particular the quality of attachment, will relate to their own experiences in childhood. Studies have demonstrated that the security of an infant's attachment is related to the mother's own level of attachment from her childhood (Mills & Allan, 1992).

Equally important to the practitioner working with physically abused children is the role of play for all children. Play is the way in which children learn, make sense of their world, relive and work through vital aspects of their lives, and communicate to others. Play is so integral to children's lives and comes so naturally to most of them that there is strong reason to be concerned when a child is unable to engage in such activity. Because children communicate through play, it is crucial that the play behaviors of children are examined and understood so that adults who are working with or advocating for them may gain perspective on the issues with which physically abused children are struggling. While there remains much to be understood about the effects of childhood physical abuse, children's ability to tell of their pain through their play is arguably the most effective means available.

A review of the play therapy literature related to physically abused children highlights a need for more research in this area (White & Allers, 1994). However, there is a growing indication in the literature of the past ten years that professionals are beginning to recognize the devastating effects of physical abuse and the effectiveness of play therapy as a treatment modality for these children. It appears that play therapists are leading the way in the field of treating physically abused children.

## PREDOMINANT PLAY PATTERNS

Play therapy is a treatment modality most suited to the needs of children because of its match with children's unique developmental needs. This is especially true for physically abused children due to the loss of trust and safety that they experience as a result of the abuse. White and Allers (1994) conducted an extensive review of the play therapy literature related to abused children. They identified two recurring play themes or recurrent patterns of play that are identified with abused children. These two play patterns are (a) unimaginative and literal play and (b) repetitive and compulsive play.

### Unimaginative and Literal Play

Experience with abused children in the play therapy setting indicates that they often have difficulty engaging in meaningful play themes. Meaningful play themes can be described as metaphoric play in which the child is creating his or her unique play and actively directing and taking part in it. As described by White and Allers (1994), some abused children cannot do this at the beginning of therapy. These children often go from one toy to another in a detached manner. They are unable to use the toys to explore or relive their life experiences. In some cases they are unable to engage with the toys or the therapist at all in the beginning of therapy. Steele (as cited in Fatout, 1993, p. 85) believed that when the child is physically abused, "…there is a deprivation of pleasure early in life, the child learns to live a more mechanical, practical, reality-oriented life."

It is apparent with these children that the trauma of the physical abuse retards their normal development and deprives them of the ability to feel safe enough to engage in the type of creative, metaphoric play that absorbs the lives of children who are not abused. White and Allers (1994) postulated that the unimaginative and literal type of play could also be the result of the physically abused child's attempt to develop a "pseudo-adult life style" (p. 392) in order to survive in a chaotic environment. Lastly, this inability to play with any intensity and meaning could be a result of neurological damage caused by the physical abuse.

**Case of Jimmy.**   Jimmy was a ten-year-old fourth grader who witnessed extreme violence in his early years. He saw his father kill his grandmother when he was three. His father was sent to jail, and Jimmy went to live with his mother. His mother eventually had two more sons with two different fathers. Both of the fathers of the two younger brothers were very physically aggressive toward Jimmy, his brothers, and their mother. All three boys received extremely harsh physical punishment from both their mother and their stepfathers.

Jimmy was seen in the playroom for one and one-half school years. For many sessions, he simply sat in a corner facing away from the counselor. He fiddled with any toy that happened to be in front of him, but he would not purposefully seek out specific toys. He rarely spoke or responded to tracking by the counselor and was never able to engage in metaphoric play. He spent several sessions attempting to fix an army tank with guns that were jammed. The counselor was quick to encourage his perseverance and his ability to fix the toy. Occasionally, Jimmy painted at the easel. His pictures were usually in black with very aggressive themes such as action figures, people getting their heads knocked off, or pictures of weapons.

At the beginning of fifth grade, Jimmy was placed in a playgroup with two other boys his age. During playgroup time, he continued to wander around the playroom, never able to engage in metaphoric play themes. When the other boys invited him to play, he sometimes joined them; however, he remained quiet, withdrawn and did not participate fully or zestfully in their play. At the end of that year, the counselor took Jimmy into the playroom alone for a final session. Jimmy painted a picture of a sunburst symbol in pastel colors that he gave to the counselor. This picture was quite a change from his usual artwork in the playroom, and perhaps represented a sense of hope. Even though physically abused children may remain quiet and withdrawn, it is important to avoid underestimating the power of the play therapist/child relationship.

## Repetitive and Compulsive Play

Experience indicates that most physically abused children, once they feel safe in the playroom environment, begin to relive the trauma of their abuse through abreactive play themes. This type of play helps the child to "recreate the traumatic event through play" (Gil, 1991, p. 30). With this type of repetitive play, children relive the trauma within their metaphoric play theme so that they can assimilate the negative emotions of the trauma in a safe playroom environment. In this type of play it often appears that the child cannot stop a play theme, and the child may use the toys to relive the trauma of the physical abuse over and over again.

Terr (as cited in White & Allers, 1994) suggested that repetitive, compulsive play can serve as the physically abused child's way of reducing stress, and it may appear strange to adults who interact with that child on a daily basis. The child may experience negative feedback from parents and teachers as a result of this type of behavior, and this constant negative feedback is retraumatizing for the child.

**Case of Gregory.**   Gregory was a six-year-old first grader. He was extremely below grade level academically, demonstrated very poor self-control with peers, and was often disruptive in the classroom. He walked with an unusual gait and had a bizarre speech pattern. These factors led the counselor and teacher to suggest to Gregory's mother that he have a medical evaluation. This evaluation revealed that Gregory had some brain damage, which his mother attributed to a severe beating Gregory had received from her ex-husband. Gregory had apparently received several blows to the head that went untreated while staying with his father the summer that he turned four years old. The medical evaluation also revealed drug and alcohol abuse by Gregory's mother while she was pregnant with him. The combination of these circumstances seemed to explain Gregory's behavior.

Gregory engaged in the same play behaviors for his first nine play therapy sessions. Consistently, he picked up a toy truck and a lamp from the dollhouse. He loaded the lamp on the back of the truck and said, "Time to go to Sears and get the lamp fixed; the lamp is broken, got to get it fixed." He then made "driving" noises while he drove the truck a few feet away. Next, he took the lamp out of the truck and set it on the edge of the table and said, "Here we are at Sears, they will fix the lamp. Get the lamp fixed." After repeating that several times, he put the lamp back in the truck, made more driving noises as he moved the truck back toward the house, and said, "Now the lamp is fixed, got to take the lamp home, it's ready to be picked up, the lamp works now." Once back at the house, he unloaded the lamp, put it where he originally found it, and then repeated the entire sequence.

Gregory repeated this play theme over 20 times per session in each of the first nine sessions. He did not engage in any other play. The counselor believed that Gregory's obsession with fixing the lamp might relate to his awareness of his own damage from the physical abuse. It is also possible that the repetitive play was a direct result of his impaired mental capacity.

Gregory had eleven sessions during that school year. The last two sessions again included taking the lamp to be fixed. However, he did spend some of his time exploring other toys. During the tenth session he painted at the easel, using each color of paint to paint circles, one on top of the other. He also played with a baton without speaking. He held it in the middle and waved it up and down for several minutes at a time.

After Gregory's eleventh session, the school year ended. At that time he was designated as eligible for a self-contained special education program. Even though Gregory was unable to continue in play therapy, the counselor did recognize a shift in his play that indicated some progress during the last two sessions.

## TYPICAL PLAY BEHAVIORS

In the literature regarding physically abused children, there seems to be some agreement as to the typical play behaviors exhibited by these children in play therapy. White and Allers (1994) compiled, from an extensive review of the literature, a list of six play behaviors of physically abused children. These are: (a) developmental immaturity, (b) oppositional and aggressive behavior, (c) withdrawn and passive behavior, (d) self-deprecating and self-destructive behavior, (e) hypervigilance, and (f) dissociation. In this section, White and Allers' (1994) listing will be used as a model to explain and describe the typical play behaviors of physically abused children.

## Developmental Immaturity

The results of abuse are devastating to the normal development of a child's emotional, social, and cognitive functioning. Fagot, Hagan, Youngblade, and Potter (1989) in their study comparing the play behaviors of sexually abused children to physically abused and non-abused children found that the abused neglected group showed clear signs of disturbance with more antisocial, disruptive, and aggressive yet passive behaviors than sexually abused children. They believe that, "disruption of play is one of the most sensitive indicators of disturbance in a child's life" (Fagot et al., p. 88). Even though there are differences in the pace of children's development, their development follows predictable stages. Howard (1986) stated that physically abused children have more behavioral problems, are more often in special education classes, and have more academic difficulties than do non-abused children. The results of Howard's study (1986) of the developmental play ages of physically abused children as compared to non-abused children found that physically abused children displayed a lower developmental play age as defined by *The Preschool Play Scale*.

Play is such an important, if not the most important, activity for the promotion of healthy development in young children. Physical abuse is a traumatic disruption to the child's play process that will have long-term, negative effects. Because physically abused children become preoccupied with the threat of physical abuse and their safety, they usually respond to the trauma with one of two extreme behavior patterns by either withdrawing or engaging in aggressive behaviors (Jones, as cited in Howard, 1986). These behavior patterns do not lend themselves to free play and creativity. Their play becomes less imaginative and joyful. This loss of the rich play experiences that non-abused children enjoy each day retards the emotional, academic, and social development of the physically abused child (Oates et al., 1985).

**Case of Mark.**   Mark was a seven-year-old who was repeating first grade. He had suffered physical abuse from his biological mother. The abuse was reported to the Department of Family and Children's Services (DFACS), and he was currently living with relatives. He began play therapy after his misbehavior in the classroom became severe. Problems included leaving the room without permission, roaming the building, and running from or refusing to obey staff members who were trying to get him back to class. He also whined, pouted, and threw tantrums in the classroom when things did not go his way. In addition, Mark showed a great deal of immaturity in his relationships with peers.

In the playroom, Mark played at a developmental level that was younger than his chronological age. He often took toys and simply banged them together, laughing at the sounds they made. He also seemed perplexed by what to do with toys such as puppets. He did not realize that he could wear the puppet on his hand and use them behind a puppet theater. He often took out the Monkeys in the Barrel game and counted the monkeys. He could not count accurately past seven. If the monkeys fell on the floor, it took him several attempts to pick them up because he could not grasp them easily. When talking to the toys, Mark often used "baby talk." In utilizing art materials, he often held the paintbrush or markers incorrectly, grasping them in his fist.

Mark's play was often focused on building things and making them "safe." He often built castles in the sand or pretended the dollhouse was a castle. He worked at making everyone safe from the "coming storms."

For a time, Mark was included in a playgroup. He had a great deal of difficulty interacting with the boys in the group. Rather than engaging in play relationships with the other boys, he chose to play alongside them. In addition, his play themes did not include any development of relationships between people or animals.

Mark continued play therapy for the remainder of the school year. He made some positive changes, but he was shuttled back and forth between relatives and his mother. When he was with his mother, she continued to physically abuse him, and that obviously was an obstacle to his development, both academically and emotionally. He was extremely fond of the counselor and had a difficult time saying good-bye to her when he moved out of district. He had the support of a caring adult through the ongoing trauma, and he was able to respond to that relationship.

## Aggressive and Oppositional Behaviors

Children who are physically abused at an early age cannot escape the overwhelmingly negative ramifications of the aggression. Reidy (1977) found that abused children are significantly more aggressive than non-abused children in the areas of fantasy, the free play environment, and the school environment.

Kindlon and Thompson (1999) cited studies indicating that kindergarteners that are spanked at home were more physically aggressive at school. Physically abused children usually have difficulty in developing positive peer relationships due to their aggression toward other children. Aggressive and oppositional behaviors are the most common play behaviors exhibited by physically abused children treated in play therapy. If children do indeed use the freedom of the playroom to relive the physical trauma, then it makes sense that aggressive play would be common. Clinical experience suggests that aggressive play is most typical for physically abused boys.

Kindlon and Thompson (1999) support this belief that boys are usually on the receiving end of harsh discipline, much more than girls. They explain that girls are physically disciplined with an "undertone of regret" (p. 53) while adults believe that boys need to be treated harshly in order to make them into men. Adults have a mistaken belief that boys are able to bounce back from the effects of abuse, and that it is for their own good.

Mills and Allan (1992) compiled a valuable review of literature regarding the longitudinal effects of aggressive behavior exhibited by boys and girls. These results indicate that early acting out behaviors can predict later difficulties with academics and relationships. These correlations were stronger for boys than for girls. In one study, aggressive behavior in childhood was linked with later pathology, but this was only true for boys, not girls. Even though it seems true that boys are particularly vulnerable to physical abuse, the fact is that both boys and girls are traumatized by physical abuse, and they develop defenses against it that can negatively affect their entire lives.

Because of the aggression that physically abused children experience at the hands of adults, some children choose to interact with authority figures in oppositional and defiant ways. These children frequently break rules and get into power struggles with various adults in their lives. In the playroom, these children typically test limits and range from being verbally to physically defiant.

Clinical experiences with physically abused children in play therapy indicate the importance of having toys that allow these children to express the anger they are feeling as a result of the betrayal of a trusted adult. The toys, combined with the safe and accepting relationship with the play therapist, enable children to manage their aggression and experience new ways of interacting that foster healthy social development.

**Case of Logan.**   Logan was a twelve-year-old female in fifth grade with a long history of abuse and neglect at the hands of her mother. Logan's older brother had many problems at school, at home, and in the community; therefore, much attention was focused on him. Logan was often an afterthought in her family. She seemed to deal with this rejection by either striving to "outdo" her brother, or assert herself as "the good one."

Logan began play therapy after severe outbursts in her classroom that included cursing, throwing items, and threatening. While she limited her play to talking nervously in the main playroom at the school, she seemed to be more comfortable in a small play corner of the counselor's office. Her play expanded in this more intimate setting.

Much of Logan's play was violent in nature. She spent part of each session in the playroom finding out how many ways she could spank the dolls from the family house. In her play, the mother doll would yell at one of the child dolls, and then Logan would smile at the counselor while telling her, "This child is really going to get it now!" Next, she demonstrated various ways she could spank the doll such as banging the doll against the side of the house, beating it with the baton, and running over it with a car. Whenever Logan thought she had discovered a better and more punishing method of spanking, she laughed, smiled and said, "This spanking is the ultimate!"

Although Logan exhibited a great deal of aggressive play, she engaged in a nurturing play theme as well. She spent quite a bit of time cleaning the toy bins and the sand trays in the counselor's office. She took great pride in putting things exactly where she thought they belonged. She also cooked for the counselor on many occasions, making sure to cook things that she thought the counselor would enjoy and inquiring if the food was to the counselor's liking.

Logan got very frustrated with toys or play themes if they did not work the way she wanted. For example, she knew how to unhook the handcuffs, but sometimes they did not come off as quickly as she desired. When this happened, she pulled on them harshly, leaving her wrists red. On other occasions, Logan had plans for her play but would abandon them in disgust because of her frustration. For example, she tried to build a staircase with large blocks so she could walk the Slinky down it. When the Slinky did not go down as planned, she knocked over all of the blocks and cursed. Logan also got out the dominoes one day, but gave them up quickly after becoming angry that some of them were missing.

Logan left the school at the end of her fifth grade year to go on to middle school. She had made great strides both in the playroom and in her classroom. By the end of the year, the aggressive play that was initially so powerful for Logan disappeared almost completely. In contrast, her nurturing play behaviors increased, and her teacher reported that Logan was calmer, able to focus on her schoolwork, and had made a few friends.

## Withdrawn and Passive Behavior

McFadden (1986) described the withdrawn and passive child as "the hider." As discussed earlier, withdrawing is a typical reaction for a child experiencing physical abuse. Avoidance, fearfulness, and isolation often characterize children's reactions to the pain of abuse and betrayal from a significant adult. These avoidance behaviors are evident in play therapy through the child's lack of interest in free play and meaningful connections with the play therapist. In fact, these children will often find a place to hide in the playroom, such as behind the puppet stage or facing away from the play therapist toward a wall or a corner.

**Case of Ryan.** Ryan was an eleven-year-old fourth grade student in a self-contained Emotional Behavioral Disorder class. The basis for his placement was his strong reaction to the breakup of his parents' marriage that led to his kidnapping by his father. His father was jailed briefly for this action. At the time of the abuse, Ryan was living with his mother and stepfather. He reported a good relationship with both parents in the home, although he said if he "messed up" he would get in "big trouble." He defined "big trouble" as getting a spanking or a "whipping."

His mother beat Ryan for the first time because of low grades he received on his report card. He came to school bleeding down his back and with his arm apparently broken in at least one place. After Ryan was seen by the school nurse and the school counselor, a report was made to the DFACS. This agency investigated in the following days, and Ryan's mother was sent to a court-mandated class on appropriate discipline for children. The court also suggested that Ryan receive services from the school, and the counselor began seeing him in the playroom.

Ryan's initial play was to bury figures in the sand without talking. He took great care to push everything down to the very bottom of the sand tray. After a few sessions, he began to talk softly to the figures as he buried them. He eventually began burying other things in the sand such as cars, a jump rope, and blocks. Ryan did not engage the counselor in conversation or play. To be so quiet in the presence of others was a definite behavioral change for this previously outgoing, exuberant boy.

When Ryan discovered a box that had some rubber insects, he acted afraid to touch the insects and began a ritual of moving the box high on a shelf each week. He always looked up to see if any of the insects were "falling out" of the box. He reported this "fear" of the "bugs" to his classroom teacher after visiting the playroom. Subsequently, the teacher told the counselor that the year before, Ryan collected dead insects, pinned them to a board, and identified them as part of a science project. He had been very proud of this project and had no apparent fear of the insects at that time, so the teacher was shocked that he was now afraid of the rubber insects in the playroom.

On the occasions when Ryan spoke to the counselor, he talked a great deal about his friend, Kevin. It was obvious that he had shared his playroom experiences with Kevin, and he reported that Kevin wanted to come with him to the playroom. When the counselor saw Kevin in the school halls or in class, Kevin asked if he and Ryan could play together in the playroom.

Eventually, the counselor offered Ryan the option of bringing Kevin to the playroom with him. He was very excited about this prospect. On their first visit together, Kevin immediately engaged in aggressive play with swords, guns, and the alligator puppet while Ryan did not play at all. He sat on the side of the room and watched Kevin, expressionless. Several times, Kevin approached Ryan and laughed at him for not participating in the play. He called Ryan a "baby" and a "wimp" while Ryan continued to sit without comment. During later visits, Ryan and Kevin played cards together. Kevin got very excited when he won a game of cards, but Ryan did not react to either winning or losing. After a few sessions with Kevin, the counselor chose to see Ryan alone again in the playroom. The counselor was uncertain as to why Ryan did not follow through behaviorally with his fervent wish to have Kevin in the playroom. She surmised that although Ryan wanted desperately to join with Kevin in a relationship, the playroom had become a special place in which he was unsure how to expand his playroom work into his friendship. It seems that once the reality of Kevin being present occurred, it was not all Ryan had envisioned. Evidently, Ryan was unable to resume his work until Kevin was no longer a participant.

Ryan continued in the playroom for almost six months until the school year ended. As time went on Ryan forgot to move the rubber insects immediately and would do so only when he happened across the box. His change in behavior suggested that Ryan was slowly conquering his fears related to the abuse.

By the time the school year ended, Ryan was interacting with the counselor by using the puppets. This desire to connect with the counselor also suggests progress for the previously withdrawn Ryan. Ryan graduated and proceeded to middle school.

## Self-Deprecating and Self-Destructive Behaviors

Children who engage in self-deprecating and self-destructive behaviors are reacting to the trauma of physical abuse by turning their anger inward (White & Allers, 1992, 1994). As opposed to acting out children who direct their emotions toward others, these children internalize their fears, anger, and hurt. They make remarks such as, "I'm stupid," "I can't do it," and "I'm ugly." As a result of the abuse, they may believe that they deserve to be hurt. They may go so far as to physically harm themselves with behaviors like banging their heads or hitting themselves.

Physically abused children will also direct their anger toward a toy in the playroom. Picking up the doll and saying, "You're a bad girl" or stabbing a puppet with the toy knife are ways that these children express the anger that they cannot express with just words.

**Case of Roderick.**   Roderick was a fifth-grade boy who was new to the school after he moved in with an aunt. His mother, who physically abused him and his four siblings, lived in another state. She had voluntarily signed over guardianship of Roderick to her sister. The DFACS was never involved with this family. The abuse was noted by Roderick's aunt and other relatives, and they offered to take him for a while to "give his mom a break." Roderick was significantly below grade level academically.

Roderick's time in the playroom was centered mostly on the things he "could not do." He was easily discouraged if something he tried did not go well the first time. For example, when he could not make the handcuffs unlock, he called himself "stupid" and threw them back on the shelf. He also tried out a game that involved using a magnetic fishing pole to catch fish. When he was unable to catch the fish he wanted to catch, he said, "I can't do this," and put it back.

Roderick played with the aggressive toys almost every week. He often aimed the toy gun at his own head and said, "The bad guys got me! I'm dead!" and threw himself to the floor. He would also use string to tie up his own hands. He sometimes used the alligator puppet to bite his own arms and legs. Roderick would make comments about not being able to save himself from the "beasts."

Sometimes Roderick engaged in conversations about his classmates and peers. He said that his friends did not really like him because he was "stupider" than the others were. When he role-played friends in the playroom, he seemed to be lacking many basic social skills. This deficit seemed to affect his ability to relate to other children his age. After several months of weekly sessions, the counselor noted that Roderick seemed more willing to take risks or try something a little longer before either mastering it or giving up. Roderick also began reporting a friendship with a girl in his class.

## Hypervigilance

Gil (1991) listed hypervigilance as a common characteristic of physically abused children. Although studies have indicated that this vigilant behavior is more common with sexually abused children (White & Allers, 1994), it is certainly important for play therapists to recognize and respect that physically abused children may spend a great deal of emotional energy on watching for environmental cues that represent physical danger. Gil (1991) suggests that play therapists should be nonintrusive with early interventions because physical abuse is an " . . . intrusive act that violates the child's boundaries" (p. 59). Clinical experience in play therapy supports our belief that safety is the critical issue for the abused child. Hypervigilant behavior is a logical coping mechanism for physically abused children to monitor their safety in the playroom.

**Case of Cindy.** Cindy was a seven-year-old second grader who lived with her father and paternal grandparents. Her parents had been divorced since she was four, and the father reported that Cindy's mother physically abused her from the age of two until the age of four. The abuse consisted of spankings with various objects (wire coat hangers, extension cords, kitchen utensils) as well as being locked in a closet or bathroom. On two separate occasions, Cindy was taken to the hospital for injuries caused by her mother. On the occasion of the second injury, a report was made to the DFACS. Cindy's father won sole custody of her in the divorce proceedings, and her mother was jailed for six months. Her father reported that Cindy had trouble sleeping and occasionally wet the bed.

When Cindy first came to the playroom she presented as a clean, bright little girl who was pleasant but a bit shy. After some hesitation in her first visit, she began to explore the room. She constantly asked the counselor for permission to play with certain toys. Cindy often phrased these questions as, "Will it make you mad if I play with this?" or "My daddy likes it when I pretend to cook for him; would you like it if I did that too?" The counselor was very aware of encouraging Cindy to make decisions for herself; however, it was quite some time before Cindy stopped asking the counselor for permission to play with certain toys.

The counselor also noticed that if any noise or distraction interrupted Cindy's play, Cindy stood perfectly still and stared at or searched for the cause of the noise. For example, if the intercom buzzed, she froze and stared at it for some time. It appeared she had a hard time relaxing before returning to her play.

Many of Cindy's play themes centered on cooking and cleaning, keeping house, and playing with the dollhouse. She acted out many scenes where she was the mother and was helping care for her family. She constantly told the other dolls and animals in her play that she loved them, and she would ask, "Do you love your mommy too?" It was noted that over time, she seemed to ask those questions less and less of her pretend playmates and her hypervigilant behaviors decreased.

At the end of the school year, Cindy and her family moved to another part of the county to be closer to her father's new job. Her father reported that she was sleeping better, her bed-wetting had virtually stopped, and her grades had improved.

## Dissociation

Snow, White, Pilkington, and Beckman (1995) believe that dissociation is not an unusual reaction to abuse, and play therapy is the logical modality for treatment of abused children. According to Gil (1991) dissociative behaviors in children present on a continuum from normal daydreaming and boredom to multiple personality disorder. She describes dissociation as allowing the child the ability to escape "...dangerous or threatening situations" (p. 77). Childs and Timberlake (1995, p. 291) believe that dissociation is a natural defense against the psychological trauma of abuse that, "solidifies into an internal system of rules and procedures which distorts cognition, inhibits the flow of information across the mind, and excludes portions of reality from conscious awareness."

Hornstein (1996, p. 31) stated that, "Preschool and early school age children in the process of personality and cognitive development are particularly apt to utilize dissociation because of the developmental lag in their elaboration of more complicated defensive possibilities." These physically abused children develop patterns of escaping the trauma of abuse by changing their mental set and escaping to a fantasy world. This becomes a habit that is transferred to their play, especially when they begin to relive the abuse through their play themes. It is critical for the play therapist to be aware of these dissociative states and marked shifts in play themes in order to be facilitative and accepting of the child's phenomenological field at any given moment.

**Case of Ali.**   Ali was a kindergarten student who had moved from another state with his pregnant mother. They had lived with his grandmother up until that time. His mother and grandmother disagreed about methods of child rearing, and he was often caught in the middle of their arguments. Ali grieved for his grandmother, who had given him a great deal of attention, and for the cousins left behind who had been his constant companions.

When Ali began to act out at school, his mother reacted in inconsistent ways. At times she was calm and talked to him in a respectful manner. At other times, she forced him to sit on a chair for long periods while lecturing him, using foul language, and insulting him. His mother was also known to grab him by his clothing and "whip" him.

At school, Ali was quick to attack other children physically. Typically, he walked into the classroom in the morning, set down his belongings, nonchalantly attempted to choke a child by the neck, and then began to eat his breakfast. He also attacked his teacher numerous times. These attacks were quick, unprovoked, and over very quickly. Ali also "heard" things that were not there. On one occasion he broke down crying, insisting that a boy at his table had called him a name. The boy in question had been working with the teacher, and she heard no verbalization from that child. Ali also attacked a student for throwing Jell-O at him. After the teacher calmed him down, Ali kept saying that "she" (meaning a female student) had thrown Jell-O at him and made him angry. The teacher checked every student in the room, both male and female, and none of them had Jell-O or anything similar to Jell-O for a snack. Ali was unable to point to the student who supposedly had the Jell-O.

In the playroom, the counselor was immediately concerned with Ali's play behaviors. On his initial visit, as he played in the sand, Ali told the counselor that he wished she could have been with him the night before. When the counselor restated his comment, Ali explained further that, "God had come again with the seven keys." As the counselor tracked his verbalizations, Ali proceeded to share that God would "come down" with the seven keys and take him into the television. Ali described how he and God would sing and dance in the television. He seemed anxious for the counselor to know that not too many people could know about the keys because then God would either stop coming or would have to visit too many people. He also asserted that his mom already knew about God coming, as if to prevent the counselor from telling his mother about his verbalizations.

Ali reported watching a great deal of television, especially wrestling shows. He reported putting himself into the role of the wrestler when he played at home. Ali told the counselor that he often had those wrestling stories in his head at school. It seemed difficult at times for him to separate the stories in his head from the reality of the moment.

Ali was seen in the playroom for many weeks. As his relationship with the counselor deepened, he shared more stories with her. The counselor continued to be concerned with his tendency to use fantasy to escape the reality of the situation. A referral was made to the (DFACS) based on these factors as well as his report of physical abuse at the hands of his mother. The day DFACS visited the home, Ali's mother abruptly withdrew him from school with no explanation.

## ASSESSMENT CONSIDERATIONS

Unless the therapist is working in a setting in which physical abuse has been confirmed before the child is ever seen, assessment is a very crucial aspect of a child practitioner's work. First, actual physical signs are the most obvious indicators of physical abuse. A child who has unexplained or poorly explained bruises, burns, or other marks, should be observed and examined carefully. These tell-tale marks often lead to a referral to the appropriate child protection agency. Sometimes, children who wear long pants, long sleeved shirts, and other clothing to cover up their body in spite of the weather are dressed to conceal the physical consequences of abuse on their bodies.

In addition to these physical signs, it is important to be able to recognize the play behaviors described in previous sections of this chapter in assessing for physical abuse. These themes emerged from an examination of the existing literature, and while the presence of these play behaviors does not indicate with absolute certainty that a child was physically abused, the possibility of abuse should be given close consideration.

Beyond the play behaviors described, there are symptoms the child may be exhibiting outside the play setting that are important to consider. Some of these symptoms vary with the child's age; the focus here will be on preschoolers and school-aged children since the age range of these groups makes play therapy interventions appropriate for them. These symptoms include:

1. Preschool and school-aged children may exhibit aggression towards self or others, or conversely, they may present in the role of victim.
2. Hyperactivity is possible and may be misunderstood as Attention Deficit Hyperactivity Disorder (ADHD) when in fact the behavior is a manifestation of the ongoing discomfort and chaos experienced by an abused child.
3. Inattention due to preoccupation may mimic Attention Deficit Disorder (ADD), primarily Inattentive Type.
4. Depression, including a loss of interest in or inability to enjoy formerly pleasurable activities is common.
5. Fearful, anxious behavior (including nightmares, fears and phobias, and/ or clinging behaviors) is also common.
6. With school-aged children, learning difficulties may be present as discussed in the introductory section.

## TREATMENT CONSIDERATIONS

When working in the playroom with physically abused children, there are several treatment issues to keep in mind. These considerations should help to make the counselor more responsive to the child's needs as well as create an environment that is more conducive to healing. These treatment issues include:

1. The playroom should be equipped with several types of toys. However, it is very important for physically abused children to have access to toys that are aggressive, toys that provide a hiding place, and toys that are nurturing.
2. The relationship between the child and the counselor is critical. However, it may be difficult for the physically abused child to establish bonds

with others. This factor may make establishing a relationship challenging to the play therapist. While all children have a need to feel acceptance and love, the severity of this need may increase depending on the experiences of the child (Malchiodi, 1990). It is important for the counselor to know this and to be patient. While the bond may be harder to come by for the physically abused child, he or she may actually be in desperate need of this bond.

3. For a physically abused child, touch can be both healing and harmful. Counselors should be sparing with their touch, as this could cross over a boundary that the child has set up for himself or herself. On the other hand, a child may show a need for physical contact during the play session. While dependency on the counselor should not be encouraged, it would be a worthy intervention for the counselor to model positive, appropriate touch when initiated by the child (Malchiodi, 1990). The child should, as always, set the tone for this element. The counselor should not attempt to initiate touch.

4. The counselor may need to be prepared to set more limits for the physically abused child in the playroom. These children may have a great deal of aggression that could result in unsafe choices, such as climbing on top of furniture. Because of this need the child may attempt to touch the counselor in an inappropriate way, such as hitting the counselor with a ball or sword, or shooting at the counselor with a gun. A child who is in need of nurturance due to physical abuse may wish to hug the counselor or sit on the counselor's lap. These and other related behaviors are all possibilities for strong and consistent limit setting by the counselor.

5. Play therapists who counsel with physically abused children must take into consideration the stress that could result from these relationships. It is always difficult to know the horrors that children experience, and it is compounded when the therapist begins to develop a meaningful relationship with the child. Good health habits, regular supervision, and healthy support from friends and family will help to prevent secondary trauma for the therapist.

## WITNESSING DOMESTIC VIOLENCE

"Aggression and acting out behaviors are currently the most common reasons for referral of young children to mental health services" (Mills & Allan, 1992, p. 1). Much of this aggression is a result of physical abuse perpetrated against children. However, there is another important area to consider when working with aggressive children in play therapy, and that is domestic violence. The exposure to violence in the home, often between parents, can be just as devastating to a child as physical abuse. In fact, it is an indirect form of child abuse.

Frick-Helms (1997) believes that exposure to domestic violence has received less attention than any other type of trauma experienced by children. The children of battered women not only witness violence between the two most significant adults in their lives, but the chances of the children not being physically abused as well are slim. Frick-Helms (1997) indicates that most children who live with battered women are abused and/or neglected themselves. In their research, Frick-Helms (1997), Kot, Landreth, and Giordano (1998), and Tyndall-Lind (1999) confirm that play therapy is an effective treatment modality for children exposed to domestic violence. It is important for play therapists working with children experiencing domestic violence and physical abuse to be aware that these children are suffering from a compounded loss. They will exhibit typical play behaviors of physically abused children and also suffer from irrational guilt that they may have caused the violence between the adults. Many of these children are uprooted with their mothers to shelters. This move from home, father, and school often leaves the child confused, angry, and afraid (Kot, Landreth, & Giordano, 1998).

## CONCLUSION

The physical abuse of children is a sad and sometimes unimaginable aspect of society that disturbs most adults deeply when they are exposed to some of the horrors that children endure. While awareness of the problem and its devastating effects is slowly increasing, the methods for preventing and remediating such atrocities are severely lagging. It seems child advocates from a variety of professions are working to bring both awareness and assistance, but the financial implications of effectively tackling such a pervasive problem, as well as some adults' desire to remain in denial about this distasteful issue, may be hindering such efforts.

Although the work yet to be done is daunting, it is rewarding to witness the strides that have been made in relatively recent times. Among these strides, there is the recognition that children are communicating their issues and attempting with courage to work through them by the means that are within a child's grasp. That is the core of the play therapy process. By providing an opportunity for and then facilitating this brave work, mental health professionals are truly partnering with the victims of physical abuse to change the malicious patterns that have invaded so many homes for so long.

In the play therapy process, it is crucial that professionals both recognize and communicate the important information that children are providing. One important way of doing this is to understand common patterns of play, the frequently seen types of play behaviors, and the typical themes that emerge during play therapy for children who have experienced physical abuse.

# REFERENCES

American Psychiatric Association. (1994). *Diagnostic and statistical manual of mental disorders* (4th ed.). Washington, DC: Author.

American School Counselor Association. (1993). *The school counselor and child abuse/neglect prevention position statement*. Alexandria, VA: Author.

Childs, L. S., & Timberlake, E. M. (1995). Assessing clinical progress: A case study of Daryl. *Child and Adolescent Social Work Journal, 12*(4), 289–315.

Fantuzzo, J., Sutton-Smith, B., Atkins, M., Meyers, R., Stevenson, H., Coolahan, K., Weiss, A., & Manz, P. (1996). Community-based resilient peer treatment of withdrawn maltreated preschool children. *Journal of Consulting and Clinical Psychology, 64*(6), 1377–1386.

Fatout, M. F. (1993). Physically abused children: Activity as a therapeutic medium. *Social Work with Groups, 16*(3), 83–96.

Fagot, B. I., Hagan, R., Youngblade, L. M., & Potter, L. (1989). A comparison of the play behaviors of sexually abused, physically abused, and non-abused preschool children. *Topics in Early Childhood Special Education, 9*, 88–100.

Frick-Helms, S. B. (1997). "Boys cry better than girls": Play therapy behaviors of children residing in a shelter for battered women. *International Journal of Play Therapy, 6*, 73–91.

Garbarino, J. (1999). *Lost boys: Why our sons turn violent and how we can save them*. New York: The Free Press.

Georgia Council on Child Abuse. (1999). *The problems of child abuse*. Atlanta, GA: Author.

Gil, E. (1991). *The healing power of play: Working with abused children*. New York: The Guilford Press.

Hornstein, N. L. (1996). Complexities of psychiatric differential diagnosis in children with dissociative symptoms and disorders. In J. L. Silberg (Ed.), *The dissociative child* (pp. 25–45). Lutherville, MD: The Sidran Press.

Howard, A. C. (1986). Developmental play ages of physically abused and non-abused children. *The American Journal of Occupational Therapy, 40*, 691–695.

Kindlon, D., & Thompson, M. (1999). *Raising Cain: Protecting the emotional life of boys.* New York: Ballatine Books.

Kot, S., Landreth, G. L., & Giordano, M. (1998). Intensive child-centered play therapy with child witnesses of domestic violence. *International Journal of Play Therapy, 7*, 17–36.

Malchiodi, C. (1990). *Breaking the silence: Art therapy with children from violent homes.* New York: Brunner/Mazel.

McFadden, E. J. (1986). Helping the abused child through play. In J. S. McKee (Ed.), *Play: Working partner of growth* (pp. 73–79). Wheaton, MD: Association for Childhood Education International.

Mills, B., & Allan, J. (1992). Play therapy with the maltreated child: Impact upon aggressive and withdrawn patterns of interaction. *International Journal of Play Therapy, 1*, 1–20.

Oates, R. K., Forrest, D., & Peacock, A. (1985). Self-esteem of abused children. *Child Abuse & Neglect, 9*, 159–163.

Parker, J. G., & Herrera, C. (1996). Interpersonal processes in friendship: A comparison of abused and nonabused children's experiences. *Developmental Psychology, 32* (6), 1025–1038.

Pelzer, D. (1995). *A child called "It."* Deerfield Beach, FL: Health Communications, Inc.

Reidy, T. J. (1977). The aggressive characteristics of abused and neglected children. *Journal of Clinical Psychology, 33*(4), 1140–1145.

Snow, M. S., White, J., Pilkington, L., & Beckman D. (1995). Dissociative identity disorder revealed through play therapy: A case study of a four-year-old. *Dissociation, 8*, 120–123.

Tyndall-Lind, A. (1999). *A comparative analysis of intense individual play therapy and intensive sibling group play therapy with child witnesses of domestic violence.* Unpublished doctoral dissertation, University of North Texas, Denton, TX.

White, J., & Allers, C. T. (1992, March). *Childhood abuse and neglect: Manifestations in children's play.* Paper presented at the American Counseling Association Convention, Baltimore, MD.

White, J., & Allers, C. T. (1994). Play behaviors of abused children. *Journal of Counseling & Development, 72*, 390–394.

# 9

# Play Therapy Behaviors of Sexually Abused Children

## MEREDITH K. ATER

S exually abused children are defined as "dependent, developmentally immature children and adolescents engaged in sexual activities that they do
not fully comprehend, or which they are unable to give informed consent,
or that violate the social taboos of family roles. The child is left powerless and
victimized by the lack of choice involved" (Federation, 1986, p. 21). With renewed feelings of confidence, sexually abused children are empowered through
play to regain control over their bodies (James, 1989).

For children, play is a natural form of expression—a special language which
is spoken through toys. With toys, children may express emotion about their
self-perception, others, and significant events they have experienced. Play helps
children explore their inner world and express their true self, which is full of
needs, as well as wishes and wants (Landreth, 1991). Play is one of the most
crucial ways "children learn that their feelings can be expressed without reprisal or rejection" (Homeyer, 1994, p. 15). Through play, children communicate what they cannot with words.

For abused children, "the goal of play therapy is to help children master
the multiple stresses of abuse and neglect and to correct or prevent deviations
in future psychosocial development. Play is particularly useful, since most abused
children, even more than children in general, express their innermost feelings
and fantasies much more readily through action than verbalization. It permits
the necessary distancing from the traumatic events by the use of symbolic materials" (Johnson, 1987, p. 1).

Through play therapy, children come to an acceptance of what has happened to them, and learn new ways of coping to protect themselves from fur-

**119**

ther abuse (Cattanach, 1992). Play provides children with courage, empowering them to heal what is hurting (Homeyer, 1994). That healing can only occur within safe boundaries is especially true for sexually abused children, whose boundaries have been violated. This safety helps children work through sexual abuse without needing, or feeling pressured to verbalize their feelings. In the playroom, sexually abused children will exhibit very different behaviors than non-abused children as they work through their own healing process (Mayer, 1985).

There are several properties of play which allow sexually abused children a sense of safety and distance while working through their trauma. Play can be **symbolic** in that a child can use a toy to represent the sexual abuser. Play can be **"as-if"** in that a child can act out events "for pretend." Play can be **projection** in that a child can put emotion onto toys or puppets that can safely act out their feelings. Play can be **displacement** in that the child can give their negative feelings to dolls or toys, instead of their own family members (Sweeney, 1997). Children will displace their trauma and conflicts onto the dolls and puppets without even realizing the connection to their own lives. "Play provides safe opportunities for reenactment, rehearsal, the practice needed to strengthen the child, and prepares them for directly dealing with the traumatic events" (James, 1989, p. 76).

## CATEGORIES OF PLAY BEHAVIOR

Children may express themselves in a multitude of ways in the playroom. The following represents the behaviors sexually abused children often exhibit in the safety of the playroom as they begin to work through their trauma, learn to gain control over their experiences, and heal.

### Abreactive Play

"When an event is too difficult or large to assimilate immediately, it must be chewed again and again" (Webb, 1991, p. 33). Sexually abused children experience a need to recreate the trauma that they have survived. When children are "ready" to begin to work on their traumatic issue, they will play out their abusive experience. When children play out a traumatic event, it will often be literal and repetitive. Actions that occurred before, during, and after the abuse are usually repeated (Gil & Johnson, 1993). "The fear seems to lessen after many repeated enactments of the stories and rituals developed in play when the power of the monster is vanquished" (Cattanach, 1992, p. 79).

Through play, children reenact situations that are important to them in reality, and as these situations are repeated, the strength of these elements becomes diminished, and they learn to actively control their feelings about the trauma (Gil, 1991). With every new repetition, children gain control and mastery over their situation. Reenacting their experiences, children become deeply involved and are able to express themselves emotionally (Schaefer, 1994). After recreating the trauma, and learning new mastery over their trauma, children may learn to "change" the ending by creating hopefulness rather than the helplessness they experienced in reality (Marvasti, 1994). Play therapy is a way for children to deal with small parts of their trauma until the experience becomes more emotionally manageable (Kelly, 1995).

## Aggressive Play

Sexually abused children will test limits as well as exhibit "acting out" behavior during the session as their way of working through trust issues with the therapist (Kelly, 1995). It is believed that children must create their own nurturing, trusting relationship before they can deal with their abuse (Brody, 1992). Sometimes children's feelings of "being bad" will show through in the therapy because they feel they are to blame—that the abuse is their fault (Cattanach, 1992).

Sexually abused children may exhibit aggressive behaviors that are somehow related to their abuse. Often, children will act aggressively due to an overidentification with the abuser, displacing the hurt they felt onto something else (White & Allers, 1994). In the case of "Tom," he used a teddy bear to "play doctor" and gave the bear "shots." As he worked through his abuse, the "shots" became more and more aggressive as he was learning to express his feelings about the abuse (Singer, 1993). In the case of "Johnny," he undressed the adult male doll, aggressively pulled on the genitalia, and attempted to stick the doll behind his legs and into his own behind. He was trying to make the doll hurt itself similarly to how he had been hurt. After his attempts failed, he inserted a knife into the doll's behind (Gil, 1991).

In the case of "Johnny," he would beat the "Larry" (perpetrator) doll with his fist and then repeatedly hit the doll's behind with his fist. After verbalizing to the therapist that he believed he was also bad, he kicked both dolls away, hurting the perpetrator and himself (Gil, 1991). An abused child might display anger by calling the therapist names, throwing toys at the therapist, or even trying to stab the therapist after stabbing the Bobo doll (Homeyer, 1994; Sweeney, 1997). During a game of "cops and robbers," the child might take on both roles in order to rob and arrest the therapist in an aggressive way (Sweeney, 1997).

Many other aggressive behaviors may be exhibited in the playroom, such as throwing objects the child has labeled as the abuser, breaking toys, brutally washing dolls, cutting off or attempting to cut off arms/legs/hair/genitals of dolls, punching the Bobo for an extended time period, or wild car chases. The child may aggressively label a doll as the perpetrator, reenact the abuse, and then have the "baby" doll hit the perpetrator doll. The child may put the perpetrator doll in "jail" and then decide to bury the doll, or may even talk to the perpetrator on the phone and verbally express feelings of anger and confused emotions (Homeyer, 1994).

## Dissociative Play

In dissociative play, the sexually abused child is able to deny and avoid the pain of the trauma by mentally escaping. Dissociation involves distancing of self from thoughts, situations, and emotions. It seems that once the play becomes too stressful and emotional, the child becomes disconnected with what is occurring in the here and now (White & Allers, 1994).

A child may be reenacting sexual abuse with dolls and become stiff and dissociated at the same instant that the perpetrator inserts a part of self into the child (Gil, 1991). The child may become quiet and possibly stare off into space while playing with water, sand, or during a specific reenactment of the abuse (Homeyer, 1994). When children dissociate in play, they are not able to hear, understand, or process what happens in the session and may eventually develop feelings of depersonalization, in which they lose sight of reality and the trauma they have experienced (Gil & Johnson, 1993).

## Nurturing Play

Nurturing play is very important for sexually abused children in helping them express their feelings of their lack of nurturing and their need for it. An example of the accompanying ambivalent feeling may be expressed as the child kisses, feeds, and then hits the baby doll—which is an example of the child's own life experience (Cattanach, 1992).

Sexually abused children might exhibit nurturing behavior by cooking a meal and feeding the therapist. Mixed feelings may be expressed as the child makes the therapist "poisoned cake" and then helps the therapist with a "magic potion" (Cattanach, 1992). Another example of this behavior is children who play "doctor" and give lots of "shots," but then "repair" and nurture their patients (Singer, 1993).

Sexually abused children often exhibit nurturing behaviors toward self and toward the therapist in the playroom. They may cuddle with a baby blanket, feed themselves with a bottle, build a soft "fort" with pillows and play inside the structure, protect a non-aggressive toy from an aggressive toy, or even play with Bobo in a gentle and tender way (Homeyer, 1994). Children might also show their desire to nurture by washing/drying the dolls and putting them to bed (Singer, 1993). Sexually abused children may make a meal to serve to the therapist, want to be held and nurtured like a baby, or even "hurt" self in order to be taken care of by the therapist (Homeyer, 1994).

## Perseveration Play

Perseveration play is usually manifested as a "routine" which appears rigid and literal. However, it differs from abreactive play in that children are not able to "change" the ending to create hope for themselves, but get "stuck" in the hope-lessness of their issue. It involves a constant, monotonous, ritualized, reenactment of the trauma that sexually abused children have experienced. The play is lacking in variety, enjoyment, and does not provide relief for children (Schaefer, 1994; Terr, 1990; Webb, 1991).

The feelings associated with this play are so strong it may feel as if it were "happening again." As children obsessively play out their experiences, stirring up their feelings of terror and helplessness, there is great risk of retraumatization. These frightening feelings may become more powerful and real than when the trauma occurred, further increasing feelings of hopelessness and lack of control (Gil, 1991; Schaefer, 1994).

Fixated on the horror of their experiences in play, sexually abused children may not be able to move forward on their own toward relief and healing (Schaefer, 1994). In this case, it may be necessary for the therapist to give some "clinical nudging" to guide the child into a position of power (James, 1989, p. 76). Active intervention by the therapist may help the child gain control and mastery over the situation, and refocus the child in the here and now, which can assist the child with trauma resolution (Gil, 1991; Schaefer, 1994). Verbalization from the therapist in the form of tracking what is being observed or encouraging the child to give the characters a "voice" in their play may help the child not to feel "stuck" in the trauma. These interventions can interrupt the child's dissociation and may help empower the child in his play (Gil, 1991). Children who have a sense of mastery over their trauma are able to play through to an outcome and exhibit control over it, feel free enough to express and release negative emotions, and have a better understanding of the sexual abuse they experienced (Schaefer, 1994).

## Regressive Play

Sometimes in the playroom, sexually abused children will exhibit regressive behaviors, acting in babyish ways that might help them "escape" from the abuse they experienced. Some examples of this are the child wanting to wear diapers, clinging to the therapist, using single baby words to communicate instead of full sentences, and "scribbling" in their art work, becoming easily frustrated with it and destroying it (Gil, 1991; Homeyer, 1994). Regressive, silly baby talk may be used by children during puppet play as a protective way to experience their emotions with the therapist (Singer, 1993).

Often, the sexually abused child will display behaviors such as feeding self with a bottle, rocking self in a chair, caring for a baby doll, or taking care of others in the doll house family. In the sandbox, the child may engage in calming, soothing behaviors, such as repetitively piling up the sand and smoothing it back out (Homeyer, 1994). Some abused children will even wet or soil themselves in the playroom, as they did at a younger age (Sagar, 1990). The child might act in an overly compliant, pleasing way or in an extremely dependent way, and may even avoid any eye contact toward the therapist (Homeyer, 1994).

## Sexualized Play

Because sexually abused children do not have a true sense of appropriate touching and boundaries, oversexualized behavior often occurs in the playroom (Sagar, 1990). In fact, sexualized play behavior is the most commonly observed behavior of sexually abused children (Homeyer, 1994).

There are three types of sexualized play that may be expressed during play therapy: abuse-reactive play, reenactment play, and symbolic sexualized play. Because of this sexualized play, the therapist faces the challenge of finding a balance between allowing children to freely express themselves and placing limits on behavior, so that children will become aware of acceptable ways of expressing their experience (Van de Putte, 1995).

Abuse-reactive play may occur when children feel that they are in a situation in which they might be abused again. As children are usually alone with an adult in the playroom, some children may display signs of hypervigilance as they anxiously anticipate sexual interaction, while some children feel they can gain control of the relationship by portraying the sexual role that they are used to with other adults (White & Allers, 1994; Van de Putte, 1995).

Abuse-reactive play may be a direct reenactment of the child's abuse and can be a true test for the therapist. Children want to know that they will still be accepted by the therapist, regardless of their sexual behavior (Van de Putte, 1995). Sexually abused children often have a sexualized image of themselves and of the therapist and assume that this relationship must also be a sexual one (White & Allers, 1994). Some children might show oversexualized behavior toward the therapist such as wanting to take clothes off in front of the therapist, wanting to openly masturbate, wanting to touch therapist's genital area, or expressing they want to be touched by the therapist in a sexual way, even to say "let's make sex" (Marvasti, 1994; Homeyer, 1994; White & Allers, 1994). Children may also want to hug and kiss the therapist, use hand puppets to kiss the therapist's face and neck, and even attempt to rub their bodies against the therapist in a stimulating way (Homeyer, 1994).

During reenactment play, children, feeling the need to express themselves to the therapist, recreate their emotional reactions and the sexual abuse using toys, dolls, or other props in combination with their own bodies. The therapist should affirm that the child is in control of this event, should respond as though the reenactment is believable, and also listen and reflect the emotions expressed during the play. At such times the child not only reenacts the traumatic experience, but also reexperiences the intense emotions and conflict of the sexual abuse (Van de Putte, 1995). An example of this type of behavior might be to put dolls in sexual positions, displaying the sexual positions the children had experienced. Children may also enact sexually abusive actions on a doll they label as "perpetrator" or pose dolls in sexually explicit ways and then take pictures of them with a toy camera (Homeyer, 1994).

Symbolic sexualized play occurs when children behave sexually during their play in order to try to gain some understanding of their sexual abuse and how it relates to their understanding of the world around them. During this type of play, children are developing a representation of themselves as having been sexually abused, an experience they begin to accept. Children play in this way to learn to understand their sexual abuse and how to maintain a new relationship to the world outside the play therapy room. They learn to gain control over their situation and learn appropriate ways of expressing themselves to others in a non-sexual way (Van de Putte, 1995).

## PLAY MATERIALS USED

Children play to communicate, using toys as their words. Therefore, specific toys are selected for the playroom that will be therapeutic for children in various ways. For sexually abused children, there are several different play materials that seem to be especially therapeutic for their healing process in the playroom.

### Sand/Water Play

Sand is a very soothing element that enables children to freely express their feelings and fantasies. Much comfort is found in smoothing out the sand and bunching it up again, or filling up cups of sand just to slowly pour the sand out again (Gil, 1991). For sexually abused children, the touching and stroking of the sand can provide them with sexual satisfaction. In fact, sometimes sexually abused children will use the sand to rub onto their thighs and genitals (Homeyer, 1994). A child may become so stimulated with the sand that it becomes difficult for the child to do anything else (Sjolund & Schaeffer, 1994).

According to Allan and Lawton-Speert (1989), sexually abused children will use sand and water in a pattern, first for sexual stimulation and then for washing and healing. They reported a case in which the child wanted to have sex with the play therapist, and when a limit was set on this inappropriate behavior, the child stimulated himself with sand instead. For a period of three months, the child would stimulate himself with sand when he did not receive what he wanted. Slowly, this child's behavior began to reflect his own healing process. Undressing in the playroom, the child would "clean" himself using wet sand without any sexual stimulation. As this washing ritual continued, the child began keeping his clothes on to wash himself, and finally he began washing other objects in the room, such as dolls, windows, and floors. The child learned to separate the "clean" and "dirty" water, using the "clean" water to wash himself and the "good guys" (Allan & Lawton-Speert, 1989).

Water can also be used in the playroom to "wash" the toys (Homeyer, 1994), and children often ritually wash their toys in the sink the same way they would like to wash themselves of their abusive experience (Sweeney, 1997). In the case of "Tom," he used water to clean all of the body parts on the doll where he had been abused (Singer, 1993). Children also may elicit the therapist's help in their cleansing ritual when they feel "dirty" or even frequently wash the therapist's hands as they wash their own (Homeyer, 1994). It can be soothing for sexually abused children just to pour the water back and forth repeatedly (Singer, 1993).

Sexually abused children may also use wet sand to drip onto another figure, make secret tunnels for hiding in the sand, make hills in the sand and poke holes in them, or put a snake or a motorcycle between their legs while in the sand. Although sand has great therapeutic value for sexually abused children, it had been found that they are able to explore and express their needs without it in the playroom (Homeyer, 1994).

### Doll/Puppet Play

For sexually abused children, the activity being created is a solution for the dolls rather than the child and this idea is what creates the distance children need to begin their healing process (Marvasti, 1994). This emotional distance helps children identify with the dolls/puppets and diminishes the fear, guilt, timidity, and various other feelings as children are able to project their conflicts outward (James, 1989). Children have the opportunity with dolls/puppets to play out the sexual abuse they experienced and recreate various outcomes that help empower them (Webb, 1991).

Sexually abused children will often use dolls to represent family members and are able to express themselves freely about the abuse. Frequently their own abuse will be reenacted with the dolls, and children may also hit-out at the dolls as they release their angry and confused feelings (Cattanach, 1992). In the case of "Jason," he used the family dolls to play out sexual activity he witnessed between his grandparents. He had the power to use the boy doll and shout through the bedroom wall, "Shut up and stop it or I'll get angry." Using the dolls, he was able to create in fantasy what he could not in reality (Cattanach, 1992, p. 60).

Often, children have confused emotions about their sexual abuse and are able to learn new information through the dolls/puppets that will help change their understanding of their experience. "A hand held by another through a puppet can be the first step towards the child learning that he or she can receive physical comfort without being expected to give anything in exchange" (McMahon, 1992, p. 177). Marvasti (1994) described a child who was able to use the dollhouse to express confused feelings about her abuse. In her scene a monster came to the house and took her father away to jail. The girl went to the monster and asked if he could give back her father and take her mother instead. In this case, the child misunderstood the sexual abuse for attention and affection from her father and was angry because her mother did not give her this "attention and affection" (Marvasti, 1994). If sex is the only way children experience affection, they will have difficulty recognizing *true* nurturing. In the safety of play, children are empowered to work out their feelings and clear up misconceptions about their trauma (Cattanach, 1992).

Using dolls, a child may vividly reveal the sexual abuse by putting the genitals of one doll in the other doll's face, or objects into the mouths to simulate oral sex, use dolls to reenact the sexual abuse medical exam, enact sexual activity with dolls/puppets, or show a doll "peeing" on another doll (Homeyer, 1994). In one reported case, a child in play therapy cut the baby doll's throat with a toy knife. This action represented what her abuser threatened to do to her if she revealed her abuse to anyone (Cattanach, 1992).

When anatomically correct dolls are used in play therapy, they are used mostly with younger children who have problems expressing themselves verbally. Younger children can show the doll doing things they cannot explain. Sometimes sexually abused children even use these dolls to play out an embarrassing situation they do not want to put into words. Older children may prefer to play with regular dolls and are able to realize similarities between the doll's feelings and their own feelings, or even use drawings to express themselves (Marvasti, 1994; McMahon, 1992).

## DRAWINGS

Expressing themselves through art can be very powerful for children who have been sexually abused. "Children may draw what they cannot say" (Johnson, 1987, p. 2).

Drawing is fun for children, the pressure of having to talk about the sexual abuse is gone, and they can explore their feelings, fantasies, and concerns. Children may use the drawings to give the therapist information about their sense of self, the traumatic events, the abuser, or any support they have received from the family (Johnson, 1987; Nickerson, 1983). Children can use art symbolically to unveil feelings of being damaged, being full of "messiness" inside, and of trying to find a way to control and take care of these feelings. Art also provides the emotional distance that enables children to address their own feelings and experiences (Sagar, 1990, p. 108).

Children who have been sexually abused will typically create art in play therapy. They tend to under or over represent the genitalia of the human figures they draw. The figures may be gender-less, or may be very seductive and have exaggerated genitalia, or may have genitals drawn away from the body (Homeyer, 1994; Johnson, 1987). Various elements may be found in their drawings, such as a face or a head with no body or only an upper half of the body (representing the loss of self), a body with no arms or legs, a body with hidden hands or a body with large parts crossed out (Homeyer, 1994). Often body parts are missing because children have difficulty dealing with body image after experiencing sexual abuse (Singer, 1993). In the case of "Sally," she was able to represent herself only as a head and a vagina after experiencing sexual abuse by her brother, who she represented as a head and a penis. This abuse left "Sally" with the understanding that her entire body was about sex and she was without a true sense of self (Cattanach, 1992).

Sexually abused children may also include sexual elements, such as drawing "sexy" people (with provocative clothing or facial features), people with genitalia, genitalia with ejaculation, people engaging in sexual activities, long phallic symbols, figures with large open mouths, or two people covered with dots (semen). Sexually abused children may use dark colors, such as red or black, or the use of red/green in drawing a house, specifically a red door on a house (Homeyer, 1994). Children may draw anatomical figures and poke/stab the genitals with a pen, or scribble through the figures, and then destroy the pictures and throw them away (Homeyer, 1994). Often, sexually abused children draw snakes and witches that symbolizes their sexual abuse, or they may subconsciously draw genitalia that they label as a cloud, tree, heart, or rainbow (Cattanach, 1992; Homeyer, 1994).

Other possible elements found in the art of sexually abused children might be the encapsulation of self in such objects as a tree, car, or house; the encapsulation of the abuser; the use of wedge shapes in house, tree, person drawings; or wedge shapes pointing towards the person's genital area (Homeyer, 1994).

In their play, sexually abused children may use serial drawings, in which every picture contains a theme that is pertinent to the child and the sexual abuse. These drawings tend to follow three stages: initial stage, middle stage, and termination stage. In the initial stage, sexually abused children's drawings show their "world," the cause of their problems, and feelings of despair and self control (Allan, 1988). Sexually abused children may draw their self-images in a cartoon-like way, which emphasizes negative characteristics they believe to be true (Homeyer, 1994). In the middle stage, drawings reflect emotion, struggle between opposites, and feelings of isolation. In the termination stage, the drawings reveal renewed feelings of self-worth, self-control, and self-mastery. Sexually abused children experience healing as their pictures change from depicting damage and hurt, to depicting repair and healthy functioning (Allan, 1988).

## SUMMARY

"The child who has experienced this devastating trauma has internalized a variety of negative messages about self, others, and the world. Play provides an opportunity to process and externalize these messages. Through play, children learn to manage the unmanageable" (Sweeney, 1997, p. 195).

Sexually abused children exhibit many different behaviors in the playroom for the rebuilding and reorientation of the self so that a person in the play can appear to be what and who they are, and feel loved and accepted as such (Sagar, 1990). Observing these behaviors is not an absolute indication that sexual abuse has occurred, but therapists should be educated as to the various forms of behavior that sexually abused children may exhibit in the playroom (Landreth, 1991). If therapists understand the many different emotionally charged behaviors of sexually abused children, they will be able to be more accepting of children and can empower them to use play to heal the deep scars of their sexual abuse.

# REFERENCES

Allan, J., & Lawton-Speert, S. (1989, December). Sand and water in the treatment of a profoundly sexually abused preschool boy. *Association for Play Therapy Newsletter, 8*(4), 2–3.

Allan, J. (1988). Serial drawing: A Jungian approach with children. In C. E. Schaefer (Ed.), *Innovative interventions in child and adolescent therapy* (p. 102). New York: John Wiley & Sons.

Brody, V. (1992). The dialogue of touch: Developmental play therapy. *International Journal of Play Therapy, 1*(1), 21–30.

Cattanach, A. (1992). *Play therapy with abused children.* Philadelphia: Jessica Kingsley Publishers.

Federation, S. (1986). Sexual abuse: Treatment modalities for the younger child. *Journal of Psychosocial Nursing and Mental Health Services, 24*(7), 21–24.

Gil, E. (1991). *The healing power of play: Working with abused children.* New York: The Guilford Press.

Gil, E., & Johnson, T. (1993). *Sexualized children: Assessment and treatment of sexualized children and children who molest.* Rockville, MD: Launch Press.

Homeyer, L. (1994). *Play therapy behaviors of sexually abused children.* Unpublished doctoral dissertation, University of North Texas, Denton, TX.

James, B. (1989). *Treating traumatized children: New insights and creative interventions.* Lexington, MA: Lexington Books.

Johnson, B. (1987, June). The use of drawings in the treatment of child sexual abuse victims. *Association for Play Therapy Newsletter, 6*(2), 1–3.

Kelly, M. (1995). Play therapy with sexually traumatized children: Factors that promote healing. *Journal of Child Sexual Abuse, 4*(3), 1–9.

Landreth, G. (1991). *Play therapy: The art of the relationship.* Muncie, IN: Accelerated Development Press.

Marvasti, J. (1994). Play diagnosis and play therapy with child victims of incest. In K. O'Connor & C. Schaefer (Eds.), *Handbook of play therapy: Vol. 2. Advances and innovations* (pp. 319–348). New York: John Wiley & Sons, Inc.

Mayer, A. (1985). *Sexual abuse: Causes, consequences and treatment of incestuous and pedophilic acts.* Holmes Beach, FL: Learning Publications, Inc.

McMahon, L. (1992). *The handbook of play therapy.* New York: Routledge.

Nickerson, E. (1983). Art as a play therapeutic medium. In K. O'Connor & C. Schaefer (Eds.), *Handbook of play therapy: Vol. 1* (pp. 234–250). New York: John Wiley & Sons.

Sagar, C. (1990). Working with cases of child sexual abuse. In C. Case & T. Dalley (Eds.), *Working with children in art therapy* (pp. 89–114). New York: Tavistock/Routledge.

Schaefer, C. (1994). Play therapy for psychic trauma in children. In K. O'Connor & C. Schaefer (Eds.), *Handbook of play therapy: Vol. 2. Advances and innovations* (pp. 297–318). New York: John Wiley & Sons, Inc.

Singer, D. (1993). *Playing for their lives: Helping troubled children through play therapy.* New York: The Free Press.

Sjolund, M., & Schaefer, C. (1994). The Erica method of sand play diagnosis and assessment. In K. O'Connor & C. Schaefer (Eds.), *Handbook of play therapy: Vol. 2. Advances and innovations* (pp. 231–247). New York: John Wiley & Sons, Inc.

Sweeney, D. (1997). *Counseling children through the world of play.* Wheaton, IL: Tyndale House Publishers, Inc.

Terr, L. (1990). *Too scared to cry: Psychic trauma in childhood.* New York: Basic Books.

Van de Putte, S. (1995). A paradigm for working with child survivors of sexual abuse who exhibit sexualized behaviors during play therapy. *International Journal of Play Therapy, 4*(1), 27–49.

Webb, N. (1991). Play therapy crisis intervention with children. In N. Webb (Ed.), *Play therapy with children in crisis: Individual, group, and family treatment* (pp. 26–42). New York: The Guilford Press.

White, J., & Allers, C. (1994). Play therapy with abused children: A review of the literature. *Journal of Counseling & Development, 72,* 390–393.

# 10

# Identifying Sexually Abused Children in Play Therapy

## LINDA E. HOMEYER

*I* dentifying child victims of sexual abuse and validating this abuse is a difficult process (Berliner, 1988; Berliner & Conte, 1993; Jackson & Nutall,
1993). The most irrevocable evidence—medical—is rare (Adams & Wells,
1993; Gray, 1993; MacFarlane et al., 1988; Meyers, 1993; Muram, 1989; Sgroi,
1982). The problem of identification is compounded by the fact that only 26%
of sexually abused children between the ages of three and seventeen years disclose sexual abuse on purpose; for preschoolers, purposive disclosure occurs
only 9% of the time (Sorensen & Snow, 1991). False accusations of sexual abuse
or misinterpretations by adults, often seen in divorce and custody cases, additionally complicate the process of validation (Berliner & Conte, 1993).

When sexual abuse was initially studied, the effects were identified by the
behavior displayed. These effects were used as behavioral indicators to assist in
identifying children who might be victims of sexual abuse. There are several
widely recognized lists of the effects of sexual abuse that serve as indicators of
sexual abuse (American Medical Association, 1985; Finkelhor, 1986; Gil, 1991;
Sgroi, 1982). These lists of behavioral indicators are commonly used by child
protective services workers, law enforcement officers, counselors, school teachers, and other professionals as "red flag" indicators. Such lists may contain as
few as six effects (Finkelhor, 1986) to as many as seventy behavioral indicators
(Lew, 1988). Any single behavioral indicator on these lists may be the result of
another stressor, such as parents' divorce, birth of a sibling, death of a significant person, or a normal reaction to various developmental stages. While any
single indicator may be explained by other causes, several indicators displayed
by a child may suggest the possibility of sexual abuse and, therefore, the need

for further exploration into the possibility of abuse (Gil, 1991; Sgroi, 1982). Currently, there is no comparable list of play therapy behaviors.

Some of the effects noted in existing lists of behavioral indicators of sexual abuse might be found in the play therapy playroom; however, most would not. Behavior of a child in the play therapy room is often different from the behavior exhibited by that same child outside the play therapy room. For example, enuresis is frequently a behavior that leads parents to take their child to play therapy. Enuresis is also a regressive behavior frequently listed as an effect or behavioral indicator of sexual abuse, particularly for young children (American Medical Association, 1985; Lew, 1988). However, in the play therapy room, enuretic behavior would not generally be seen. Nevertheless, an enuretic child will express self in any of a number of ways. Enuresis, for the child being sexually abused, can be an attempt at keeping oneself safe by trying to keep the abuser at a distance: "If I'm wet with urine, the abuser won't want to touch me." The child's play therapy behavior may take the form of keeping the play therapist (adult) at a distance by playing out of the sight of the play therapist or frequently going in and out of the play therapy room (Everstine & Everstine, 1989; Gil, 1991).

Although there have been several studies of the play therapy behavior (PTB) of maladjusted children in general (Hendricks, 1971; Howe & Silvern, 1981; Moustakas, 1955; Oe, 1989; Perry, 1988; Withee, 1975), there have been no studies to identify the specific play therapy behaviors of sexually abused children. Children are frequently referred to play therapy with the hope that within the safety of the therapeutic setting the child will disclose sexual abuse, should such exist. Additionally, children who are being seen for a presenting problem other than sexual abuse, may begin displaying behavior that the play therapist interprets as reflective of sexual abuse. However, without any research on such behaviors, the play therapist may find it difficult to make a professional assessment, comply with state laws regarding the reporting of abuse, or otherwise handle the case appropriately. Thus, the identification of specific play therapy behaviors associated with sexual abuse is needed to assist mental health professionals in identifying, protecting, and providing needed therapeutic intervention for children who have been sexually abused.

## PLAY THERAPY SCREENING INSTRUMENT FOR CHILD SEXUAL ABUSE

The *Play Therapy Screening Instrument for Child Sexual Abuse* (PTSI-CSA), based on Homeyer's (1995) research, identifies play therapy behaviors consistent with and highly correlated with children who have been sexually abused. It helps play therapists in the difficult process of identifying children who may be sexually abused. The PTSI-CSA is to be used when the play therapist begins to question whether the child's play therapy behaviors may reflect sexual abuse. As a screening instrument, if the child is identified as *high-risk*, a referral should be made for a more thorough and formal sexual abuse assessment.

The PTSI-CSA is a fifteen-item instrument. Each item is a specific, spontaneous, behavior exhibited by a child in a play therapy session. The instrument discriminates between sexually abused children and nonsexually abused children in the play therapy setting. The play therapist must indicate if a child has, or has not, displayed each specific behavior. It is for use in nondirective play therapy sessions, or can be used to assess spontaneous behaviors that are expressed by the child in a more directive play therapy session. Figure 10.1 lists the fifteen items.

---

**Play Therapy Screening Instrument for Child Sexual Abuse**
By Linda E. Homeyer, Ph.D.

Child: _____

Completed by _____ Date _____

Has this play behavior been seen? (yes or no)             Y    N

1. Uses hand puppets to kiss therapist on face/neck .............. 0    0
2. On phone, screams hate to a person then expresses love before
   hanging up................................................. 0    0
3. Sexual gesture(s) when talking about home situation or someone
   at home ................................................... 0    0
4. Re-enacts sexual abuse medical exam ......................... 0    0
5. Hits or attempts to cur off doll's penis or breasts.............. 0    0
6. Pretend doll is "peeing" on another doll ...................... 0    0
7. References of "peeing" & "pooping" .......................... 0    0
8. Asks to be covered with a blanket ........................... 0    0
9. Figure is drawn, scribbled or ripped up, destroyed, thrown away . 0    0
10. Draws figures with large open mouths ....................... 0    0
11. Draws with large parts of bodies crossed out .................. 0    0
12. Encapsulates self in drawing, cutting off lower half of body...... 0    0
13. Stabs/pokes drawings of genitals with pencil .................. 0    0
14. Draws a figure with displaced body parts ..................... 0    0
15. Draws a male with a penis .................................. 0    0

**Total number of items checked in the Y (yes) column** _____

Comparison Child's Score (subtract) _____

**Total Difference Score** _____

A **Total Difference Score** of **4 or more** identifies the child as ***High Risk*** for sexual abuse. The child should then be referred for an assessment of sexual abuse.

---

**FIGURE 10.1.** Play Therapy Screening Instruments for Child Sexual Abuse (PTSI-CSA), by Linda E. Homeyer, Ph.D. These results are not diagnostic. The PTSI-CSA is intended to identify children who should receive additional assessment for possible sexual abuse.

## Items of Play Therapy Behavior

Following are descriptions of the fifteen play therapy behaviors that may occur in the playroom. For rating purposes, the play must be spontaneous, not in response to the direction or leading of the play therapist. The play behavior may stand alone, that is, the entire play sequence is comprised of an individual specific play therapy behavior listed below. For example, a child may reenact a sexual abuse physical examination. The play sequence begins with the child taking the medical kit from a shelf of toys, selecting a doll, and then proceeding to reenact a sexual abuse examination. When the examination is completed, the child leaves that play and shifts to some other, unrelated play. Or, more typically, the play is embedded within a larger sequence of play. An example might be a child who is well into a sequence of household play. The child appears to be in the role of the mother, cooking food and then feeding the children/dolls. After the meal, all but one child/doll is put down for a nap. The mother then takes the child/doll to the doctor. The child-client then shifts roles and becomes the doctor. The doctor proceeds to conduct a sexual abuse medical examination on the child/doll. After the examination is complete the child-client again shifts to the role of mother and takes the child/doll home. Once home, the mother lovingly and caringly puts the child/doll down for her nap. This sequence of play is much longer and is surrounded by other, extended play resulting in the sexual abuse physical examination being only one part of the sequence.

Some play therapy behaviors may be violent (such as the child pretending to kill the perpetrator), gruesome (using pliers and screwdrivers as implements in the sexual abuse examination), or repulsive (such as repetitive reenactment of the sexual abuse). However, the play is tied to some aspect of the child's sexual abuse experience or the child's perception of self because of the abuse. Additionally, the child's affect may be incongruent with the content of the play. Being flat, light, or seemingly frivolous would not be unusual. Many children are not able, at first, to express their real feelings, and need to stay well defended in order to begin playing out difficult material. The congruence will come at a later time in the therapeutic process. For example, a child may initially laugh and joke around while initially punching Bobo (bop bag) in the genital area. Later, when the child is more able to tolerate his own level of anger at the perpetrator and realizes the play therapist's ability to accept his behavior, the child will become more congruent. The play therapist should also be aware that the child may dissociate during the enactment of some play behaviors.

Children carefully observe the reaction of the play therapist to the content of their play or words, testing to see if they will still be accepted. Many sexually abused children realize they have caused parents to cry, other significant adults to become angry or upset when communicating aspects of their abuse. Consequently, children who have been sexually abused often protect themselves from additional rejection, or from being the causative of another person's distress. For these reasons, the play therapist who works with children who have been sexually abused needs to maintain a nonjudgmental, accepting, presence in the play room.

**1. Uses hand puppets to kiss the therapist on face/neck.** Children often use a puppet as a way, through play, to come close to the play therapist and decide how safe it is to be near the play therapist. Once close to the play therapist, children typically have the puppet bite the play therapist. Sexually abused children may have the puppet kiss the play therapist on the face or neck. Although often used in an initial session, the kissing play might also occur later, within the context of another play sequence.

**2. On the phone, screams "hate" to a person then expresses love before hanging up.** This play behavior occurs when the child is pretending to talk with a person on a telephone. The child may begin the conversation with shouting and screaming about hating a person, however, before the conversation is over, the child states how much she loves the person. This play may occur within a longer sequence of play. The content of the conversation may have nothing to do specifically with sexual abuse, simply the contrasting juxtaposition of hate and love. The sexually abused child may have many persons with whom she has conflicted feelings, such as the perpetrator, a non-protecting parent, and herself.

**3. Sexual gestures when talking about home situation or someone at home.** This behavior can be overt or very subtle. During this play, the child talks about her home or someone at home. It may be a conversation with the play therapist or the child talking to herself in the midst of other play. This play may take place at the dollhouse, in the kitchen area, while drawing, or other play. While the verbalization is occurring, the child also performs sexual gestures. The sexual gesturing may take the form of rubbing of her genitalia, masturbating, or holding her body in a provocative posture. The sexual gestures may be out of the conscious awareness of the child.

**4. Re-enacts sexual abuse medical exam.** Using the medical kit is common for children in play therapy. Children typically use the medical instruments to doctor dolls, themselves, or the play therapist. Children often use the medical instruments much like they use puppets, to checkout the safety of the play therapist. In this case, children may demonstrate knowledge of a sexual abuse exam. A sexual abuse exam would include examination of genitalia. The child might manipulate the doll to take the knees to chest position. This position has the doll lying on its' stomach, side, or back with the doll's knees pulled up to its chest. (In a medical exam this provides the physician a better view of the anus [stomach and side] or hymen [on back].) The child may or may not talk during this play. It's also possible the child may show signs of dissociation. The child may use a doll, teddy bear, or other toy as the object to which the sexual abuse medical examination is happening.

**5. Hits or attempts to cut off doll's penis/breasts.** In this play therapy behavior the child attacks sexual body parts. The child may select a doll or other toy that might represent a person, such as a teddy bear or Bobo. The doll does not have to be anatomically detailed. The child hits, punches, kicks, or pretends to cut off the doll's penis or breasts (or area where the body parts would be). The child might use a knife, sword, or other toy to pretend to cut off body parts. As with other play therapy behaviors, this play may be embedded within a broader play sequence.

**6. Pretends doll is peeing on another doll.**   As in the above play therapy behavior, the term *doll* is used loosely. The child may use another toy, such as a teddy bear. The child plays out having one doll urinate on a second doll. This, however, is more likely a reenactment of ejaculation, or a golden shower as labeled by some in the sexual abuse field.

**7. References of peeing & pooping.**   The child makes verbal references about urinating and defecating. This may be in reference to what the child is playing out. It may also refer to the child sharing the enuresis or encopresis that he is experiencing at home, school, or daycare. The child might also talk about it in a joking manner, as if to test the reaction or tolerance of such content by the play therapist. Sexually abused children often urinate and defecate in their beds as an attempt to keep the perpetrator from coming into their beds. Children who are sexually abused may also urinate from anxiety. This is often seen by the many bathroom breaks children may need during play therapy. The resulting anxiety of their dealing with issues in session often result in a need to urinate.

**8. Asks to be covered with a blanket.**   The child is involved in play during which he asks the play therapist to cover him with a blanket. The play probably will have thematic overtones of either nurturing or regression. The play may, alternatively, be about hiding or needing to be protected or cared for. As a part of a longer sequence of play, the play therapist might miss this play behavior.

The remainder of the play therapy behaviors involve some form of artwork. As with the items above, the specific drawing (painting, coloring, etc.) may be within a larger piece of artwork or art activity. One or more of items 9 through 15 may be part of the same drawing. For example, a child might draw a figure with a large open mouth (item 10) and then rip it up and throw it away (item 9).

**9. Figure is drawn, scribbled or ripped up, destroyed, thrown away.** Children often destroy their artwork when they are frustrated with their attempt to get it just right. Children also destroy their artwork when the content becomes too threatening or anxiety producing. In this case, the accompanying affect may be any one of the following. At any time during the process of drawing, painting, or coloring, the child stops creating the work and begins obliterating the drawing by scribbling on it, ripping it up, until it is destroyed. Throwing the artwork away can take the form of actually depositing the work into the wastebasket, throwing it across the room, or leaving it in a crumpled ball on the art table.

**10. Draws figure with large, open mouth.**   This item pertains to a human figure being drawn. The mouth on the face is large and open. The presence or absence of teeth is not significant. The face may be drawn alone on the paper or as one part of a larger, more complex drawing.

**11. Draws with large parts of body crossed out.**   For this item to be scored, the child first draws a body, and then crosses out sections of the figure's body. The areas crossed out might be the lower torso, chest, or face. It might be all of the drawing below the waist. Or, it could be any combination. It is as if the child, upon viewing the completed drawing, needs to destroy parts of it. Should the child go on to rip up the drawing and then throw it away, item 9, rather than this item would be scored.

**12. Encapsulates self in drawing, cutting off lower half of the body.** Encapsulation is surrounding a figure in a drawing on all four sides. In this item, it is surrounding the child's drawing of herself on all four sides and having the bottom side of the encapsulation occur in such a way that the figure is not shown from the waist down. This may be as simple as drawing only the head and shoulders of oneself within a box or oval. Or, it may be a more complex drawing, perhaps of the family eating dinner, and the child draws herself at the table so only the top half of her body is showing. Or, it could be a drawing of the child at school, sitting at a desk. Again, only the chest, shoulders, and head of the child is showing in the drawing.

**13. Stabs/pokes drawings of genitals with pencil.**   In this item, the child pokes at or stabs at a drawing with a pencil. The child might also use a marker, crayon, or other drawing instrument to attack the drawing of genitalia. The drawing may be of a figure with genitals (breasts, penis, vaginal area) or the drawing may be only of genitalia.

**14. Draws a figure with displaced body parts.**   Displaced body parts are defined as body parts out of their usual or appropriate place, either on the figure or elsewhere in the drawing. For example, a child draws a human figure and places the facial features (eyes, nose, and mouth) on the paper near the figure, but not on the figure's face. Displacement also means the purposeful absence of a body part. For example, a child might make a detailed drawing of a human figure, but leave an open space where the crotch should be. The figure is clearly missing the connecting line between the legs although other parts of the drawing were completed with detail and care.

**15. Draws a male with a penis.**   This is only too straightforward. The child draws a male figure and adds a penis. The child might make this drawing, then poke or stab at the penis with the pencil, marker, or crayon. In this case, the play therapist would score both this item and item 13. Or, the child might create this drawing and then cross out this or other parts of the figure. In such a case, both this item and item 11 would be scored.

Table 10.1, *Understanding Children Who Have Been Sexually Abused,* places the fifteen items of play therapy behavior of the *PTSI-CSA* in context of the results of sexual abuse. The chart is divided into four therapeutic issues identified by Finkelhor and Brown (1985): Traumagenic Sexualization, Stigmatization, Betrayal, and Powerlessness. The first column, Causative Experiences, lists a variety of possible events the sexually abused child may have experienced. The second column, Psychological Consequences, lists the possible psychological and emotional impact of the causative experiences. The third column, Child's Behaviors, lists many of the behaviors typically exhibited by sexually abused children in their regular environments (home, school, daycare, etc). These behaviors are linked to the corresponding psychological consequences and causative experiences. The fourth column, Child's Play in Play Therapy, relates the child's play therapy behaviors to causative experiences, psychological consequences, and behavior in the child's environment. This table is provided to assist the play therapist in understanding how the child's play therapy behavior may be tied to the child's previous experience and the emotional and psychological consequences of that experience.

The reader should note that behaviors may be listed with more than one therapeutic issue. It is possible that the same play behavior may have more than one meaning. It is the play therapist, in the session, understanding the child's world, who can tell the difference. For example, the meaning attached to a child destroying a drawing may be the child's expression of anger at being betrayed by the perpetrator or non-protecting parent (the drawing being of the perpetrator or non-protecting parent, respectively). Or, the child may destroy a drawing of himself because the child now believes he is to blame or he has high levels of shame (stigmatization).

A caution is necessary. The table should not be used to prove a direct cause–effect correlation. The variables of sexual abuse are many and complex. Children are very idiosyncratic. Each child expresses his or her own experience, and perception of that experience, in a very individualized way. The table is provided to assist the play therapist in understanding *possible* connections between the play therapy behavior and the complex factors of the child's experience and it's psychological consequences.

## RESEARCH AND DEVELOPMENT OF THE PTSI-CSA

### Phase One: Survey Research & Factor Analysis

The first phase in the process of developing the PTSI-CSA was survey research (Homeyer & Landreth, 1998). The original list of play therapy behaviors (PTBs) was developed from a review of the professional literature regarding the treatment of sexually abused children in play therapy. This list contained 115 items. A panel of experts, in the areas of play therapy, art therapy, and sexual abuse of children, reviewed the list. They added, deleted, and reworded items, resulting in a final list of 178 items.

TABLE 10.1. Understanding Children Who Have Been Sexually Abused

| Causative Experiences | Psychological Consequences | Child's Behaviors | Child's Play in Play Therapy |
|---|---|---|---|
| **Traumagenic Sexualization** | | | |
| developmentally inappropriate sexual activity | confusion & misconceptions regarding sexual behavior & morality | preoccupation with sex | kisses therapist with a puppet |
| repeatedly rewarded for sexual activity | unusual emotional associations to sexual activities | repetitive sexual behavior | uses sexual gestures when talking about the abuse and/or home situation |
| exchange of affection, attention, privileges and/or gifts for sexual behavior | confusion between sexual intimacy & emotional intimacy | use of sexual behavior to manipulate others | pretends doll is "peeing" on another doll |
| parts of child's body fetishied: given distorted importance & meaning | frightening memories & events associated with sexual activity | advanced sexual knowledge | draws figure with large, open mouths |
| use of force and/or threats | flashbacks | forcing sexual activity with peers and/or younger children | draws males with penis |
| | negative body image | promiscuous | |
| | negative attitude toward sexuality | hypervigilance | |
| | sexual identity confusion (particularly in boys) | | |
| **Stigmatization** | | | |
| abuser blames child for sexual activity | child incorporates negative connotations into self-image: | gravitation toward others who feel stigmatized to reduce feelings of isolation, leading to criminal activity, prostitution, drug or alcohol abuse | asks to be covered with a blanket |
| pressure for secrecy | blame | | makes references to "peeing" and "pooing" |
| negative attitudes reinforced by family and/or community | shame | self-destructive behavior, such as suicide | draws figure, scribbles, rips it up, destroys it, and throws it away |
| blaming the child for the abuse | guilt | | draws self-encapsulated, cuts off lower half of body |
| | reduced moral standards | | draws figure with large parts of body crossed |
| | "spoiled/damaged" goods | | |
| | sense of being different | | |

*(Continued)*

## TABLE 10.1. Continued

| Causative Experiences | Psychological Consequences | Child's Behaviors | Child's Play in Play Therapy |
|---|---|---|---|
| **Betrayal** | | | |
| a person:<br>upon whom the child is dependent caused harm<br>manipulated or lied about moral standards<br>who is loved treated child with callous disregard<br>who should have protected and/or believed child did not distances self from child after disclosure | inability to trust others<br>inability to feel safe in a relationship<br>negative self-image<br>reduced level of self-worth | depression and grief reactions resulting from loss of trusted figure(s)<br>extreme dependency and clinginess (especially in young children)<br>impaired judgement in trustworthiness of adults<br>placing self in relationships that are physically, psychologically, and sexually abusive<br>hostility & anger & mistrust<br>anti-social behavior, delinquence | on the phone, screams hate to the abuser, then expresses love before hanging up<br>draws figure, scribbles, rips it up, destroys it, and throws it away<br>stabs/pokes drawings of genitals with drawing instrument (pen, pencil, crayons)<br>hits and/or attempts to cut off doll's penis/breasts |
| **Powerlessness** | | | |
| violation of physical boundaries<br>violation of emotional boundaries<br>child's will, desires, and sense of efficacy are repeatedly ignored<br>impact of level of threat and/or manipulation<br>attempts to stop abuse are ineffective<br>inability to make other adults believe them | fear, anxiety<br>impaired coping skills<br>impaired sense of control of one's self & world<br>inability to cope with environment<br>need to compensate for pain of powerlessness | nightmares, phobias, hypervigilance, clinging behavior, somatic complaints<br>revictimization<br>despair, depression, suicidal behavior<br>learning problems<br>running away<br>unusually high need to control or dominate (especially males)<br>aggressive, delinquent behavior<br>bullying behavior, re-victimizing others | hits and/or attempts to cut off doll's penis/breasts<br>reenacts sexual abuse exam<br>stabs/pokes drawings of genitals with drawing instrument (pen, pencil, crayons) |

* *Note.* The data in columns 1–3 are from "Impact of Child Sexual Abuse: A Review of the Literature," by D. Finkelhor and A. Browne, 1985, *Psychological Bulletin, 99,* pp. 66–77. Adapted with permission.

The first draft of the survey instrument comprised of these 178 items was field tested with thirty selected play therapists identified on the basis of their professional status as play therapists. These play therapists resided in Texas and California, many specialized in play therapy in their graduate programs, and were currently seeing a large number of sexually abused children in play therapy. The field test participants completed the instrument and made written comments regarding clarity and usability. Based on their clinical experience with sexually abused children, the participants rated each PTB using the Likert scale categories: 1 (Never), 2 (Very Seldom), 3 (Seldom) 4 (Often) 5 (Very Often). In order to identify possible significant behavior connected with gender or age, the participant-play therapist rated each PTB four times for boys, ages 3–6; girls, ages 3–6; boys, ages 7–10; girls, ages 7–10.

Ten demographic questions regarding the participant-play therapist also were asked: gender; age; highest academic degree; discipline; job setting; experience in conducting play therapy; training in play therapy, number of graduate courses, clock hours in professional workshops/conferences; number of sexually abused children in play therapy (individual cases); average number of sessions with sexually abused child clients; and what percentage of (the participant's) weekly practice is with sexually abused children in play therapy.

Twenty-one returned field test surveys were analyzed by using Principal Components Analysis with Varimax Rotation, a type of factor analysis. Items with a loading of ±.50, rather than the lower, typical, ±.30, (Tabachnick & Fidell, 1983) were retained. This resulted in 140 items to be retained and 38 items to be dropped. The panel of experts reviewed the 38 items and unanimously agreed that they should be dropped. The factor analysis of the field test survey using the higher loading resulted in a stronger, more powerful, and shorter instrument, of 140 play therapy behavior items (Homeyer & Landreth, 1998). The complete list of 140 items can be found in the Appendix.

The second, and final, draft of the survey instrument was sent to the 2,541 members of the Association for Play Therapy (APT). The APT membership consisted of a wide range of mental health professionals such as counselors, social workers, psychologists, psychiatric nurses, and psychiatrists. A large percentage (46.18%), of the 786 APT members who replied were not seeing sexually abused children in play therapy. This left a total of 423 (53.82%) completed surveys. In order to ensure the strongest and most robust findings possible, only the data from the 249 play therapists most experienced in working with sexually abused children (16 or more) were used (Homeyer & Landreth, 1998).

Principal Components Analysis with Varimax Rotation was applied to the 140 play therapy behavior survey items to cluster highly interrelated PTBs. A key finding was that all 140 items were interrelated to each other and clustered on Factor One. For a more detailed report of the resulting analysis, the reader is referred to previous publications by Homeyer (1995) and Homeyer and Landreth (1998).

An important finding of the research at this phase was that there are identifiable PTBs of sexually abused children. This large number of PTBs provides some insight into the difficulty that play therapists have had in identifying sexually abused children. There are, simply put, a very large number of PTBs that, in some way, relate to the play of sexually abused children.

### Phase Two: Development of the Screening Instrument

It was clear the 140 PTBs were highly interrelated. The next phase was to identify the play therapy behaviors that would differentiate between sexually abused and nonsexually abused children in play therapy.

The list of 140 items had a reliability coefficient of .98. Item analysis was used to reduce the number of items. Only those items with a high individual reliability coefficient (plus/minus .60) were retained. The resulting list of 17 items had a reliability coefficient of .97. These 17 items were used in a pilot study. Analysis of the pilot study data showed that fifteen of the seventeen items could discriminate between sexually abused child clients and nonsexually abused child clients (Homeyer, 1997a, 1997b).

The fifteen-item screening instrument was completed by 103 play therapists. The play therapists scored both a sexually abused client and a nonsexually abused client. The play therapist indicated the client's gender, status (current or terminated case), and age group (3–5 years, 7–10 years). The play therapy behaviors could have been seen in one session or across several sessions. A Paired Differences $t$-test was applied to the data. Statistical significance between the ratings of the sexually abused and nonsexually abused child clients was found.

An order effect was found, based upon which type child-client was scored first. When the sexually abused child was scored first, an average of 2.8 items were identified as spontaneously displayed by a sexually abused child in play therapy and 1.15 items displayed by the nonsexually abused child ($p = .0012$). When the nonsexually abused child was scored first, an average of 4.6 items were scored as displayed by the sexually abused child in play therapy as compared to .95, or less than one item, by the nonsexually abused child ($p = .0000$). An alpha level of .05 was used for all statistical analysis. Further data analysis found that client gender (male/female), age (3–6 years or 7–10 years), and/or status (current client or terminated client) had no impact on the order effect. The order effect is sufficiently significant to impact the use of the screening instrument. The immediate practice effect of scoring the items on a nonabused client before scoring the child the play therapist wants to screen, is important in the use of this instrument.

## USING THE PTSI-CSA

### Administration Scoring

The PTSI-CSA is to be used with boys and girls, three years old to ten years old. It is administered and scored in a two-step process. Because of the order effect, discussed above, a comparison child must be scored first. Use of the screening instrument is invalid if this first step is skipped.

### Step one:

 A. Select a nonsexually abused client to serve as the *Comparison Child Client*. A nonsexually abused client is defined as a child who is in play therapy for a reason other than sexual abuse, and is not in a high risk category for sexual abuse, such as a sibling of a sexually abused child or a victim of family violence.

 B. Check any of the fifteen play therapy behaviors seen during play therapy session(s) with this child. An item is scored *Yes* if it has been observed during a play therapy session. An item is scored *No* if it has not been observed during a play therapy session. Scoring may occur within a single session or across several sessions.

 C. Total the number of *Yes* responses.

### Step two:

 A. Select the client to be screened.

 B. Check any of the fifteen play therapy behaviors seen during play therapy. The scoring process is the same as above: An item is scored *Yes* if it has been observed during a play therapy session. An item is scored *No* if it has not been observed during a play therapy session. Scoring may be done within a single session or across several sessions.

 C. Total the number of *Yes* responses.

 D. Subtract the *comparison child score* from the total score of the *child being screened*. This will provide the *total difference score*.

## Interpretation

If the *total difference score* is four or more, the child is considered *high risk* for being the victim of sexual abuse. Further assessment for possible sexual abuse should occur as soon as possible. A forensic interview or sexual abuse assessment is recommended.

## CASE EXAMPLE

### Initial session

The child has been exploring the room, picking up toys, manipulating them, labeling the toys she knows (this is a phone) and nicknaming others (this is a bongie thing for a Slinky). She continues to work her way around the room, interacting easily with the toys and the play therapist. She brings some toys toward the play therapist, some she simply handles, labels, and returns to the shelf. After about fifteen minutes:

(C is used to designate the child and T for the play therapist.)

C: (*She works her way to the easel. She looks at the paintbrushes, then at the play therapist.*)

T: You're wondering if you can paint. In here, that's something you can decide.

C: Oh-h-h, I'd like that. (*She turns back to the easel and pulls out a paintbrush.*)

T: You decided to paint.

C: I'm gonna be careful.

T: You don't want to get paint on you. But that's special paint that washes right off!

C: (*She begins to carefully paint a typical scene: first a brown house, then she selects yellow for a sun.*)

T: You picked another color for that.

C: (*Finishes the sun, then selects black to paint a person next to the house.*)

T: Now you're painting something else.

C: (*When the person is just about completed, she begins painting over the figure.*)

T: Something about that you didn't like.

C: (*She gets more paint on her paintbrush. No longer careful, the paintbrush full of paint, drips globs of black from the paint cup to the paper. Her breathing increases, she begins to shift her weight from one foot to another and back again.*)

T: You want to get that all covered up.

C: (*She nods in agreement. The paint now totally obliterates the figure and part of the house. She works quickly and haphazardly to take the paper off the easel. The paint-heavy paper flops onto itself, and she lets it fall to the floor. She then goes to the sandbox.*)

**NOTE: This qualifies as item #9: Figure is drawn, scribbled or ripped up destroyed, thrown away. Item #9 would be scored as Yes on the PTSI-CSA.**

The child plays in the sand, mostly moving sand around with her hands, pouring sand through the funnel, feeling the falling sand with her hand. After a few minutes she returns to the shelves of toys and continues to explore, and works her way around to the dollhouse. About ten minutes before the end of the session she is at the dollhouse.

C: (*She sits on the floor at the dollhouse and begins to pickup the dollhouse dolls.*) Where's the daddy? Here he is! (*She picks him up.*)

T: You found him.

C: Daddy's gonna keep um safe. Where's the kid? The mom is gonna find her . . . oh, she'll get in trouble!

T: That kid will be in trouble.

C: Time for bed. (*She begins undressing the dolls, places the naked daddy and mom together on one bed.*)

T: You know just how they look when they go to bed.

C: (*She begins arranging furniture.*) Here's the kid! (*She begins to undress the kid doll. Moves doll into the bathroom. Looks up to the therapist.*) She's peeing now. (*Then, looking back to the doll, places doll in bathtub.*)

**NOTE: This qualifies as item #7: References to peeing and pooping. Item #7 would be scored as Yes on the PTSI-CSA.**

T: You know just how to get her ready for bed.

C: (*Child places doll in a bed in a second bedroom. She then continues to arrange the furniture, placing lamps on end tables, putting chairs at the table in the kitchen, etc. She has her other hand between her legs, at her crotch, rubbing herself.*)

**NOTE: This qualifies as item #3: Sexual gestures when talking about home situation or someone at home. Item #3 would be scored as Yes on the PTSI-CSA.**

C: (*Before the play therapist could respond to the rubbing, the child inadvertently hits the side of the dollhouse with her shoe, making a thump sound, startling herself.*) It's a monster!

T: Oh, there's a monster!

C: The monster waked them up! (*C looks directly at T, getting and keeping eye-to-eye contact.*) It's a REAL monster!

T: That's scary!

C: I know what she can play with, she can play in my sandbox!

T: You've got an idea of what to do.

C: (*She picks up the kid doll and goes to the sandbox. She again moves the sand around with her hands for a few moments, then fills the bucket with the sand, places the doll on top.*)

T: You found something for the kid. And, Jessie, we have five minutes left in the playroom today.

C: Mom can play here, too! (*She carries the bucket over to the dollhouse, places mom in the bucket, on top of the sand. Then she adds a lamp, a chair, a bed, and continues to place furniture in the bucket until it's full to overflowing.*)

T: You're putting lots of things with them.

C: Something woke her up. It was a surprise.

T: She didn't know it was going to happen.

C: Nope. (*Child then leaves the bucket at the dollhouse and plays in the sandbox until the session is done.*)

## Session #2

Again C begins the session by exploring the toys. C appears relaxed and at ease. Then she gets to the puppets.

C: (*Puts the alligator puppet on her hand and comes to the therapist. This is the first time C has come directly to the therapist. C has the puppet kiss the therapist on neck.*) He loves you.

T: He loves me and gave me a kiss.

**NOTE: This qualifies as item #1: Uses hand puppet to kiss therapist on the face/neck. Item #1 would be scored as Yes on the PTSI-CSA.**

C: Yup! (*Child turns around, returns the alligator puppet to the puppet rack, and checks-out some of the other ones. The turtle puppet, which can pull its head and feet into its shell, seems to be especially intriguing to her. She then continues to explore the room without settling into any lengthy play. After about ten minutes she begins play in the sandbox that focuses on need for protection. She buries a farmer figure in the sand, then adds one animal after another indicating they all need protection from the farmer who is going to shoot them. This play continues throughout the remainder of the session.*)

## Session #5

Client has established a pattern of spending her first few minutes of the session generally exploring the room. It seems to help her transition from her external world to the world of the playroom. Today she wanders until she sees the baby bottle.

C: (*She picks up the baby bottle, fills it with water, and continues to suck on it as she moves around the room. Coming to Bobo (bop bag) she kicks him in the groin, then immediately feeds him from her baby bottle.*)

T: You kicked him right there.

C: (*She nods and kicks him again, a karate-like kick.*) That makes me feel better.

T: You like kicking him.

C: (*She continues to kick Bobo several times.*)

T: You can kick him over and over.

C: (She goes over and picks up a sword. Then returns to Bobo.) I'm gonna chop off his wienie.

T: You're gonna chop it right off.

This play continues for about thirty minutes. She goes from chopping off the wienie to chopping through Bobo's head from the top all the way down, to cutting his head off.

**NOTE: This qualifies as item #5: Hits or attempts to cut off doll's penis/breasts. Item #5 would be scores as Yes on the PTSI-CSA.**

In this case example, the play therapist, after session #5, was concerned about possible sexual abuse. The play therapist began the screening process by selecting a client who had been referred because of problems resulting from the death of a beloved grandmother. This child would serve as the comparison child client. The play therapist scored the comparison client's play behaviors. In this case, the only item on the PTSI-CSA that was checked *yes* was item #2. The child was still angry because her grandmother went away (died).

The play therapist then scored the child-client she was concerned about. As indicated above, five items were scored yes. Items #1, 3, 5, 7, and 9.

Subtracting the comparison child's score (1) from the case study's child score (5) resulted in a total difference score of 4. The score of four was sufficient to provide the parents with referrals for a forensic sexual abuse assessment.

## LIMITATIONS OF THE PTSI-CSA

To date there is no standardized instrument, interview protocol, or investigative approach that guarantees to discover the truth, 100% of the time, about whether or not sexual abuse has occurred. Sexual abuse is not like other physical or mental disorders. No blood test can reveal it; no single set of symptoms or syndromes, identifies it. Whenever the attempt is made to discover whether a child has been sexually abused, there is a dilemma: What if we suspect abuse where there is none (false positive) and subject the child and his or her family to all that occurs in a sexual abuse investigation. Or, worse yet, label a person as a perpetrator, when he or she is not.

On the other hand, what if we are too cautious and make no referral, even if we have concerns and it turns out that the child has been sexually abused. Or, we do the best we can with all available resources, based on the most recent research in the field, and we still cannot verify abuse when in fact it is occurring (false negative).

### False Positives

A false positive on the PTSI-CSA would be a case where the total difference score is 4 or higher, the child is referred for a child sexual abuse assessment, but is, in fact, not sexually abused.

**Type I False Positive.** There are limitations to the use of any list of behavioral indicators: The behavior may be a response to a wide variety of possible stressors. This is also true of the play therapy behaviors on this instrument. It is possible for a child to have a total difference score of 4 or higher and NOT be sexually abused. Thus, it should be stressed that this is a screening instrument only, to be used as a way to seek out the source of a particular child's behavior, and is not a diagnostic instrument.

**Type II False Positive.** Child victims of sexual abuse are often intimidated or threatened into not talking about the abuse. Also, for any of many other reasons, the sexually abused child refuses to disclose during a sexual abuse assessment. Therefore, a child might be a victim of sexual abuse, score as *high risk,* and still not be identified during the formal sexual abuse investigation/assessment. Even a skilled, experienced forensic interviewer cannot force a child to disclose sexual abuse if the child does not want to do so. Sorensen and Snow (1991) found that 72% of sexually abused children deny abuse in their first interview. A sexually abused child may deny or not disclose abuse in a manner in which the interview can confirm abuse. As such it would be logged as a false positive, but in fact *not be false*. This is part of the ongoing difficulty in the work of trying to identify, and protect, sexually abused children. Short of physical evidence, or the confession of the perpetrator, there is little to be done to help children who are unable or unwilling to provide a verbal disclosure of abuse.

### False Negative

A false negative would occur with the PTSI-CSA when the child is sexually abused, but the total difference score is 3 or lower. Therefore, no referral for further exploration of possible sexual abuse would take place. However, studies suggest that up to 30% of sexually abused children do not exhibit behavioral indicators (Kendall-Tackett, Williams, Finkelhor, 1993). Why these children do not is not clearly known. Some children may mask their response to the abuse, while others may be more resilient to the effects of the abuse. Therefore, a sexually abused child may not have a score sufficient to result in a referral.

### Other limitations

When this instrument was being developed, the children's demographic information was not identified. More research needs to occur to explore the impact of the client's socioeconomic status and cultural background. It is proposed, however, that since gender and age did not impact the fifteen items, socioeconomic status and cultural background may not either. Still, further study is needed.

Additionally, the demographic variables of the play therapists should also be explored. The participants in the final stage of this research lived in a large southwestern state, presumably both urban and rural areas. However, the influence of the play therapist's gender, socioeconomic status, and cultural background is not known. The amount of play therapy training and experience might also impact the ability of the play therapist to identify the play therapy behaviors and influence the use of the screening instrument. This should be explored as well.

## SUMMARY

Children use behavior, both in and out of the play therapy room, to communicate. It is the responsibility of adults in the child's world to assist in understanding that communication. Children who have been (or are being) sexually abused may not be able to communicate that to others. The child being sexually abused may have been threatened not to tell, or children may not be able to express their experience because the experience is too overwhelming or beyond their ability to express. The PTSI-CSA provides the play therapist with another tool. It can be used both in an attempt to understand children's play in the playroom as well as to comply with legal and ethical requirements to report abuse.

The PTSI-CSA is an empirically researched screening instrument. The fifteen items of play therapy behavior that make up the screening instrument can identify children who are at high risk of being sexually abused. Once a child is identified as high risk, the child can then be referred for a more formal sexual abuse evaluation. The user should also be aware of the possible false negatives and false positives findings.

Additional research is needed to refine this instrument and develop norm groups. Play therapists are encouraged to use this instrument and to work on developing other instruments. Play therapy is an exciting and valuable treatment modality for children. However, the development of statistically sound, standardized instruments for use in play therapy is needed.

## REFERENCES

Adams, J., & Wells, R. (1993). Normal versus abnormal genital findings in children: How well do examiners agree? *Child Abuse & Neglect: The International Journal, 17*(5), 663–675.

American Medical Association (1985). AMA diagnostic and treatment guidelines concerning child abuse and neglect. *Journal of the American Medical Association, 254,* 796–800.

Berliner, L. (1988). Deciding whether a child has been sexually abused. In E. B. Nicholson & J. Bulkley (Eds.), *Sexual abuse allegations in custody cases: A resource book for judges and court personnel* (pp. 48–69). Washington, DC: American Bar Association.

Berliner, L., & Conte, J. (1993). Sexual abuse evaluations: Conceptual and empirical obstacles. *Child Abuse & Neglect: The International Journal, 17*(1), 111–125.

Everstine, D., & Everstine, L. (1989). *Sexual trauma in children and adolescents: Dynamics and treatment.* New York: Brunner/Mazel.

Finkelhor, W. (1986). *A sourcebook on child sexual abuse.* Newbury Park, CA: Sage.

Finkelhor, D., & Browne, A. (1985). Impact of child sexual abuse: A review of the literature. *Psychological Bulletin, 99,* 66–77.

Gil, E. (1991). *The healing power of play: Working with abused children.* New York: Guilford Press.

Gray, E. (1993). *Unequal justice: The prosecution of child sexual abuse.* New York: The Free Press.

Hendricks, S. (1971). A descriptive analysis of the process of client-centered play therapy (Doctoral dissertation, North Texas State University, 1971). *Dissertations Abstracts International, 32,* 3689A.

Homeyer, L. (1995). *Play therapy behaviors of sexually abused children.* Unpublished doctoral dissertation, University of North Texas, Denton, TX.

Homeyer, L. (1997a). Research update: Development of a child sexual abuse screening instrument, On-going research. *Texas Association for Play Therapy Newsletter, 5*(3), 3–4.

Homeyer, L. (1997b). Play therapy behaviors of sexually abused children, *Play Notes: Georgia Association for Play Therapy Newsletter, 2*(1), 2.

Homeyer, L., & Landreth, G. (1998). Play therapy behavior of sexually abused children. *International Journal of Play Therapy, 7* (1), 49–71.

Howe, P., & Silvern, L. (1981). Behavioral observation during play therapy: Preliminary development of a research instrument. *Journal of Personality Assessment, 45,* 168–182.

Jackson, H., & Nutall, R., (1993). Clinical responses to sexual abuse allegations. *Child Abuse & Neglect: The International Journal, 17,* 127–143.

Kendall-Tackett, K., Williams, L., & Finkelhor, D. (1993). Impact of sexual abuse on children: A review and synthesis of recent empirical studies. *Psychological Bulletin, 113*(1), 164–180.

Lew, M. (1988). *Victims no longer: Men recovering from incest and other sexual child abuse.* New York: Harper & Row.

MacFarlane, J., Feldmeth, J., Saywitz, K.,

Damon, L., Krebs, S., & Dugan, M. (1988). *Child sexual abuse: The clinical interview.* New York: Guilford.

Meyers, J. (1993). A call for forensically relevant research. *Child Abuse and Neglect: The International Journal, 17*(5), 573–579.

Moustakas, C. (1955). The frequency and intensity of negative attitudes expressed in play therapy: A comparison of well-adjusted and disturbed young children. *The Journal of Genetic Psychology, 86,* 309–325.

Muram, D. (1989). Child sexual abuse: Relationship between sexual acts and genital findings. *Child Abuse & Neglect: An International Journal, 13,* 211–216.

Oe, E. (1989). *Comparison of initial session play therapy behaviors of maladjusted and adjusted children.* Unpublished dissertation, University of North Texas, Denton.

Perry, L. (1988). *Play therapy behavior of maladjusted and adjusted children.* Unpublished doctoral dissertation, University of North Texas, Denton.

Schwartzenberger, K., & Sweeney, D. (1992). *Play therapy and storytelling with children in foster care.* Paper presented at the 9th Annual Association for Play Therapy Conference, Nashua, NH.

Sgroi, S. (1982). *Handbook of clinical intervention in child sexual abuse.* Lexington, MA: Lexington Books.

Sorensen, T., & Snow, B. (1991). How children tell: The process of disclosure in child sexual abuse. *Child Welfare, 60*(1), 3–15.

Tabachnick, B., & Fidell, L. (1983). *Using multivariate statistics.* New York: Harper & Row.

Withee, K. (1975). A descriptive analysis of the process of play therapy. (Doctoral dissertation, North Texas State University, 1975). *Dissertations Abstracts International, 36,* 6406B.

# APPENDIX

## Toy Play

1. hitting a male doll's buttocks
2. harshly washing a doll
3. pulling hair while combing doll's hair
4. throwing all the toys on the floor
5. cutting/sawing off limbs from stuffed animals/dolls
6. non-accidental breaking toys
7. baby doll hitting father/mother doll
8. car chases with exaggerated speed and handling
9. untamed horses
10. play which backs toys into corner
11. killing aggressor symbol
12. burying/hiding figures
13. hits adult dolls against hard surfaces: wall, floor, wooden stove
14. feeding self with the baby bottle
15. rocking self in a chair while holding a soft toy or doll
16. dollhouse play of feeding, cleaning, caring for the children
17. bathing, combing hair, diapering, and changing clothes of a baby doll
18. rolling on Bobo, soothing behavior
19. cuddling in a baby blanket
20. placing an aggressive toy to protect a non-aggressive toy
21. enacting sexual activity with animal toys/puppets
22. enacting sex play with dolls, pressing genitals of one doll to another doll's face
23. show sexual intercourse positions
24. taking pictures of dolls in sexually explicit poses with a pretend camera
25. inserting objects in own/toy's mouth, simulating oral sex
26. persistent masturbation
27. needing to go to the bathroom in the middle of play, symbolic of abuse
28. undressing and exploring genital areas of dolls
29. hitting/attempting to cut off doll's penis/breast
30. pretending doll is "peeing" on another doll
31. washing toys before using them
32. frequent washing of hands during session, own and/or therapist's
33. child washing own body and/or genitals
34. killing a toy, then bringing back to life
35. toy/symbol keeps changing identity/behavior from good to bad: friendly snake wraps around your neck; doctor cuts out hearts/kills; parenting figure who doesn't protect/hurts
36. building then destroying
37. washing of toys and/or play room

38. obsessive neatness: appears to be more worried about putting toys back than playing freely
39. compulsive sorting, naming exploring toys

### Sand Box Play

40. repetitively filling and emptying cups of sand
41. smearing self with sand
42. making secret tunnels for hiding
43. building hills out of wet sand and poking holes in each of them
44. rubbing sand on genitals and thighs
45. covering genitals and thighs with sand
46. placing a snake or motorcycle between one's legs
47. dripping wet sand on a figure
48. washing self/parts of body with sand (clearly cleansing, not sexualized play)

### Art

49. figure with displaced body parts
50. figure is drawn, scribbled on, ripped up, destroyed, thrown away
51. figures surrounded by circles or boxes
52. hands that are large, club-like, or shoot bullets
53. figures with large open mouths
54. asymmetrical/leaning figures
55. large parts of bodies crossed out
56. figure of self in elaborate clothes, to cover self
57. smearing self with clay
58. repetitive use of material: smoothing clay, shading in drawings
59. color, mutilate, crumple and throw away anatomical drawings
60. face only, no body
61. figure with only upper half of body
62. encapsulate self in drawing, cutting off lower half of body
63. two people in bed covered with dots, i.e. semen
64. drawing males with penises
65. draw genitalia, but labeled as a tree, cloud, heart, rainbow
66. people with genitalia
67. inclusion of long phallic shapes
68. genitalia with ejaculation
69. genitals drawn away from body
70. torsos with blood running down legs
71. people engaging in sexual activities
72. drawings of figures with emphasized cheek markings/make-up
73. stabbing/poking drawing of genitals with pen

## Toward the Therapist

74. rubbing their body against the therapist
75. attempting to 'mount' the therapist
76. touching/grabbing the therapist's breasts or genitals
77. hugging therapist around waist, face in crotch
78. spitting
79. wanting to kiss and hug
80. using hand puppets to kiss therapist on face and neck
81. taking off underwear
82. saying they want to please
83. trying to second-guess what therapist wants
84. wanting to be covered with blanket
85. wanting to be fed by the therapist
86. initiating hide-and-seek
87. displays of anger: attempting to bite, hit, spit on therapist
88. calling the therapist names
89. stabbing at therapist
90. hiding/burying toys from therapist
91. starting to be aggressive, then stopping
92. hurting self in minor ways to get nurturing from therapist
93. wanting to be held and rocked like a baby, while sucking on a baby bottle
94. asking to be covered with blanket
95. feeding the therapist
96. wanting to be "put to sleep"
97. getting self dirty and asked the therapist's help in cleaning
98. scaring therapist by yelling "Boo," then comforting by patting on shoulder saying, "are you okay?"
99. giving money to therapist, then robbing
100. frightening figure does pleasant things to therapist: monsters kissing therapist
101. asking therapist to play, but therapist's character always gets hurt
102. starting an aggressive gesture then changing mid-movement
103. unable to tolerate being alone with the therapist for an entire session
104. huddling on the floor away from the therapist
105. need to be rescued/saved: climbing on furniture; drawing a figure, then telling therapist the figure is lost and instructs it be found

## Verbalizations

106. identifying toy as perpetrator, putting the toy in jail, later burying it
107. on phone, screams hate to the perpetrator then expresses love before hanging up
108. use of only single words

109. requesting a sexual activity like "let's make sex"
110. attempting/requesting permission to remove some/all clothing
111. requesting therapist remove clothing
112. referring to self as "a sexy lady"
113. references to "peeing and pooing"
114. sexual gestures when talking about abuser or home situation: rubbing doll between legs while talking; inserting finger in doll's mouth or rectum
115. no verbal interaction
116. reenacting the sexual abuse medical exam

## Child's Presentation

117. being in a trance-like state, while playing with water and sand, or while reenacting the abuse
118. appearing glassy-eyed, stiff, and holding one's breath
119. sitting in a chair, staring off into space
120. appears to be cut off from reality and in a world of their own
121. incongruent presentation of self: voice/words are bright/positive but eyes are hooded and body constricted; or, lilting/smiling face while talking/ playing out horrible or frightening play
122. needing to go to the bathroom excessively
123. hiding for most of the session

## Themes of Play

124. good guys/people vs. bad guys/people
125. God vs. Devil
126. building new homes
127. taming wild animals
128. fixing things
129. drawings with themes of damage & violation
130. treating self as a "bad child"
131. guilt and shame
132. punishment
133. love, seduction, and sex
134. need for protection: baby animal seeking protection from bigger/stronger
135. rescue & danger: monster threaten, super heroes/good figures help
136. good figures unavailable for help: call the doctor who cannot come because doctor is on vacation or at lunch
137. being lost/burying: lost puppies
138. medical/healing play: giving shots/bandaging/medicine
139. identification with aggressor: taking role or aggressor/evil character
140. hopelessness: fighting/earthquake in which no one wins/survives

# 11

# Diagnostic Assessment of Children's Play Therapy Behavior

LESSIE H. PERRY
GARRY L. LANDRETH

A persistent and perplexing problem for child therapists has been the difficulty in adequately assessing in a comprehensive way the total behaviors considered to be characteristic of children. Of specific concern has been the need for a method or instrument that would provide the therapist with quantifiable means for deriving meaning from children's play behaviors. It is generally recognized and accepted by authorities in the field of child therapy that children's play can be a window to understanding children's experiential and psychological world. Children express their world through play in often open but potentially complex and profound ways, and the therapist is called on to translate those play behaviors in ways that help not only him- or herself but also others to better understand the psychological needs of the child. Play offers a unique psychological tool for viewing the world through the eyes of the child.

## CHILD'S PLAY

The use of play in counseling children was an inevitable process because play provides a natural bridge to the counselor. In play therapy, counselors use children's concrete language as portrayed in play rather than limit children's communication to words, which are adults' abstract and symbolic language. An example of how children portray their world can be seen in the following descriptions of children's play behavior in a play therapy experience.

### Audrey

Audrey, five years old, painted two pictures, using all the colors at the easel and placing one color on top of the other, mixing the colors together. When the therapist asked what title she wanted on her paintings, she said, "This one is 'Messy Makeup' and that one is . . . (pausing and then nodding) . . . 'Lovely makeup.'" As she painted, she asked what colors she should use, and as she finished, she disclosed, "I'm not a good painter. . . . I can't get it (the painting) down. You get it, and put it so it can dry, but don't mess it up!"

Audrey moved on to the sandbox and the kitchen area and prepared some "sand food with lots of sugar." As she dished out her cooked food, she turned to the therapist and said, "Do you want to come have supper with me?"

The therapist, in a stage whisper replied, "What shall I say?"

"Say 'yes,'" directed Audrey and with a slight change in her voice continued, "My husband is dead, and I hate to eat alone."

Audrey then played doctor using the doctor kit with the therapist as the patient. She placed the stethoscope on the therapist's chest and listened.

"Well, what do you think?" inquired the therapist.

Audrey stepped back, frowned, and shook her head saying, "You're sick, real sick. You have to stay in the hospital six more weeks."

Audrey moved to the table where she had laid out the thermometer, syringe, microscope, reflex hammer, and eyeglasses. She took the various instruments and checked the therapist's temperature, knee reflexes, ears, and then listened with the stethoscope again.

Audrey moved back to the table, turned to the therapist and declared, "I don't hear anything. You're sick. You're bad sick." She paused and pronounced, "You're dead!"

"Oh, I'm bad sick and now I'm dead" reiterated the therapist.

For the third time, Audrey listened to the therapist's chest with the stethoscope, and this time remained right by the therapist's knee and said, "You're okay now. You can leave. You can go out."

The therapist smiled and replied, "Oh, I'm all right and I can leave now."

### John

John, four years old, spent the initial fifteen minutes of his first play session exploring the play therapy room. He tried on the firefighter hat and the cowhand hat ("just like the one at Miss Ann's" [his daycare teacher]). He played briefly with the colored markers, the telephones, the Lego blocks, the dollhouse, and the playdough, which he labeled "mud." John's language at times slipped into very babyish speech patterns: "I'm little baby John . . . Coo ca coo. . . . I'm not nothing. . . . Pooh, pooh. . . . I like my little baby, John, coo ca coo."

John returned to the table where he had left the playdough. He took two tiny baby doll figures and pushed their feet into the playdough, saying, "He's got his feet in the mud and he doesn't want to get out—never." The therapist reflected this commentary back to John. John pushed the baby figure further in the playdough and said, "The baby is down to his butt in the mud. . . . He's way, way, way, way down in the mud." The therapist again restated the child's play and comments. Pushing the babies further into the "mud," John shouted, "Pooh, pooh," and began jumping around the room, banging on the toy shelves, throwing the farmer hat and yelling.

The therapist observed, "you get excited when you put those babies way down in the 'mud.'"

John stopped the frantic play and declared, "Now I'm going to get them out." He returned to the table and began taking the babies in and out of the playdough. He commented, "They have a mess on them. . . . It's yucky mud. . . . It's green. . . . I've never seen green mud . . . Baby wants to get out, . . . Mr. Policeman! . . . Policemen are nice. . . . They are strong. . . . It's a mud jungle." John's play gradually increased in intensity and he began moving the babies more quickly in and out of the "mud." "Help me. Help me. Help me," he kept repeating. As he removed one baby, he said, "Thank you. . . . Help my baby brother. . . . Thank you, baby brother." Taking a plastic knife he cut the playdough, explaining, "I am going to cut up that mud. . . . You bad mud. . . . Don't you do my babies that way. I don't like you. . . . He's crying. . . . One time I saw Santa Claus mud cry."

The therapist replied, 'Mmmmhh sounds like you have seen lots of different things."

John turned to the therapist, smiled an engaging smile and said, "I want you to play with me." The therapist smiled back and nodded. Again, John repeated a similar fantasy scene. This time, the baby figures were pushed down in the "mud" and covered with the playdough can. His running dialogue got louder and louder: "Help get us out of here, coo, ca. . . . Get me out of here. Get me out of here! Get me out of here! Get me out of here!!! I'm mad at you. . . . I'll cut you up! The mud wants me to cut him up." John continued cutting the "mud" until all the playdough was cut into many tiny pieces. He then turned from the table, put on the farmer hat, picked up the stethoscope, and began examining the therapist's eyes and ears.

## Meaning in Play

As therapists, what do we make of all this play? Clinicians are always in the process of experiencing the play of their clients for diagnostic, interpretative, and evaluative purposes. Play is children's natural mode of communication (Axline, 1947). Young children do not possess the needed degree of language ability or cognitive skills to communicate with such an abstract means as words

(Piaget, 1951). Toys are their words, and play is their symbolic language of self-expression (Ginott, 1982). Like speech and social living, play develops from the child's encounter with the environment (Behar & Rapoport, 1983). Moustakas (1953) described play as an expression of the child's emotional inner world. According to Frank (1976), even if play becomes warped, stunted, or distorted, play remains creative because children are actively constructing their own unique life space by imposing meaning, form, and significance on situations and relating themselves to those self-imposed meanings in their own idiosyncratic way.

Because play offers a unique psychological tool for viewing the world through the eyes of the child, what did Audrey and John tell about themselves? Three months prior to beginning play therapy, Audrey's father was involved in an automobile accident in which one man died and her father suffered near fatal injuries. Audrey's father had spent the past three months in the intensive care unit in a hospital 60 miles from home. He had a series of operations and skin grafts and had been confined in an area in the hospital where Audrey was not permitted to enter. Audrey's mother had spent most of the time at the bedside of her husband. Audrey was staying with an aunt and saw her mother only occasionally.

Audrey had visited her father in the hospital for the first time two days prior to the recorded session. Her father had a tube in his nose for feeding purposes, an intravenous tube in his arm, a tracheal opening in his neck, bandages on his body and face, and was breathing with the help of a respirator. At the time of the hospital visit, the doctor said Audrey's father would have to spend 6 more weeks in the hospital.

In the playroom, Audrey was playing out her experiences, as well as her feelings, understandings, attitudes, and desires about her life experiences. If the therapist had asked Audrey to verbally describe what it was like for her mother and father to be gone for 12 weeks, it is doubtful she would or could have said, "I am so lonely. Sometimes I think my daddy is dead and I'm afraid." If Audrey had been questioned about her visit to the hospital, she may not have been able to describe the experience. Through play, however, she could become the doctor and pronounce others sick, or dead, or even well enough to leave the hospital. She could do to others what had been done to her. She was no longer the passive participant; Audrey was the active designer and ended the story as she hoped and dreamed.

John had been referred for play therapy as a result of suspected sexual abuse at a childcare center. John's mother also reported that John had talked about"real people being mean" and about his fear of being "trapped." During the week following the session described, John told his mother about his teacher making fun of him when he soiled his pants, tying him naked to his chair, and getting him to suck on her breast "cause I was a baby." In his own creative way, John was expressing his inner emotional life, his life space as he perceived it.

In a symbolic manner, John reenacted his abuse. He stuck the babies in the "mud" just as he had been "stuck" or tied to his chair in his dirty pants. His cry for help to the "policeman," and his plea for justice to "not do my babies that way" were John's deep longings for safety and protection. Direct verbal expressions of those longings are beyond the capabilities of a child his age but are easily enacted through fantasy play. Even the act of minutely cutting the "yucky mud" was an act of destroying the mess he was in. He no longer experienced the role of the victim. Rather, he took control and felt empowered through the play.

## PLAY THERAPY OBSERVATION INSTRUMENT

Empirical research in the area of play therapy remains sparse, due, in part, to a lack of objective behavioral instruments (James, 1977). Because children's play is highly variable and directly affected by the immediate situation, the use of an observational instrument of play therapy activities can add information and understanding to children's therapy activities and thereby enable therapists to be more sensitive and therapeutically responsive to children's statements about themselves and about their world. The Play Therapy Observational Instrument (PTOI), developed by Howe and Silvern (1981) and adapted by Perry (1988–1989), is a rating scale of play therapy behavior, which offers therapists a useful and readily usable tool for codifying behavior in the playroom.

Howe and Silvern (1981) initially constructed a 31-item rating instrument as a result of an extensive review of the literature in which they identified behaviors described as indicators of important clinical concepts. The results of Howe and Silvern's study indicated that 13 of the 31 behaviors were scored with an inter-rater agreement within a 1-point range of 80% or better and with an intraclass correlation of at least .48 across seventy-six 12-minute play segments.

Those reliable scores also formed three theoretically meaningful subscales, which are similar to dimensions of playroom behavior outlined by major schools of play therapy as important to psychodiagnosis, therapy process, and outcome. The subscales of the PTOI are social inadequacy, emotional discomfort, and use of fantasy. Table 11.1 contains the behaviors included in each of the three subscales of the PTOI. A maladjustment subscale was also evident and consisted of all the behavioral items in the social inadequacy subscale and all but one item—"talk about worries and troublesome events"—of the emotional discomfort subscale. Because the maladjustment subscale represented an overlap of behaviors in the other subscales, the maladjustment subscale was omitted in this chapter.

The reader might find it helpful to peruse the PTOI Rating Form in the appendix at the end of this chapter, as a means of providing a structure through which to interpret and integrate the content of the PTOI subscales described and illustrated in the following section. The number in parentheses following each behavior corresponds to the item's PTOI rating form number.

### Social Inadequacy Subscale

**Use of Incoherent or Bizarre Content (1).**   This item assesses children's ability to express themselves understandably and coherently or to conceptual-

---

**TABLE 11.1. Behavioral items of selected PTOI subscales**

---

Social inadequacy subscale
1. Incoherent or bizarre content(1)
2. Therapist excluded from activities (2)
3. Therapist's interventions met with hostility or withdrawal (3)
4. Body stiffness(12)

Emotional discomfort subscale
1. Quality and intensity of affect—mood (4)
2. Aggression toward the therapist (5)
3. Conflicted play (10)
4. Playdisruption (11)
5. Talk about worries and troublesome events (13)

Use fantasy play subscale
1. Abrupt fluctuations between fantasy and reality(6)
2. Time spent concentrating play on characters rather than things (7)
3. Variations in fantasy story scenes (8)
4. Qualitatively different fantasy role (9)

---

*Note.*The parenthetical numerals following each item refer to the item numbers appearing in the PTOI rating form in the Appendix to this chapter.

ize the world in a way that is not so repugnant or bizarre as to be unfathomable. Comprehensible play sequences would be composed of a chain of thought expressed in a readily grasped manner. Disjoined, psychotic-like trains of thought would be judged incoherent or bizarre. Examples of bizarre play would include a child doing things such as pretending to eat feces or a baby brother's head, screaming at the sight of a puppet's face, claiming that the eyes were the eyes of a monster who is sucking out the child's heart. The distinguishing element of bizarre behavior is that the play is statistically infrequent and would be considered very grotesque and pathological if it occurred in an adult's fantasy. Examples of play therapy behaviors indicative of this dimension follow:

> Lon played out a story of a boy who meets a witch who grants him his wish. He wished for the ants to stop chewing up his heart and intestines and throwing up all over his head.

> Lewis began playing with the school bus, saying, "Go to school, kids. Go away. No, stop. Pointed nails, eyeballs, stop biting. What' that? Got'em dead. Go ahead. Stop."

**Therapist Excluded from the Child's Activities (2).** This item rates children's unwillingness to interact with the therapist. Such refusal of social interaction hinders children's social growth and their learning of social skills and perspective of others. Examples of exclusion of the therapist would be a child hiding behind the easel, silently staring out the window, or playing in a manner that prevents the therapist from seeing the play activity. Other examples are a child's solitary play or avoidance of any play activity. Interventions initiated by the therapist are not considered behavior depicting therapist's inclusion in the child's activity. Activities structured to include the therapist would entail the therapist playing a character in a play, being the audience for a puppet show, and being a participant in a game or verbal exchange. Commentary by the child describing what he or she is doing in the playroom or sharing with the therapist some experience, thoughts, or concerns would also be examples of including the therapist in the play activities. Examples of play therapy behaviors indicative of this dimension follow:

> Ryan took the army men and equipment to the sandbox and said to the therapist, "You take these men and things and set up your camp on this side."

> Jane moved about the room, picking up many of the toys and commenting, "I have one of these at home. . . . Lynn has this. . . . I know how to do this. I'm going to paint a rainbow message."

> Jacob sat on the floor with the army men arranged in a battlefield setting. He positioned himself with his back to the therapist and did not respond, verbally or nonverbally, to the therapist's comments.

> Ryan and Jane have included the therapist; Jacob has not.

## Therapist's Interventions Met with Rejection, Hostility, or Withdrawal (3).

This item rates children's use of hostility toward the therapist's interventions as a defense against exploration of their feelings and conflicts. Verbal rejection would be denying that an interpretation of reflection is true, telling the therapist to shut up, or screaming or banging on the drums to drown out the therapist's intervention. Ignoring the therapist's reflections or interpretations are not rated as rejections except when the children are asked questions or are given alternative behavioral outlets, such as shooting the darts at the "Bop Bag" or the target rather than shooting the therapist. Behavioral rejection would be trying to hit or throw something at the therapist, or making a mess when the therapist insisted that the therapy time was up and the child must leave the room. Examples of play therapy behaviors indicative of this dimension follow:

> Jake was headed for the Bop Bag with the hammer and a nail. The therapist said, "You would like to hammer that nail into that Bop Bag, but that bag is not for nailing. That block of wood is for nailing." Jake screamed, "Shut up, you S.O.B." He then put his hands over his ears.

> Jeremy screamed, yelled, and kicked the therapist when she restrained him from leaving the playroom. He ran around the room, throwing toys at the therapist, and clearing the toy shelves with huge sweeps of his arm.

## Degree of Body Stiffness (12).

This item evaluates the stiffness in fine and gross body movements. The general constrictiveness of the child's movements and general level of rigidness of the child during the session are key factors to be assessed. Examples of play therapy behaviors indicative of this dimension follow:

> Laurie spent ten minutes standing in the middle of the room, turning slowly around, her eyes scanning the room and the toys but never touching any toy. Layne stood close by the therapist, talking quite rapidly, yet standing very still and erect. Even when Layne moved more into the playroom, his body was stiff and controlled.

### Emotional Discomfort Subscale

**Quality and Intensity of Affect (4).**   The overall emotional temperament of the child during the play segment is assessed in this behavior. This is not a rating of the types of emotional conflict that are depicted in the play or speech but rather the affect of the child while expressing and experiencing the play enactment. For instance, children could be working through very angry feelings toward their siblings but still be in an extremely elated mood while doing so. Dysphoric feelings are generally acknowledged as unpleasant and would include anxiety, fear, anger, frustration, and sadness. Children who display flat affect—that is, children who do not readily reveal their inner feelings—are rated the highest score on this behavior item. Examples of play therapy behaviors indicative of this dimension follow:

> Jo picked up the baby doll, then dressed and fed the baby, and then began to fuss at the doll because the baby would not sit still and cried all the time. Jo scolded, "You're a bad child. I'm going to have to spank you, you bad girl." Jo then spanked the baby repeatedly. She grinned broadly and laughed and seemed to enjoy punishing the baby. (The child would be rated as experiencing positive affect while portraying a play sequence containing conflict.)

> Wayne had the father doll throw the furniture all around the dollhouse. The father doll then hit all the other dolls one by one. His face and body showed no emotion. His affect was flat.

**Aggression Toward the Therapist (5).**   This item assesses children's use of aggression as a defense for protecting themselves from close human contact, exploration of more frightening impulses and desires, and feeling of frustration. Expressions of aggression may be couched in fantasy play, as when the therapist becomes the "bad guy" and gets "killed to death" with the cowboy guns by a puppet. Aggressive behaviors are categorized as either high- or low-level aggression. Verbal hostility or undermining the playroom limits, such as pouring sand on the floor, are examples of low-level aggression. Overt hostility, such as physically attacking the therapist, is rated a high-level expression of aggression. This item rates children's aggression directed toward the therapist, not the general level of aggression.

Examples of play therapy behaviors indicative of this dimension follow:

> Danny did not want to stay in the playroom. He screamed and yelled. He cursed the therapist and threw a pot from the stove at her. He kicked her leg and bit her hand when she prevented him from leaving. (In this example, the child's screaming, yelling, and cursing would have been rated as low-level aggression. The physical assault on the therapist would be rated as high-level aggression.)

> Jane picked up the machine gun, pointed the gun at the therapist, and pulled the trigger again and again. She then took the dart gun and shot the therapist with a dart. The therapist said, "I am not for shooting. I know you would really like to shoot me, but I'm not for shooting with the dart gun. You can shoot me with the machine gun, or you could pretend that the Bop Bag is me and shoot me there." Janie grinned, loaded the dart gun, aimed at the therapist and fired again. (Shooting the therapist with the machine gun is considered a symbolic expression of aggression. A high-level expression of aggression was evident as Janie broke a known playroom limit and shot the therapist the second time with the dart gun.)

**Frequency with which Behaviors are Expressive of Conflict (10).**   This dimension of behavior assesses children's ability and willingness to communicate attitudes and feelings about their problems through speech and play activities and to permit their behavior to be directed by their conflicts. Play that permits the therapist to perceive something of the child's issues or conflicts would be included in connection with this item. The issues might be from the symbolic and original nature of the play themes, as well as the conversation and emotions of the fantasy characters. Another example would be children communicating their experience of conflicts in real life events. Ritualized play and stereotyped speech would not be considered an example of this behavior. Speech and play more idiosyncratic to the child's personality and expressing strong dysphoric feelings would be considered expressing of conflicts. Examples of play therapy behavior indicative of this dimension follow:

> Jan fantasized a story theme in which the mother was constantly working and directing others. The father in the story was always working at the office, promising to be home and to help with the work, but never following through. The mom would scold the father and finally said, "I don't believe a word of what you say, Herbert Evarts. You never keep your word. I can't depend on you anymore."

> Jennie told the therapist about Johnny, who was her boyfriend at school. She said, "He's sexy and he likes to see my 'private part' but I can't tell Mom cause you know what she'd do. She would get real mad."

**Frequency and Degree of Play Disruption (11).**   This behavioral item assesses how children are able to use fantasy and reality-based play to protect themselves from anxiety disruptions that might be inherent in the painful content of the play activity. Erikson (1963) defined play disruption as the "sudden and complete diffuse inability to play" (p. 223). He believed that play disruption occurred when the subject matter of the play suddenly becomes too painful for the child. Children seem to switch from the *microsphere*, the play world in which they are immersed, to the world shared with others, the *macrosphere.* The anxiety that surrounds this switch leads to the cessation of the child's play and is the key factor in distinguishing play disruption. The signs to look for are points where the child is intensively involved in play and abruptly stops at a point that appears to be especially threatening for the child. Facial expressions suggestive of fear or despair, stiffening of the body, staring into space, sudden concern with realistic aspects of the environment, sudden interest in unrelated objects, and request to leave the room, are behaviors that might indicate play disruption. Examples of play therapy behaviors indicative of this dimension follow:

> Mattie enacted a scene of a house full of sleeping people. She stuck the heads of the toy tiger and the elephant in the window of the house and made them roar. Mattie then made the little girl doll jump out of the house and fall onto the trucks that were setting out across the room. Mattie abruptly went to the easel and painted a rainbow. Fifteen minutes later, she returned to the dollhouse with a She-Ra doll, who saved the animals from being killed by the people in the house.

> Mack had spent two minutes trying to make the Slinky® somersault down the building block staircase he had constructed. He gradually appeared more anxious and uncomfortable. He suddenly jumped up and said, "I have to go to the bathroom."

**Talk About Worries and Troublesome Events (13).** This behavioral item assesses the frequency with which the child talks about negative feelings and troubles in the first person without the protection of fantasy play. The child must use personal pronouns, such as I, my daddy, my sister, my teacher, and so on. Examples of play therapy behaviors indicative of this dimension follow:

> Joe tried to open the jar of fingerpaint and failed to do so and said, "I can't open this jar. I don't know how."

> Jennifer told about going to the beach with her school class and picking up shells and walking on the beach for hours. She then said in a very soft voice, "They (her classmates) all laughed at me because I couldn't keep up with them. Nobody really likes me. That's okay. I don't like them either!"

## *Use of Fantasy Subscale*

**Time Spent in Fantasy Play Versus Reality Play (6).** The make-believe, dramatic nature of the play characterizes the fantasy form of play. In fantasy play, children construct a story, either pretending to be a character or using dolls or other toys to symbolically represent characters or props in the scene. At times, children may even portray parts of themselves or of significant people in their lives in their stories. Often, the theme of the fantasy can be symbolic of children's conflicts in real life. Fantasy play provides children with a protection from directly acknowledging their conflicts, feelings, attitudes, and impulses, which might be too threatening for them to express directly. Reality play would include telling the therapist about an experience, playing with the bowling set, shooting at the dartboard. For example, the children would be rated as being engaged in fantasy if, during bowling, they kept score for themselves and the therapist and then presented the winner with a trophy. If children move a plane around the room and make sounds like an engine, they would be rated as being engaged in fantasy play. Examples of play therapy behaviors indicative of this dimension follow:

> Emily played in the sandbox, slowly sifting the sand through the strainer into the bucket. She then filled the food cans with sand and the syrup bottle with water and made a "secret recipe." (The first part would be rated reality play and the latter part would be rated fantasy play.)

> Allan took the dragon and monster puppets and had them shake hands, bow to each other, and then fight until the monster killed the dragon. Though no verbalization accompanied the play scene, the imagination was evidence that fantasy was presented.

## Time Spent Concentrating Play or Speech on Characters Rather Than on Things (7).

This item assesses the degree to which children choose activities that facilitate or avoid working on interpersonal or familial concerns. Examples of play concentrated on things would be throwing the ball, painting a picture without people or animals, building a block building, or setting up the dollhouse furniture but including no dolls, animals, or puppets. Behavior concentrated on characters would be conversations about family or personal experiences, playing with dolls or animals, taking a role, or playing a game with the therapist. Examples of play therapy behavior indicative of this dimension follow:

> Bill spent ten minutes very carefully arranging and rearranging the army equipment into two sets of army camps in the sandbox. He did not introduce any of the soldiers into the scene, nor did any of the equipment portray any action or sounds. Bill's behavior concentrated entirely on inanimate objects. He gave no indication of his beliefs or emotions in any interpersonal situation.

> Zella arranged the dollhouse furniture as though she was the mover. She took the doll family and played out a story of a family moving into a new house. In contrast to Bill's behavior, Zella's play gave the therapist an opportunity to see the child's conceptualitzation of her family's reaction to moving into a new house and her portrayal of how she would behave if she were the furniture mover.

**Number of Variations of Fantasy Stories and Scenes (8).** This behavior measures the degree to which children use fantasy to work on various aspects of a problem. A *story* would be a dramatic account of two or more events with one or more characters. A *scene* is dramatic portrayal of an event or a specific circumstance. Two scenes are part of the same story if one or more characters are the same or if an episode is the logical sequence of another. In order to score children as enacting two different stories, the episodes portrayed would need different plots and different characters. Examples of play therapy behavior indicative of this dimension follow:

> Wanda enacted a family moving into a new house, the children enrolling in a new school, and the father and mother going to work and leaving the children at home to take care of themselves. This enactment would be rated as one story with three scenes.

> Terry enacted a story of a mother taking care of the baby and the father going to the store for some groceries. Terry then became Cinderella and had to clean and cook for the wicked witch and the stepsisters. Such a portrayal would be rated as two different stories being presented.

**Number of Qualitatively Different Fantasy Roles (9).** This item evaluates the degree to which children learn to see their conflicts from different perspectives and their willingness and ability to identify with various positions and attitudes. The enactment of roles involves a dramatic impersonation through physical or verbal portrayal, or using toys in a symbolic portrayal. A *role* can be as broad as an aggressor, criminal, or victim, or as specific as a sister or teacher. In order to be rated as portraying two roles, children must pretend two different attitudes, such as a dinosaur and a little child being killed by the dinosaur. If the child pretends to be a dinosaur, a tiger, and a monster, the child would be assessed as identifying with one role—the role of the aggressor. Examples of play therapy behaviors indicative of this dimension follow:

> Adam put four of the "scary monsters"—snake, spider, dinosaur, and wolf—in the sandbox. He took the army bomber, the cowboy pistol, the knife, the machine gun, and the rope, and killed each monster with a different weapon. Adam was a marine, a sheriff, Rambo, a policeman, and a soldier. Adam was playing the part of one role: the aggressor.

> David placed the dolls representing mother, father, brother, and baby in the car and played out a scene of a camping trip to the lake. With a noticeable change in his voice, he spoke for each family member as the story progressed. David would be rated as portraying four characters.

### Using the PTOI

The PTOI was designed to be used in rating 12-minute segments of a videotaped play therapy session. Though the instrument has not been used in research settings via the direct observation of an ongoing session, such a use would be a logical step in the development of this scale. The rater views a 12-minute segment and then selects a descriptive number that best represents the frequency and/or intensity of the child's play behavior as represented in each subscale item (see scale in the appendix at the end of this chapter). The authors of this chapter found that, as a segment was viewed, a stopwatch was needed to record the time involved in some behaviors, such as Items 1, 2, 6, 7, and 10, and tally marks were needed to indicate the frequency of other behavioral items, such as Items 3, 5, 6, 8, 9, 11, and 13. The following is a description and a verbatim transcript of a 12-minute segment of an initial 36-minute play therapy session with a seven-year-old girl who was experiencing very poor school performance, unsatisfactory peer relations, and a disruptive family life. "C" is used for the child's name, and "T" for the therapist's name. The transcript begins 12 minutes into the session.

**A Case Example.**   C went to the stove and ran her hand over the top as she talked to T. C talked quite softly, and her hands moved constantly as she talked. Her eyes moved furtively around the room and frequently checked with T as she talked.

C:  Last time, when I was here (*the experience C referred to is unknown because C had not been seen in play therapy prior to this session*), I cooked things and had things and something like that, I made cookies, sold them . . . something like that. But I was scared to death. (Opens the door to the oven.) We had one of these. We had a 'frigerator we played with, too.

T:  So you have seen one of those things before, too!

C:  I've seen lots of things. One of my friends in my classroom . . . his name is Jeffrey. . . . He loves dinosaurs.

T:  Oh. (*C looks at T and smiles broadly.*)You think you would really like them.

C:  Someone stole one of his dinosaurs…at the party. (*C goes to shelf and places her hands on the xylophone.*) I used to have one, but I can't find it (*Takes the xylophone to the stovetop*)

T:  Sometimes things get lost.

C:  (*Plays the xylophone.*) Also lost that little thing that . . . I don't know what it was . . . er, er. (*C looks around the room, then points to Slinky toy on a shelf.*) You've got the same thing!

T:  Oh, you see one over there, too.

C:  Yeah. I'll find it. (*C looks around in other parts of the room.*) I think you have it! (*C sways nervously, with her hand over her mouth.*)

T:  (*T apparently misunderstood the child.*) You're looking around to see if there might be something else.

C:  (*Walks to a toy shelf and pats the Slinky.*) See here it is. I had one of those. Someone took it or stole it. I lost it.

T: You were kind of disappointed when that happened. (*C returns to the xylophone and plays a recognizable tune.*) You know just how to make that work.

C: (*Plays the musical scale on the xylophone, double-sounding the scale—first a harmonious tune, then a tune that is not harmonious.*) Uh! Somebody doesn't know how it works, and she goes like that. (*Giggles*)

T: Kinda funny to you.

C: Yeah, kinda funny. (*C puts xylophone back to the original spot on the shelf, goes to the easel and touches the paint brushes.*) Can I take these and paint on this (*indicating the easel*)?

T: In here, you can decide.

C: No . . . ah. . . . er. (*Walks stiffly and slowly around the room.*)

T: Sometimes, it's hard to decide.

C: Yeah. (*Pointing to the puppet stage and looking at the puppets lying on the shelf.*) Are these the puppets that [are] suppose to go with that?

T: In here, you can decide what to do with those.

C: I like this one. (*Puts a female puppet with yellow hair . . . to be designated as P1 . . . on her right hand.*)

T: You found one you really liked.

C: Yeah. I've got his little one at my house, and he plays like this. (C puts puppet behind her back and sways as she talks.) I kind of talk back to it, too. And at Pete's house, too.

T: Sounds like you really like to do that.

C: Yeah. (*Goes behind the puppet stage.*) I'm going to hide it.

T: Oh, so you're going where I can't see you.

C: Nope, you can't see me. (*Giggles.*) I can see me.

T: But you know you're back there.

C as P1: (*Pokes P1 past the stage curtain.*) Hello.

T: Oh, I see somebody.

C/P1: (*Moves puppet as she role plays*) My name is Cindy. Is anybody else out there?

T: You're just wondering if anybody is out there watching?

C/P1: (*C speaks a sentence or two too softly to be heard.*) I'll tell you a story.

T: Sounds like you would really like to tell me a story.

C: Once upon a time, there was an old ghost. Every day, he went "Boo!" and that scared everybody out of the house. . . . Well I'm going to tell my friends. (*C reaches for Puppet 2.*) Sorry she's not here. So if you'll hold my station. . . . Don't worry, I'll be here in a minute.

T: Sounds like you've got an idea for what to do next. (*C leaves P1 hanging on the stage ledge. Working behind the curtain, C puts P2 on her right hand.*)

C/P2: Looks like someone's coming to see me today. So I need to go get somebody so I can play my game. Let's see . . . er . . . ah . . . yeah. Let's see if she'll come now or not. (*Whispers*) Let's see. Be quiet she might come now. (*C pulls P1 behind the curtain and places her on her left hand.*)

T: Sounds like something's going on.

C/P1: (*From backstage*) Shhh! (*Excitedly announces*) She's coming!

T: She's coming (*P1 and P2 appear in front of the curtain.*)

C/P2: My name is Ducky. My hair is red. (*In point of fact, the puppet's hair is black, but T's hair is red.*)

C/P1: I better go get lunch.

C/P2: Okay.

C/P1: Have to go. Bye, bye. (*P1 exits.*)

C/P2: Bye. Oh, this is an old friend of mine that everybody plays [with] in our story. So ready to go? On with the story. Deejay, Deejay (*P2 says two or three nonsense words and turns to see P1 exit*). Bye, Francie. Well, I have an old friend of mine (*reaches for another puppet*). She's almost like a sister like me but you can't tell cause er . . . ah . . . there's not a lot of people. (Takes P2 backstage.) So if you'll hold your attention, she may be out soon . . . in a minute.

T: So if I'm patient, I'll get to see you. (*P2 and P3 enter.*)

C/P3: Hello.

C/P2: I called you, Randolph.

C/P3: Oh, I use that name. I didn't know. I was in a meeting. I didn't know if you called my name or not. My hair is a mess. My hair is red. (*P3 does have red hair.*)

C/P2: I better get going to jury duty, too. (*P2 exits.*)

C/P3: (*Turns to watch P2 exit.*) Who was that? (*P3 moves to the opposite side of the stage from T.*) What's your name? I have an old friend, Johnny. Hmmm, hmmm. (*Moves close to T.*) What's your name?

T: My name is Peggy.

C/P3: (*P3 sways, bows head, moves furtively, hides face with hands, and speaks in an Elmer Fudd sounding voice*). Gosh, I like that name. Wish I had a pretty name like that.

T: You really like that name.

C/P3: (*Excitedly*) Yeah, yeah! (*Very softly*) Can I have a picture of you? You look pretty.

T: Hmm, you would even like to have my picture.

C/P3: Yeah, yeah. Well I need to go. I need to get . . . (*C reaches for another puppet.*)

T: Sounds like you have something to do. (*C lays P3 on ledge of the stage as she puts P4 on her hand. She then puts P3 back on. Both puppets are behind the curtain.*)

C/P3: (*P3 is heard from backstage.*) She wears glasses, too.

T: So some people have glasses.

C/P3: She wears real glasses. Here she comes. (*P4 appears in front of curtain.*)

C/P4: Oh, hi. (*Speaks rather slowly and with some hesitation*) I'm not a beautiful lady. We . . . I wear this pretty hat 'cause it's soooo pretty. Well, I love it because my grandmother gave it to me, but it's for boys though. I look like a boy too with glasses.

T: So even though it's for boys, a girl can wear it if she...

C/P4: (*interrupting*) Yeah, well I have to leave here pretty soon. I must go. Some. . . . Sorry.

C/P3: (*Turns and heads backstage, calling*) Oliva, Oliva!

C/P4: (*Annoyed*) What do you want?

C/P3: (*From backstage*) Someone's out there to see you.

C/P4: (*Sounding pleased*) Someone out there to see me. Well, I'll be right back. (*P4 exits.*)

A puppet off stage: I think Oliva died. (*P5 is thrown from backstage to the floor in front of the puppet stage.*) Oh! She died!!

T: Ummm, somebody died. (*P1 and P4 reappear.*)

C/P1: Oh no!! She died!

C/P1 and C/P4: (*Hugging and clasping each other in sorrow and wailing*) Waaaa,waaaaah! (*P1 and P4 disappear behind the curtain.*)

T: You think that would be real sad.

C/P1 and C/P4: (*P3 is thrown from backstage onto the floor. P1 and P4 reenter, crying.*) Oh, no Brownie died, too! What are we going to do? Waaaah!

T: Somebody else died. (*P1 and P4 go behind curtain again.*)

C/P4: No, no! Someone's in the house! Waaaa, waaah! (*P4 is thrown onto the floor in front of the puppet stage.*)

C/P1: (*Reappears crying.*) Waaa, waaah!

C/P1: (*Exits and from backstage screams*) Quick, quick. Gotta get. . . . Yaaaaaah! (*P1 is thrown onto the floor.*)

C: (*From backstage, using her own voice and laughing nervously*) Too late!

T: Looks like they all died.

C: (*C sticks head out between the stage curtains.*) The end.

C plays the xylophone in a random manner, then a scale, followed by a double-stroked scale, and then the scale up and down. She then plays a melody that sounds like a familiar children's song.

T: You know how to play some songs on it, too. (*C smiles.*) You really like to play.

C: (*Using a long block in place of the xylophone mallets*) I can do it with this.

T: Hmmmm, you figured out another way to do it.

C: (*Picks up cymbals*) What are these? These are things drummers have. Hmmmm. (*Taps cymbals lightly together.*) I'd like to do it loud.

T: You would really like to do that.

C: Yeah.

T: Well, you can decide.

C: (*In an incredulous voice*) Loud?

(*C hesitates then lays the cymbals back on the shelf.*)

T: You were really kind of wondering if I thought it (*banging the cymbals loudly*) might be okay.

C goes across the room and begins to stack the cardboard bricks one on top of the other.

## PTOI RATING OF THE CASE EXAMPLE

The PTOI requires the rater also to view the child's play, so some limitations are inherent in presenting only a verbatim account and then evaluating the play segment, which also considers nonverbal behaviors. A number value representing the chosen response for each behavior and an accompanying explanation of the reasoning underlying the choices are as follows (see PTOI scale items in the appendix at end of this chapter):

Item 1. Bizarre content/incomprehensible play sequence. Rating = 1. Though there were points in the child's dialogue that were difficultto follow, the difficulty seems to rest in the child's anxiety level rather than in any manifested psychotic train of thought.

Item 2. Exclusion of the therapist. Rating = 1. C included the therapist for nearly the whole time by means of sharing her experiences, asking directions, telling a story, and staging a play.

Item 3. Rejection of interventions. Rating = 1. None of the therapist's interventions were denied by the child. On the contrary, there was a preponderance of "yeah" in response to T's commentary.

Item 4.   Mood.Rating = 4. This behavior requires visual input to determine the item's appropriate rating number. Occasionally, when playing the xylophone, C appeared uneasy and uncertain, and she giggled at points in her play that indicated a degree of anxiety, such as when all the puppets died. There was evidence of both pleasant and dysphoric emotions.

Item 5.   Aggression toward the therapist. Rating = 1. Though C accused T of taking her thing, C never directed aggression toward the therapist.

Item 6.   Time spent in fantasy versus reality. Rating = 3. To rate this item, the session must be viewed and a record of time spent in reality and fantasy noted. C spent 5½ minutes in reality play and 6½ minutes in fantasy. Because a rating of 4 states that the child must clearly spend more time in fantasy, the third statement on this scale item would be the more accurate descriptor of C's play.

Item 7.   Time spent on characters rather than on things. Rating = 5. C spent nearly the entire time talking about herself, her experiences and friends, and on the characters in the fantasy play. Only during the brief occasions when C played the xylophone did she concentrate on things. Even as C played, she made comments about people, such as "she played like this" and "I can do this."

Item 8.   Fantasy scenes and stories. Rating = 3. This behavioral item presented some difficulty for discriminating stories versus scenes in stories. The parade of puppet characters certainly suggests a series of scenes within one story theme. The story within a story might be suggested in the form of the "ghost story" and could be viewed as two separate story themes. The conclusion of the series of puppet vignettes in which there is something scary and all the puppets die, however, suggests a similar type of theme, so the third descriptor statement was selected for this item.

Item 9.   Number of roles. Rating = 5. Though C used puppets in her story, most puppet characters appeared to have similar characteristics. The roles identified were the ghost storyteller and other similar "sister" types of characters, the ghost, the dying victims, and finally the mourners. Four different positions were portrayed, so response 5 was selected.

Item 10.  Behavior expressive of conflict. Rating = 4. C's play presented a series of conflicts (e.g., "I was scared to death." "Someone stole his dinosaur at the party." "I lost my thing.I think you took it." "The ghost went 'Boo.'" "I'm not a beautiful lady." "That's a silly joke." "No, no.That's not the way you do it." "She died. Waaa, waaa! What will we do? They all died. That's too sad. They all died on the same day.").

Item 11.  Play disruption. Rating = 1. This behavior must be determined in part through observing the child's level of anxiety and noting any sudden switch in play activity or inability to continue on a particular theme. Though C's play included many instances where anxiety was exhibited, she continued her play activity and reached a satisfactory resolution in each play representation.

Item 12. Body stiffness. Rating = 2. Visual evaluation is essential in rating this behavior. C appeared stiff and constricted in her body movements prior to and following her fantasy play. Fantasy seemed to offer C a mechanism for self-expression without feelings of self-consciousness.

Item 13. Negative talk about self, feelings, or worries. Rating = 4. Negative statements and expressions of worries appeared in the following examples: "I was scared to death." "Someone stole it. I lost it." "I can't get this (puppet) on." "That's too sad."

The number values, which precede the descriptor that best describes each behavioral item composing a particular subscale of the PTOI, are summed to determine a subscale score. Howe and Silvern (1981) also suggested that all the items on the emotional subscale and the social inadequacy subscale, with the exception of Item 13, "negative talk about self," can be combined to form a maladjusted subscale.

Table 11.2 contains C's rater-determined raw scores for each behavioral item, the range of scores possible for each item, the sum of C's raw scores for each subscale, and the possible range of scores for each subscale. Standard scores and norms have not been obtained, due to the limited research using the PTOI. Examination of the ratings given to C's play, however, provides much informa-

**TABLE 11.2. C's PTOI subscale scores as determined by raters**

| PTOI Subscale | C's Scores | Range of Scores Possible |
|---|---|---|
| Social inadequacy | | |
|   Bizarre content | 1 | 1–5 |
|   Therapist excluded | 1 | 1–5 |
|   Interventions met with hostility | 1 | 1–5 |
|   Body stiffness | 2 | 1–3 |
|   Total | 5 | 4–18 |
| Emotional discomfort | | |
|   Mood | 4 | 1–6 |
|   Aggression toward therapist | 1 | 1–5 |
|   Conflictual play and speech | 4 | 1–5 |
|   Play disruption | 1 | 1–5 |
|   Talk about worries | 4 | 1–4 |
|   Total | 14 | 5–25 |
| Use of fantasy | | |
|   Time spent in fantasy vs. reality | 3 | 1–5 |
|   Time spent on characters vs. things | 5 | 1–5 |
|   Number of stories/scenes | 3 | 1–5 |
|   Number of roles | 5 | 1–5 |
|   Total | 16 | 4–20 |

tion for detailed assessment of the child, planning of therapeutic treatment, and prognosis.

C's score on the social inadequacy subscale indicates the child's frequent use of social interaction to deal with her life situation. She presented herself as a compliant child, eager for the social support of the therapist, yet her body stiffness expressed a noticeable degree of uneasiness. C will probably respond in a positive manner rather rapidly to the therapist's warm and accepting attention during play sessions. It can be noted, as is often the case, that compliant, socially dependent children will also express a high degree of conflict in their play. Feelings of dependency are most often accompanied by feelings of anger, as children's sense of inadequacy fan the fires of uncertainty and self-doubt, which hide beneath the surface of apparent complicity.

The score on the emotional discomfort subscale reflects the degree to which C is willing to disguise her emotions, displaying little affect even in the midst of frequent talk about her worries and negative experiences. Her affect appeared split from her cognition. Her mood did not match her words except when she was in fantasy. In fantasy, her characters displayed a wide range of emotions—surprise, shock, happiness, fear, pleasure, sadness, and anger.

The score on the use of fantasy subscale is near the top of the range and verifies that fantasy is a vehicle for C to work through her concepts surrounding her life experiences and feelings about herself and her world. Her continued extensive use of fantasy in the play sessions could be expected, especially scenes depicting conflict and accompanying dysphoric emotions. C can express through fantasy what is too threatening to address in reality.

## RESEARCH AND DEVELOPMENT

Research has established support for the use of the PTOI as a measure of children's emotional well-being. Perry (1988–1989) correctly identified 23 of 30 children as adjusted or maladjusted when subscale scores were computed for the second 12 minutes, as well as for the entire 36-minute initial play therapy session. Her analysis showed that the play behaviors on the emotional discomfort subscale were the behaviors that discriminated the two groups of children. Maladjusted children's play expressed significantly more dysphoric feelings, conflictual themes, play disruptions and negative self-disclosing statements than were expressed by the play of well-adjusted children. Further item analyses (unpublished) of these data found 90% of the maladjusted and adjusted children, or 27 of the 30, correctly classified when seven behavioral items were weighted and entered into a discriminant function analysis. Maladjusted children evidenced a higher number of rejections to therapist's interventions, a predominance of dysphoric feelings, more time spent in fantasy than reality, more time spent on characters as opposed to things, a greater number of scenes and stories, frequent play disruptions, and more negative talk about themselves and their experiences.

Howe's study (1980–1981), on the other hand, found psychopathological behaviors present during the first 12 minutes of an initial play session. Aggressive children were identified by their aggressive behavior toward the therapist, frequent play disruptions, conflicted play, negative self-disclosures, and high level of fantasy play. Withdrawn boys presented bizarre play, rejection of therapist's interventions, and dysphoric play content. Well-adjusted children exhibited lower levels of emotional discomfort, social inadequacy, and fantasy play. Withdrawn girls could not be differentiated from well-adjusted girls during the first 12 minutes. No differences were found among the diagnostic groups during the second 12 minutes. Pathological behaviors re-appeared during the third segment, and by the last 12 minutes, all disturbed children exhibited higher levels of social inadequacy and dysphoric content than well-adjusted children. Howe's study suggests that differential diagnoses of withdrawn and aggressive children are possible. Further research may find that the play therapy behaviors of children differ along a line similar to the more subtle differential diagnoses found in the DSM-IV (American Psychiatric Association, 1994).

These studies are encouraging, however the use of the PTOI is limited to two published research findings, and more study is needed to refine the instrument and develop norms. Man factors are present that can, and often do, affect the behavior presented in the therapy room. When assessing children's behavior, developmental norms must be established. Developmental factors, such as the age and cognitive maturity of the child, affect play. Differences in the play therapy behavior of boys and girls also must be examined. The relationship of play behavior and the socioeconomic status and cultural background of the children's parents must be explored in more detail. Perry (1988–1989) found that children whose parents held professional jobs rated lower on the use of fantasy scale and higher on the social inadequacy scale than children whose parents held the lower-rated occupations. Therapist's characteristics such as gender, age, cultural background, socioeconomic status, level of training and expertise, and theoretical posturing may influence the child's play and must be researched.

The role of the therapist and the physical setting of the playroom are variables influencing the child's play and should be standardized. As the development of the PTOI proceeds and the PTOI is used in the initial diagnostic interview, the counselor is directed to maintain the therapist's role as described by Axline (1947) and Moustakas (1953), to use only reflective and tracking interventions, and to follow the limit-setting procedure outlined by Bixler (1982). These guidelines provide minimum intrusion into children's play and permit children to communicate themselves with as little psychodynamic influence as possible. Though the overall dimensions of the playrooms will vary, the playroom should be equipped with the range of toys recommended by Landreth (1991).

# REFERENCES

American Psychiatric Association. (1987). *Diagnostic and statistical manual of mental disorders* (3rd ed., rev.). Washington, DC: Author.

Axline, V. (1947). *Play therapy*. Boston: Houghton-Mifflin.

Behar, D., & Rapoport, J. L. (1983). Play observation and psychiatric diagnosis. In C. E. Schaefer & K. J. O'Connor (Eds.), *Handbook of play therapy* (pp. 193–199). New York: Wiley.

Bixler, R. H. (1982). Limits are therapy. In G. L. Landreth (Ed.), *Play therapy: Dynamics of the process of counseling with children* (pp 173–188). Springfield, IL: Charles C. Thomas.

Erikson, E. H. (1963). *Childhood and society* (2nd ed.). New York: Norton.

Frank, L. K. (1976). Validity of play. In C. S. Schaefer (Ed.), *The therapeutic use of child's play* (pp. 71–78). New York: Aronson.

Ginott, H. G. (1982). A rationale for selecting toys in play therapy. In G. L. Landreth (Ed.), *Play therapy: Dynamics of the process of counseling with children* (pp. 160–172). Springfield, IL: Charles C. Thomas.

Howe, P. E. A. (1980-1981). Patterns of playroom behavior in disturbed and adjusted preschool children (Doctoral dissertation, University of Colorado, 1980). *Dissertation Abstracts International, 42*, 374B.

Howe, P. A., & Silvern, L. E. (1981). Behavioral observation during play therapy: Preliminary development of a research instrument. *Journal of Personality Assessment, 45*, 168–182.

James, D. (1977). *Play therapy: An overview*. New York: Dabor Science Publishers.

Landreth, G. L. (1991). *Play therapy: The art of the relationship*. Muncie, IN: Accelerated Development.

Moustakas, C. E. (1953). *Children in play therapy*. New York: McGraw-Hill.

Perry, L. H. (1988–1989). Play therapy behavior of maladjusted and adjusted children. (Doctoral dissertation, University of North Texas, 1988) *Dissertation Abstracts International, 49*, 2937A.

Piaget, J. (1951). *Play, dreams and imitation in childhood*. New York: Norton.

# APPENDIX
## *Rating Form for Selected Scales of Howe and Silvern's PTOI*

1. Comprehensibility of play sequences, interactions; bizarre content
    1. *Always* comprehensible and never uses bizarre content
    2. Incomprehensible occasionally *or* uses bizarre content occasionally
    3. Incomprehensible occasionally *and* uses bizarre content occasionally
    4. Incomprehensible and/or bizarre a good deal of the time
    5. Bizarre and incomprehensible for nearly the entire time
2. Frequency with which activities exclude the therapist[1]
    1. Activities include therapist for nearly the whole time
    2. Clearly spends more time in activities with therapist
    3. Spends about half the time in solitary activities
    4. Clearly spends more time in solitary activities
    5. Therapist included in activities for *no more than 2 minutes*
3. Frequency of rejections of T's interventions
    1. Rejects no more than 2 of therapist's interventions
    2. Clearly accepts more interventions than he/she rejects
    3. Rejects about half of therapist interventions
    4. Rejects more interventions than he/she accepts
    5. Rejects nearly all therapist interventions: *accepts no more than 2*
4. Mood
    1. Seems extremely elated and delighted for virtually the entire time
    2. Occasionally seems extremely elated
    3. Seems happy and pleased most of the time
    4. Vacillates between being happy and dysphoric
    5. Appears to be experiencing a predominance of unpleasant feelings
    6. Unclear
5. Frequency and degree of aggression directed at therapist[1]
    1. *Never* directs aggression at the therapist
    2. Occasionally direct low-level aggression toward the therapist
    3. Persistently directs low-level aggression *or* directs high-level aggression at therapist *once or twice*
    4. Frequently directs high-level aggression at therapist
    5. Persistently directs high-level aggression at therapist
6. Frequency of fluctuations between fantasy play and reality
    1. In reality nearly the whole time, 1 or 2 slips into fantasy
    2. Clearly spends more time in reality, occasional slips into fantasy
    3. Spends nearly equal time slipping in and out of fantasy
    4. Clearly spends more time in fantasy, occasional slips into reality
    5. In fantasy nearly the whole time, 1 or 2 slips into reality

7. Time spent concentrating play on characters rather than on things[1]
   1. Spends nearly the whole time concentrating play on things
   2. Spends most of time concentrating play on things
   3. Spends about half the time on things rather than on characters
   4. Clearly spends more time on characters than on things
   5. Spends virtually the whole time on characters
8. Number and variations in scenes from fantasy stories
   1. Enacts *no* fantasy scenes
   2. Enacts 1 scene or repeats same scene with slight variation
   3. Enacts 2 or more different scenes from the same story
   4. Enacts 2 different stories, each having different characters, plots
   5. Enacts 3 or more different stories
9. Number of roles identified with during fantasy play
   1. Identifies with no role or character
   2. Identifies with 1 role or many characters representative of 1 role
   3. Identifies with 2 different roles
   4. Identifies with 3 different roles
   5. Identifies with 4 or more different roles
10. Frequency with which behavior is expressive of conflicts
    1. Behavior is nonexpressive for nearly the entire time
    2. Behavior is nonexpressive most of the time; occasionally expressive
    3. Behavior expressive about half the time
    4. Behavior expressive most of the time; occasionally nonexpressive
    5. Behavior expressive for almost the whole time
11. Frequency and degree of play disruption
    1. *Never* evidences play disruption
    2. Abruptly stops play *once* or *twice* but *resumes* that play momentarily
    3. Abruptly stops play *3 or 4 times* but *resumes* that play momentarily
    4. Abruptly stops play *once but unable to resume* that play activity
    5. Abruptly stops play *2 or more times* but *unable to resume that play*
12. Noticeable stiffness in fine and gross body movements[1]
    1. Rarely, if ever, appears stiff, rigid, and constricted
    2. Occasionally appears stiff, rigid, and constricted
    3. Appears stiff, rigid, and constricted for most of time
13. Frequency of negative talk about self, feelings, worries
    1. *Never* makes negative talk statements
    2. *One* negative statement
    3. *Two* negative statements
    4. *Several* negative statements

---

[1] PTOI Items 2, 5, 7, and 12 were revised by Perry (1988–1989).

# PART III

# INNOVATIVE PROCEDURES
# IN PLAY THERAPY

# 12

# Child-Centered Group
# Play Therapy

## GARRY L. LANDRETH
## DANIEL S. SWEENEY

*J*ust like childhood itself, child therapy is a journey—a process of exploration in which the therapist has the special privilege of partnering. It is within
this partnership, or relationship, that hurting children find healing and a
sense of self. For some children, this journey comes within an individual
relationship with a play therapist; while for other children, it includes a relationship with other children as well as the therapist.

Child-centered group play therapy is indeed a journey of exploration, as
children find within themselves the resources to solve problems and heal. The
counseling approach, developed by Carl Rogers (1951) and adapted by Virginia
Axline (1947) to counseling with children focuses on providing a permissive
and growth-promoting atmosphere in which children can reach their full potential. The play therapist is interested not in the child's problem, but in the
child. The play therapist is not therapeutically prescriptive, but prescriptively
therapeutic. The play therapist is not focused on directing the therapeutic process, but on facilitating a process that will unfold as the therapist trusts the
inner person of the child. It is a journey of self-exploration and self-discovery.

The child-centered group play therapist should be a person trained in play
therapy and group therapy. These skills, however, remain secondary to the play
therapist's attitude as Landreth and Sweeney (1997) point out: "Child-centered

play therapy is not a cloak the play therapist puts on when entering the play-room and takes off when leaving; rather, it is a philosophy resulting in attitudes and behaviors for living one's life in relationships with children. It is both a basic philosophy of the innate human capacity of the child to strive toward growth and maturity and an attitude of deep and abiding belief in the child's ability to be constructively self-directing. Child-centered play therapy is a complete therapeutic system, not just the application of a few rapport-building techniques" (p. 17).

## CHILD-CENTERED THEORY

Child-centered play therapy is based upon the theoretical constructs of client-centered therapy developed by Carl Rogers (1951). These constructs were applied to working with children through play therapy by Virginia Axline (1947), a student and colleague of Rogers. The child-centered approach to play therapy, like client-centered therapy is based upon a process of being with children as opposed to a procedure of application. It is not so much a process of reparation as it is a process of becoming. Rogers (1986) summarized the essence of the approach: "The person-centered approach, then, is primarily a way of being that finds its expression in attitudes and behaviors that create a growth-producing climate. It is a basic philosophy rather than simply a technique or a method. When this philosophy is lived, it helps the person expand the development of his or her own capacities. When it is lived, it also stimulates constructive change in others. It empowers the individual, and when this personal power is sensed, experience shows that it tends to be used for personal and social transformation" (p. 199).

It is this *formative tendency* that all persons—indeed, all of nature—possess that forms the foundation for the child-centered approach to working with children. The child-centered theory of personality structure is based on three central constructs: the organism, or person, the phenomenal field, and the self (Rogers, 1951).

### The Organism

The organism is all that a child is, consisting of the child's self-perceptions including thoughts, feelings, and behaviors, as well as the child's physical constitution. Because the person is always in the process of developing, the child is " . . . a total organized system in which alteration of any part may produce changes in any other part" (Rogers, 1951, p. 487). This developmental process in children is emphasized, as every child "exists in a continually changing world of experience of which he is the center" (p. 483). Children interact with and respond to this personal and continually changing world of experience.

Therefore, a continuous dynamic intrapersonal interaction occurs in which every child (organism), as a total system, is striving toward actualizing the self. Landreth and Sweeney (1997) posit that this dynamic and animated process is an internally directed movement toward becoming a more positively function-ing person, toward positive growth, toward improvement, independence, ma-turity, and enhancement of self as a person. The child's behavior in this process is goal-directed in an effort to satisfy personal needs as experienced in the unique phenomenal field that for that child constitutes reality (Landreth, 1991).

## Phenomenal Field

The phenomenal field consists of everything that is experienced by the child. These experiences include everything happening within an organism at a given time—whether or not at a conscious level, internal as well as external—includ-ing perceptions, thoughts, feelings, and behaviors. Essentially, the phenomenal field is the internal reference that is the basis for viewing life; that is, whatever the child perceives to be occurring is reality for the child. This points to a fun-damental rule of thumb in child-centered play therapy, which is that the child's perception of reality is what must be understood if the child and behaviors exhibited by the child are to be understood.

Whatever the child perceives in the phenomenal field, therefore, assumes primary importance as opposed to the actual reality of events. The magnitude of emotion that a child experiences corresponds to the perceived significance of the behavior, which is focused on maintaining and enhancing the organism. Rogers (1951) proposed that "behavior is basically the goal-directed attempt of the organism to satisfy its needs as experienced in the field as perceived" (p. 491). Reality is therefore determined individually and subjectively. This con-cept is central to child-centered play therapy.

The behavior of any child, or group of children, must always be under-stood by looking through the eyes of a child. Thus, the therapist intentionally avoids judging or evaluating even the simplest of the child's behaviors (i.e., a picture, stacked blocks, a scene in the sand) and works hard to try to under-stand the internal frame of reference of each child in the group (Landreth & Sweeney, 1997). If the therapist makes contact with the person of the child, the child's phenomenal world must be the point of focus and must be understood. Children are not expected to meet predetermined criteria or fit a set of precon-ceived categories (Landreth, 1991).

## Self

The third central construct of the child-centered theory of personality struc-ture is the self. Self is that differentiated aspect of the phenomenal field that develops from the child's "evaluational interactions with others" (Rogers, 1951, p. 498). The consequence of how others perceive a child's emotional and be-havioral activity and accordingly react involves the formation of the concept of "me." The self is formulated as an "organized picture, existing in awareness as figure . . . or ground . . . , of the self and the self-in-relationship . . . , together with the positive or negative values which are associated with those qualities and relationships, as they are perceived as existing in the past, present, or future" (p. 501).

According to Rogers (1951), even very young infants engage in a process of "direct organismic valuing," beginning with such simple experiences as, "This taste bad, and I don't like it," even though they may lack descriptive words or symbols that match the experience. This is the beginning of a natural and continuous process in which children positively value those experiences that are perceived as self-enhancing and place a negative value on those that threaten or do not maintain or enhance the self.

This process of evaluation—by parents, others, and self—points to one of the key benefits in child-centered group play therapy. As children develop, they experience parents and others, and symbolize themselves as good or bad dependent on these evaluations. To preserve a positive self-concept, the child may distort such experiences and deny to awareness the satisfaction of the experience (Rogers, 1951). "It is in this way . . . that parental attitudes are not only introjected, but . . . are experienced . . . in distorted fashion, as if based on the evidence of one's own sensory and visceral equipment. Thus, through distorted symbolization, expression of anger comes to be 'experienced' as bad, even though the more accurate symbolization would be that the expression of anger is often experienced as satisfying or enhancing" (Rogers, 1951, p. 500). The group play therapy experience provides the opportunity for children to be viewed by the child-centered therapist as a positive and growing self, while also experiencing the evaluation of the other group members within an atmosphere of permissiveness and acceptance.

Rogers (1951) hypothesized that the self grows and changes as a result of continuing interaction with the phenomenal field. In the child-centered group play therapy process, *the group itself is the phenomenal field*. The group fosters a growth-producing climate, and the child's interactions with it facilitate the child's concept of self. Rogers described the structure of the self-concept as "an organized configuration of perceptions of the self which are admissible to awareness. It is composed of such elements as the perceptions of one's characteristics and abilities; the percepts and concepts of the self in relation to others and to the environment; the value qualities which are perceived as associated with experiences and objects; and the goals and ideals which are perceived as having positive or negative valence" (p. 501). This not only speaks to the child's behavior being consistent with the child's concept of self, but also the ability of the group to facilitate positive change in self-concept.

An understanding of Rogers' (1951) propositions regarding personality and behavior is key to understanding the child-centered approach to treatment. Boy and Pine (1982, p. 47) provided a paraphrase and synopsis of Rogers' propositions, which furnishes a summary for viewing each child as:

- Being the best determiner of a personal reality
- Behaving as an organized whole
- Desiring to enhance self

- Goal-directed in satisfying needs
- Being behaviorally influenced by feelings that affect rationality
- Best able to perceive the self
- Being able to be aware of the self
- Valuing
- Interested in maintaining a positive self-concept
- Behaving in ways that are consistent with the self-concept
- Not owning behavior that is inconsistent with the self
- Producing psychological freedom or tension by admitting or not admitting certain experiences into the self-concept
- Responding to threat by becoming behaviorally rigid
- Admitting into awareness experiences that are inconsistent with the self if the self is free from threat
- Being more understanding of others if a well integrated self-concept exists, and
- Moving from self-defeating values toward self-sustaining values.

# CHILD-CENTERED GROUP PLAY THERAPY

Child-centered group play therapy combines the distinct advantages of child-centered play therapy with the recognized benefits of group process. Landreth (1991) provided a definition of play therapy that adapts well for the group play therapy process: "Play therapy is defined as a dynamic interpersonal relationship between a child and a therapist trained in play therapy procedures who provides selected play materials and facilitates the development of a safe relationship for the child to fully express and explore self (feelings, thoughts, experiences, and behaviors) through the child's natural medium of communication, play" (p. 14).

## Child-Centered Play Therapy

Virginia Axline (1947) concisely clarified the fundamental principles that provide guidelines for establishing and maintaining a therapeutic relationship and making contact with the inner person of the child in the play therapy experience. Landreth (1991, pp. 77–78) revised and extended Axline's eight basic principles as follows:

- The therapist is genuinely interested in the child and develops a warm, caring relationship.
- The therapist experiences unqualified acceptance of the child and does not wish that the child were different in some way.
- The therapist creates a feeling of safety and permissiveness in the relationship so the child feels free to explore and express self completely.
- The therapist is always sensitive to the child's feelings and gently reflects

those feelings in such a manner that the child develops self-understanding.

- The therapist believes deeply in the child's capacity to act responsibly, unwaveringly respects the child's ability to solve personal problems, and allows the child to do so.
- The therapist trusts the child's inner direction, allows the child to lead in all areas of the relationship and resists any urge to direct the child's play or conversation.
- The therapist appreciates the gradual nature of the therapeutic process and does not attempt to hurry things along.
- The therapist establishes only those therapeutic limits that help the child accept personal and appropriate relationship responsibility.

These principles all point to the development and maintenance of a strong therapeutic relationship. This therapeutic relationship is, in fact, so powerful that it is the central factor determining the success or failure of therapy. Moustakas (1959) believed that "through the process of self-expression and exploration within a significant relationship, through realization of the value within, the child comes to be a positive, self-determining, and self-actualizing individual" (p. 5).

In the child-centered approach to play therapy, the focus is on the child rather than on the presenting problem. It is assumed that the therapist who concentrates upon assessment and diagnosis has a greater likelihood of losing sight of the child. Symptoms may be important, but not as important as the child. Although interpretation of play behaviors is interesting, it generally serves the need of the therapist and not the child. This relationship is therefore focused on the present, living experience (Landreth, 1991, p. 79):

person . . . . . . . . . . . rather than . . . . problem
present . . . . . . . . . . . rather than . . . . past
feelings . . . . . . . . . . . rather than . . . . thoughts or acts
understanding . . . . . . rather than . . . . explaining
accepting . . . . . . . . . rather than . . . . correcting
child's direction . . . . . rather than . . . . therapist's instruction
child's wisdom . . . . . . rather than . . . . therapist's knowledge

This relationship develops as the therapist communicates understanding and acceptance. Children begin to recognize their inner value when the play therapist responds sensitively to the inner emotional part of their person by accepting and reflecting feelings, whether verbally or nonverbally expressed. The child-centered play therapist generally avoids asking questions, for several reasons. Questions tend to take children out of their world of affectivity and into the world of cognition, which defeats the developmental rationale for using play therapy. Questions also tend to structure the relationship in the direction of the therapist placing the focus on the therapist rather than the child. This naturally interferes with the process of the child's play. The value of symbolic expression and the safety of therapeutic projection may be eliminated through the asking of too many questions.

Child-centered play therapy avoids any kind of evaluation. Children are encouraged, but not praised, because praise establishes an evaluative pattern. It is important to note that evaluative statements deprive the child of inner motivation. Additionally, the child-centered play therapist avoids interfering with the child's play. This does not eliminate participation in the child's play, which can be done at the direction of the child, though it should be noted that the more the therapist becomes involved in the child's play, the more difficult it is to keep the child in the lead. Interference, however, may involve offering solutions or suggestions, or allowing the child to manipulate the therapist into becoming a teacher or doing things for the child. Assistance can be provided in the exceptional circumstances when the child has tried and truly cannot do something alone. Children do not learn self-direction, self-evaluation, and responsibility when the therapist evaluates or provides solutions.

## DIAGNOSIS AND TREATMENT PLANNING

Although it may be considered important to discuss the issues of diagnosis and treatment planning because of the current climate of the mental health field, these are clearly not the central issues in child-centered play therapy. Person-centered therapy views diagnosis and evaluation as distracting and potentially detrimental to the client (Rogers, 1951). The focus of the child-centered play therapist is on the inner person of the child; it is on what the child is capable of becoming as opposed to the child's ways of being in the past. The children in the therapeutic play group are the focus, the problems for which they have been referred are not. Essentially, knowledge about the problems is not at all necessary to establish a therapeutic relationship with children, and may in fact be a substantial distraction.

"Maladjustment," therefore, should be viewed within the context of the developing relationship and as resulting from a state of incongruence between the self-concept of a child and the experiences of the child. Incongruence between a child's self-concept and a child's experience will naturally result in an incongruence of behavior, thus causing what would be labeled maladjustment. The group play therapy process for children provides the environment in which these incongruences can be processed, as children are given opportunity to experience affirmation of their needs of growth and self-realization.

Axline (1947) suggested that an "adjusted person seems to be an individual who does not encounter too many obstacles in his path—and who has been given the opportunity to become free and independent in his own right. The maladjusted person seems to be the one who, by some means or other, is denied the right to achieve this without a struggle" (p. 21). She further explained the differences between well-adjusted and maladjusted behavior:

> When the individual develops sufficient self-confidence . . . consciously and purposefully to direct his behavior by evaluation, selectivity, and application to achieve his ultimate goal in life—self-realization—then he seems to be well adjusted.
>
> On the other hand, when the individual lacks sufficient self-confidence to chart his course of actions openly, seems content to grow in self-realization vicariously rather than directly, and does little or nothing about channeling this drive in more constructive and productive directions, then he is said to be maladjusted. . . . The individual's behavior is not consistent with the inner concept of the self which the individual has created in his attempt to achieve complete self-realization. The further apart the behavior and the concept, the greater the degree of maladjustment. (pp. 13–14)

The setting of treatment goals in the child-centered group play therapy process must take into consideration this perspective on maladjustment. Just as diagnosis is generally eschewed in the person-centered process, the setting of specific treatment goals is seen as antithetical to the natural and unfolding process of therapy. Children are in a state of constant change and continuous development, and are themselves considered to be the most appropriate determiner of change within self. Therefore, the therapy process is not an application of prescriptive goals and treatment but a discussion of growth and change that proceeds from the internal frame of reference of the developing individual. When this process is indeed child-centered, therapy and therapeutic growth are not dependent on the therapist but the child. The child's self-concept and perception of others become less dependent on the attitudes of other people, and the child can build self-confidence and an ability for self-direction. The child is able to "own" his or her own feelings and behaviors, and feels in greater control, more empowered, and more congruent.

The establishment of specific treatment goals, therefore, is not an aspect of child-centered group play therapy. Such establishment would be incongruent with the philosophy of child-centered theory, as described by Landreth and Sweeney (1997):

> The central hypothesis governing what the therapist does is an unwavering belief in the child's capacity for growth and self-direction. The establishment of specific treatment goals would be a contradiction of this belief. Goals or objectives of treatment imply that the therapist knows where the child should be and that there is a specific structure by which to get there. The play therapist is not wise enough to know where another person should be in his or her life or what that person should be working on or toward. Life is much too complex to be understood by diagnosis and controlled by a prescription for growth. Further, the child is the best determiner of what should be focused on in play therapy. How can children learn self-direction if even their play is directed? Diagnostically based treatment goals usually result in the therapist's being focused on the treatment goal. Such an approach would be much too structuring and would restrict the creative potential of the child and the relationship. (p. 38)

Although specific and prescriptive treatment goals are not established for children in the child-centered group play therapy process, there are broadly defined therapeutic objectives that are considered congruent with the child-centered theoretical and philosophical approach. According to Landreth (1991, p. 80):

> The general objectives of child-centered play therapy are consistent with the child's inner self-directed striving toward self-actualization. An overriding premise is to provide the child with a positive growth experience in the presence of an understanding supportive adult so the child will be able to discover internal strengths. Since child-centered play therapy focuses on the person of the child rather than the child's problem, the emphasis is on facilitating the child's efforts to become more adequate, as a person, in coping with current and future problems which may impact the child's life. To that end, the objectives of child-centered play therapy are to help the child
>
> 1. Develop a more positive self-concept
> 2. Assume greater self-responsibility
> 3. Become more self-directing
> 4. Become more self-accepting
> 5. Become more self-reliant
> 6. Engage in self-determined decision making
> 7. Experience a feeling of control
> 8. Become sensitive to the process of coping
> 9. Develop an internal source of evaluation
> 10. Become more trusting of self .

Within the framework of these general objectives, children in group play therapy are free to work on specific problems, which is often the case. It is important to underscore that this is the child's choice and not a result of the therapist's direction, suggestion, or implication. The group play therapist believes in and trusts the child's capacity to set his or her own goals and direction: "In this view, no attempt is made to control a child, to have the child be a certain way, or to reach a conclusion the therapist has decided is important. The therapist is not the authority who decides what is best for the child, what the child should think, or how the child should feel. If this were to be the case, the child would be deprived of the opportunity to discover his/her own strengths" (Landreth, 1991, p. 81).

## THERAPEUTIC LIMIT SETTING

The group play therapist must be an expert limit-setter. The presence of two or more children in the playroom magnifies (sometimes exponentially) the need for limits to be set. An exploration of the child-centered approach to group play therapy would be incomplete without a discussion of the role of therapeutic limit setting as a facilitative dimension in the process. As noted, children do not grow where they do not feel safe. And children do not feel safe, valued, or accepted in a completely permissive relationship. Moustakas (1959) summarized the importance of limits as a vital and necessary part of relationships:

> Limits exist in every relationship. The human organism is free to grow and develop within the limits of its own potentialities, talents, and structure. In psychotherapy, there must be an integration of freedom and order if the individuals involved are to actualize their potentialities. The limit is one aspect of an alive experience, the aspect which identifies, characterizes, and distinguishes the dimensions of a therapeutic relationship. The limit is the form or structure of an immediate relationship. It refers not only to a unique form but also to the possibility for life growth and direction rather than merely to a limitation. . . . In a therapeutic relationship, limits provide the boundary or structure in which growth can occur. (pp. 8–9)

The purpose for limits in the group play therapy process emphasizes the child-centered group play therapist's focus on the process rather than specific behaviors. Just as the focus of the group process is not on specific behaviors but the relationship and the underlying affective element relative to the behaviors, the child's desire to break the limit in the group is always of greater importance than the actual breaking of a limit. The various purposes for setting limits can be summarized as follows (Axline, 1947; Bixler, 1949; Ginott, 1994; Landreth, 1991; Moustakas, 1959; Landreth & Sweeney, 1997):

- Limits define the boundaries of the therapeutic relationship.
- Limits provide security and safety for the child, both physically and emotionally.
- Limits demonstrate the therapist's intent to provide safety for the child.
- Limits anchor the session to reality.
- Limits allow the therapist to maintain a positive and accepting attitude toward the child.
- Limits allow the child to express negative feelings without causing harm, and the subsequent fear of retaliation.
- Limits offer stability and consistency.
- Limits promote and enhance the child's sense of self-responsibility and self-control.
- Limits promote catharsis through symbolic channels.
- Limits protect the play therapy room.
- Limits provide for the maintenance of legal, ethical, and professional standards.

Permissiveness is a crucial element of the group play therapy process. These are not, however, completely permissive relationships in the playroom. Children are not allowed to do just anything they may want to do. The group play therapist should establish a prescribed structure that provides boundaries for the relationship. Limits inherently need to be set on the following: (1) behavior that is harmful or dangerous to any children in the group or the therapist, (2) behavior that disrupts the therapeutic routine or process (continually leaving playroom, wanting to play after time is up), (3) destruction of room or materials, (4) taking toys from playroom, (5) socially unacceptable behavior, and (6) inappropriate displays of affection (Landreth & Sweeney, 1997).

As important as therapeutic limits are, it is equally important that they should not be set until they are needed. Providing a long list of prohibited activities at the beginning of the first group play therapy session would definitely not encourage or facilitate exploration and expression by the children. When children are allowed to express themselves affectively, there is greater opportunity for significant learning and growth. This can certainly be hampered by a preliminary dissertation on restrictions.

When limits are needed in the group process, the therapist should take a matter-of-fact and a firm approach. This is necessary so that the child will not feel chastised. The therapist's role is obviously not parental and authoritative, but rather facilitative yet structured. While there are usually more limits set in group play therapy than individual, they should nevertheless be as minimal as possible. Limits should also be specific, rather than general (generality makes for unclear boundaries), total rather than conditional (conditional limits are confusing and can lead to power struggles), and enforceable. Landreth and Sweeney (1997) note, "Since boundaries have previously been determined, the play therapist can be consistent and thus predictable in setting limits. This consistency and predictability help the child to feel safe. It is within this structure that the feeling of permissiveness is more important than actual permissiveness. When limit setting becomes necessary, the child's desire to break the limit is always the primary focus of attention because the child-centered play therapist is dealing with intrinsic variables related to motivation, perception of self, independence, need for acceptance, and the working out of a relationship with a significant person" (p. 49).

## RATIONALE FOR UTILIZING GROUP PLAY THERAPY

Although efficiency in terms of saving therapist time has often been considered a major attraction of group play therapy, the placing of several children in a group provides advantages beyond expediency. Group play therapy can give children the kinds of experiences that help them learn to function effectively, to explore their behavior, to develop tolerance to stress and anxiety, and to find satisfaction in working and living with others. If a group play therapy approach is to be employed, it would seem logical to assume the play therapist should understand the rationale for placing children in groups before this approach is attempted.

The presence of another child or several children enhances the therapeutic relationship by facilitating the following dimensions of the play therapy experience (Axline, 1947; Ginott, 1994; Schiffer, 1969; Slavson, 1964):

- It is less threatening for the child to enter the new experience in the company of two or three other children.
- The presence of several children facilitates the establishment of a desired relationship between the therapist and each child.
- The presence of other children diminishes tension and stimulates activity and participation.
- The presence of other children increases spontaneity.
- The therapeutic process is enhanced by the fact that every child can be a giver and not only a receiver of help.
- The group accelerates the child's awareness of the permissiveness of the setting.
- Children are forced to re-evaluate their behavior in the light of peer reactions.
- Group play therapy provides a tangible social setting for discovering and experimenting with new and more satisfying modes of relating to peers.
- The presence of several children serves to tie the therapy experience to the world of reality.
- The group provides opportunity for vicarious and direct learning (problem solving, alternative behaviors, and so on).
- The therapist is provided insight into how the child may be in the "real world."

## GROUP STRUCTURE AND LOGISTICS

The structure of a child-centered play therapy group is not based on the application of techniques. Thus, the child-centered group play therapist does not enter the group with a specific agenda. Therapeutic change is a result of a therapeutic relationship; that is, the children in the group will change in response to the group participants and the environment created by the therapist. The considerations discussed in this section are important, but can not replace the curative value of the play therapy relationship

### Group Selection and Size

Child-centered play therapy groups should be appropriately structured in terms of the selection of group members and the size of the group. A group that consists of the wrong mix of children, or is too large, will diminish the ability of the therapist to create a warm, accepting, and growth-promoting environment. The selection process, therefore, is a crucial element to the success of the group. Generally, since child-centered theory is focused on the child and not on the problem, groups are not specifically organized around a diagnosis.

However, there are general considerations for placing children in group play therapy. According to Ginott (1994), children generally recommended for group play therapy are withdrawn children, immature children, children with phobic reactions, children with "pseudo assets" (children who are too good, obedient, orderly, over generous, and too concerned with pleasing adults), children with habit disorders, and children with conduct disorders. Ginott also noted that children with intense sibling rivalries, sociopathic children, children with accelerated sexual drives, children who persistently steal, and extremely aggressive children are not recommended for group play therapy. These children's behaviors may have possible destructive effects on other children in the group. For example, sexually abused children should not be placed with non-sexually abused children because they may abuse such children. Another category of children not recommended for group play therapy is children with gross stress and trauma reactions. Generally, children in categories not recommended for group play therapy have such intense personal needs that they need the complete and undivided attention and focus of the play therapist all to themselves. Therefore, they should be placed in individual play therapy.

Several issues related to group selection should be considered. Initially, it should be emphasized that the primary screening mechanism for group therapy membership is an individual play therapy session with each child. Children may be referred from individual therapy, or placed immediately into a group following an initial session. Parent and teacher interviews are also helpful in group placement, although there may be a tendency for the referring parties (children rarely self-refer) to be problem-focused rather than child-focused.

An initial consideration in determining group membership will be the age of the children, who should generally be within one year of one another. The developmental differences between young children two or more years apart can be substantial. Developmental or psychological age is more important than chronological age, but the physical maturity of the child must also be considered. A developmentally delayed boy who is larger and stronger than younger boys at a similar level may be problematic.

When considering the gender mix of a play therapy group, it is generally not an issue of import until children reach nine years of age. As children enter the middle school years, psychosocial development, particularly in terms of relating to the other gender, becomes a matter of concern and gender should not be mixed. Prior to age nine, it is recommended that groups be generally gender balanced if both boys and girls are included. A group of four is better balanced with two boys and two girls than with three boys and one girl.

Another consideration in group play therapy is the size of the group. An initial rule of thumb is that the younger the children, the smaller the group. Play therapy groups may have only two or three children, depending on the needs and ages of the children, and the size of the facility. Since child-centered group play therapy focuses on the creation of a therapeutic environment in which children can actualize their potential, the larger the group, the more challenging it will be for the therapist to create these conditions. Groups larger than five children are not recommended.

## Group Playroom and Materials

The physical setting for group play therapy is also important. A designated play-room is recommended, but a designated section of a larger room (such as a classroom) may also be used. A major consideration is a setting that affords privacy and is large enough to afford a certain degree of freedom within the context of limitations on destructiveness. A room that is too small restricts children's expressions and may promote frustration. Likewise, a room that is too large may encourage too much activity and inhibit the development of a relationship with the therapist or other children because too little contact and interaction occurs.

In play therapy, toys are considered to be children's words and play is their language, therefore careful attention should be paid to the selection of toys and materials that allow for children's self-directed activity and facilitate a wide range of feelings and play activity (Landreth, 1991). It should be recognized that not all play media encourages children's expression or exploration of their feelings, needs, and experiences. As noted, it is not play therapy to simply provide a random collection of toys coupled with an "adult" therapy approach. Additionally, play therapy is not used as a method for learning or for the child to get ready to do something else. The purpose is not to engage the child in some play behavior in preparation for trying to get the child to talk, tell about something that has happened, or describe something the child wants in life. This may naturally occur within the unfolding of the process, but is never a goal. The child's play is the message, and the toys are the tools. Landreth's chapter on playroom and materials in his book *Play Therapy: The Art of the Relationship* (1991) has an extensive listing of toys suitable for play therapy.

Play materials should be simple, generic, and safe. Toys that are too complicated or mechanical, involve complex structure, or that require the play therapist's assistance to manipulate are not appropriate because their potential to frustrate children may enable dependence in children who already feel helpless or inadequate. Therefore, as Landreth (1991, p. 116) notes, toys and materials selected should:

- Facilitate a wide range of creative expression
- Facilitate a wide range of emotional expression
- Engage children's interests
- Facilitate expressive and exploratory play
- Allow exploration and expression without verbalization
- Allow success without prescribed structure
- Allow for noncommittal play.

## Length, Frequency, and Duration of Sessions

The length of child-centered group play therapy sessions should also be considered. This is variable and may relate to the setting of the groups—with groups being held in schools having a shorter time limit, groups held concurrently with parent sessions being limited to the therapeutic hour, and so on. The general rule of thumb is to establish the length of the group session based upon the ages of the group members, noting that the younger the children, the shorter the session—reflecting the children's shorter attention span. The most effective time frame for preschool and primary grade children would be 30- to 45-minute sessions. Some groups should perhaps meet twice a week.

In the process of child-centered group play therapy, the frequency and duration of therapy is established by the needs of the child and not the agenda of the therapist. As Axline (1947) pointed out, the child-centered play therapist does not hurry the process along: "If the therapist feels that the child has a problem and she wants to attack the problem as soon as possible, she must remember that what she feels is not important. If the child has a problem, he will bring it out when he is ready. The problem of maladjustment is so complex that one cannot draw a simple circle around some singular experience and say, 'This is it'" (p. 126).

Play therapy groups are generally held once or twice a week, although this structure is certainly flexible. The needs of the child group members should take precedence over any prescribed group schedule, which is admittedly for the professional convenience of the counseling setting or the therapist. It must be remembered that the developmental and emotional needs of children do not necessarily follow the prescribed structure of the adult service providers. Additionally, it must be remembered that a week in a child's life is not equal to the same amount of time in an adult's life. A week in the young child's life can feel like a very long time, and this must be considered when scheduling children.

Also, the intense emotional needs of the child resulting from certain life experiences must be taken into account. The traumatized child may be seen two or three times a week in the first few weeks and then move to a schedule of once-a-week sessions, in addition to or prior to placement in a play therapy group. Intensive short-term groups, meeting two to five times per week may be very effective. Kot (1995) reported positive results on the efficacy of short-term, intensive (12 sessions in two weeks), child-centered play therapy with children who had witnessed domestic violence and were temporarily residing in women's shelters. Although this research involved individual play therapy, it points to the significant potential for short-term intensive therapeutic play groups.

Tyndall-Lind (1999) studied the effectiveness of short-term (12 sessions in two weeks) child-centered group play therapy with children who had witnessed domestic violence and were temporarily residing in women's shelters. She reported the treatment group displayed a significant increase in self-concept, a significant decrease in behavior problems, a significant decrease in both externalizing and internalizing behavior problems, and a significant decrease in aggression, anxiety, and depression.

The duration of the group play therapy process will also vary. This may relate to play groups meeting in different settings (schools, hospitals, and so on) and to the severity of the presenting issues. Gumaer (1984) noted that most research indicates that for group counseling to be effective with children, a minimum of ten sessions is necessary. This points to the need for adequate time for a therapeutic rapport and environment to be established, adequate time for the natural growth process, and adequate time for termination. To reiterate, this timetable is best established by the needs of the children, although logistical constrictions must be considered.

## CASE EXAMPLE

Child-centered play therapy views children within the framework of *emotionalized attitudes*, as discussed by Axline (1955):

> In psychotherapy, we are dealing with emotionalized attitudes that have developed out of the individual's past experiencing of himself in relation to others. These emotionalized attitudes influence his perception of himself as either adequate or inadequate, secure or insecure, worthy of respect or not worthy of respect, having personal worth or deficient in this basic feeling. His perception then, in turn, determines his behavior. The individual's behavior at the moment seems to be his best efforts to maintain and defend his selfhood and so maintain a psychological identity and a resistance to threats against his personality. Consequently, the child who is emotionally deprived and who has had experiences that seem to form and reinforce feelings of inadequacy and lack of personal worth learns the kind of behavior that protects his self-esteem and lessens the impact of threats against his personality. . . . He may refuse to behave in certain ways that are expected or demanded by others in order to maintain a self with integrity. (p. 619)

In the following case example, three children (Randy, age 7; Judi, age 7; and Steve, age 8) are meeting for the first time in a play therapy group at an elementary school. The have all been referred because of so-called "socialization problems." Randy has been described as an anxious child who does not have any friends, Judi as an introverted child who relates more to adults than to children, and Steve as a somewhat hyper child who tends to annoy his peers. Since it is difficult to describe child-centered group play therapy without giving specific examples, in keeping with the person-centered characteristic of illustrating principles through verbatim accounts (Raskin & Rogers, 1989), the following is a brief transcript of some of the therapeutic interactions with the children in the playroom.

### Initial Session

Therapist: Randy, Judi, and Steve— this is our playroom, and you can play with the toys in a lot of the ways you would like to.

The child-centered group play therapy approach is permission-giving. The therapist uses each child's name, which honors each child, and establishes the egalitarian status of each group member.

Steve: (*rushing into the room toward the sandbox*) I want to play in the sand!

Therapist: Steve, it looks like you've got something in mind. (*Judi moves slowly into the room while looking at the toys.*) Judi, it looks like you're checking out the toys on that shelf.

Judi: Yeah, I guess so. (*Judi has reached out tentatively to touch the cash register, but has pulled her hand back. Randy is still standing next to the door, furtively glancing around.*)

Therapist: Judi, it seems like you're wondering if it's OK to play with that. In here, you can choose what to play with. Randy, it looks like you're wondering about this place.

Steve: (*Grabs the rubber snake and runs across the room, poking the snake at Randy's face. Randy cringes and tries to fend off the snake.*)

Therapist: Steve, it looks like you would like to scare Randy with that snake, but he is trying to tell you he doesn't like what you are doing. He wants you to stop.

It is not unusual to have children of varying levels of emotional and sociable levels.

In group play therapy, it becomes very important to use the child's name, so that each group member is aware of who is being addressed. Steve has an intentional plan, and the therapist needs to acknowledge this. At the same time, the other children need to be responded to. It can be a temptation to respond primarily to the most active and vocal children, but therapeutic responses should be spread out equally among the group members.

The initial session of group play therapy is often tentative and exploratory for the children. They are not just exploring the playroom, but also checking out the therapist and the other children.

The therapist's voice tone should match the voice tone and activity level of the child. The response to Judi is warm and empathic, but places the responsibility for making the choices onto her. It might be tempting for the therapist to give Randy a specific invitation to play, because of his tentativeness. He should be allowed to make this choice himself.

Recognition of feelings is key to the child-centered approach. Verbalizing Randy's nonverbal message helps Steve to hear Randy's message and gives Randy the needed support that he is understood.

Steve: (*Leaves Randy and with great glee begins chasing Judi around the room as she screams: "Quit that!"*)

Therapist: Steve, you're having lots of fun chasing Judi; but Judi, you are telling him you don't like what he is doing.

Tracking of activity and responding to feelings is the same as in individual play therapy, just more so. It is important that both children be responded to equally. Both children need to know they have been heard and understood.

(*Steve drops the snake on the floor and goes back to the sandbox. Judi picks up some puppets and begins to make a puppet show. Randy plays with a toy in the corner behind the easel stand, out of sight.*)

Therapist: So, Steve, you decided to do something else; and Judi, you decided to play with the puppets.

Recognizing that children have made a decision affirms their strength. No response is made to Randy because he seems to need to be left alone at the moment. The therapist is keenly sensitive to where he is and what he is doing but respects his choice to hide.

Randy: (*sits on the floor under the easel looking out at the group*)

Judi: (*continues puppet story, saying to the therapist*) Good morning. I'm the lion. (gives a loud roar)

Therapist: Good morning lion. That's a big roar.

The therapist can interact without structuring.

(*Other interactions occur as Judi develops the puppet story.*)

Therapist: Randy, it looks like you decided to sit right there.

Nonevaluative recognition communicates acceptance of his decision to sit and look.

Steve: (*has been digging in the sand, burying toy soldiers and says to no one in particular*) I'm going to bury all of these guys.

Therapist: (*to Steve*) Yep, looks like you've buried a bunch of them.

Toys are not labeled until the child identifies the item.

Randy: (*emerges from under the easel, joins Steve and begins digging in the sand*)

The activity of other children in group play therapy invites and entices shy, quiet children. Randy relaxes enough to begin playing.

Steve: (*to Randy*) Hey! Neat! You can dig the holes, and I'll bury these guys.

Steve's statement is encouraging to Randy, and helps him feel included.

Therapist: Randy, you've decided to play in the sand with Steve—and Steve, sounds like you like that!

A simple tracking of the play activity provides affirmation of the choices made by the children, particularly Randy.

Steve: (*grabs the sand pail and yells*) This is going to be a bomb! (*holds bucket up high and drops it on the floor as Randy protests*)

Therapist: Steve, I know that was fun for you, but the sand is for staying in the sandbox. You wanted the bucket— but Randy, you are telling Steve you want to play with it.

The therapist shows understanding of each child's behavioral and emotional message, and sets an appropriate limit. The limit setting follows the A.C.T. model, proposed by Landreth (1991). This highly effective models includes: (1) A–Acknowledging the child's feelings (it is important to begin the setting of limits by continuing reflection and acceptance), (2) C–Communicating the limit (in a neutral and nonpunitive manner), and (3) T–Targeting an acceptable alternative (which recognizes that the child still has a need to express self and can do so within acceptable boundaries). A limit that is set objectively, with acceptance, and without disapproval is most often received and responded to by children with compliance.

Randy: (*picks up bucket and begins to fill it with sand again*) I'm going to build a castle.

Steve: These soldiers can guard the castle.

Steve's aggression has subsided because he has been allowed to act it out, and he joins in the play activity in a helpful way.

Judi: (*stands watching the boys*) There needs to be a family living in the castle. (*She retrieves the doll family from the dollhouse and adds them to the castle scene.*)

Therapist: You're all making that castle just the way you want it to be.

The therapist's comment empowers the children, recognizing their own decision making, effort, and creative ability. This comment also affirms their working together, while not providing praise and approval. The child-centered play therapist does not evaluate, and focuses on the effort rather than the product. The difference between encouragement and praise is key in the child-centered group play therapy process. By focusing on the effort the therapist can make self-esteem building statements without creating the leading and approval-seeking dynamic that comes from statements of praise. It also models this important dynamic for the group members in their interaction with each other.

Judi, Randy, & Steve: (*almost in unison*) Yeah!

## General Comments

In an initial session, the child-centered group play therapist is focused on creating an environment of acceptance that promotes the inherent growth-producing tendencies of the children. The therapist is thus concerned with being sensitive to each child's feelings and perception, helping the child to feel safe, making emotional contact with the child, and returning responsibility for self to the child. "The building of a relationship begins with what the child sees and perceives in the therapist and is dependent on the therapist's sensitivity to the child's experiencing at the moment. Making contact with the child means responding with gentleness, kindness, and softness to the child's communication of self. Through the process of accepting the child's attitudes, feelings, and thoughts, the therapist enters the child's world. Once contact with the child has been made in this way, a trusting relationship can begin to develop" (Landreth, 1991, p. 157).

Each child in the case described here reacted differently to the therapist's communication of this message. Although this was an initial session, some of the previously stated benefits of child-centered group play therapy are already evident. Randy demonstrated movement from being generally anxious in the group to interacting with the other children. His physical movement from distance to closer proximity to the therapist and the other children was one example of the benefit of placing shy, anxious children in play therapy groups. Steve's aggressive behavior was ameliorated by the group, particularly by the therapist giving expression to the displeasure of the other children at some of his behaviors. He was given the opportunity to reevaluate his acting out behaviors in the presence of Randy and Judi, as well as the therapist. Judi begins by playing alone and seeking to engage the therapist, which is typical of her introverted behavior outside of the playroom where she attempts to relate primarily with adults. She, too, is drawn into the play process.

## CONCLUSION

In the child-centered group play therapy process, children experience an environment that is marked by warmth and acceptance and promotes safety and growth. This environment allows children the opportunity to discover that their peers may be struggling too, which helps to deconstruct the barriers that children have of feeling alone in their pain. A sense of belonging develops, and children learn appropriate ways to relate within and outside the playroom. Gumaer (1984) summarized the value of child-centered group counseling:

> Group counseling provides a lifelike representation of children's everyday world. The small group situation is a microcosm of the child's real world. Children interact in group therapy, share their lives and receive feedback from peers about their feelings, thoughts, and behavior. They relate interpersonally and learn to identify effective and ineffective social skills. Children learn about themselves by hearing other children's perceptions of them. They learn how they are similar and different, and that is all right to be unique. Children learn they must conform and cooperate in some instances, but also that original and creative thinking is appreciated and supported. (p. 213)

All children experience a need to feel understood and accepted. In the group-centered approach to play therapy, children experience a consistent and accepting response from the therapist, regardless of their presenting problem, degree of normality, or extent of personal adjustment. The play therapy experience allows children to communicate about these issues in their own natural medium. The group experience allows children to process these issues on both an intrapersonal and an interpersonal level. The child-centered therapy process takes the focus off of the therapist and allows the children to experience self-exploration, self-discovery, and self-realization. It is the actualization of empowerment.

## REFERENCES

Axline, V. (1947). *Play therapy: The inner dynamics of childhood*. Boston: Houghton Mifflin Company.

Axline, V. (1955). Play therapy procedures and results. *American Journal of Orthopsychiatry, 25*, 618–626.

Bixler, R. (1949). Limits are therapy. *Journal of Consulting Psychology, 13*, 1–11.

Boy, A., & Pine, G. (1982). *Client-centered counseling: A renewal*. Boston: Allyn and Bacon.

Ginott, H. (1994). *Group psychotherapy with children: The theory and practice of play therapy*. Northvale, NJ: Jason Aronson, Inc.

Gumaer, J. (1984). *Counseling and therapy for children*. New York: The Free Press.

Kot, S. (1995). *Intensive play therapy with child witnesses of domestic violence*. Unpublished doctoral dissertation, University of North Texas, Denton.

Landreth, G. (1991). *Play therapy: The art of the relationship*. Muncie, IN: Accelerated Development, Inc.

Landreth, G., & Sweeney, D. (1997). Child-centered play therapy. In K. O'Connor & L. Braverman (Eds.), *Play therapy: Theory and practice* (pp. 17–45). New York: John Wiley & Sons.

Moustakas, C. (1959). *Psychotherapy with children: The living relationship*. New York: Harper & Row.

Raskin, N., & Rogers, C. (1989). Person-centered therapy. In R. Corsini & D. Wedding (Eds.), *Current psychotherapies* (4th ed., pp. 155–194). Itasca, IL: F. E. Peacock Publishers, Inc.

Rogers, C. (1951). *Client-centered therapy*. Boston: Houghton Mifflin Company.

Rogers, C. (1986). Client-centered therapy. In I. Kutash & A. Wolf (Eds.), *Psychotherapist's casebook* (pp. 197–208). San Francisco: Jossey-Bass.

Schiffer, M. (1969). *The therapeutic play group*. New York: Grune & Stratton.

Slavson, S. R. (1964). *A textbook in analytic group psychotherapy*. New York: International Universities Press.

Tyndall-Lind, A. (1999). *A comparative analysis of intensive individual play therapy and intensive sibling group play therapy with child witnesses of domestic violence*. Unpublished doctoral dissertation, University of North Texas, Denton.

# *13*

# Intensive Short-Term Group Play Therapy

ASHLEY TYNDALL-LIND
GARRY L. LANDRETH

*I*n striving to extend and intensify the effectiveness of play therapy, many traditional concepts must be reconsidered and reconstructed. Existing lockstep patterns of scheduling should be reexamined. Play therapists are encouraged to re-orient their thinking in the area of effect of time lapse between play therapy sessions to consider the worthwhileness of condensing of sessions into a shorter span of time. Positive results from several studies support deviation from the traditional one session per week. If ten sessions of play therapy over a two week period could achieve results similar to that of ten sessions in ten weeks, then a child would be better adjusted and more productive eight weeks sooner.

We do not know what the human organism is capable of assimilating nor the amount of time needed by children between play therapy sessions to process changes facilitated during the play therapy sessions. Condensing the time between sessions reduces the element of time and can intensify the therapeutic process through increased involvement of the children. The approach, traditionally, would seem to indicate play therapists consider time as being a therapeutic agent, when the relationship with the play therapist and the dynamics of the process of the session are the healing agents.

It just may be that the traditional once-a-week scheduling of play therapy clients is based more on the convenience of the therapist's schedule than on the emotional needs of children. When a child has experienced a crisis or trauma, the play therapist should consider intensive play therapy in which the child is scheduled for play therapy sessions two or three times a week for the first two weeks in order to speed up the therapeutic process. Intensive play therapy is also recommended for a child who is already being seen in play therapy and has such an experience. If there has been a death in the family, major car accident, sexual or physical abuse, domestic violence, attack by an animal, bombing, or other stressful life event resulting in psychic trauma, a week between sessions can be an eternity for a child in crisis.

Several variations of the intensive play therapy model have been utilized at the Center for Play Therapy at the University of North Texas. One unique model has been the scheduling of some carefully selected children for several play therapy sessions in one day. A few children have been scheduled for play therapy sessions in the morning and in the afternoon for three days. Some children have been scheduled for three 30-minute play therapy sessions each day for three days with a 30- to 45-minute break between sessions. An interesting observation is that the play therapy process for each of these sessions appears to be quite similar to the process that occurs in once-a-week sessions. For example, the process of exploration described by play therapists for a typical third session is similar to what occurs in session three of three sessions scheduled in one day. Parents have reported positive behavioral changes for children in these experiences.

Intensive short-term therapy is not a new concept in the field of psychotherapy. In fact, for the past forty years clinicians have examined issues related to the intensity and length of treatment in an attempt to maximize therapeutic effectiveness and to facilitate client relief. Marathon groups of the 1960s highlighted dramatic positive effects of intense short-term therapy. These groups were intense therapeutic experiences that extended 24 to 48 hours without a break. They were based on the premise that intense therapeutic interventions yielded longer lasting and more beneficial results. During these intensified sessions, participants' defenses broke down, truthfulness and openness increased, and personal growth was stimulated in a more rapid fashion (Capuzzi & Gross, 1992). Landreth (1966) was one of the first to investigate the effectiveness of collapsing the time between group counseling sessions with adolescents. In the late 1970s and early 1980s, the field of adult counseling continued to experience growth in the use of intensive psychotherapy for adults (Davanloo, 1980; Malan, 1976; Sifneos, 1979). However, to date there have been few models of short-term or intensive therapy that are specifically designed to meet the needs of children. "Child therapists have had little choice but to expand upon existing crisis intervention techniques, adapt an eclectic, improvisational approach, or try to modify a brief adult treatment mode" (Sloves & Peterlin, 1993).

A few short-term and intensive treatment interventions for children in crisis were reported in the early 1990s. Of particular interest is a study conducted by Saravay (1991), who found short-term sibling group play therapy was an effective intervention with two preschool brothers following a sudden parental death. Treatment included six play therapy sessions focusing on clarification of cognitive confusion, provision of age, appropriate information about death, facilitation of the grieving process, and identification of feelings associated with loss. Progress, as a result of this intervention, included a decrease in nocturnal awakening, complete relief from nightmares, a reduction in the intensity of the expression of anger, an increase in positive peer relations, and an increase in autonomous daily functioning. Sibling participation in treatment appeared to stimulate personal healing, and it appeared to expedite the healing process. Each sibling served as a catalyst and a sounding board for the other, with each reflecting the other's experience.

Hofmann and Rogers (1991) utilized intensive group play therapy in working with traumatized children who had been displaced from their homes due to an earthquake. Play therapy groups met on a daily basis for four days with a session duration of 4–6 hours. Group membership was limited to children between the ages of 2 and 12, who were forced to reside in a crisis shelter. Each day, the groups engaged in structured play activities which encouraged the children to utilize art supplies, spontaneous dialogue, and toys to express their initial fears related to their trauma. Positive outcomes included an increased sense of control, mastery over the crisis, decreased anxiety, and an understanding of the traumatic episode. The intensity of the group was amplified by combining several children who had similar trauma experiences, by providing children with a daily treatment regimen, by structuring the sessions to incorporate 4–6 hours of group play therapy and by facilitating structured group activities focused on the crisis. Combining a variety of intensifying strategies enabled the children to maximize the benefits of the limited intervention window.

More recently, Kot, Landreth, and Giordano (1999) studied the effectiveness of intensive individual play therapy with child witnesses of domestic violence versus a wait list control group. Children between the ages of 4 and 9 participated in 45-minute individual play therapy sessions on a daily basis, for twelve consecutive days. Kot found that child witnesses of domestic violence showed significant improvement in self-concept, a reduction of externalizing behavioral problems, improvement in behavior problems overall, and showed a significant improvement in play proximity.

Tyndall-Lind (1999) found that intensive sibling group play therapy with child witnesses of domestic violence maximized the effects of play therapy as an intervention. She utilized three intensifying strategies: group play therapy, sibling dyads, and daily treatment. Children who received intensive sibling group play therapy for 45 minutes on twelve consecutive days, showed improvements in self-concept, a reduction in total behavior problems, a reduction in externalizing behavior problems, a reduction in internalizing behavior problems, a reduction in aggression, and a reduction in anxiety and depression.

## GROUP THERAPY:
## APPLICATIONS IN INTENSIVE PLAY THERAPY

The foundations of group therapy, play therapy, group play therapy, and sibling group play therapy are key elements in facilitating intensive short-term group play therapy. Each component adds to the intervention unique dynamics that serve as therapeutic agents.

## Group Therapy

Within the past twenty-five years, group therapy has received increased empirical attention due to the curative factors inherent in the group process. Yalom (1970) identified ten such factors: (a) the imparting of information; (b) the instillation of hope, which allows children to feel they have control over their lives; (c) universality, which helps children to realize that other children have experienced similar situations; (d) altruism, which provides children with a non-threatening opportunity to give and receive; (e) corrective recapitulation of the primary family group, which allows children to work through family dynamics within the group system; (f) development of socialization techniques; (g) imitative behavior, which provides children with positive therapeutic adult role models; (h) interpersonal learning; (i) group cohesiveness; and (j) catharsis.

## Play Therapy

Play serves to protect the child who has limited ego strength by providing the child with the opportunity to work through external difficulties without having to identify and label the painful incident as his or her own. This process allows children to work through extremely traumatic events without being further challenged to communicate these confusing events to adults (Terr, 1990). This point can be clearly exemplified by the following case illustration.

John, an eight-year-old boy coping with an extremely volatile home environment, had expressed suicidal ideation and was referred for treatment. Due to the extreme nature of John's emotional condition, he was immediately engaged in intensive sibling group play therapy. Emotionally overwhelmed, John was unable to label his emotions or to articulate his concerns. Instead, through the course of play therapy, John represented his mood and expressed his concerns through the use of daily artwork. Each day he painted a picture of "his house." During initial sessions, John's art work depicted a house that was black and falling down. It was raining in the picture and a lightning bolt had struck the house. As a result, the house was "burning to the ground." John soon began to give the house a brighter representation. By the sixth session, John's house was an orangish-brown and it had a tree next to it; however, a very large rain cloud produced pouring rain. By the final session (the tenth in 10 days), John painted a brightly colored house with a tree and a rainbow in the sky. It was still drizzling "to water the tree" and the mood of the picture was certainly one of hope. His mother reported that he "was less tearful and that he appeared to be much happier." John was able to address feelings of fear, sadness, anger, and guilt related to family violence through his daily paintings. His severe anguish about the "destruction" of his family and his home life was processed in a manner that protected his fragile ego.

The process of the play activity provided the distancing from the actual experience that enabled John to deal with an intense emotional experience on a daily basis without being overwhelmed by the experience. It is this dynamic that allows for the reduction of time between sessions and the assimilation of the experience by the child. A child intuitively knows how much of an experience he is ready to cope with at any given time. Therefore, a child-centered approach to play therapy is needed in intensive short-term play therapy experiences, because in this approach, "The therapist trusts the child's inner direction, allows the child to lead in all areas of the relationship and resists any urge to direct the child's play or conversation" (Landreth, 1991, p. 78).

## Advantages of Group Play Therapy

Group play therapy combines the therapeutic elements of group therapy and the unique communication style used in individual play therapy to provide a foundation for an extremely dynamic intervention. Ginott (1994) cited numerous advantages of group play therapy in working with children. First, within the group play therapy arena, children are provided with opportunities for multilateral relationships that are unavailable to them in individual play therapy. Group play therapy allows children to identify with the therapist and with other members of the play group. Secondly, group play therapy provides two media of catharsis—play and verbalization. This allows the child to utilize the method with which he or she feels most comfortable. Third, group play therapy provides children with vicarious catharsis. As one child explores an issue, the other children can benefit from the events that take place by indirectly experiencing the outcome. Fourth, group play therapy is representative of a miniature society in which children can test out new patterns of behavior. This arena also provides motivation and support for change. Finally, children are exposed to a new quality of intimate relationships. They learn that they can get close without being hurt or rejected (Ginott, 1994).

An additional benefit of group play therapy is the reduction of repetitious play that may be caused by traumatic reenactment (Terr, 1991). The collaboration of several children provides the opportunity to jointly utilize resources to establish a therapeutic and progressive expression of troubling situations (Slavson, 1968). All of these factors serve to enhance the effectiveness and productivity of time spent with the child in therapy. Providing group play therapy, rather than individual play therapy, may serve, in many cases, as a tool to increase the effectiveness of counseling and to enhance in assimilation of intrapersonal insight.

Further, group play therapy adds an additional intensifying dynamic to working with children experiencing social or family difficulties by creating a microsocial environment where the children are able to create positive social interactions without having to rely on generalizability from the therapeutic environment to the more realistic social environment or family environment. Children who participate in intensive group play therapy are able to actually experience a new social dynamic within the session, while children in individual play therapy only have access to a positive relationship between the therapist and the child. The child must internalize experiences from the therapeutic relationship and generalize it to another social context. Within the context of group play therapy, the therapist often serves as a representation of the parent figure or social mediator. During the play therapy sessions, the child is able to experience acceptance and nurturing, thereby restructuring the child's perception of the caregiving role. This relationship becomes a powerful tool for therapeutic change in children.

In addition, group play therapy decreases feelings of isolation and secrecy for children coping with issues such as familial AIDS, child sexual abuse, family drug use, and family violence. Group play therapy provides children with an open forum where they can begin to openly express the difficulties that they may be experiencing. This is especially true in sibling group play therapy. Although, individual play therapy addresses this issue by helping the child to feel safe with the therapist, it does not directly assist any members of the family in becoming more open about their difficulties. In group play therapy the therapist is available to mediate potentially harmful interchanges and to protect the nurturing environment of the playroom when the children risk expression.

## Sibling Group Play Therapy

It should be taken into account that children who are coping with family difficulties may more directly benefit from the intensity offered in intensive sibling group play therapy because the development of a trusting and understanding relationship has already been established between siblings. Often this relationship has been intensified through the experience of similarly traumatic events within the family of origin. The preexisting bonded relationship perhaps allows children to demonstrate and acknowledge a loving connection, thereby developing a non-threatening support system and enhancing therapeutic exploration and catharsis within the group context (Leavitt, et al., 1996; Leavitt et al., 1998). In individual play therapy or in non-sibling group play therapy, the child lacks the advantage of having a partner that has knowledge of previous events.

In intensive sibling group play therapy, aggressive feelings and behaviors are humanized and remediated in the here and now. In individual play therapy, children are not faced with solving interpersonal conflicts. This dynamic in sibling group play therapy has the potential to more easily tap into feelings and behaviors associated with person to person aggression. Siblings that address family difficulties as a unit have fewer difficulties in generalizing information to the family unit outside of the therapeutic hour. For example, during parent consultation with a mother of two young girls concluding intensive sibling group play therapy, the following event was proudly relayed. The children's mother reported overhearing her younger daughter verbally and physically annoying her older daughter in the back seat of the car while driving to school. The older daughter was clearly annoyed with the younger child and perceived her interactions to be an extreme nuisance. However, rather than engaging in the typical response of hitting her, the older daughter stated, "Stop buggin' me! I know you just want my attention, you can just tell me you want to play!" The mother reported that this type of interaction was representative of entirely new behavior between the siblings. It should be noted, however, that these behaviors had been apparent for some time during the play therapy sessions. After becoming comfortable with rehearsed play behaviors, the children were able to readily practice the new behaviors with one another outside of the sessions with little discomfort or unpredictability in familial response.

## INTENSIVE SHORT-TERM GROUP PLAY THERAPY TREATMENT FORMAT

Intensive short-term group play therapy is a complex and multifaceted intervention designed to more effectively address emotional and behavioral concerns of children. Establishing a clear therapeutic understanding of the intensive group play therapy structure and rationale is imperative to the facilitation of an effective and well rounded intervention. More specifically, proper group selection, size, and structure are essential to effective remediation of therapeutic concerns. Since intensive short-term group play therapy requires advanced clinical skill, it is important to acquire training in the use of group play therapy procedures and the use of playroom materials.

### Group Selection

The first step in initiating intensive short-term group play therapy sessions is to identify group members that will complement and assist one another in the therapeutic process. This means that children that participate in any form of intensive short-term group play therapy must be consistent in their attendance. If one group member repeatedly misses therapy sessions, the others are dramatically impacted. As mentioned earlier, sibling group play therapy often resolves this dilemma. Typically, if one sibling is absent or ill, the sibling also misses therapy. Another way to ensure consistency is to perform the sessions at school or in the family home. This would involve getting consent from the parents and/or the school system and would require that you assemble portable playroom supplies in a mobile tote bag. Conducting the sessions at school or at home also assists the play therapist in achieving a greater appreciation of the children's environment and level of coping. Additionally, intensive short-term group play therapy is highly conducive to working with children who are hospitalized, in residential treatment, group home placement, or shelter care due to their ability to consistently and actively participate in the therapeutic process on a daily basis.

Although children should generally be no more than one year apart in age in play therapy groups, sibling groups have much more flexibility in age range because the children have a daily relationship and they are already functioning as a unit outside of the counseling session. Sibling group interventions can be productive even when there is an age gap that spans up to six years. Issues related to gender and group composition are dealt with in the previous chapter.

## Group Size

Group size is another consideration that dramatically impacts the clinician's ability to properly manage therapeutic interactions within the group play sessions. Intensive short-term play therapy is extremely intense and progresses very rapidly. Therapists often have a sense of being drained and tired at the end of a therapeutic session. It is not because the dynamics are any different from weekly group play therapy sessions, but rather because the children are working at such an intensive pace, and they are often addressing crisis issues. It is important to keep up with the central theme being expressed and to identify the most productive therapeutic response in line with the stage of recovery. With the need for extreme clinical focus, it is recommended that there be *no more* than four children to a group. However, two children in a group is optimal. Siblings will actively recreate the family dynamic regardless of how many siblings are involved. Non-sibling groups with three older children can result in triangulation and two-against-one teasing teams.

## Group Structure

Intensive short-term group play therapy can be structured in a variety of ways depending on the family's schedule and the level of crisis exhibited by the child. Most literature considers brief or short-term therapy to be defined as twelve sessions or less. Ten to twelve sessions can allow a child adequate time to progress through treatment stages of engagement, self-discovery, change, and termination (Mann, 1973; Sloves & Peterlin, 1993). There are four characteristics associated with intensive short-term group play therapy: number of sessions per week, length or duration of sessions, inclusion of siblings or other group members with the same or a similar experience, and structuring of sessions. These factors are considered to be intensifying strategies and they can be varied in a number of ways. The standard model calls for daily, child-centered group play therapy sessions which are 45 minutes in duration for twelve consecutive sessions. This structure is the most intense format due to daily contact with the children and due to the non-directive nature of the sessions. Children are able to address concerns as they perceive them, and they control the structuring play themes to replicate *their* experience of the crisis. Sessions that are not structured by the therapist allow the child to pace the sessions as fast or as slow as needed to accommodate their level of functioning and to protect their ego strength.

Utilizing daily treatment provides a powerful view into the child's reality. Themes are more readily evident and seem to flow from one session to the next.

Often themes or play scenarios pick up where they left off the day before. A tea party that has been disrupted due to the conclusion of one session is very likely to resume the next day. Additionally, trust develops rapidly because of the daily consistency. When children are exposed to one another daily for extended periods of time, an in-depth level of intimacy that fuels therapeutic self-discovery is facilitated.

This model can be modified by providing play therapy sessions two or three times weekly rather than daily. The length of the sessions can also be adjusted, increasing standard sessions from forty-five minutes to one hour and a half for older children. It is not advisable to lengthen the sessions more than one hour and a half. Unlike adults who participated in the marathon groups of the '60s, children become tired, agitated, and lose focus. Sessions that are too long begin to focus on teasing or whining rather than on treatment issues.

A final method of manipulating the format of intensive short-term group play therapy is to structure the sessions. Structuring play sessions requires the therapist to design specific scenarios, select materials, and control the parameters of a narrative session. This intervention should be used very sparingly and should be conducted with forethought and precision. Because this technique relies on the therapist's understanding of how the child perceives a given event, there is a lot of room for error. Additionally, since it is difficult to judge a child's ego strength during an intake session or even within a more extensive evaluation period, structuring is not recommended for children needing therapy for the first time. While structuring can expedite treatment, much training is needed to successfully facilitate therapeutic structuring of a crisis event.

## Materials and Techniques

Many of the same techniques and materials used to facilitate long term play therapy with an individual child or with a group may be utilized in intensive short-term play therapy. It is important to remember that if the child has experienced a trauma, provisions should be made to incorporate toys and materials that can adequately express the child's experience. For example, if the child has experienced a medical emergency, the therapist should include an ambulance and medical supplies that the child may have encountered while at the hospital.

A procedure that is used in individual play therapy which has an expanded application when used in group play therapy is identification of themes and enlarging the meaning. The group may identify a central theme that is addressed by all members, but each individual will participate in the larger theme in their own unique way. Over the course of treatment, each individual may demonstrate a consistent way of participating in group events. This is reflective of internal and personal struggles and they can be identified as individual themes. For example, children coping with family violence may be preoccupied with safety and self-preservation, which are believed to be representative of high levels of anxiety pertaining to safety from the abusive parent. Group play themes typically revolve around shielding oneself from harm and gaining mastery and control over an otherwise frightening situation. These children may engage in elaborate play with weapons and shields, and they may establish secret, protected hiding places for themselves and for the toys that are representative of themselves. These types of play behaviors allow children to restructure their reality so as to experience control and psychological safety (Frick-Helms, 1997).

Within the consistent group theme of safety and protection, one child may repeatedly perform heroic, lifesaving feats, while another child typically falls victim to the "bad guys." Their individual themes reflect their own experiences within the family unit. Although they work together on a central theme of safety and self-preservation, they each demonstrate individual themes of power and control and victimization respectively. It is important to respond to both sets of themes. The therapist may engage the children in the above scenario by making general theme statements such as "This is a very dangerous situation" *and* by making individual theme statements such as "You really feel like you're in control. Nothing can get you!" (directed toward the heroic child). Both of these themes enlarge the meaning for the child and help the child to personalize and apply the play material to the child's perception of reality.

Pacing within a group play therapy session refers to both the pace that each child uses to engage in play *and* the pace at which the children engage with one another. For example, a child can be so absorbed in the urgency of individual exploration of the playroom that he or she virtually ignores the other children in the room. The child may be moving quickly about the room and verbalizing pleasure and excitement but not engaging with the other children. The child's individual pace would be described as rapid but pacing between the group members would be slow or nonexistent. It is important that the therapist mirror the pace of the individual when communicating with only one child, but mirror the pace of the group when communicating with more than one child at a time. This allows the children to feel connected and understood as an individual and as a group member.

"Bridging" is a concept that applies only to group play therapy. This is a response in which the therapist identifies behaviors or emotions that the children may have in common. The application of this response can be broadened to incorporate behaviors and emotions that group members display as opposite from other group members. This technique is particularly useful in assisting children to understand the impact that their behavior has on others in their social environment. This response can be readily exemplified by the following play scenario conducted with two female siblings.

Initial behavioral assessments revealed that the older child, Jessica, tended to cope with emotional distress by isolating and withdrawing. The younger of the two, Brittany, appeared to manage anxiety with behavior that was impulsive and aggressive. In the initial sibling play therapy group sessions, Jessica reacted as though she was overwhelmed by her sister's behaviors. She often retreated behind the easel to color or to hold a teddy bear while Brittany raced around the room exploring every detail of the play equipment. Frequent bridging statements might be: "Jessica, you really feel anxious and overwhelmed when your sister races around the room exploring all of the toys. But, Brittany, you're excited about all of the new things in this room."

By the fourth session, Jessica had established her corner of the room and had portioned off a section that she labeled as "her house." Additionally, she stated that "No one is allowed to visit." Yet her sister persistently barged into "her house" without an invitation. These behaviors were bridged by comments like: "Jessica you really want some private space of your own, and Brittany, you want to play in her house, too. You *both* want it your way." (This response demonstrates the use of bridging opposites as well as commonalities.)

As sibling group play therapy sessions continued, both children became more aware of how their behavior impacted others and they became more perceptive about what motivates other people's actions. Previously, both children had assumed that their sibling was simply trying to annoy them. They eventually gained a greater appreciation of underlying feelings for one another.

Videotaping play therapy sessions is also a recommended play therapy procedure when engaging in intensive short-term group play therapy. The videotaped sessions can be used in a variety of ways. First, videotaped sessions can be reviewed by group participants. This may be the first time they are able to see themselves as others see them. Often this intervention comes about at the request of the children when they know that they are being videotaped. When they view the video, they should have the liberty to fast forward through sections and pause wherever they chose. This allows the children to focus on and discuss emotions or behavioral interchanges that are most important to them.

Additionally, videotaped sessions are extremely important for therapist self monitoring. Review of sessions at a later period often reveals themes that may have been missed during the actual session. A review can also reveal personal issues that may have been touched upon within the therapist and that have been inadvertently expressed through facial expressions or body posturing. The therapist can objectively view the session pace and practice better responses. This is a particularly useful technique when engaging in intensive short-term group play therapy because themes develop and shift so rapidly. It is often easy to miss important therapeutic opportunities due to the rapid pace of the sessions.

## PRACTICAL APPLICATIONS IN INTENSIVE SHORT-TERM GROUP PLAY THERAPY

When conducting group play therapy, most clinicians will be faced with the day-to-day challenges inherent in play therapy with more than one child. Two common issues confronted in intensive sibling group play therapy include bathroom breaks and group member absenteeism. It is inevitable that a child will require a bathroom break at some point during treatment. Most play therapy rooms do not have the luxury of a bathroom inside the playroom, therefore bathroom breaks become more complicated events due to the need to supervise all of the children that are participating in the group session. Some clinicians choose to stand in the playroom doorway, keeping one eye on the group and one eye on the bathroom door. This is not a recommended method of managing bathroom breaks. The therapist will certainly have a difficult time facilitating therapeutic interactions without full and focused attention on the children remaining in the session. Often children recognize that they are not being attended to and choose to act out in order to gain more attention. When the therapist turns to address concerns within the group, the child in the bathroom has, for all intensive purposes, been abandoned. The child may feel betrayed if complications are experienced in the restroom and the therapist is unavailable or inattentive.

The most effective method of coping with bathroom breaks is to make a clear statement that all of the group members stick together, no matter what. So, if one child must go to the bathroom, the therapist sets a clear limit "It's time for a bathroom break, you can choose to hold hands to walk to the bathroom or you can choose to walk on your own." Other group members may take advantage of the break to use the restroom as well. This has the additional advantage of avoiding several trips to the bathroom. Using this procedure, bathroom breaks are usually not disruptive because group cohesion has not been impacted. Group members often continue with the same play theme once they have returned to the playroom.

While bathroom breaks are typically not disruptive, group member absenteeism does have a profound impact on the children in the group. It is important to make it clear to parents that consistency is extremely important and unplanned absenteeism can negatively impact all of the participants. It is best to plan for unavoidable absenteeism well in advance, thereby preparing the other members and the absent group member. Childhood illnesses and family emergencies, however, are often unpredictable and therefore a plan of action should be prepared in advance. Despite an absent group member, sessions should proceed even if only one participant is present. Cancellation suggests to the child who is present, that he or she is not important.

When beginning a group play session in which a member is absent, it is necessary for the therapist to inform group members that a child will be absent. However, the therapist should avoid a lengthy explanation of the reason for the missed appointment. When the absent child returns, if the group members are still interested, the child should have the option of whether to state the reason for the absence. The therapist may be prodded by the other children to disclose the reason for the absence when the child is not present; however, confidentiality should be protected by suggesting that the missing group member will need to answer their questions and they can ask upon the child's return. With younger children, this is usually not an issue. If a child is regularly absent, the therapist should recommend that the child continue treatment in individual therapy to preserve the integrity of the group and to enhance the effectiveness of treatment for all of the children involved.

If a child must unexpectedly terminate therapy, it is always best to request at least two termination sessions; however, this is not always possible. When the family has confirmed the need for immediate termination, it is appropriate for the therapist to state that the child will not be returning. At this time, it is important to allow time for expression of emotion. The therapist may choose to handle questions about the sudden termination by reflecting the children's disappointment, sadness, and surprise, rather than by directly answering questions related to the child departing the group.

## REFERENCES

Capuzzi, D., & Gross, D. (1992). *Introduction to group counseling*. Denver, CO: Love Publishing.

Davanloo, H. (1980). *Short-term dynamic psychotherapy*. New York: Jason Aronson.

Frick-Helms, S. (1997). "Boys cry louder than girls:" Play therapy behaviors of children residing in a shelter for battered women. *International Journal of Play Therapy, 6*(1), 73–91.

Ginott, H. C. (1994). *Group psychotherapy with children: The theory and practice of play therapy*. Northvale, NJ: Jason Aronson.

Hofmann, J., & Rogers, P. (1991). A crisis play group in shelter following the Santa Cruz earthquake. In N. B. Webb (Ed.), *Play therapy with children in crisis: A casebook for practitioners* (pp. 379–395). New York: Guilford Press.

Kot, S., Landreth, G., & Giordano, M. (1999). Intensive play therapy with child witnesses of domestic violence. *International Journal of Play Therapy, 7*, 17–36.

Landreth, G. (1966). *Group counseling and varied time effects*. Unpublished doctoral dissertation, University of New Mexico, Albuquerque.

Landreth, G. (1991). *Play therapy: The art of the relationship*. Muncie, IN: Accelerated Development.

Leavitt, K., & Gardner, S., Gallagher, M., & Schamess, C. (1998). Severely traumatized siblings: A treatment strategy. *Clinical Social Work Journal, 26*(1), 55–70.

Leavitt, K., Morrison, S., Gardner, S., & Gallagher, M. (1996). Group play for cumulatively traumatized child survivors of family

AIDS. *International Journal of Play Therapy, 5*(1), 1–17.

Malan, D. H. (1976). *The Frontier of brief psychotherapy*. New York: Plenum.

Mann, J. (1973). *Time-limited psychotherapy*. Cambridge, MA: Harvard University Press.

Saravay, B. (1991). Short-term play therapy with two preschool brothers following sudden parental death. In N. B. Webb (Ed.), *Play therapy with children in crisis: A casebook for practitioners* (pp. 379–395). New York: Guilford Press.

Sifneos, P. E. (1979). *Short-term dynamic psychotherapy*. New York: Plenum.

Slavson, S. (1968). Play group for young children. *Nervous Child, 7*, 318–327.

Sloves, R., & Peterlin, K. B. (1993). Where in the world is...my father? A time limited play therapy. In T. Kottman & C. Schaefer (Eds.), *Play therapy in action: A casebook for practitioners* (pp. 301–344). Northvale, NJ: Jason Aronson.

Terr, L. C. (1990). *Too scared to cry: Psychic trauma in childhood*. New York: Harper & Row.

Terr, L. C. (1991). Childhood trauma: An outline and overview. *American Journal of Psychiatry, 148*, 10–20.

Tyndall-Lind (1999). *A comparative analysis of intensive individual play therapy and intensive sibling group play therapy with child witnesses of domestic violence*. Unpublished Dissertation, University of North Texas, Denton.

Yalom, I. D. (1970). *The theory and practice of group psychotherapy*. New York: Basic Books, Inc.

# 14

# Short-Term Play Therapy

## SHAUNDA PETERSON JOHNSON

*P*lay therapists today, along with other mental health professionals, must recognize managed care as a dominant force in the mental health care industry. Professionals are often required to defend their practice to managed care organizations that are concerned with cost-effective, goal-oriented, time-limited therapy (Cummings, 1995). Play therapists must actively educate themselves about current research on outcomes of short-term play therapy for two reasons: (a) to provide managed care organizations and other professionals research-based evidence of the effectiveness of play therapy as a treatment modality for children, and (b) to combat the common belief that effective play therapy requires a lengthy commitment (Landreth, Homeyer, Glover, & Sweeney, 1996).

A concise definition of short-term play therapy currently is not available in the research literature. "Many therapists consider eight to ten sessions a long-term case; others do not see 2 years or more of treatment as excessive" (O'Connor, 1991, p. 306). Within the context of this chapter, short-term play therapy is defined by twelve or less play therapy sessions. This chapter documents the effectiveness of short-term therapy, including individual play therapy, group play therapy, and filial therapy as useful interventions with children experiencing a wide range of difficulties.

## ABUSE AND NEGLECT

"Abuse and neglect cause serious inner conflicts and relationship problems for children, and play therapy provides the modality necessary for children to develop adaptive and coping mechanisms on their own terms and at their own emotional pace" (Landreth et al., 1996, p. 1). Maintaining an awareness that the child sets the pace of therapy provides a vantage point from which to consider short-term play therapy as a useful intervention. The results of several studies have demonstrated the effectiveness of short-term play therapy with abused and neglected children (Klem, 1992; Perez, 1987).

Klem (1992) used a structured play therapy approach with a developmentally delayed six-year-old boy who was able to use the play therapy setting to disclose and explore physical and sexual abuse that he had experienced. During the first play therapy session the boy used a dollhouse and doll figures to repeatedly reenact the abuse. The availability of the dollhouse in therapy provided the child with a means to communicate his fears related to the abuse. By the fourth session, Klem noted that the child had developed a stronger sense of safety and control.

Perez (1987) studied the effect of short-term individual and group play therapy with sexually abused children. Fifty-five children ages four to nine years, and identified as sexual abuse victims, were divided into three groups. The first group participated in individual play therapy, while the second group participated in group play therapy. The third group served as a control and received neither individual nor group play therapy. The treatment groups received twelve sessions of play therapy, conducted once a week for one hour. At the end of twelve weeks, the children who received either individual or group play therapy showed significant increases in scores on a measure of self-mastery. The self-concept measures of children in both treatment groups also increased, whereas the self-concept measures of the control group decreased. The results of this study support the use of short-term play therapy as a beneficial intervention with male and female sexually abused children despite their age, current home environment, or varied abuse experiences.

## AGGRESSION AND ACTING OUT

Aggressive behavior by children often stems from unexpressed wants, desires, or feelings. Once a child has been given an opportunity to express negative feelings or needs, and remains accepted, the child will feel the freedom to experiment with more effective behaviors. Short-term play therapy, as described by Levy (1939), can provide aggressive children with just such an opportunity for expression.

Levy (1939) reported positive results after ten sessions of release play therapy with a two-year-old child exhibiting severe temper tantrums and behavior problems. Levy proposed that the child's problems were related to rigid toilet training imposed by a strict caregiver when the child was one-year old. The use of a potty chair and clay as play materials allowed the child the freedom to self-regress, releasing her anxiety over physical demands imposed on her at an earlier age. The child's mother reported that soiling behavior had ceased by the tenth session of play therapy. Parent reports also indicated that the child displayed positive changes in her attitude, compliance with parents, and relations with peers.

## EMOTIONALLY DISTURBED AND SCHIZOPHRENIC CHILDREN

Play therapy provides a safe, consistent setting in which emotionally disturbed children can play out their intense emotions and better learn to cope with their environment (Landreth et al., 1996). Gumaer (1984) conducted a study using developmental group play therapy with eight emotionally disturbed children, ages 8 and 9 years old. Gumaer divided the participants into two groups and met with each group for 45-minute sessions, once a week for 12 weeks. The sessions were designed to meet certain goals by following an outline of specific activities, such as expressing emotions through pantomime. The participants completed a self-concept evaluation prior to and following treatment. Disregarding one child who did not accurately complete the scale, the remaining children displayed an increase in self-concept. The children's teacher reported that the children evidenced fewer discipline problems and displayed more developmentally appropriate behaviors toward teachers and peers. During the twelve sessions of group play therapy, the children were provided an opportunity to develop socialization skills and transfer these skills to their daily lives.

Short-term play therapy is not only applicable for children experiencing emotional disturbances, but also for children with mental disorders as severe as schizophrenia. Irwin (1971) conducted six sessions of child-centered play therapy with a sixteen-year-old girl hospitalized for schizophrenia. At the onset of therapy Jane made no eye contact with others, exhibited a total lack of affect, and displayed a lack of control of her bladder or bowel movements. She remained in bed all day, presented with an expressionless stare, and would only speak the word "yellow." By the third play therapy session, hospital staff reported that Jane was choosing to leave her room during the day, and by the fifth play therapy session Jane was reading aloud in front of other hospital patients. Furthermore, she made eye contact with the therapist and smiled when the therapist reflected her feelings. A two-month follow-up found Jane attending school and continuing to display remarkable progress.

## ENCOPRETIC PROBLEMS

Encopretic children often experience peer rejection and lower self-esteem as a result of their condition, which is difficult to conceal. Play therapy allows the child to work through the many emotions associated with encopresis (Landreth et al., 1996). Knell and Moore (1990) employed a cognitive-behavioral approach in working with a five-year-old boy with primary nonretentive encopresis and a language deficit. At the onset of therapy, the child refused to have bowel movements in the toilet and frequently soiled his clothes. The child's language deficit made play therapy a particularly appropriate treatment. Knell and Moore noted that after twelve sessions of play therapy, the child consistently used the toilet for bowel movements, and after fourteen sessions no soiling accidents were reported. The child's improvement was readily apparent with short-term play therapy. Furthermore, a follow-up at 8 months and again at 45 months indicated lasting positive results of play therapy.

## FEAR AND ANXIETY

Play therapy provides a safe, accepting environment in which children are free to express their fears and anxieties. Similar to aggressive behavior, once fear or anxiety has been expressed the child may experience a sense of control and feel free to move toward healthier development. Research has suggested that short-term therapy, as few as three sessions (Levy, 1939), can be an effective intervention for dealing with children's fear and anxiety.

Barlow, Landreth, and Strother (1985) found eight weekly sessions of child-centered play therapy to be effective with a four-year-old child experiencing Trichotillomania (pulling out and then eating her own hair). Play therapy allowed Nancy an opportunity to process her inner conflicts within the safety of a therapeutic relationship. For the first time, Nancy felt the freedom to express her inner self without fearing limits or disapproval from her mother or grandmother. During eight sessions of play therapy, she never attempted to pull her hair out while in the playroom. Furthermore, by the seventh session new hair growth covered Nancy's head, providing strong visual evidence of the effectiveness of short-term play therapy.

Three sessions of release play therapy allowed a two-year-old boy to release his anxiety over being hit and scratched by another child. Shortly after the traumatic incident, Paul began stammering and displayed a fearful disposition. The therapist used a form of release play therapy in which the traumatic event was symbolically reenacted with Paul until he could release his anxiety through aggression. Following the third play therapy session, Paul's mother reported that he had stopped stammering and did not display a fearful attitude. He had released his anxiety surrounding the traumatic experience by acting out aggressively in the playroom. A one-year and two-year follow-up indicated that Paul did not revert to stammering and was developing normally (Levy, 1939).

Machler (1965) reported positive results after five consecutive sessions of play therapy using puppets to help a ten-year-old girl that was experiencing school phobia. Puppets representing the characters in the story of Pinocchio provided Nora with a metaphor through which she could work through her problems concerning fear of school and feelings toward her parents. By the fifth session, Nora no longer exhibited school phobia; instead, she voiced enthusiasm to the therapist about her learning experiences at school.

Straughan (1964) studied the effect of a behavioral approach to improve the interaction patterns between an eight-year-old girl and her mother. At the onset of play therapy, the child was reported to persistently exaggerate or lie and she had few positive peer relationships. It was suspected that parent–child interactions, characterized by anxiety and stress, were negatively impacting the child's behavior. In a total of five sessions, the mother and child each met with a therapist. Initially, the mother and her therapist observed the child's play discussing principles of play therapy such as limit setting, and allowing the child to lead the play. Beginning in the first session, the mother and her therapist spent an increasing portion of each session in the playroom with the daughter and her therapist. The mother received feedback from her therapist regarding appropriate facilitative responses to her daughter's free play. By the fifth and final session, the child demonstrated noticeably improved behavior at school and at home. She had increased social interaction and decreased behavioral problems. An eight month follow-up indicated that the child continued to display improvement.

Milos and Reiss (1982) studied the effectiveness of play in reducing separation anxiety in two to six-year-old children. Thirty-two boys and thirty-two girls were divided into four groups, including: free play, directed play, modeling, and a control group. The children participated in three, 10-minute individual play sessions that were spaced several days apart. Toys provided to the children in the treatment groups were related to separation anxiety caused by being dropped off at nursery school. After three sessions, there was a noticeable reduction in anxiety among children in the treatment groups. The researchers did not discover a significant difference in decrease of anxiety among the three treatment groups. Although, the directed group engaged in more play related to separation when compared to the free play group. The researchers found children with higher quality play related to separation experienced lower levels of anxiety. The child's emotional investment in the play itself was the most critical factor (not whether the play sessions were directive or nondirective) in allowing the children to work through their separation anxiety.

Conn (1941) worked with a nine-year-old girl who was afraid of the dark due to a fear of being kidnapped. The therapist used structured doll play to illustrate the child's problems, and to allow the child to explore the cause of her fears. The dolls provided Harriet with a safe emotional distance from which to discover the root of her problems and to deal with her fears. By the third session Harriet was able to approach bedtime without a fear of darkness or kidnappers. Conn's study provided evidence of improvement by the child after only a few sessions, although therapy continued for at least seven months. His use of structured play therapy fits this author's definition of short-term play therapy in that it consisted of nine total sessions, although treatment spanned a lengthy period of time.

## FILIAL THERAPY

Short-term therapy has proven to be effective not only in play therapy with children but also in filial therapy with parents. The filial therapy model developed by Landreth (1991) is based on a ten-week training program that emphasizes strengthening the parent–child relationship through the use of both didactic and dynamic components. Parents are trained in child-centered play therapy skills, including: reflecting feelings, conveying acceptance, and establishing appropriate limits. Filial therapy provides an emotional support system for parents and promotes the development of healthy parenting skills (Bratton & Landreth, 1995).

Glass (1987) studied the effects of the Landreth (1991) filial therapy training model as an intervention for building children's self-concepts. Twenty-seven parents and twenty children, ages five through ten, who volunteered for filial therapy training were chosen as the participants in the study. Fifteen parents were placed in the experimental group and twelve parents in the control group. The filial therapy training consisted of ten sessions, once a week for two hours. In addition, the parents organized a thirty-minute play session, once a week, at home with their children. Glass found that both parents and children that participated in filial therapy demonstrated increases in self-concept when compared to the control group. Although the increases in self-concepts were not statistically significant, Glass suggested that parental acceptance gained in filial therapy could continue to positively impact the children's self-concepts in the future. In other words, long-term benefits may be derived from short-term filial therapy.

Glazer-Waldman, Zimmerman, Landreth, and Norton (1992) conducted a study using the Landreth (1991) filial therapy training model as an intervention with parents of chronically-ill children. The participants consisted of six parents whose children were diagnosed with asthma, cerebral palsy, muscular dystrophy, and a severe feeding disorder. The parents participated in ten sessions of filial therapy training, once a week for 2 hours. The researchers attempted to measure both the parents' and the child's perception of current anxiety, and the parents' level of acceptance and behavior toward their child. Results did not show statistically significant outcomes; however, qualitative research findings indicated that the parents effectively learned the skills associated with child-centered play therapy. The parents reported positive changes in their children and themselves after engaging in the filial therapy training. Each of the parents noted an improved relationship with their children.

Bratton and Landreth (1995) studied the effectiveness of the Landreth (1991) filial therapy training model with single parents. Forty-three people participated in the study; twenty-two were assigned to the experimental group and twenty-one were assigned to the control group. The participants in the experimental group received ten sessions of filial therapy training, for two hours once a week, in addition to engaging in weekly 30-minute play sessions with one of their children. Bratton and Landreth found that parents in the experimental group displayed (a) significantly increased levels of empathic behavior toward their children, (b) significantly increased attitudes of acceptance toward their children, (c) significantly reduced levels of parenting related stress, and (d) significantly decreased perception in the number of their child's problematic behaviors.

Glover (1996) studied the effects of the Landreth (1991) filial therapy training model with Native American parents. Eleven parents in the experimental group received ten weekly 2-hour filial therapy training sessions and participated in weekly 30-minute play sessions with one of their children. Ten parents in the control group received no treatment. Parents in the experimental group significantly increased their level of empathy in their interactions with their children. There were positive trends in parental acceptance, parental stress, and children's self-concepts.

Yuen (1997) utilized the Landreth (1991) filial therapy training model to study the effectiveness of filial therapy with immigrant Chinese parents. Eighteen immigrant Chinese parents in Canada comprised the experimental group, which participated in ten weekly 2-hour filial therapy training sessions. The experimental group participants also engaged in weekly 30-minute play sessions with their child of focus for the study. Consistent with Tew's results, Yuen found that the experimental group (a) displayed significantly reduced parental stress, (b) displayed significantly improved level of acceptance toward their children, and (c) reported significantly less problematic behaviors with their children. Yuen also found that the parents in the experimental group exhibited an increased level of empathic behavior in interactions with their children, and the children in the experimental group displayed a significant increase in self-concept.

Tew (1997) also studied filial therapy with families with chronically-ill children, utilizing the Landreth (1991) filial therapy training model. Twelve parents in the experimental group received ten sessions of filial therapy training, once a week for 2 hours. In addition, they participated in weekly 30-minute play sessions with one of their children. Eleven parents in the control group did not receive treatment. Statistical analysis showed that the experimental group (a) significantly reduced their parental stress, (b) significantly improved their level of acceptance toward their children, and (c) reported significantly less problematic behaviors with their children.

Harris and Landreth (1997) utilized the Landreth (1991) filial therapy training model with incarcerated mothers to determine the effectiveness of filial therapy in increasing empathic interactions with their children, increasing acceptance level toward their children, and reducing parenting related stress. Participants in the study included twenty-two incarcerated mothers, twelve in the experimental group and ten in the control group. The researchers employed an intensive training format in which participants received ten sessions of filial therapy training, twice a week for five weeks. Parents in the experimental group participated in 30-minute play sessions, twice a week, with their child of focus. Analysis of the research instruments showed that the mothers in the treatment group (a) displayed a significant increase in empathic behaviors toward their children, (b) displayed a significant increase in acceptance of their children, and (c) reported a significant decrease in the number of problematic behaviors their children were experiencing. Researchers did not find a significant reduction in the treatment group's level of parental stress.

Chau and Landreth (1997) examined the effectiveness of the Landreth

(1991) filial therapy training model with Chinese parents. Eighteen parents in the experimental group received ten weekly 2-hour filial therapy training sessions and conducted a weekly 30-minute play session with one of their children. Sixteen parents in the control group received no treatment. Parents in the experimental group significantly increased their empathic behavior and attitude of acceptance toward their children and significantly reduced their level of parental stress.

Landreth and Lobaugh (1998) studied the effects of the Landreth (1991) filial therapy training model with incarcerated fathers as a method of improving the parent–child relationship and building the child's self-esteem. The participants in the study consisted of thirty-two incarcerated fathers, sixteen in the experimental group and sixteen in the control group. The participants in the experimental group received ten sessions of filial therapy training, once a week for ninety minutes; in addition, these fathers conducted weekly 30-minute play sessions with their child of focus for the study. The fathers in the control group did not participate in training; however, they each met in a playroom with their designated child ten times during visiting hours. Landreth and Lobaugh found that children whose fathers were in the filial therapy training displayed significant improvement in self-concept. The fathers who received filial therapy training illustrated decreases in parental stress and increases in unconditional love, acceptance of their children's feelings and individuality, and awareness of their children's needs for independence.

Costas and Landreth (1999) investigated the effectiveness of the Landreth (1991) filial therapy training model with non-offending parents of children who had been sexually abused. Fourteen parents in the experimental group received ten sessions of filial therapy training once a week and had weekly 30-minute play sessions with their child of focus for the study. Twelve parents in the control group received no training. Experimental group parents significantly increased their empathetic behavior and attitude of acceptance toward their children and significantly reduced their level of parental stress. Measures of children's anxiety, behavior adjustment, emotional adjustment, and self-concept indicated positive trends.

Kale and Landreth (1999) investigated the effectiveness of the Landreth (1991) filial therapy training model with parents of children experiencing learning difficulties. Eleven parents in the experimental group received ten weekly 2-hour sessions of filial therapy training and conducted a weekly 30-minute play session with one of their children. Eleven parents in the control group received no treatment. Experimental group parents significantly increased their attitude of acceptance toward their children and significantly decreased their level of stress related to parenting.

## GRIEVING CHILDREN

According to Landreth et al. (1996), "Children do not generally experience acute pain in lengthy periods, but rather in short bursts, almost as though their attention span for pain is short" (p. 135). This description of children's grief reactions is highly compatible with the principles of short-term play therapy. Researchers have studied the effects of individual play therapy (LeVieux, 1994) and group play therapy (Tait & Depta, 1994) with bereaved children.

LeVieux (1994) used a child-centered approach to play therapy with a five-year-old girl grieving the loss of her father. At the onset of therapy, Celeste was described as stubborn, uncooperative, moody, and depressed. The total number of sessions that LeVieux worked with Celeste is unclear; however, by the seventh session, Celeste's mother reported notable changes in her daughter. Celeste and her mother were able to more easily discuss the father's death, and Celeste became capable of verbally and symbolically expressing her sadness and anger surrounding her father's death. The research implied that through play therapy, Celeste was able to process her repressed emotions and regain a sense of control in her life.

Tait and Depta (1994) conducted a study using group play therapy with bereaved children, ranging in age from seven to eleven-years old. The ten children included in the group had all experienced the loss of a close family member, usually a parent. During eight total treatment sessions, the therapist employed a wide range of activities in the session, including drawing, charade games, clay work, family sculpting, puppetry, storytelling, and writing letters to the deceased family member. The children in the group gained support from their peers and the co-facilitators of the group. The study suggested that through group play therapy the children were able to move from a state of feeling angry, depressed, withdrawn, and abandoned toward a sense of feeling normal and in control of their lives.

## HEARING IMPAIRED CHILDREN
## WITH BEHAVIORAL DIFFICULTIES

Play therapy is a well-suited intervention for hearing impaired children because of the lack of emphasis on verbalization. Oualline (1975) conducted a study of short-term therapy with twenty-four hearing impaired children, ages four through six years, exhibiting behavioral disturbances. The participants were assigned to either a treatment group or a control group. The treatment group received ten weekly 50-minute sessions of individual child-centered play therapy. The control group received thirty minutes of individual unstructured play time with an untrained supervisor. Statistical analysis indicated that children participating in play therapy significantly improved on a scale measuring social maturity. Furthermore, reports by parents and teachers indicated that seven of the children involved in play therapy displayed an increase in positive behaviors following the treatment.

## HOSPITALIZED CHILDREN

Hospitals provide an excellent site to implement short-term play therapy, based on the length of stay of many children. Hospitals can be frightening and unusual places for children, however, play can offer the child a sense of familiarity. Play therapy in a hospital setting allows children an opportunity to release anxiety and regain a sense of control or mastery over their environment.

Acord (1980), Barton (1962), and Garot (1986) reported successful studies based on a limited number of sessions of play therapy with hospitalized children. Acord (1980) facilitated four play therapy sessions in the hospital, followed by two sessions in the home for a five-year old boy suffering injuries from an automobile accident. Jason was able to play out his fear of injections by using a stuffed bear and a syringe. Barton (1962) cited the case of Kathy, also a five-year-old child, who participated in two play therapy sessions while she was hospitalized for open-heart surgery. Distrust and hostility characterized Kathy's first hospital visit and for that reason play therapy was recommended. During the play sessions Kathy was able to work through her feelings of anger toward her mother, as well as build a sense of trust in the hospital staff. She moved from feeling hostile and distrusting to cheerfully looking forward to visiting her friends at the hospital. Garot (1986) conducted two sessions of play therapy with a five-year-old girl hospitalized because of an infected lymphangioma. Brandy presented with high levels of fear and stress related to the IV (intravenous) treatments, anxiety over separation from her parents, and a poor self-image. Garot maintained that after two sessions Brandy's anxiety and stress were significantly lessened, and her self-acceptance improved. In each of the above cases (Acord, 1980; Barton, 1962; Garot, 1986) short-term play therapy was effective as a means for children to play out their fears and anxieties, thus reducing the trauma associated with hospitalization.

Cassell (1965) conducted a study involving children hospitalized for cardiac catheterization. Forty children, ages 3 through 11, were divided between an experimental group and a control group. The experimental group received two sessions of puppet therapy, one prior to the catheterization and one following the catheterization. The control group received standard hospital treatment. Results of the two sessions showed that children taking part in the puppet therapy exhibited less emotional distress during the cardiac catheterization and displayed more acceptance of returning to the hospital for future medical care.

Daniel, Rae, Sanner, Upchurch, and Worchel (1989) studied the effectiveness of play therapy on the psychosocial adjustment of hospitalized children with acute illnesses. Forty-six hospitalized children participated in the study. Participants were randomly assigned to one of three experimental groups, or a control group that received no treatment. The three experimental groups included: therapeutic play, diversionary play, and verbal support. The therapeutic play group employed nondirective child-centered play therapy. Toys associated with hospitals were included in the play materials. The diversionary play group participated in structured activities, such as games and puzzles. The researcher did not provide verbal support or therapeutic interventions with this group. The verbal support group discussed their thoughts and feelings surrounding their hospitalization; however, they were not permitted to participate in any play behaviors. Participants were administered a pre-test prior to being assigned to one of the four groups, and a post-test on their third day in the hospital. Analysis of research instruments indicated that the children participating in nondirective play therapy exhibited a significantly reduced level of self-reported fear, and an increase in somatization. No significant differences were found regarding level of fear for the diversionary play group, verbal support group, or control group. It is significant to note that after only three days as a pediatric patient, the children who received child-centered play therapy were less fearful about their experience in the hospital.

Ellerton, Caty, and Ritchie (1985) conducted an analysis of play interviews with ten chronically-ill children, ages 2 to 6 years old, hospitalized for a minimum of 21 days. A maximum of six play interviews was conducted with each of the children involved in the study. The play interviews consisted of providing the child with a suitcase of toys including familiar toys, family dolls, and clinical equipment. Initially, each of the toys was identified by the researcher to the child; however, the remainder of the session was nondirective. The researchers analyzed all behavior identified as intrusive, and discovered that 9 of the 10 children had themes of intrusion (injections, medications, temperature taking, and tube-feeding) in their play. The children studied were receptive to using their few play sessions as a means to express their worries about medical procedures. Play therapy in hospital settings offers children an opportunity to project their fear and anxiety onto the toys and regain a sense of control in an unfamiliar environment.

Zilliacus and Enberg (1980) took a different approach to short-term play therapy in hospitals. The researchers set up a play therapy program in the hospital waiting room of a children's hospital. Children could choose to participate in play activities in the hospital waiting room as well as on the individual wards. The researchers surveyed twenty-one hospital staff members and one hundred parents whose children had participated in the hospital's play therapy program. Eighty percent of the parents surveyed reported that play therapy was effective in decreasing their child's fear or anxiety. The hospital staff members also reported positive attitudes toward the play therapy program, in that children were more at ease and parents were easier to approach.

## READING DIFFICULTIES, SELF-CONCEPT, AND SELF-ESTEEM

Research suggests that there is a correlation between emotional problems and reading difficulties. Poor reading skills, associated with feelings of frustration and failure, can negatively impact a child's self-esteem. Researchers have found school-based short-term play therapy to be an effective intervention for improving reading skills (Axline, 1947; Bills, 1950) and building self-esteem (Crow, 1990; Gould, 1980).

Axline (1947) conducted a study using child-centered play therapy to promote reading readiness among school-aged children. Thirty-seven children were selected for the study based on the criteria of serious reading maladjustment. Axline later concluded that most of the children chosen for the study also experienced serious emotional difficulties. The children's emotional problems appeared to manifest, in part, as a deficit in reading readiness. The thirty-seven participants were placed in the same classroom, which was oriented toward personal expressiveness, problem solving, goal clarification, and positive interpersonal communication. Four children in the class received eight sessions of individual play therapy for 30 minutes once a week. After four months, all of the children were administered reading and IQ tests. Approximately 21 of the 36 students left in the study demonstrated improved reading skills in each of three areas including words, sentences, and paragraphs. Axline found that three of the four children who received play therapy had notably increased their IQ score. The fourth child did not show an increase in IQ score; however, her initial score was 126. Axline's study suggests that a therapeutic classroom environment in conjunction with short-term play therapy can positively impact both the emotional development and reading ability of school-aged children.

A second research study by Bills (1950) examined child-centered play therapy as an intervention for third grade children experiencing reading difficulties. The participants included eighteen children in a class specifically for students designated as slow learners. Eight of these children served as a treatment group and ten served as a comparison group. The study was composed of three phases that were each thirty school days in length. During the first phase of the study, the children were administered oral and silent reading pre-tests and post-tests to ascertain a baseline for comparing reading abilities. In the second phase of the study, the treatment group received six weekly individual child-centered play therapy sessions, and three weekly group child-centered play therapy sessions. At the conclusion of the third phase of the study, the children were once again administered the oral and silent reading exams. Each participant in the treatment group demonstrated increased reading skills at the end of both the second and the third phase of the study. Although no play therapy was involved in the third phase of the study, the children continued to show improvement. Bills also found six of the eight children in the treatment group showed not only academic improvement but also personal improvement, displaying the pervasive effect that short-term play therapy can have on the life of a child.

Gould (1980) researched the effectiveness of group play therapy and discussion groups, within an elementary school setting, to increase the students' self-concepts. Twenty-one children identified as having low self-images were assigned to each group: experimental, placebo, or control. Children in the experimental group were placed in groups of three or four and received twelve weekly sessions of nondirective play therapy. The children in the placebo group were placed in groups of seven and engaged in twelve weekly discussion groups. The control group did not participate in play therapy or discussion groups. Gould found that the play group and the discussion group indicated positive change according to the Piers-Harris Children's Self-Concept Scale. The greatest improvement in self-concept occurred in the children who were involved in group play therapy.

Crow (1990) studied the effect of play therapy as a means to increase the self-concept of poor readers. The participants included students from two schools; one school's students served as a control group and the other school's students served as the experimental group. Twelve students in the experimental group received ten sessions of play therapy, 30 minutes once a week. Prior to and following treatment, the children were administered instruments to evaluate reading achievement, self-concept, and locus of control. Following treatment, the participants in play therapy displayed a statistically significant increase in self-concept. The treatment group also demonstrated an improvement in internal locus of control, as compared to the control group that did not show an improvement. While all twelve children in the experimental group evidenced progress in reading ability, there was not a significant difference in progress between the children in the experimental group and the children in the control group. Crow noted that aside from the measured factors, several children who received play therapy displayed improvements in attention span, ability to focus, self-confidence, and self-control. The 30-minute sessions utilized by Crow blended easily into a classroom schedule, encouraging the future use of short-term play therapy as a powerful intervention for children with both academic and emotional difficulties.

## SELECTIVE MUTE CHILDREN

Similar to working with hearing impaired children, play therapy is an effective intervention with children who are selective mutes because of the lack of emphasis on verbalization. Axline (1948) reported significant progress in working with a five-year-old boy that would not speak and exhibited undersocialized behavior. Billy had developed normally until age 3, when he ceased talking and walking, and reverted to infantile behaviors. By the fourth session of nondirective play therapy, Billy's mother noticed dramatic improvements in his behavior at home. She reported that he appeared more relaxed and exhibited less regressive behavior. By the fifth play therapy session, Billy's school also reported positive changes in his behavior. The total number of sessions that Billy engaged in is unclear; however, improvement clearly took place within the first few sessions. Furthermore, a one-year follow up indicated that Billy was happy, well adjusted, and succeeding academically.

## SOCIAL ADJUSTMENT PROBLEMS

Gould (1980) suggested that all children could profit from engaging in play therapy, as an opportunity to exercise social skills within a controlled setting. Group play therapy, in particular, offers children a chance to hone new social skills, recognize their competencies, gain peer acceptance, and build self-control (Landreth et al., 1996). Pelham (1972), Smith (1988), and Trostle (1988) all studied the effect of short-term group play therapy with children experiencing social adjustment problems.

Pelham (1972) studied the use of group and individual self-directive play therapy with socially immature kindergarten students. The participants in the study were described as socially immature by their kindergarten teachers. The control group included eighteen children who did not receive treatment. In the treatment group, nine children participated in group play therapy (three children in each group) and eight children participated in individual play therapy. Pelham facilitated six to eight 45-minute sessions with each child. When compared to the control group, children participating in either individual play therapy or group play therapy: (a) demonstrated improvement in social maturity, (b) scored higher on a measure of self-concept that was linked to the child's ability to be flexible when faced with new experiences, and (c) displayed significantly improved behavior in the classroom.

Smith (1988) conducted a study of group play therapy, comparing the effectiveness of a directive approach to a nondirective approach with children experiencing social adjustment difficulties. Smith organized three groups of six students, ages 7½ to 9½ years old. Two children identified as aggressive and four children identified as withdrawn were included in each group. The first group received directive, problem-focused play therapy. The second group participated in nondirective play therapy, and the third group operated as a control. The two treatment groups were involved in therapy for 10 weeks receiving twelve, 45-minute sessions. Participants in the directive group engaged in specific activities that emphasized getting acquainted, developing social skills, exploring feelings, examining alternatives, accepting consequences of choices, and learning to define problems. Smith found that the children participating in directive group play therapy obtained significantly greater scores on a scale measuring social status, when compared to the other two groups. The directive and the nondirective play therapy group were found to have significantly higher scores than the control group on measures of self-concept and social adjustment. Overall, the children receiving directive play therapy scored higher than the children receiving nondirective play therapy on all three scales: social status, social adjustment, and self-concept.

Trostle (1988) studied short-term group play therapy as an intervention to facilitate greater self-control and social acceptance in bilingual children. Trostle's study included forty-eight Puerto Rican children, ranging in age from 3 to 6 years old. Twenty-four children were divided into six groups receiving ten weekly 40-minute play therapy sessions. The remaining twenty-four children served as a control group. Results suggested that children participating in play therapy demonstrated significant gains in self-control and displayed a more advanced developmental level in both fantasy and reality play. Greater acceptance of others was a characteristic developed by boys in the play therapy group, when compared to girls in the play therapy group or any member of the control group.

Trostle's findings demonstrate support for the use of play therapy with minority children who may experience social adjustment problems due to feeling unlike their peers. After only ten sessions of group play therapy, the children demonstrated developmental gains that led to a greater acceptance of self and others.

## SPEECH DIFFICULTIES

The achievement of normal developmental tasks, such as speech, can be hindered when a child is experiencing emotional difficulties. The positive therapeutic relationship developed in play therapy provides an environment conducive to healthy emotional development. Kupperman, Bligh, and Goodban (1980) studied the use of speech Theraplay to remediate the articulation disorders of six children, ages 3 to 6 years old, attending a university speech clinic. The sessions were conducted over a course of six weeks with each child receiving two 30-minute speech Theraplay sessions per week. In contrast to other research studies, the clinician did not use props or toys in the therapy process. Typical interaction with the children involved behaviors such as smiling, cooing, singing, or playing peek-a-boo. In an effort to build the child's self-esteem, the clinician provided the child with unconditional acceptance and offered high affect responses. Results showed a reduction in misarticulated items by all six children. The Theraplay sessions appear to have provided the child with an intensive, short-term, positive relationship in which the child was able to stimulate or restimulate normal speech development.

## TRAUMATIZED CHILDREN

In studying the reactions of traumatized children, research indicates that "the natural reaction of children is to reenact or play out the traumatic experience in an unconscious effort to comprehend, overcome, develop a sense of control, or assimilate the experience" (Landreth et al., 1996, p. 241). Children strive to heal themselves through repeatedly reenacting the traumatic experience. Short-term play therapy, as described by Allan and Berry (1987), Kot (1995), and Tyndall-Lind (1999) can provide traumatized children with an opportunity to play out traumatic events.

Allan and Berry (1987) utilized sand play as a means of working with a second-grade boy experiencing difficulties that were likely related to dramatic changes in his family environment. James participated in ten sand play therapy sessions. At the onset of therapy, James was described as aggressive, impulsive, and lacking in social skills; his sand play reflected themes of confusion and chaos. As therapy progressed, his sand play appeared more organized and moved toward illustrating order and family unity. Sand play provided James with an opportunity to work through unresolved trauma and to gain a sense of control over his environment. At the conclusion of therapy, teachers reported that James displayed less aggressive and impulsive behavior and had increased his positive social skills.

Kot (1995) conducted an intensive version of short-term child-centered play therapy. Twenty-two children, ages 3 through 10, who had witnessed domestic violence were included in the study. The children were evenly divided between an experimental group and a control group, both receiving services from a domestic violence shelter. In addition to shelter services, the experimental group participated in twelve, 45-minute play therapy sessions over a two week period. Analysis of research instruments showed that the experimental group displayed a significant increase in their self-concept and significant progress in their play behavior regarding play themes and physical closeness. The experimental group also showed a significant decline in both externalizing behavior problems and total behavior problems.

Tyndall-Lind (1999) conducted a comparative analysis of child-centered intensive individual play therapy and child-centered intensive sibling group play therapy with child witnesses of domestic violence. The individual play therapy treatment group consisted of ten child witnesses of domestic violence, while the comparison group was obtained from the 1995 Kot study. In addition to basic shelter services, over a two week period the treatment group received twelve 45-minute sibling group play therapy sessions. Statistical analysis indicated that children in the treatment group, when compared to the control group, displayed (a) a significant increase in self concept, (b) a significant decrease in overall behavior problems, (c) a significant decrease in both externalizing and internalizing behavior problems, (d) a significant decrease in aggression, anxiety, and depression. Intensive sibling group play therapy and intensive individual play therapy were found to be equally effective with children who witnessed family violence.

## WITHDRAWN CHILDREN

Withdrawn children may be particularly challenging in short-term play therapy because of their general lack of involvement. Short-term therapy with this population may be more efficient in groups because the other children serve as a catalyst for the development of therapist–child relationships.

Axline (1948) employed her child-centered approach to help a five-year-old boy who was extremely withdrawn. At the onset of therapy, Billy would not verbally communicate with other children or his teacher. If approached by another child, Billy would hide his face and curl up on the ground. Axline conducted at least ten individual sessions that were 45 minutes once a week. By the fifth play therapy session, both his mother and his teacher reported a significant increase in social interaction and decrease in regressive behavior. During the sixth through the tenth session, Billy appeared to relax and displayed confidence in his interpersonal interactions. Prior to termination of individual therapy, Billy participated in group play therapy to facilitate the further development of his social skills.

# SUMMARY

Obviously, short-term play therapy is not recommended for all children and all difficulties. The number of play therapy sessions needed will depend on a multitude of factors including the child's age, emotional maturity, family stability, severity of trauma, duration of the trauma as in the case of sexual abuse, and parent's response to the child's difficulty. Each child is unique and the decision regarding number of play therapy sessions must be made on a case by case basis. The number of sessions needed cannot be determined on the basis of an initial diagnosis.

The results of these research studies suggest that short-term play therapy may be recommended for the following possible diagnoses see below (American Psychiatric Association, *Diagnostic and Statistical Manual of Mental Disorders*, 4th Edition):

| | |
|---|---|
| 293.89 | Anxiety Disorder Due to a General Medical Condition |
| 295.90 | Schizophrenia, Undifferentiated Type |
| 300.00 | Anxiety Disorder (Not Otherwise Specified) |
| 300.02 | Generalized Anxiety Disorder |
| 300.23 | Social Phobia Generalized |
| 300.29 | Specific Phobia, Situational Type |
| 307.0 | Stuttering |
| 307.7 | Encopresis |
| 309.21 | Separation Anxiety Disorder |
| 309.3 | Adjustment Disorder with Disturbance of Conduct |
| 309.40 | Adjustment Disorder with Mixed Disturbance of Emotions and Conduct |
| 312.39 | Trichotillomania |
| 312.9 | Disruptive Behavior Disorder |
| 313.23 | Selective Mutism |
| 315.00 | Reading Disorder |
| 315.31 | Expressive Language Disorder |
| 995.5 | Physical and Sexual Abuse of a Child |
| V61.20 | Parent–Child Relational Problems |
| V61.81 | Relational Problem (Not Otherwise Specified) |
| V62.82 | Bereavement |
| V71.02 | Child or Adolescent Antisocial Behavior |

The case reports and research studies presented in this chapter provide research-based evidence of the effectiveness of short-term therapy in individual play therapy, group play therapy, and filial therapy. However, there is a continuing need for play therapists to develop a standard definition of short-term play therapy to elucidate the results of research outcome studies. Agreement among professionals about specific criteria on whether short-term therapy is judged by number of sessions or length of treatment would benefit this area of research.

While the field of play therapy could benefit from further empirical research, current studies and case reports indicate that short-term play therapy can have long-lasting effects on the lives of children experiencing a wide range of problems.

## REFERENCES

Acord, L. T. (1980). One five-year-old boy's use of play. *Maternal Child Nursing Journal, 9,* 29–35.

Allan, J., & Berry, P. (1987). Sand play. *Elementary School Guidance and Counseling, 21*(4), 301–307.

Axline, V. (1947). Nondirective therapy for poor readers. *Journal of Consulting Psychology, 11,* 61–69.

Axline, V. M. (1948). Some observations on play therapy. *Journal of Consulting Psychology, 12,* 209–216.

Barlow, K., Landreth, G., & Strother, J. (1985). Child-centered play therapy: Nancy from baldness to curls. *The School Counselor, 34*(1), 347–356.

Barton, P. H. (1962). Play as a tool of nursing. *Nursing Outlook, 10,* 162–164.

Bills, R. E. (1950). Nondirective play therapy with retarded readers. *Journal of Consulting Psychology, 14,* 140–149.

Bratton, S., & Landreth, G. (1995). Filial therapy with single parents: Effects on parental acceptance, empathy, and stress. *International Journal of Play therapy, 4*(1), 61–80.

Cassell, S. (1965). Effects of brief puppet therapy upon the emotional responses of children undergoing cardiac catheterization. *Journal of Consulting Psychology, 29* (1), 1–8.

Chau, I., & Landreth, G. (1997). Filial therapy with Chinese parents: Effects on parental empathic interactions, parental acceptance of child and parental stress. *International Journal of Play Therapy, 6* (2), 75–92.

Conn, J. (1941). The treatment of fearful children. *American Journal of Orthopsychiatry, 11,* 744-751.

Costas, M., & Landreth, G. (1999). Filial therapy with nonoffending parents of children who have been sexually abused. *International Journal of Play Therapy, 8*(1), 43–66.

Crow, J. (1990). Play therapy with low achievers in reading. (Doctoral dissertation, University of North Texas, 1989). *Dissertation Abstracts International, 50*(09), B2789.

Cummings, N. A. (1995). Impact of managed care on employment and training: A primer for survival. *Professional Psychology, Research and Practice, 26*(1), 10–15.

Daniel, C. A., Rae, W. A., Sanner, J. H., Upchurch, J., & Worchel, F. F. (1989). The psychosocial impact of play on hospitalized children. *Journal of Pediatric Psychology, 14*(4), 617–627.

Ellerton, M. L., Caty, S., & Ritchie, J. A. (1985). Helping young children master intrusive procedures through play. *Children's Health Care, 13*(4), 167–173.

Garot, P. A. (1986). Therapeutic play: Work of both child and nurse. *Journal of Pediatric Nursing, 1*(2), 111–115.

Glass, N. M. (1987). Parents as therapeutic agents: A study of the effect of filial therapy. (Doctoral dissertation, University of North Texas, 1986). *Dissertation Abstracts International, 47*(07), A2457.

Glazer-Waldman, H., Zimmerman, J., Landreth, G., & Norton, D. (1992). Filial therapy: An intervention for parents of children with chronic illness. *International Journal of Play Therapy, 1,* 31–42.

Glover, G. (1996). *Filial therapy with Native Americans on the Flathead reservation.* Unpublished doctoral dissertation, University of North Texas, Denton.

Gould, M. F. (1980). The effect of short-term intervention play therapy on the self-concept of selected elementary pupils. (Doctoral dissertation, Florida Institute of Technology, 1980). *Dissertation Abstracts International, 41*(03), B1090.

Gumaer, J. (1984). Developmental play in small group counseling with disturbed children. *The School Counselor, 31*(5), 445–453.

Harris, Z. L., & Landreth, G. L. (1997). Filial therapy with incarcerated mothers: A five week model. *International Journal of Play Therapy, 6*(2), 53–73.

Irwin, B. L. (1971). Play therapy for a regressed schizophrenic patient. *JPN and Mental Health Services, 9*, 30–32.

Kale, A., & Landreth, G. (1999). Filial therapy with parents of children experiencing learning difficulties. *International Journal of Play Therapy, 8*(2), 35–56.

Klem, P. R. (1992). The use of the dollhouse as an effective disclosure technique. *International Journal of Play Therapy, 1*, 69–73.

Knell, S. M., & Moore, D. J. (1990). Cognitive-behavioral play therapy in the treatment of encopresis. *Journal of Clinical Child Psychology, 19*(1), 55–60.

Kot, S. (1995). *Intensive play therapy with child witnesses of domestic violence.* Unpublished doctoral dissertation, University of North Texas, Denton.

Kupperman, P., Bligh, S., & Goodban, M. (1980). Activating articulation skills through Theraplay. *Journal of Speech & Hearing Disorders, 45*(4), 540–548.

Landreth, G. L. (1991). *Play Therapy: The art of the relationship.* Muncie, IN: Accelerated Development.

Landreth, G. L., & Lobaugh, A. (1998). Filial therapy with incarcerated fathers: Effects on parental acceptance of child, parental stress, and child adjustment. *Journal of Counseling and Development, 76*(2), 157–165.

Landreth, G. L, Homeyer, L. E., Glover, G., & Sweeney, D. S. (1996). *Play therapy interventions with children's problems.* Northvale, NJ: Jason Aronson.

Levy, D. (1939). Release play therapy in young children. *Child Study, 16*(1), 141–143.

LeVieux, J. (1994). Terminal illness and death of father: Case of Celeste, age 5½. In N. B. Webb (Ed.), *Helping bereaved children: A handbook for practitioners* (pp. 81–95). New York: Guilford.

Machler, T. J. (1965). Pinocchio in the treatment of school phobia. *Bulletin of the Menninger Clinic, 29*(4), 212–219.

Milos, M. E., & Reiss, S. (1982). Effects of three play conditions on separation anxiety in young children. *Journal of Counseling and Consulting Psychology, 50*(3), 389–395.

O'Connor, K. J. (1991) *The play therapy primer: An integration of theories and techniques.* New York: John Wiley & Sons.

Oualline, V. J. (1975). *Behavioral outcomes of short-term nondirective play therapy with preschool deaf children.* Unpublished doctoral dissertation, North Texas State University, Denton.

Pelham, L. E. (1972). Self-directive play therapy with socially immature kindergarten students. (Doctoral dissertation, University of Northern Colorado, 1971). *Dissertation Abstracts International, 32*(07), A3798.

Perez, C. (1987). A comparison of group play therapy and individual play therapy for sexually abused children. (Doctoral dissertation, University of Northern Colorado, Greeley, 1987). *Dissertation Abstracts International, 48*, 12A.

Smith, L. (1988). The relative effectiveness of two group play therapy approaches in modifying the social adjustment of primary-grade children. (Doctoral dissertation, Pacific Graduate School of Psychology, 1987). *Dissertation Abstracts International, 48*(07), B2112.

Straughan, J. (1964). Treatment with child and mother in the playroom. *Behavior Research and Therapy, 2*, 37–41.

Tait, D. C., & Depta, J. (1994). Play therapy group for bereaved children. In N. B. Webb (Ed.), *Helping bereaved children: A handbook for practitioners* (pp. 169–185). New York: Guilford.

Tew, K. L. (1997). *The efficacy of filial therapy with families with chronically ill children.* Unpublished doctoral dissertation, University of North Texas, Denton.

Trostle, S. L. (1988). The effects of child-centered group play sessions on social-emotional growth of three-to-six-year old bilingual Puerto Rican children. *Journal of Research in Childhood Education, 3*(2), 93-106.

Tyndall-Lind, A. (1999). *A comparative analysis of intensive individual play therapy and intensive sibling group play therapy with child witnesses of domestic violence.* Unpublished doctoral dissertation, University of North Texas, Denton.

Yuen, T. C. (1997). *Filial therapy with immigrant Chinese parents in Canada.* Unpublished doctoral dissertation, University of North Texas, Denton.

Zilliacus, K., & Enberg, S. (1980). Play therapy in the pediatric outpatient department. *Paediatrician, 9*, 224–230.

# PART *IV*

# PLAY THERAPY WITH SPECIAL POPULATIONS

# 15

# Play Therapy with Aggressive Acting-Out Children

## SHAUNDA PETERSON JOHNSON
## PATRICIA CHUCK

*I*n recent years, one of the most common referrals of children to mental health services is for aggressive and acting-out behaviors. Often, these be haviors are displayed in the classroom, serving as sources of constant disruption, as well as danger toward others. With juvenile crime on the rise, there is a great need for screening and intervention with children at an early age. In addition, professionals and clinicians in the field must be educated in how to understand and best work with the aggressive child. This chapter presents an overview of the following: (a) aggressive acting-out children's needs and behaviors, (b) rationale for the use of play therapy with this population, (c) aggressive behaviors exhibited in the playroom, (d) limit setting, (e) play materials utilized for the expression of aggression, (f) stages during the therapeutic process, (g) and case studies that provide documented effectiveness of play therapy with aggressive acting-out children.

## AGGRESSIVE ACTING-OUT CHILDREN

A child who engages in aggressive, acting-out behavior may be using the aggression as a shield to protect against feeling unwanted, unimportant, unloved, or unlovable. An aggressive child may feel incapable of attracting the genuine interest or caring of others and therefore, may initially reject the play therapist as a way to protect himself. At such times, it is important that the play therapist remain sensitive to and focused on the child's feelings about himself. The child's acting-out behavior is not a personal reaction to the therapist.

At an early age, aggressive children have commonly experienced some type of injury to the self involving the parents, such as a serious disappointment in the family, loss of a sense of safety or protection, abuse or neglect, loss of attention from a parent because of a divorce, parental depression, or birth of a sibling. The child may remain fixated at the developmental level in which the traumatic event occurred, experiencing difficulty differentiating various degrees of threat to the self. A fragile self-concept tends to leave the child constantly on guard to defend against criticism or perceived attacks by others. The child's lack of connectedness with others and a negative self-concept often create a "narcissistic vulnerability" (Willock, 1983, p. 389) in the child's personality. Tied to this sense of vulnerability are feelings of anger, depression, and distress that the child defends against by developing a callous attitude and engaging in distinctly antisocial behaviors.

Aggressive acting-out children depend on their self-protection mechanisms to provide themselves with a sense of security that they are lacking. For these children, aggression often becomes the child's most reliable defense for coping with the world. Feeling threatened by the intimacy of a therapeutic relationship, the child will more than likely be skeptical and resistant to a therapist who is perceived as trying to change the child's behavior. The child may feel suspicious of any question or comment made by the therapist. Furthermore, difficulties might arise based on the therapist's reaction to the child's aggression. Many play therapists experience difficulty in appropriately responding to a child who directs physical aggression toward them.

## RATIONALE FOR USING PLAY THERAPY WITH AGGRESSIVE ACTING-OUT CHILDREN

Aggressive, acting-out children are notably one of the most difficult populations that play therapists encounter (Willock, 1983). However, play therapy is well suited to meet the needs of aggressive children (Landreth, Homeyer, Glover, & Sweeney, 1996). Play is a child's most natural means of self-expression and is an essential component of childhood development (Landreth, 1991). Through play a child is able to release pent-up feelings of anxiety, disappointment, fear, aggression, insecurity, and confusion. Bringing these feelings to the surface encourages the child to deal with them, learn to master them, or abandon them (Axline, 1969). Through symbolic representation, the child gains a sense of control over events that seem uncontrollable in reality. Often, children are unable to verbally express what they are feeling; thus, in play therapy toys serve as children's words and play serves as their language. Toys are used by children to express thoughts, feelings, and actions that the child is unable to express in reality (Landreth, 1991). An aggressive acting-out child uses play as a language for expressing negative feelings.

An inability to express emotions, especially those emotions connected to traumatic events, has been linked to aggressive acting-out behaviors (Ginsberg, 1993). When a child is able to release and express strong negative emotions, and remains accepted by the therapist, the emotions lose some of their intensity and the child experiences less disturbance (Moustakas, 1953). The playroom provides a safe place for a child to release these feelings and to reenact experiences. Within a nonthreatening therapeutic environment, the child is free to express and explore inner thoughts, feelings, experiences, and behaviors. The release of aggression allows the child to reduce inner frustration. Being able to release or express the emotion has a cathartic effect and allows the child to move beyond maladaptive behaviors to a more effective way of functioning. The symbolic nature of play allows children to transfer strong feelings, such as anger, fear, anxiety, guilt, or frustration, onto toy objects instead of real people. Children are protected from their own strong actions and emotions connected to traumatic experiences because their feelings are acted out in fantasy rather than reality (Landreth, 1993a).

In responding to an aggressive acting-out child in play therapy, the therapist should strive to meet the child's inner needs underlying the behavior. The focus of play therapy is to gain an understanding of the child, not to merely stop the undesired behavior (Landreth et al., 1996). When the therapist relates to the child with genuine acceptance and respect, this sends a message that the child is a worthwhile individual. The therapeutic relationship is then used as a testing ground for the child to build self-esteem and explore more constructive ways of dealing with the environment. With aggressive children, the play therapist must consistently strive to identify with their internal frame of reference in order to understand their external reactions to the world. "Once the feelings and needs behind aggressive acts have been accepted and allowed to be expressed, children are able to go on to explore more positive behaviors" (Landreth et al., 1996, p. 15).

A typical concern surrounding the expression of aggressive, acting-out behavior in the playroom is whether the child will continue these socially unacceptable behaviors outside of the playroom. Dorfman (1958) proposed several answers to these concerns. First, children in play therapy are neither praised for specific behaviors nor encouraged for particular verbalizations or actions. Because of this, children develop an awareness that they are responsible for their own behavior. Second, children recognize that being in the playroom is unlike daily life. Third, simply restricting certain behaviors outside of the playroom does not eliminate the child's need for that behavior. The therapist's acceptance of the total child, despite any problems, allows the child the freedom to expose inner emotions. In order to be certain of the therapist's acceptance, the child may test the therapist by demonstrating parts of his or her personality which are frequently rejected. Fourth, the therapist's acceptance of the child appears to decrease aggressive behavior, rather than increase aggressive behavior. Finally, the playroom is not a place of complete freedom. The therapist carefully sets limits and boundaries around the child's inappropriate behavior.

## LIMIT SETTING WITH AGGRESSIVE
## ACTING-OUT CHILDREN

Limit setting is an area of particular concern when working with aggressive acting-out children. The physical safety of the child, therapist, and the playroom must be protected through appropriate limit setting. Through setting limits, the therapist is able to preserve feelings of acceptance, empathy, and positive regard for the aggressive acting-out child. It would be virtually impossible for the therapist to remain warm, empathetic, and accepting of a child who attacks the therapist causing physical pain or discomfort. The therapist would have difficulty accepting a child who is allowed to pull the therapist's hair, paint his face, rip his clothes, or destroy his glasses (Ginott, 1994). Undoubtedly some type of anger or resentment would surface in the therapist that could be interpreted by the child as rejection.

Therapists should not allow the child's actions to push them beyond a level that can be tolerated, thereby inhibiting positive acceptance of the child. However, it is imperative that the therapist be able to demonstrate a certain degree of tolerance, and that the therapist's personal needs do not interfere with the child's need to be messy or destructive (Landreth, 1991). "The therapist must be able to accept the hypothesis that the child has reasons for what he does and that many things may be important to the child that he is not able to communicate to the therapist" (Axline, 1955, p. 623).

Preventing the child from physically harming the therapist or destroying toys by setting limits helps the child develop a sense of security and consistency in the child–therapist relationship (Axline, 1955). "Children do not feel safe, valued, or accepted in a completely permissive relationship" (Landreth, 1993a, p. 23). A goal of limit setting is to promote the child's release of aggression through symbolic expression, rather than direct acting-out. For example, a child who is angry at his mother can punch, stab, or shoot a doll that symbolically represents the child's mother (Ginott, 1994). When children are able to symbolically express their negative feelings, they are freed from potential anxiety or guilt over actually harming someone or something.

It is important to note that while the therapist limits the child's undesirable behavior, the therapist allows the child to express feelings through verbal and play outlets. Limits help strengthen the child's self-control as the child learns to differentiate between desires and actions. Whereas all feelings are accepted, the child learns that feelings may not always be acted on in any chosen manner. "By accepting the child's feelings and preventing his undesirable acts, the therapist reduces the child's guilt and at the same time turns his wishes in the direction of reality controls" (Ginott, 1994, p. 105).

Bixler (1949) maintained that the foundation for working with aggressive children lies in a strict adherence to limits on behavior in conjunction with an acceptance of the child's feelings that motivate the behavior. Moreover, Landreth (1991) has consistently maintained that the child's need to violate a limit is of greater therapeutic value than the child's actual behavior. Within the therapeutic relationship, it is of critical importance that the therapist continually seek an understanding of the meaning of the aggressive behavior to each individual child. When limits are necessary, Landreth's (1991, p. 223) ACT model of therapeutic limit setting is recommended.

A—Acknowledge the child's feelings, wishes, and wants.
C—Communicate the limit.
T—Target acceptable alternatives.

## AGGRESSIVE BEHAVIORS IN THE PLAYROOM

Aggressive acting-out children present the play therapist with quite a challenge. In addition to an awareness of the therapeutic relationship, therapists must be conscious of protecting themselves, the child, and the playroom. It is not unlikely that an aggressive child would choose to destroy the playroom before the child would choose to talk about feelings (Willock, 1983). During the initial play therapy sessions, the emotions of distressed children are most often diffuse and undifferentiated. Negative feelings are typically expressed by these children (Moustakas, 1953).

> Attitudes of hostility, anxiety, and regression are pervasive in their expression in the playroom. Children are frightened, angry, or immature without definitely focusing their feelings on any particular person or persons or emotional experiences. They are often afraid of almost everything and everybody and sometimes feel like destroying all people, or merely wish they would be left completely alone, or wish to regress to a simpler, less demanding level of adjustment. (Moustakas, 1953, p. 7)

Therapists must be prepared to encounter a variety of aggressive acts, including biting, spitting, kicking, hitting, obscenities, or flying toys (Willock, 1983). O'Connor (1986) identified the following as hostile behaviors in the play room: yelling, shooting the dart gun, striking an object, throwing objects, acting out others' deaths, discussing hurting someone or revenge, demanding the therapist perform some behavior, and discussing the child's own misbehavior that resulted in punishment. Anger might be expressed by the child through attempts to beat, smash, destroy, rip, or crush the materials in the playroom (Moustakas, 1953). Initially, the child's actions may appear to be random and without purpose. However, Moustakas (1953) maintained that as the child experiences greater trust and acceptance from the therapist, the child's anger will appear more focused. As the therapeutic relationship develops, expressions of aggression become less diffuse and are more directly connected to a specific person or experience. As the child releases negative feelings, the feelings become less severe and as a result are easier for the child to manage. Willock (1983) proposed that it is the therapist's constant striving to understand the meaning behind the child's aggressive, acting-out behavior that maintains a therapeutic environment in the midst of the seeming chaos.

# PLAY MATERIALS

"Shooting, burying, biting, hitting, and stabbing are acceptable in the playroom because they are expressed symbolically" on toys (Landreth, 1991, p. 122). A wide variety of play materials can be utilized to facilitate the child's expression or symbolic representation of aggression, frustration, or hostility. Landreth (1993b) suggested the following toys as appropriate for acting-out or release of aggression: a bop bag, a rubber knife, guns, toy soldiers, and an alligator puppet. The alligator puppet is selected because it can be used to act out aggressive acts such as chomping, biting, or crunching. Landreth (1993b) also suggested less structured items such as a clay, blocks, sand, and puppets or dolls.

Clay is both a creative and an aggressive play material because a child can pound, mash, roll out, and pull apart the clay with great passion and intensity. Blocks can also be used as a creative material for constructively building something, as well as a tool for releasing aggression through destruction by knocking over or kicking down the blocks. Sand provides an outlet for aggression by providing the child with a place to bury dolls and other toys. Puppets and dolls can be used by children to symbolically represent their family, thus helping children express experiences with sibling rivalry, family conflicts, anger, fear, frustration, and violence. Puppets and dolls can serve as a buffer between the child's fantasy play and reality (Landreth, 1993b). In addition to the previously mentioned play materials, playrooms should include inexpensive items, such as egg cartons or popsicle sticks that can be broken, smashed, or thrown by the child. According to Landreth (1991), every play therapy experience should have some item that can be destroyed, such as egg cartons. Bursting balloons, tearing newspaper, and wadding paper can also facilitate the expression of emotions that accompany aggression.

# TOOLS FOR SYMBOLIC EXPRESSION OF AGGRESSION IN THE PLAYROOM

A wide variety of tools have been cited in the literature as effective in facilitating the symbolic expression of aggression. These tools include: doll play (Cohn, 1962; Landreth, 1991), puppetry (Howells & Townsend, 1973; Landreth, 1991; Yura & Galassi, 1982), artwork (Manning, 1987; Neibauer, 1988; Salant, 1980), and games (Reid, 1993; Willock, 1983).

## Doll Play

Doll play " . . . allows a child to create a miniature world in which his own motives, thoughts, and emotions can dictate what actions will occur" (Cohn, 1962, p. 241). In a child's world, as opposed to an adult's world, fantasy and reality are much more closely integrated; thus, acting out a scenario in play is comparable to taking the action in reality. Doll play allows children to engage in spontaneous aggressive behavior. The dolls represent persons in the child's environment, therefore, fantasy acts of aggression can be symbolic of aggressive acts in reality (Cohn, 1962).

The therapist may choose to present doll play to the child in either a structured or unstructured manner. In unstructured doll play, the child decides how to play with the dolls. In structured doll play, the therapist may present the child with a situation and request the child to act out a resolution to the conflict. Alternately, the therapist may conduct an "interview" with the doll, allowing the child to provide the doll's answers (Cohn, 1962).

Children who are exposed to aggression or violence in their homes will typically play aggressively with the dolls in the playroom. Cohn (1962) reported that children whose home environments have been characterized by high frustration and punishment, engage in aggressive doll play more frequently and with more intensity than children from homes with less frustration and punishment. Additionally, girls who were severely punished by their mothers exhibited the most aggressive doll play when compared to other girls. Boys who highly identified with their aggressive father exhibited the most aggressive doll play.

## Puppetry

Puppets in the playroom provide the aggressive child with another avenue for symbolically expressing aggression. Puppets have been found to reduce anxiety between the child and therapist by allowing the child to focus on the actions of the puppets (Howells & Townsend, 1973). A variety of puppets should be available for the child to utilize during play. A structured approach for using puppets might entail the therapist suggesting a scenario for the child to act out, while an unstructured approach would allow the child to independently develop puppet play (Yura & Galassi, 1982). Yura and Galassi described a scenario in which puppets were used to help an aggressive child learn coping skills other than fighting. The therapist took an active role by playing either the hostile or victimized puppet. The child played the opposite role. Puppets provide a nonthreatening atmosphere, by allowing children to attribute feelings to the puppet instead of acknowledging the feelings as their own.

## Artwork

Aggressive, acting-out children may respond to artwork with either enthusiasm or fear. Creating a piece of art requires assertiveness and organization. This may present quite a challenge to the child who is controlled by anger. Art can help neutralize aggression by allowing the child free expression. "When an aggressive child faces a white piece of paper, the first image he sees is his own emptiness. What follows is a courageous and painful search for self" (Neibauer, 1988, p. 13).

In a study of aggressive children's artwork, Neibauer (1988) found that children's approach toward art can take a variety of forms. One child may be drawn toward the permissiveness of abstract art. Another child may be attracted to stereotypical positive images, such as happy faces, hearts, or rainbows, to disguise hostile impulses. Through artwork, a child may illustrate self, whether the paint is cautiously smeared or aggressively scribbled. "Their anger is not expressed on paper but rather acted out on paper" (Neibauer, 1988, p. 9).

Manning (1987) examined drawings created by abused children and children from violent families and found that aggression was most often depicted in artwork by exaggerated size of figures, inclement weather, and drawings with items falling or hanging over a child's head. Heavy outlining was also found in the children's artwork, which was interpreted as their attempt to establish boundaries. Moreover, people were rarely depicted in the children's drawings. Manning interpreted this as the children's attempt to either distance themselves from relationships or to withdraw from an abusive or violent environment. Salant (1980) maintains that a child's first drawing in therapy typically illustrates the problem. For example, an aggressive young boy's first picture in therapy depicted a volcano spewing hot ashes and steam. This drawing symbolically showed the boy's own explosive rage.

Destruction and violence are often themes in an aggressive child's artwork. The therapist must be keenly aware of whether the child is using these hostile images as a means to release inner aggressive drives or as a defense mechanism to protect against feelings of mistrust and fear. As with doll play or puppets, art offers the aggressive child a vehicle to express inner emotions while maintaining a safe distance from fears and threats of reality (Neibauer, 1988).

## Games

Play therapists typically utilize board games, card games, "street" games, and games that involve fine and gross motor skills. Contrary to unstructured play, games require a child to employ more self-control, reason, and social skills. Games provide particularly effective techniques in working with aggressive acting-out children over the age of nine who have difficulty with peer relations. Because playing a game requires more than one person, the game provides a mechanism for a child to learn appropriate social skills for interacting with others. By adhering to the rules of the game, the child learns to constructively deal with anger, frustration, or hostility in a socially acceptable manner. The child quickly discovers the consequences of inappropriate behavior through feedback from other players (Reid, 1993).

Games offer experience with sublimation of basic impulses, while simultaneously providing permissible outlets for strong emotions, such as anger or hostility. Games may provide the child with a stepping stone for learning to control basic aggressive impulses. Research has shown that board games and card games led by an adult, have been more successful in reducing severe aggressive behaviors than behavioral or cognitive techniques (Reid, 1993).

Games are familiar to children, and may make a child feel safe in a seemingly anxiety-provoking situation (Reid, 1993). For an aggressive child, structured activities such as board games or cards, may feel safer because the games are less likely to stimulate intense emotions. However, the therapist should be aware that a child may hide behind these structured activities to resist a therapeutic relationship. The child may use the game as a shield against the threat of emotional closeness (Willock, 1983). Landreth (1991) cautions when choosing playroom materials, that games might inhibit the child's range of creative or emotional expression, as well as reduce the level of exploratory play.

# STAGES OF PLAY THERAPY
# WITH AGGRESSIVE ACTING-OUT CHILDREN

Play therapy provides a safe environment for the aggressive child to express feelings of pain, anger, and confusion. The materials in the playroom allow the child to both directly and symbolically work through these negative feelings by acting out traumatic events. In a study of aggressive and withdrawn patterns of interaction among maltreated children, Mills and Allan (1992) reported four stages children typically work through during the play therapy process.

## Establishment of the Relationship

During the first stage of play therapy, the therapist facilitates a secure and accepting environment in which the child feels safe to explore thoughts and feelings. The therapist also sets limits to further create feelings of security in the child. The therapist recognizes and accepts that a child from a family where acting out and aggression is the norm, may feel comfortable with aggressive or combative play. In this initial stage, the child reacts with anxiety and is unable to tolerate close proximity with the therapist. When the child feels safe, dramatic/symbolic and regressive play appears. The child may use toys to act out family experiences as in the case described by Mills and Allan (1992) of a young boy from a violent, abusive, and neglectful home. The boy acted out scenes symbolic of hurt and caring, such as punching a baby doll and then cuddling it, and staging fights between action figures and then bandaging their wounds.

## Testing Limits

The second stage of play therapy constitutes a major shift in the aggressive child's behavior. Here, the child attempts to test the limits of the therapist's acceptance, usually by engaging in behaviors that are least tolerated in the child's home environment. The child unconsciously tests whether or not the therapist will continue to be accepting of the child as a person, regardless of behavior in the playroom. As the child experiences acceptance from the therapist, despite noncompliant or aggressive behavior and emotions, the child's defenses weaken. The child wants to trust the therapist, but feels anxiety due to previous disappointing experiences with adults. The child experiences a strong occurrence of ambivalent feelings during this stage, while on the brink of breaking through defenses and feeling trust for the therapist. The child learns that it is safe to express positive as well as negative feelings.

### Working on Personal Needs

This is the true working stage of therapy. Here, the child will typically engage in more interaction with the therapist, through eye contact and closer physical proximity. The child may use art, toys, and even drama to continually create distance from painful feelings. The child may also direct anger and frustration over events at home toward the therapist. As the child progresses through the third stage, aggressive behavior typically declines, possibly leaving the child with a first true friendship. During this stage, the child may also exhibit increased confidence, sharing, and improved interpersonal skills.

### Consolidation and Termination

During this final stage, the child displays distinct progress, moving from inappropriate and aggressive behaviors to socially acceptable behaviors. The child has developed interpersonal skills and may actively verbalize issues involving the home and classroom. The child may display an increased ability to learn, creating a positive effect in the child's school environment. The child may also exhibit sensitivity to others through play, and an increased ability to develop friendships. This is the termination and consolidation phase of therapy and it is important that the therapist utilize a termination process that does not leave the child feeling abandoned.

## GROUP PLAY THERAPY
## WITH AGGRESSIVE ACTING-OUT CHILDREN

As in individual play therapy, group play therapy can provide an environment in which children may release emotions and excess energy. The power of the group situation allows children to receive immediate peer feedback about perceived behaviors. Group play provides a forum for children to learn socially acceptable ways of interacting with others. A sense of group loyalty, rules, norms, and identification with peers may develop as a result of group play (Johnson, 1988). In addition, group play therapy reduces repetitive play. In individual play therapy, children may engage in the same activity during every session. For example, a child may choose to draw and never try painting, or may play with the trucks and never touch the dolls. This may be due to a lack of ingenuity or security in the child. In a group, children learn from one another how to use a variety of materials and engage in numerous activities, thereby increasing each child's opportunity for new creative outlets (Ginott, 1994).

Careful consideration is necessary when assembling a play therapy group involving the aggressive child. A therapeutic group is most effective when it consists of children with varying presenting problems. This exposes all children in the group to behavior that is both dissimilar and complimentary to their own. The aggressive child needs to be placed with groupmates who are strong, but not overbearing or hostile. The effective play therapy group allows children to become both active and reflective. The atmosphere in the group must continually vacillate between high levels and low levels of tension and anxiety. A group composed entirely of acting-out children would contradict therapeutic goals. Aggressive children stimulate and reinforce each other, creating a continual state of disturbance and struggle in the group. Ginott (1994) suggested that only one aggressive child should be placed in a play therapy group of four or less children, while no more than two aggressive children should be placed in a group with five members. It is important to note that aggressive children are not incapable of enjoying close, personal relationships; however, they may lack the skills to form relationships that are rewarding.

## RESULTS OF PLAY THERAPY WITH AGGRESSIVE ACTING-OUT CHILDREN

Empirical research and case studies are essential components in providing validation and support for the use of play therapy as a treatment modality for aggressive acting-out children. The following case reports and research studies provide documented effectiveness of individual play therapy and group play therapy with aggressive acting-out children.

### Darren: Acting-Out

Darren, an eight-year-old boy, was referred to counseling because of aggressive acting-out at school. Over a period of fifteen play therapy sessions, the therapist tracked behaviors, reflected feelings, set limits, and made interpretations relevant to the child's play. During the thirteenth session, the strong child–therapist relationship that had developed allowed Darren the freedom to express his pain, aggression, and confusion surrounding his parents' separation. Consequently, his negative feelings were neutralized and his behavior outside of therapy was positively impacted. One year post-therapy, Darren still displayed more adjusted conduct and coping at home and at school (Allan & Brown, 1993).

### Lucy: Loss of Control

Lucy, a six-year-old girl, was placed in an institution after being abandoned by her mother. She was referred for play therapy because of loss of self-control following her mother's visits. Lucy's first therapist met with her for five sessions, followed by seventeen sessions with a second therapist. Lucy's play exhibited contrasting themes of nurturing and aggression. She did not speak or interact directly with her therapist until the eighteenth session when a second child was introduced to the session. At this time, Lucy engaged the therapist in conversation and displayed affection through hugs and kisses. She maintained this behavior during her final four sessions. Lucy chose a variety of toys to work through her inner struggle and feelings of abandonment. She also became able to request affection for the first time. The therapist was able to offer Lucy a secure relationship where her basic needs were met. Lucy decided on her own when she was ready to terminate play therapy. Lucy's teachers reported that she showed definite progress in that she became better able to manage her behavior in school and was able to maintain self-control after seeing her mother (Miller, 1948).

### James: Aggressive

James, a four-year-old boy, was referred to play therapy because he exhibited behavior problems, including aggression, fear of animals and the dark, noncompliance with parents and teachers, unsatisfactory peer relations, and insufficient dietary habits. James' strict home environment did not encourage the expression of his feelings, which often manifested in disagreeable or controlling behaviors. In the playroom, James primarily played with the sand and the water. Initially, he was very cautious about mixing the sand and water, careful to leave the playroom clean, and rarely involved the therapist in his play. There were two significant turning points in James' therapy. First, through sand and doll play, he was able to work through feelings of aggression toward a new sibling and move toward more nurturing behavior typical of an older child. Second, he was able to experience out-of-control feelings and then move on to create a more safe, nurturing environment. This was displayed through a session in which James aggressively threw sand and water around the playroom and then carefully pretended to drive children safely home in a school bus. Following this session, James did not attempt to clean up the mess, instead he seemed proud of his hard work. Although sand and water were allowed to be thrown around the room in this case, the play therapist is encouraged to exercise caution and to be aware of when appropriate limits should be defined. Through the child-centered approach to play therapy, James was able to deal with his feelings of anger, fear, and a need for control. He was free to explore more appropriate avenues for expressing his feelings resulting in an improved self-concept and enhanced peer relations (Par, 1990).

### A Play Therapy Group: Disruptive Classroom Behavior

A group of deprived second graders who exhibited disruptive classroom behavior were chosen to participate in a study on the effects of developmental play group counseling. The participants included fifty-six children that were divided into groups of four and then randomly assigned to a developmental play group, child-centered play group, or control group. The two treatment groups received fourteen sessions of group play therapy, 45-minute sessions twice a week for seven weeks. The developmental play group required structured, verbal inter-action. The group focused on learning to verbalize and explore feelings through taking turns as an observer, listener, or speaker. In the child-centered play group, the children were self-directed and the therapist focused on observing, listen-ing, and reflecting behaviors and emotions. The children were free to use the session to meet their own needs. The results of the study found that the chil-dren in the play group were the only participants to show significant reduction in disruptive classroom behavior. For eight weeks following the study, the chil-dren in the play group consistently maintained their improved behavior (Gaulden, 1975).

## Jane: Temper Tantrums

Play therapy was utilized to help a two-year-old child exhibiting severe temper tantrums. Jane began displaying behavior problems at 12-months during toilet training with her nanny. The nanny was highly authoritarian in nature and very strict with Jane. Complete toilet training was achieved when Jane turned two, however, extreme temper tantrums ensued. In play therapy, the use of clay and a potty chair as play materials allowed Jane the freedom to self-regress. Jane's mother reported that soiling behavior had ceased by the tenth session of play therapy and therapy was terminated. In a total of ten sessions, Jane was able to act out her frustrations and exhibited positive changes in her attitude, compli-ance with parents, and relations with peers (Levy, 1939). This case illustrates that positive results can be achieved in a short period of time, even with chil-dren experiencing severe problems.

## Oppositional Defiant Disorder Children

A study by Beers (1985) found that play therapy, when used in conjunction with parent counseling, was helpful in establishing positive interactions between a group of parents and their children who had been diagnosed with Oppositional Defiant Disorder. After eight weekly sessions of play therapy with the children, as well as counseling sessions with the parents, results indicated significant im-provement in the interactions between parents and their children. The results of this study lend support to the power of play therapy with acting-out children, when combined with parental involvement.

## Betty: Acting-Out

Betty, a six-year-old girl, was referred to play therapy by her parents because of extreme acting-out behaviors such as temper tantrums, pulling out her own hair, aggression toward her sibling, and beating her head on the floor. Betty's mother had suffered the loss of a close relative shortly after Betty's birth and became severely depressed. She turned toward Betty for comfort, and in the process, neglected to appropriately nurture Betty.

Betty had a history of using art to express emotional pain, and her parents brought over one thousand pictures and paintings to the initial parent consultation. Overriding themes of doom and despair were evident in her artwork, with many images of skulls and ghosts. The play therapist felt that Betty unconsciously needed to paint in order to survive and the images themselves represented symbols of Betty's inner fears.

A wide variety of toys and art materials were provided as play materials for Betty. During the initial stages of therapy, Betty's play exhibited themes of nurturing and unconscious fears. The play therapist initiated storytelling with a fairy tale focus to allow Betty to interpret these stories and thus, process inner fears. As therapy progressed, a therapeutic bond was secured between Betty and the play therapist and Betty was then able to more openly express her emotions. Betty also became increasingly aggressive toward the play therapist by ordering her around and throwing toys at her.

During Betty's treatment, the play therapist also worked with Betty's parents and teachers to gain further relevant information about Betty and to enhance therapeutic objectives. As therapy continued, Betty's artwork reflected remarkable changes in her life. Images of ghosts and ghouls were replaced with scenes of animals, friends, and ice skating. The play therapist described a cardboard box that held profound meaning concerning Betty's progress. Betty initially used the box as a cradle. The play therapist interpreted this as symbolic of the womb. Later, this box became a pirate ship displaying a death emblem. Toward the end of therapy, this box became a playhouse with an open door. At this time, the aggressive behaviors Betty was referred for dissipated. A few years later, a follow-up revealed Betty's continued success (Ude-Pestel, 1977).

### Billy: Aggressive

When Billy was five years old, his mother brought him to counseling to help deal with his anger and aggressive behaviors. Billy's home was characterized by emotional abuse, with frequent verbal arguments between his parents. The therapist saw Billy in child-centered play therapy, once a week for eight months.

During the initial session, Billy appeared to enjoy the freedom of the playroom. He stated, "I like this place. I like the gun, mom doesn't let us have guns." For the next several weeks, aggression was the predominant theme in Billy's play. He would act out "battle scenes" in the sandbox involving shootings and car crashes. While acting out the scenes, Billy was silent. His sandplay appeared symbolic of his home environment in which family members "walked on eggshells" never knowing when a conflict might surface.

Billy quickly moved into the second stage of play therapy, where he began testing the limits of the therapist's acceptance. Billy used verbal questions, as opposed to acting-out, to test limits in the playroom. He asked, "What if I dumped out the sand on the carpet?" and "Can I pour the sand on you?" When a limit was set on the amount of water allowed in the playroom, Billy threatened, "If you don't get me more, you're fired!" By the fifth session, Billy took action for the first time. He was able to appropriately release his anger by ripping up a phone book in the playroom. During this session, Billy frequently said, "I don't like it here" and "I hate you." He also began to throw objects, usually toward the therapist's feet. The therapist focused on allowing Billy a place where he was free to express his thoughts and feelings, while setting appropriate limits on his behaviors. Billy struggled with differentiating feelings from limits in the playroom. He asked the therapist, "Remember, you said nothing would make you mad. Well, if you wouldn't be mad then I could dump it (sand) out of the sandbox. You wouldn't have to cover it up."

In the eighth session, Billy narrated his sand play, naming "good guys" and "bad guys." Without looking at the therapist, Billy handed her a figure and said, "You have a good guy." After this session, Billy's mother reported that she felt as if a "light had gone off" and she was feeling positive about Billy's progress. By the thirteenth session, Billy stated, "I like this place." However, he continued to struggle with experiencing strong ambivalent feelings. Billy frequently "fired" the therapist, and he often stated "I choose to end my play time." However, he never chose to walk out of the playroom before the session ended. Billy struggled with his need for power. He would state to the therapist, "I make the rules in here, and I can do what I want." Billy was able to feel in control and to establish a sense of security, that he did not have at home, by striving to be powerful in the playroom.

As Billy moved into the third stage of play therapy, he began to show evidence of social interest. He brought a stick of gum to the therapist and proudly gave it as a gift. He invited the therapist to play koosh ball with him. He also told the therapist about a girl in his class that he thought was lucky for winning a prize. Billy stated, "I bet that was hard to do!" Billy began sitting near the therapist during the play therapy sessions. During the seventeenth session, Billy was lying on the floor near the therapist's feet. He told the therapist in a soft voice, "Do you know what? I'm in the first grade. . . . My brother skipped the first grade." After making this statement, Billy abruptly sat up and asked, "Is it time to go yet?" Billy had begun to reveal his inner pain and allowed himself to be close to the therapist. For the next several sessions, Billy reverted to saying that he hated the playroom.

In the twentieth session, it seemed clear that Billy had moved into the final stage of play therapy when he looked directly at the therapist and said, "You know Shaunda, I don't like talking. Sometimes when I talk I don't feel good." At age six, Billy had already learned that if you don't talk about your feelings, maybe you do not have to feel them, you can try to pretend they aren't there. Billy's emotionally abusive home environment prevented him from learning to freely express his emotions. The playroom had been a place where Billy had to face his feelings, something that had never been safe for him to do before. Play therapy was helping Billy develop a greater understanding of himself. During the twenty-first session, he stated "I'm mad at my mom 'cause I don't like coming here . . . but I still love her." In the twenty-sixth session, Billy excitedly talked about his new toy at home. He stated, "Mom can help me with things I can't do.

I'm going to share with my brother. . . . I bought it because he likes it." Billy had developed a sensitivity to others and improved interpersonal skills.

As termination was nearing, Billy's mother described Billy as "shining" more. She informed the therapist, "Billy doesn't get quite as angry, he deals with it in a much different way now. He uses words. He tells me and shows me what he wants and needs." After eight months of child-centered play therapy, not only did Billy display a reduction in aggressive behavior, but also an increase in positive behaviors at home and at school. Upon termination, his mother agreed to enroll in filial therapy to further strengthen her relationship with Billy.

## CONCLUSION

While the field of play therapy could benefit from further empirical research, current studies and case reports indicate that play therapy is an effective treatment for children experiencing a wide range of aggressive acting-out behaviors. The documented effectiveness of play therapy has been demonstrated through a number of different theoretical positions and through a wide variety of approaches (Landreth, et al., 1996). However, what better testimony to the effectiveness of play therapy than the words spoken by a child.

> It's not me against all the people in the world that I hate and despise. You make it turn out again and again that it's me against myself. All of a sudden I feel all of my feelings—and sudden like I just wish I'm not the way I am. I wish I had a feeling of being strong deep inside of me without threats and being afraid really. I feel like I'm too little for too big a world. I don't want to always make war with myself. (Axline, 1955, p. 626)

Documented research suggests that play therapy can be an effective treatment intervention with aggressive acting-out children, provided counselors are well trained and amply prepared to respond to the special needs of the aggressive child.

## REFERENCES

Allan, J., & Brown, K. (1993). Jungian play therapy in elementary schools. *Elementary School Guidance and Counseling, 28*(1), 30–41.

Axline, V. (1955). Play therapy procedures and results. *American Journal of Orthopsychiatry, 25,* 618–626.

Axline, V. (1969). *Play therapy* (revised edition). New York: Ballantine Books.

Beers, P. (1985). Focused videotape feedback psychotherapy as compared with traditional play therapy in treatment of the oppositional disorder of childhood. (Doctoral dissertation, University of Illinois at Urbana-Champaign). *Dissertations Abstracts International, 46*(04), B1330.

Bixler, R. H. (1949). Limits are therapy. *Journal of Consulting Psychology, 13*(1), 1–11.

Cohn, F. S. (1962). Fantasy aggression in children as studied by the doll play technique. *Child Development, 33,* 23–250.

Dorfman, E. (1958). Play therapy. In C. Rogers

(Ed.), *Client-centered therapy* (pp. 235–277). Boston: Mifflin.

Gaulden, G. L. (1975). Developmental-play group counseling with early primary grade students exhibiting behavioral problems. (Doctoral dissertation, North Texas State University). *Dissertation Abstracts International, 36*(05), A2628.

Ginott, H. G. (1994). *Group psychotherapy with children: The theory and practice of play therapy.* Northvale, NJ: Jason Aronson.

Ginsberg, B. G. (1993). Catharsis. In C. E. Schaefer (Ed.), *The therapeutic powers of play* (pp. 107–141). Northvale, NJ: Jason Aronson.

Howells, J. G., & Townsend, D. (1973). Puppetry as a medium for play diagnosis. *Child Psychiatry Quarterly, 6*(1), 9–14.

Johnson, M. L. (1988). Use of play group therapy in promoting social skills. *Issues in Mental Health Nursing, 9,* 105–112.

Landreth, G. L. (1991). *Play therapy: The art of the relationship.* Muncie, IN: Accelerated Development Press.

Landreth, G. L. (1993a). Child-centered play therapy. *Elementary School Guidance and Counseling, 28,* 18–28.

Landreth, G. L. (1993b). Self-expressive communication. In C. E. Schaefer (Ed.), *The therapeutic powers of play* (pp. 41–63). Northvale, NJ: Jason Aronson.

Landreth, G. L., Homeyer, L. E., Glover, G., & Sweeney, D. S. (Eds.). (1996). *Play therapy interventions with children's problems.* Northvale, NJ: Jason Aronson.

Levy, D. (1939). Release therapy in young children. *Child Study, 16*(1), 141–143.

Manning, T. M. (1987). Aggression depicted in abused children's drawings. *Arts in Psychotherapy, 14,* 15–24.

Miller, H. E. (1948). Play therapy for the institutionalized child. *Nervous Child, 7,* 311–317.

Mills, B., & Allan, J. (1992). Play therapy with the maltreated child: Impact upon aggressive and withdrawn patterns of interaction. *International Journal of Play Therapy, 1*(1), 1–20.

Moustakas, C. E. (1953). *Children in play therapy: A key to understanding normal and disturbed emotions.* New York: McGraw Hill.

Neibauer, M. (1988). Aggressive children and their art: The aesthetic search for self. *Pratt Institute Creative Arts Therapy Review, 9,* 4–13.

O'Connor, K. (1986). The interaction of hostile and depressive behaviors: A case study of a depressed boy. *Journal of Child and Adolescent Psychotherapy, 3*(2), 105–108.

Par, M. A. (1990). Sand and water play: A case study. *Association for Play Therapy Newsletter, 9*(1), 4–6.

Reid, S. (1993). Game play. In C. E. Schaefer (Ed.), *The therapeutic powers of play* (pp. 323–348). Northvale, NJ: Jason Aronson.

Salant, E. (1980). Case study: The collaborative use of art and play in the treatment of a preschool child. *American Journal of Art Therapy, 19*(4), 93–97.

Ude-Pestel, A. (1977). *Betty: History and art of a child in therapy.* Palo Alto, CA: Science and Behavior Books.

Willock, B. (1983). Play therapy with the aggressive, acting-out child. In C. Schaefer & K. O'Connor (Eds.), *Handbook of play therapy* (pp. 387–411). New York: John Wiley & Sons.

Yura, M. T., & Galassi, M. D. (1982). Adlerian usage of children's play. In G. L. Landreth (Ed.), *Play therapy: Dynamics of the process of counseling with children* (pp. 130–136). Springfield, IL: Charles C. Thomas.

# 16

# Play Therapy
# with Autistic Children

WYNNE MITTLEDORF
SHIRLEY HENDRICKS
GARRY L. LANDRETH

*A*utism is a disorder that has long baffled medical and mental health professionals. As might be expected, many forms of treatment have been applied and studied in an effort to help autistic persons. Educational programs, behavior modification, and other treatment methods have received significant attention. A survey of literature revealed, however, that little research exists on the use of play therapy with autistic children. Notably missing in the literature are references that specifically address the use of child-centered play therapy with autistic children.

The training for most mental health professionals has consisted largely of verbally based interactions. Consequently, they experience great difficulty in communicating or establishing a relationship with children who do not typically communicate by verbal means. This is especially true with autistic children who for a multitude of reasons, many of which we do not scientifically understand, do not rely on verbal expression for communication. Play is the most natural thing all children do, and autistic children engage in their own self-involved play through which they express themselves and communicate with their world. Although much of the play of autistic children is ritualistic, it is, nevertheless, play and is their way of declaring themselves.

Play is the language of children, and when toys or play media are used, the item can become the words of children conveying vast resources of messages, which cannot be communicated verbally. Useful toys or play items are not necessarily what would be thought of in the traditional sense, but rather are any items that children use for play or expressive purposes.

Children can ascribe their own personal meanings to nondescript items. The therapist may not understand what meaning an item has for a child, but it does potentially possess some meaning to the child. The therapist's job is to make contact with autistic children through the medium chosen by the children and with which they are most comfortable. Once play is viewed as having meaning, the therapist is much more likely to sense the inner rhythm of the child since children's play activity expresses the inner rhythm of their emotional life.

## AUTISM DEFINED

Autism is a disorder that is commonly diagnosed in infancy or early childhood. Parents report being worried about the child's social interactions and lack of interest in affection and people. This disorder can have characteristics that range from mild, moderate, or even of the severe magnitude. One common characteristic among these children is their inability to play and interact with other children in a social setting.

According to the *Diagnostic and Statistical Manual of Mental Disorders*, Fourth Edition, 1994 (DSM-IV), "the essential features of Autistic Disorder are the presence of markedly abnormal or impaired development in social interaction and communication and a markedly restricted repertoire of activity and interests" (p. 66). There may be impairments in reciprocal social interactions and the use of nonverbal behaviors to regulate social interaction and communication. "There may be a failure to develop peer relationships appropriate to developmental level that may take different forms at different ages. There may be a lack of spontaneous seeking to share enjoyment, interests, or achievements with other people" (p. 66). There may also be a lack of social or emotional reciprocity.

Autistic children also have delays in their communication skills. "There may be a delay in, or total lack of, the development of spoken language. In individuals who do speak, there may be a marked impairment in the ability to initiate or sustain a conversation with others" (DSM-IV, 1994, p. 66). When their speech does develop, it may be abnormal in pitch, rate, intonation, or rhythm. Repetitive language may also emerge, and the child may repeat certain phrases or words in inappropriate settings.

"Individuals with Autistic Disorder have restricted, repetitive, and stereotyped patterns of behavior, interests, and activities" (DSM-IV, 1994, p. 67). They also display a restricted range of interests and are often preoccupied with one narrow interest. An example of this may be an extreme focus on transportation vehicles. Their play may focus solely on one object for hours at a time. In addition, these children may exhibit body movements that include hands, or the whole body. Examples include rocking, swaying, walking on tiptoes, and constant clapping.

Most children with autism fall into the category of mental retardation. According to the DSM-IV (1994), "approximately 75% of children with Autistic Disorder function at a retarded level" (p. 67). IQ scores can vary, and most autistic children have uneven cognitive and intelligence skills.

Autism occurs more frequently in boys than girls and is characterized by a lack of social relationships/isolation/withdrawal, lack of communication/language skills (both expressive and receptive), persistent, compulsive ritualistic behaviors (sometimes self-destructive), and extreme rigidity or resistance to change. Autism is a disorder of infancy/early childhood, with characteristics emerging between birth and 3 years of age (DSM-IV, 1994). The prognosis is considered to be poor (Paluszny, 1979) but there is increasing optimism regarding successful treatment. There is disagreement as to whether autism is of organic, psychological, or mixed origins (Bromfield, 1989), but this is not vital to the discussion at hand.

## PLAY BEHAVIORS

Black, Freeman, and Montgomery (1975) stated that "unless a child develops appropriate play skills through his interaction with his environment and the objects in it, his social development is severely impaired and inappropriate patterns of behavior are reinforced" (p. 363). They examined play behavior of autistic children in four different environments.

> The play behavior, defined as interaction with peers and objects, of five autistic children was systematically observed in four environments, i.e., a stark environment, a theraplay unit, a playroom, and an outside play deck. The preliminary results suggested that (1) with some children environment has little or no effects on their play behavior; (2) with multiple objects, autistic children frequently related to the objects rather than to their peers; (3) object play was most frequently at the manipulative stage and often included repetitive and negative behavior; (4) within a confined space with no objects present, autistic children frequently engaged in solitary repetitive behavior; and (5) within a confined space designed to facilitate a movement flow (theraplay), autistic children modeled and imitated and were involved in gross motor play together. (p. 363)

Typical autistic behaviors, such as twiddling fingers, flapping hands and arms, rocking, etc., show up in play, but there are other unique behaviors observed in the play of autistic children. Rogers and Fine (1977) found autistic children will maintain greater personal distance from a therapist (as compared to a differentially disturbed child or a normal child). Their play is more often solitary or parallel rather than social (Black, Freeman, & Montgomery, 1975) and, in general, they play less than normal children (Jarrold, Boucher, & Smith, 1993). Autistic children use toys less, and their functional play skills are limited (Black et al., 1975; Jarrold et al., 1993). Libby, Powell, Messer, and Jordan (1997) examined pretend play in children with autism and reported, "Children with autism are not devoid of all skills relating to pretense although there is clearly a problem in spontaneous production" (p. 367). They concluded that children with autism are capable of comprehending play acts and predicting the outcomes of pretend transformations.

Another significant feature of the play of autistic children is that symbolic play, defined as pretending an object is something else, attributing false/absent properties to a thing or using imaginary objects, rarely occurs spontaneously. Libby, et al. (1997) found that "children with autism could imitate symbolic play acts. Furthermore, they performed better than children with Down's syndrome and normal development who had comparable verbal mental ages" (p. 375). In conclusion, they stated that "when isolated play acts were presented, children with autism were, in fact, more likely to imitate these actions than the other two groups of children" (p. 379). Conversely, it was found that "when the pretend acts were embedded in a script the children with autism do less well than the other two groups" (p. 379).

It appears that many autistic children are capable of symbolic play, but only with initial training and/or ongoing assistance (Jarrold et al., 1993; Lanyado, 1987; Voyat, 1982). This is a significant factor to be considered in play therapy with autistic children since symbolic play is considered by some play therapists to be the "container" of the children's emotions. Just what serves as the "container" of autistic children's emotions has yet to be explored. The lack of symbolic play is also a significant treatment issue in general as there is growing evidence of a strong connection between symbolic play and language development.

## PLAY THERAPY WITH AUTISTIC CHILDREN

### Theoretical Orientation and Approach

The majority of play therapy experiences with autistic children reported in the literature, whether traditional play therapy or quasi therapy, are based on a psychodynamic/analytic perspective. This is interesting as this approach is traditionally thought to require a high degree of verbal communication and this population is decidedly verbally non-communicative. Several of the most recent articles in the literature describe behavioral approaches involving play. Whatever the theoretical orientation, there seems to be widespread agreement on the need to establish the core conditions of relationship therapy in work with autistic children.

Bromfield (1989) concluded that

> Play therapy with a high-functioning autistic child can be a labored experience, but one which can be highly profitable for child and therapist. Assuming and nonintrusively seeking meaning in the child's behaviors and unusual verbalizations conveys an interest in the child's communication as well as helps the therapist to feel less lost, bored, or helpless. Nowhere is the need for therapist patience more critical. Preconceived notions of what constitutes

valuable fantasy or play will blind the therapist to what is there and workable. If indeed, as some say, the autistic child's inner life is barren, is that empty feeling (which quintessentially defines the child's identity) not in need of validation, empathy, and self inquiry? (p. 451)

**Traditional play therapy.**   Three articles were located in the literature, which offer descriptions of traditional play therapy with autistic children (Bromfield, 1989; Lanyado, 1987; Lowery, 1985). Bromfield's (1989) play therapy with a high-functioning autistic child focused on entering the child's world in order to begin to understand the meaning of the child's often confusing speech and behavior. Bromfield described an incident where he imitated the child's obsessive sniffing of objects by using a puppet to sniff an object in a similar way. This small act, and the simple verbal reflection that accompanied it, seem to have caught the child's attention and elicited a coherent response. Bromfield also recorded the use of frequent reflection of content and emotion in the child's play as well as occasional simple interpretations. Bromfield successfully engaged the child by following the child's lead in communicating through initially complex and indirect channels such as puppets, note writing, and play telephones. Over the course of therapy (three years), the child began to communicate more directly and more often. According to Bromfield (1989, p. 448), "Therapy permitted Tim to have his fantasies which effectively served as a place in which he securely could be in control."

Lowery (1985) and Lanyado (1987) also presented case studies of play therapy with autistic children. They describe initial attempts to engage the child through rudimentary sign and body language, such as pointing. Both also indicated that they relied on reflection and simple interpretation as their primary techniques. Lowery described unsuccessful attempts at redirecting a child away from perseverative behaviors toward more symbolic play. Both seem to indicate that they were eventually able to enter the child's world and to make contact with the child. Both authors seem to think this was the basis for any further therapeutic gains.

**Group play therapy.**   Wolfberg and Schuler (1993) recommend the use of group play therapy with autistic children and emphasized the importance of integrated groups that include a higher proportion of children who are more "socially competent" (p. 469). They matched normal children with autistic children and carefully chose materials to facilitate play and interaction. The adult facilitators provided support and guided participation to encourage appropriate interaction.

Further support for the use of integrated play groups with autistic children comes from Mundschenk and Sasso (1995). They trained non-handicapped children to interact with an autistic child in a group setting. While the adult therapist's involvement in the group interaction was minimal, it seems that the design could be easily modified to accommodate facilitation of the play activities by a play therapist.

MacLennan (1977) summarized two early reports of group activity therapy with autistic children. The reports each involve homogeneous groups of young autistic children. One study involved traditional psychoanalytic play therapy with the initial focus on containment of chaos, and later on toileting and separation/individuation issues. In the second study the only intervention mentioned was use of primitive games. It is notable that no toys other than the children's own transitional objects (teddy bears, etc.) were used in this study.

**Multi-discipline approach.** Voyat (1982) described a multi-discipline approach to treatment involving play therapy, special education, and life skills training. The program included traditional play therapy, classrooms for autistic children with specially trained teachers, and paraprofessional therapeutic companions for the children in the classroom, at home and on outings. Voyat considered play therapy to be the core of the program, but did not give details on methods of implementation. A number of other experts similarly advocate including play therapy in intensive, multi-discipline programs but do not provide further details or give more specific recommendations.

### Effectiveness of the Various Forms of Play Therapy

**Traditional play therapy.** It is difficult to evaluate the effectiveness of traditional play therapy because it is presented almost exclusively in case study form. Bromfield (1989), Lanyado (1987), and Lowery (1985) reported improvement in their clients in the areas of language development, social interaction, and reduction of stereotypic behaviors. Bromfield (1989) found that these gains transferred to settings outside the playroom. Rogers and Fine (1977) reported a decrease in personal distance and movement in and out of close contact with the therapist by an autistic child after five months of twice weekly play sessions. These changes seem to indicate improved tolerance for social interaction.

**Group play therapy.** Wolfberg and Schuler (1993) reported a high degree of success with their integrated play group model, which was designed to promote gains in symbolic play skills and social interaction. As described, improvement in these areas seems quite positive. They also reported language gains and reduction in aberrant behaviors. In addition, improvements seem to have generalized to other settings. Mundschenk and Sasso (1995) also reported improved social interaction among autistic children and that the gains generalized well.

**Multi-discipline approach.** Voyat (1982) reported dramatic changes in the behaviors of autistic children. Evidence indicates that multi-discipline programs including at least 15 hours per week of therapeutic activities are among the most effective (Rogers, 1996).

### Implications

It appears that any number of approaches to treatment can facilitate improvement in autistic children. It seems likely that different forms of treatment or applications of play therapy might prove more effective in ameliorating different aspects of the syndrome. Wenar and Ruttenberg (1976) compared the overall effectiveness of various treatment programs. They determined that, while theoretical orientation, treatment mode, and setting were factors in effectiveness, the most important factor was the manner in which the treatment was administered. They discovered that among the therapists working in different types of programs, techniques were similar (e.g., educators used behavior modification, therapists used teaching, etc.). The differences in the various programs showed up more in the attitudes and skills of the staff and the level of structure, etc. They concluded that treatment in general is more effective with younger children (ages 3–6) than with older children (ages 7–9). Rogers (1996) confirmed the need for early diagnosis and treatment and also noted that the most effective programs had low client to therapist ratios, indicating that individual attention is beneficial for autistic children. Individual and small group play therapy seem to be effective methods for providing that attention.

## Principles for Application

There is agreement in the literature regarding the importance of a phenomenological approach in therapy and in attempting to enter the autistic child's world (Bromfield, 1989; Lanyado, 1987; Lowery, 1985; Voyat, 1982; Webster, Konstantaress, Oxman, & Mack, 1980). Voyat (1982) asserted that therapists must learn the autistic child's private language that is expressed through play in order to be helpful. This seems to suggest that the use of child-centered methods (i.e., permissiveness, reflection, tracking, etc.) are vital in the stages of play therapy.

There is also agreement in the literature that therapy with this population is a slow and laborious process, requiring a great deal of patience (Bromfield, 1989; Lowery, 1985; Wenar & Ruttenberg, 1976). Improvements lauded in a year of work with an autistic child take place spontaneously in normal children in a much shorter period of time (Wenar & Ruttenberg, 1976). Therapists must avoid viewing the child's initial isolation as personal rejection (Lowery, 1985), taking care not to push the child into contact, waiting until the child is ready. The labor of patience required extracts a high toll on the therapist and a high potential for burnout exists in therapists working with this population. Preventative measures seem advisable.

It also seems advisable for professionals to keep in mind that, while autistic children can and do make substantial improvements with treatment, their social and play skill may never look completely normal. If the overall goal of treatment is to help children maximize their potential and lead more functional lives, then even small gains can be celebrated as great victories as in the following case example.

## THE CASE OF BRAD

### A Shaky Beginning

As I entered the reception area, I saw a thin almost fragile blonde five-year-old boy. His empty stare seemed to indicate lack of acknowledgment of people or objects in his environment. As his mother helped remove his coat, Brad's barely audible voice was heard saying, "Cheryl Crane, Cheryl Crane." He was reading the name plate of the receptionist.

The usual introductions and explanations were made. Brad willingly took my hand and left for the playroom, located on the 3rd floor of an old house. There was limited strength felt as his limp hand lightly grasped mine. Holding on to the rail with one hand and my hand with the other, the climb began. Brad immediately began counting each step "one, two, three," etc. As each level was reached, I knelt down and said to Brad, "Yes, you and I have climbed eight steps." This continued until at last the 3rd floor playroom was reached. Upon entering the playroom, Brad immediately sat on the floor and began playing the xylophone. As he played he counted "one, two, three, etc." Again feeling a need to make contact with Brad as he played, I sang "la la." Without looking at me, Brad began softly singing with me.

Someone had mistakenly left a digital clock on a table in the playroom. Brad seemed mesmerized by the clock. He stated five-second intervals and minute changes. I attempted to intervene by asking if it were okay to unplug the clock. Brad compliantly said "Yes." When the clock was unplugged, Brad became semi-hysterical—screeching, crying, and flaying his hands. Had this been a later session, I would have chosen to work through Brad's anger, frustration, and disappointment. However, this was the first session and the relationship was tenuous at best. I plugged in the clock again, moved to sit very close to Brad and began rubbing his back. His physical reaction indicated he was trying to shrug off the physical contact and wanted it discontinued. With minimal interference I continued to occasionally rub Brad's back. Torn between the desire to respect Brad's space and with the desire to make some kind of contact, I felt the occasional physical contact was in order.

For twenty-five minutes, Brad told the five-second intervals and minutes as shown on the digital clock. He talked softly to himself in nonsense syllables. Some echolalia was also noted.

After the session, I sat with Brad in the reception room, waiting for his mother who was habitually late for appointments. Brad read aloud the titles of books on the shelf, looked at the clock on the wall, spotted the desk calendar, went to the desk and began turning the calendar pages and reading numbers. Again trying to make contact, every time Brad came to multiples of 10, I rubbed his back. He began to look at me at these times, leaned over to be touched and then lightly touched me. Although there was physical contact, little strength was felt in Brad's touch.

### Presenting Problems

Brad had been referred by his father. The stated concerns were lack of language development, possible retardation, encopresis, and a mild form of cerebral palsy. Although psychological data was available from a psychiatrist, I chose not to review the material until I had seen Brad for three or four sessions. Often having information prior to seeing the child increases the inclination to develop a mental image of the child and the child's problems. Prejudging tends to set up certain expectancies that seem to decrease the flexibility and openness of the counselor. Acknowledging the fact that data can be beneficial, it is believed that diagnostic data is not a prerequisite for admission to play therapy.

From the first meeting with a child in the reception area, one of the therapist's main functions is to make contact with the child. The building of a relationship begins when therapist and child first meet. For a large number of children, simple introductions and brief explanations are sufficient. Parents may be invited to accompany the child and counselor to the playroom but to leave immediately. For other children, particularly self-insulated or isolated children, making contact with them is a major and arduous task. Such was the case with Brad.

Unmet affectional needs of children tend to either cause them to isolate or insulate self or to strike out against the world and everyone in it. Other factors also contribute to a self isolation that seems to say, "I'll be my own source of emotional nourishment." Consequently, some of these children develop their own language, talk to self, have great difficulty giving or receiving affection, and engage in ritualistic behaviors. The other type, the striking-out child, seems to be saying, "At any cost, no matter how painful, I will have some physical contact." In Brad's case, the former was true. Brad's ritualistic behaviors took many forms. Obsession with numerical things has been noted.

Brad seemed unaware of objects in space. He seemed unaware of the toys on the floor, often stumbling and stepping on them without acknowledging their presence. This concerned me because of Brad's slight motoric problems; it could be a safety factor. His lack of awareness of body and objects in space were indicative of a limited sense of self. He seemed to feel disembodied: his bodily experiences and actions did not seem part of himself.

## Self-Rejection

Although Brad was encopretic, he requested to be taken to the bathroom, and I accompanied him to the bathroom. Brad was most reluctant to hold his penis and did so only after much encouragement. He seemed to be attempting to deal with the anxiety aroused by his penis and bodily functions by dissociating himself from them. During the second session, the bathroom trip was repeated. This time Brad grasped his penis but pulled, tugged, and twisted it roughly. Attempting to aid Brad, I made several comments, "It is part of you, Brad. It is your penis. You use it when you go to the bathroom. It hurts to twist and tug on it."

In succeeding sessions, Brad appropriately handled bathroom behavior. Occasionally, when Brad soiled his pants in the playroom, I encouraged him to go to the bathroom. His usual response was "No!" Constipation and encopresis were problems. Trusting in Brad's abilities to decide some things for himself, no pressure was used. For several weeks, Brad's refusal to accept my suggestion to go to the bathroom resulted in soiled pants. Any attempt to discuss or explore the issue resulted in further withdrawal on Brad's part. The ritual of Brad indicating the need to go to the bathroom, my encouraging the same, Brad's refusal, my accepting his choice was repeated. A hint of acceptance of social standards was seen when Brad chose to change the ritual. Instead of refusing to go to the bathroom, he grasped my hand saying "Shirley will help." Accompanying Brad to the bathroom was not enough. "Shirley will stay" and I did. Brad experienced great pain with bowel movements even though the physician found no physical cause and his diet was monitored to help alleviate his discomfort.

## Making Contact

It is of paramount importance to be genuine and real with all children, particularly with this sensitive, perceptive child. Brad's limited acknowledgment of what he saw, felt, and heard made it difficult to ascertain just how he was perceiving me and the situation.

Brad's entry into the playroom typically followed a ritualistic pattern. First, he would play the xylophone and with me sing "la la's." Next, he would read the coloring book *Cinderella*. (It was later determined that this five-year-old child was reading on a seventh grade level with very limited comprehension.) Sometimes a page would be missing—children were permitted to take colored pages home. Brad would stare into space, repeat the words from the missing pages, and continue. Accepting Brad's need for ritualistic play and feeling the need to make contact, I made sound effects where appropriate—such as wind blowing, owl screeching, etc. When I momentarily hesitated to make sound effects, Brad waited patiently and a faint grin was seen. The first sense of joy was observed during the reading of the coloring book. Brad made good eye contact, grinned broadly, and eventually joined in the making of the sound effects.

Whether Brad became tired of the coloring book story or whether he desired to extend the "game" was unclear when he chose to bring two additional books into the playroom. (Rarely is the use of books and reading same encouraged during play therapy sessions. Children can hide behind books. In Brad's case, concreteness and sameness seemed important. Books served to accomplish these goals.) Brad read the two books with great animation. When additional sound effects seemed warranted, he would pause, glance at me, and wait for me to respond. Brad's increased desire for close physical contact was expressed during the "reading" periods. Initially, he preferred to lean against my chair. Slowly he eased closer to me until he was sitting on my lap. As I rubbed his back, he nestled closer still attending to his "reading" yet obviously hungry for physical warmth and contact.

## Brad's Tentative Acceptance of Self and the Therapist

Some time was spent in front of the one way mirror—pointing to parts of Brad's body and to me to help Brad gain some sense of his physical self. He was anxious and insecure, even about his own body. It was during these times that the first gleeful laughter was heard. At the end of one session, having spent a good amount of time at the mirror, we started downstairs. Brad gently tugged on my arm, pulled me down to his size and timidly placed a light kiss on my cheek.

During one session, Brad went to the puppet shelf and announced, "Animals." Putting each puppet on his hand in succession, he said "Pardon me, Mr. Dragon. Could I ask you a couple of questions?" "Pardon me, Mr. Leopard," etc. until all of the puppets had been used. I responded each time, "Yes, you may ask me any question you'd like." The results were the same—no response. As Brad was engaging in the puppet play, I asked, "Wonder what question you'd like to ask?" The response was a definite "No." I responded "No question. I say, Mr. Dragon, it's nice to see Brad today." A large smile slowly crept across his face.

Nonsense syllables were prominent in Brad's speech. Most of the time Brad's nonsense syllables were barely whispered, hardly audible. One day I was able to hear and repeated the syllables. Sheer delight crossed Brad's face and his body relaxed. He came to me, put his hands on my knees and looking into my face said nonsense syllables over and over. As each "sentence" was finished, I repeated same. Brad's voice grew louder and louder, he shrieked with delight; clapping his hands, he danced around and around the room.

As might be expected, the next session began with nonsense syllables. With great uncertainty and much difficulty, I attempted to help Brad understand that it was OK to use those words in the playroom, but in class and at home others might not know what was being said. (There was a need to tie the playroom activities to the world of reality for Brad. Imagine the reaction of peers, etc., to a child yelling nonsense syllables.)

In later sessions, Brad would occasionally express nonsense syllables which were then repeated by me. The message from Brad seemed to be that we had some secret, and he needed to check on my memory of same.

## What Brad Learned

Brad occasionally glanced at the paints and easel in several sessions. Yet he made no movement in that direction. My comments such as "Kind of looking at the paints-trying to decide" met with no verbal or physical response. In one session after a similar interaction, Brad said, "Shirley will help." I knelt beside Brad who was standing near the easel. Very gently I placed a brush in Brad's hand and guided the green paint onto the paper. Brad seemed totally awed by this experience. As each color was splashed on the paper, Brad's smile and eyes became larger and larger. In later sessions Brad stood in front of the easel and said, "Shirley will help." After a few painting sessions, Brad began to print by himself, though he continued to want me by his side painting with my own brush.

Only a few of the dynamics involved in Brad's case are reported here. The limited episodes and excerpts are mere illustrations of the results of believing in the child and regarding the child with dignity and self-worth. The therapist's attitude, characterized by warmth and caring plus patience in allowing Brad to unfold at his own pace, were powerful determinants in aiding Brad in finding his own strength.

Various theoretical approaches would view the dynamics quite differently. For the behaviorists, the hugs and sound effects might be viewed as reinforcing perseveration. Repeating the nonsense syllables might be viewed as reinforcing inappropriate behavior. For those of psychoanalytic orientation, the problem of encopresis might be seen as fixation at the anal stage. In addition, the physical contact—hugs—might be seen as working on transference. From a clinical standpoint, diagnosis and labeling might be the first order of business. Labeling Brad "autistic" could well have resulted in different intervention strategies.

My attitude of respect for, acceptance of, and faith in Brad allowed him "to be." In this safe, supporting, and emotionally nurturing relationship, Brad gained a sense of self both in the physical and emotional sense. He learned he did not have to give up all of his "unique" behaviors, (i.e., nonsense syllables) but rather to engage in those behaviors with a few selected others. He learned the joy of trying some new behaviors and mastering some. He learned an increased sense of "I am."

## Epilogue

The epilogue is short, not sweet. After approximately eighteen months of play therapy, often biweekly, Brad and his family moved to another city. By then, Brad was experiencing academic success and some social success in a mainstreamed behavior disorder classroom. Brad still needed additional play therapy. Whether he received any is questionable; no requests for Brad's records were ever received by school personnel or by me for Brad's records. Allen (1942) stated that one hour of play therapy can have a dramatic positive impact on a child's life. I believe this to be true.

I often wonder where Brad is and how he is doing. Though I desperately tried to maintain some degree of objectivity with Brad, I must admit I was too emotionally involved at times. He tugged at my heart strings so. His loneliness, isolation, need for love and affection, sensitivity, and intelligence, plus his frail physical slate touched me deeply.

## REFERENCES

Allen, F. (1942). *Psychotherapy with children*. New York: Norton.

American Psychiatric Association. (1994). *Diagnostic and statistical manual of mental disorders* (4th ed.). Washington, DC: Author.

Black, M., Freeman, B. J., & Mongomery, J. (1975). Systematic observation of play behavior in autistic children. *Journal of Autism and Childhood Schizophrenia*, 5(4), 363–71.

Bromfield, R. (1989). Psychodynamic play therapy with a high-functioning autistic child. *Psychoanalytic Psychology*, 6(4), 439–453.

Jarrold, C., Boucher, J., & Smith, P. (1993). Symbolic play in autism: A review. *Journal of Autism and Developmental Disorders*, 23(2), 281–307.

Lanyado, M. (1987). Asymbolic and symbolic play: Developmental perspectives in the treatment of disturbed children. *Journal of Child Psychotherapy, 13*(2), 33–44.

Libby, S., Powell, S., Messer, D., & Jordan, R. (1997). Imitation of pretend play acts by children with autism and Down's syndrome. *Journal of Autism and Developmental Disorders, 27*(4), 365–382.

Lowery, E. F. (1985). Autistic aloofness reconsidered. *Bulletin of the Menniger Clinic, 49*(2), 135–150.

MacLennan, B. W. (1977). Modifications of activity group therapy for children. *International Journal of Group Psychotherapy, 21*(1), 85–96.

Mundschenk, N. A., & Sasso, G. M. (1995). Assessing sufficient social exemplars for students with autism. *Behavioral Disorders, 21*(2), 62-78.

Paluszny, M. J. (1979). *Autism: A practical guide for parents and professionals.* Syracuse, NY: Syracuse University Press.

Rogers, A. L., & Fine H. J. (1977). Personal distance in play therapy with an autistic and symbiotic psychotic child. *Psychotherapy: Theory, Research and Practice, 14*(1), 41–48.

Rogers, S. J. (1996). Brief report: Early intervention in autism. *Journal of Autism and Developmental Disorders, 26*(2), 243–246.

Voyat, G. (1982). Symbolic play in the treatment of autism in children. *New York University Education Quarterly, 13*(4), 11–15.

Webster, C. D., Konstantareas, M. M., Oxman, J., & Mack, J. E. (Eds.). (1980). *Autism: New directions in research and education.* New York: Pergamon Press.

Wenar, C., & Ruttenberg, B. A. (1976). The use of BRIAC for evaluating therapeutic effectiveness. *Journal of Autism and Childhood Sczophrenia, 6*(2), 175–191.

Wolfberg, P. J., & Schuler, A. L. (1993). Integrated play groups: A model for promoting the social and cognitive dimensions of play in children with autism. *Journal of Autism and Developmental Disorders, 23*(3), 467–488.

# 17

# Play Therapy for Children with Chronic Illness

## ELIZABETH MURPHY JONES

"**I** don't care if you don't like it! You have to eat it!" exclaimed Angela, a seven-year-old child with insulin-dependent diabetes mellitus. "I'll make you eat it even if you hate it!" she continued, as she pushed a plastic slice of pizza down the mouth of a rubber alligator. The play therapist replied, "The alligator has to eat, even if he doesn't want to. You are making him!" Angela continued to push food violently into the alligator's open mouth. The therapist reflected, "Sometimes you have to do things you don't want to, and it makes you so angry!" Suddenly, Angela paused. She looked up at the therapist thoughtfully, and said in a soft voice, "Yeah. The alligator is sad. He has diabetes." The therapist nodded understandingly as Angela jumped up and walked toward the therapist saying, "Let's play with the dollhouse now!"

This chapter focuses on the unique needs of chronically ill children like Angela in play therapy. Specifically, it addresses the issues facing children and families suffering from chronic illness, the importance of play for chronically ill children, and the efficacy of play therapy with this group of children. Finally, the practice of child-centered play therapy with this special population is illustrated in case study examples.

## CHRONIC ILLNESS IN CHILDHOOD

### The Challenges Facing Chronically Ill Children

Children who suffer from chronic illnesses are often a neglected segment of our society. Although medical advances and technology have allowed children who might not have survived decades ago to live healthy, productive lives, chronically ill children and their families are faced with a host of rigorous demands and stressors associated with managing their illness. These children and families must endure financial strains, daily medical procedures, dependence on medical services and personnel, family tension, and uncertainty about the future.

Although the number of children who die as a result of chronic illness has markedly decreased, the incidence of chronic illness in childhood remains stable (Perrin, 1985). Approximately 10 to 15 percent of the childhood population suffers from chronic illnesses such as cystic fibrosis, spina bifida, sickle cell anemia, leukemia and other cancers, asthma, juvenile diabetes, or hemophilia (Perrin, 1985). Among these children, about one to two percent live with severe chronic illness, requiring significant health care (Perrin, 1985). In other words, an estimated 7.5 million children in the United States live with chronic illness, with approximately one million of these being severe disorders (Hobbs, Perrin, & Ireys, 1985). Unlike adult illness, each of these conditions that appear in children are relatively rare, therefore, families with chronically ill children may have difficulty locating adequate health care at diagnosis, appropriate support services, and long term management may be difficult to find in certain geographical areas.

## Medical Play

In recent years, hospitals have become increasingly aware of the psychosocial, educational, and recreational needs of their pediatric patients. Hospitalization requires children to relinquish their freedom, sense of control, and privacy, while demanding that they undergo frightening and occasionally painful experiences. Acute physical illness can create severe stress for children due to their limited knowledge of the hospital environment, their cognitive development, and their separation from family and school settings. The stress of a severe illness can result in feelings of depression and anxiety within the child, which may manifest in behaviors such as withdrawal, regression, decreased cooperation, aggression, disruptive behavior, and sleep disturbances (Cooper & Blitz, 1985). These behaviors impact the ability of the medical staff to adequately care for these children, thus making the hospital stay a significantly negative experience for both the child and the family.

Koocher and O'Malley (1981) found that children's ability to anticipate stressful events, gain a sense of mastery, and express negative thoughts and feelings, increased their ability to cope with difficult experiences. Adams (1976) reported that children benefited from therapeutic play activities, as they were able to express their anxiety in a language that was developmentally appropriate: the language of play. According to Billington (1972), "play is a natural function of any child, whether well or sick. It does not stop when he enters the hospital" (p. 90).

## The Language of Play

Play is a child's natural medium for self-expression. In play, children are given the opportunity to "play out" feelings and problems so that they become more manageable (Axline, 1969). Play provides children with opportunities to develop a sense of mastery of self and environment, test reality, express needs and wants, confront fears and anxieties, and become active in an environment that they can control (Landreth, 1991). According to Erikson (1963) play is the child's first experience in creating situations and to master reality by experimenting and planning. Piaget (1962) emphasized the importance of the symbolic nature of play for children, as it is an assimilation of concrete and abstract thought. Piaget considered play to be integral to development as it provides the child opportunities for mastery, experimentation, and self-expression.

Play is, for children, an experience they can control and manipulate entirely. In play, children can express unpleasant thoughts and feelings in a nonthreatening environment, and solve problems independently. As children begin to feel more in control of their lives through the active process of play, they begin to feel more secure in their lives (Landreth, 1991). According to Erikson (1963), as children are able to express fantasies, fears, and conflicts through play, they are better able to cope with these dimensions and to compensate for deficits and frustrations, therefore, moving toward more emotionally mature behavior.

## Child-Centered Play Therapy for Children with Illness

The child-centered play therapy approach is based on the philosophical belief that children have the capacity within themselves to grow, develop, and solve problems when they experience an environment of safety and trust. In this approach, the establishment of an accepting and permissive relationship between the child and the play therapist is considered to be crucial. The play therapy environment is characterized by freedom, acceptance, and permissiveness where the child "learns to accept himself, to grant himself the permissiveness to utilize all his capacities, and to assume responsibility for himself" (Axline, 1969, p. 27).

For children with chronic illness, this environment of freedom and acceptance is particularly significant. Children who receive long-term medical care often experience a loss of control, privacy, and freedom of choice. In fact, in young children, it has been shown that repeated or lengthy periods of hospitalizations are related to developmental delays, anxiety, and failure to develop a sense of mastery or control of self (Bolig, Fernie, & Klein, 1986). This failure "to develop, maintain, or regain a feeling of control only increases susceptibility to other physical and psychological disorders" (Bolig et al., 1986, p. 101). In health care, medical procedures are externally directed and are not controlled by the child, thereby fostering an external locus of control. These experiences profoundly influence the child's sense of control, often leading to feelings of helplessness, anger, and anxiety. Children who develop an internal locus of control are more likely to comply with medical prevention and treatment because they believe in their own capacity to control events and consequences in their lives (Bolig et al., 1986). Therefore, "an internal response pattern is increasingly viewed as critical to recovery" from illness (Bolig et al., 1986, p. 103).

Child-centered play therapy is based on the assumption that the child has the ability to be self-directive, and it is this capacity that leads the child toward greater maturity and understanding of self and internal sense of control. Therefore, child-centered play therapy provides maximum opportunity for children to gain or continue to maintain control during medical treatment. In this relationship, ill children have an opportunity to control events, ideas, relationships, and outcomes through the process of integration of experiences and expression of feelings in a permissive and accepting environment (Landreth, 1991).

## The Effectiveness of Play Therapy for Children with Chronic Illness

Play therapy has been shown to be an effective treatment for hospitalized children undergoing medical procedures. Ellerton, Caty, and Richie (1985) found that nine out of ten hospitalized patients with chronic illnesses played out intrusive medical procedures, particularly injections of medicine during non-directive play therapy sessions. These results indicate children's need to express their anxieties and fears regarding medical procedures and the benefit of play therapy in the hospital setting.

Similarly, Garot (1986) and Daniel, Rae, Sanner, Upchurch, and Worchel (1989) found that play therapy significantly decreased children's anxiety and fearfulness in the hospital environment. Zilliacus and Enberg (1980) studied the effectiveness of a hospital play program implemented in a hospital waiting room for children admitted to the hospital, children receiving outpatient services, and siblings of hospital patients. Interviews with one hundred parents whose children participated in the play program indicated that eighty percent of those parents felt that the play therapy program was effective in decreasing the children's tension. In addition, eighty-eight percent of these parents reported that they benefited from watching the play sessions as well.

In other studies, play therapy has been shown to be an effective treatment for children diagnosed with chronic illness. Bentley (1975) provided play therapy for a young boy suffering from severe, persistent asthma and eczema. In therapy, the child was able to express himself through the play materials, engaging in play with aggressive and nurturing themes. Bentley reported that following therapy, the child's parents reported no serious asthma attacks. This case study illustrates the significance of the relationship between a child's emotional and physiological health.

Short term play therapy has been shown to be an effective means of reducing fears in children who are suffering from a medical condition. Acord (1980) conducted six play sessions with a boy who was hospitalized as a result of injuries following an automobile accident. These play sessions were comprised of projective play, where the child was able to project his fear of injections onto dolls and this significantly decreased his anxiety about intrusive medical procedures. Barton (1962) utilized toys that represented a hospital setting to treat a child who was hospitalized for heart surgery. Prior to play therapy, this child exhibited behavioral problems such as aggressive hostility toward hospital staff, and she demonstrated a high level of distrust of the hospital environment. After three child-centered play therapy sessions, including a structured re-enactment of the surgical procedure, this child demonstrated a significant decrease in anxiety. After discharge from the hospital, the child requested a visit to the hospital to see her hospital friends. It was determined that this brief intervention was effective in allowing the child to release her anxiety and to develop a sense of mastery and self-control in the hospital environment.

Studies involving larger numbers of children have also shown the efficacy of play therapy in reducing anxiety in children hospitalized for medical procedures. Cassell (1965) conducted two individual structured medical play sessions with twenty children undergoing cardiac catheterization in which she acted out the medical procedure with the use of puppets. When compared with the control group, these children showed less emotional disturbance during the cardiac catheterization, and they expressed greater willingness to return to the hospital for further treatment. Similarly, Clatworthy (1981) provided daily play therapy sessions for fifty-nine children who were hospitalized for two to four days utilizing play materials such as medical toys, dolls, puppets, and art supplies. The results of this study indicated that the children who received short-term play therapy sessions exhibited a significantly lower level of anxiety when compared to the control group.

## Filial Therapy for Children with Chronic Illness

Filial therapy, developed by Bernard and Louise Guerney in the 1960s, is based on the principles of child-centered play therapy outlined by Axline (1969) and utilizes parents as therapeutic agents with their children. The model developed by Landreth (1991) includes ten weekly filial therapy group sessions led by a play therapist trained in filial therapy and weekly play sessions at home between the parent and child. During these thirty minute play sessions, parents utilize child-centered play therapy principles of reflecting feelings, accepting their children's feelings, setting therapeutic limits, and encouraging their children's self-direction.

Glazer-Waldman, Zimmerman, Landreth, and Norton (1992) and Tew (1997) have documented the effectiveness of Landreth's (1991) model of filial therapy with parents of chronically ill children. Specifically, Glazer-Waldman et al. (1992) found that all parents who participated in the filial therapy program indicated significant changes in their relationships with their children. Tew (1997) found a significant decrease in parental stress and problematic behavior in chronically ill children, and a significant increase in parental acceptance of their child following filial therapy.

## THE PRACTICE OF PLAY THERAPY
## FOR CHILDREN WITH CHRONIC ILLNESS

Chronically ill children may be seen in play therapy in a variety of settings and circumstances. They may be seen in schools by school counselors; hospitals by counselors, psychologists, or child life specialists; camps or schools where children with medical illnesses are in attendance; or private practices. Chronically ill children may be referred for behavioral, emotional, or adjustment difficulties, and as a preventative measure as the child and family adjust to the demands of managing childhood illness.

Regardless of the environment or the circumstances of the referral, it is important for the play therapist to balance the unique needs of the child and the impact of the child's illness in order to provide an appropriate and effective therapeutic experience for the child. The following cases illustrate the effectiveness of child-centered play therapy with two special children.

## THE CASE OF ALAN

Alan, age 10, was diagnosed with cerebral palsy as a toddler. He was referred for play therapy by his mother, who reported that his behavior was uncontrollable at home and at school. He was seen by a child psychiatrist who diagnosed him with Oppositional Defiant Disorder. His physical and occupational therapists refused to continue his therapy sessions until he received counseling due to a recent increase in aggressive behavior. When Alan arrived with his mother for the initial parent interview, he sat in the corner of the waiting room, with stiff braces on his legs, searching the faces of the clinic staff with great anticipation. When he reached out to shake the therapist's hand, it was apparent that he had chewed his fingernails until there was nothing left at the end of his fingers. Throughout his initial visit, Alan asked questions to his mother and the therapist incessantly, such as "What is your name?", "What is your name?", "When are we going home, Momma?", "When are we going home, Momma?"

During the initial parent interview, Alan's mother reported that his cerebral palsy had caused Alan to be severely delayed developmentally, he was diagnosed as mentally retarded, and he received both physical and occupational therapy for his motor impairment. Alan's recent aggression had made it impossible for her to transport him to school or his doctor's appointments. Her voice shook with sadness as she explained that Alan was a loving and affectionate child, but that his behavior had become increasingly antagonistic and physically aggressive in recent months. She believed that Alan was significantly distressed, but she said, " I just don't know how to reach him. He doesn't talk to me like my other children." During this meeting, the therapist and his mother agreed that Alan should begin play therapy.

## Case History and Background

In order to gain a better understanding of Alan's experience in play therapy, some knowledge of Alan's family environment and his medical background is needed. Alan was diagnosed with cerebral palsy as a toddler, when his mother noticed that he was not developing normally. At the time of his diagnosis, Alan lived with his biological mother, father, and older sister. Alan's father left the family in the early years of Alan's life, and he did not remain in contact with the family. At the time Alan began play therapy, he lived in a small apartment with his biological mother, his older sister, age 15, his stepfather, and a half brother, age 2. Alan's mother did not work outside the home in order to be available to transport Alan to several doctor's appointments each week. Alan attended physical therapy two times per week to improve his gross motor skills, and although he wore braces on both legs, he was able to walk independently. Alan attended public school where he was placed in special education classes for developmentally delayed children.

At the beginning of therapy, Alan was learning the alphabet and beginning to read simple words. Alan's mother reported that at school, he was disruptive in the classroom, as he frequently refused to comply with classroom rules. Alan's teachers reported that he sometimes became physically abusive to both teachers and classmates.

During the year that Alan received play therapy, his family structure changed several times. His stepfather, whom his mother reported was diagnosed with alcoholism and bipolar disorder, left home three to four times for extended periods of time, often leaving the family without financial resources. In addition, a male friend of Alan's mother moved into the home, and he helped to support the family when Alan's stepfather was out of the home. Alan's sister, who cared for Alan as a frequent baby-sitter, attempted suicide and was hospitalized for several weeks. These events were significant losses for Alan. Although he had difficulty understanding the complexity of the family's difficulties, he clearly reacted to the emotional environment in the home.

Alan's mother was a bright, articulate woman, who was extremely invested in the upbringing of her children. In the initial parent interview, she communicated her desire to provide for her children an environment of love and acceptance and described her own childhood as being characterized by criticism and blame. As a result, she was committed to staying at home with her children, so that she might "be there" when they needed her. During the first parent consultation, she spent a great deal of time telling the therapist the things that Alan couldn't do that she must do for him. It was clear that Alan's mother had a strong commitment to doing anything she could for Alan. Prior to beginning therapy, Alan's mother took an authoritarian approach to parenting, and she communicated her sense of pride in being "in control" of the household. However, she reported that Alan's behavior had become unmanageable in the weeks preceding therapy. He had become physically aggressive toward her and she had resorted to spanking him when he disobeyed her, although clearly, she did not feel comfortable with this method of discipline.

Alan was seen in play therapy for twenty-five sessions over a period of one year. Although weekly play therapy was recommended at the onset of therapy, Alan's mother had difficulty attending the regular appointments due to financial constraints (no money for gasoline) and family conflicts. Alan's play therapy sessions began in a small playroom equipped with several categories of toys including nurturing toys (dolls, animals), aggressive toys (toy gun, toy soldiers), real-life toys (family figures, dollhouse, telephone, medical kit, pots and pans), and toys for creative expression (art supplies, paints, Play-Doh) as recommended by Landreth (1991). However, at the tenth session, Alan requested to play in the therapist's office, which had a small box containing a few of the toys outlined above. This environmental shift proved to be helpful for Alan, as there was a significant decrease in stimuli in the therapy office. He became less anxious and more expressive in the new environment, and he did not request to return to the playroom. Therefore, the remainder of the play therapy sessions were conducted in the therapy office with a small group of toys. In addition to play therapy, Alan received physical therapy and psychiatric medication management throughout the year of therapy. He was prescribed medication for attention difficulties and feelings of anxiety and depression. Throughout his therapy, the play therapist kept in contact with Alan's child psychiatrist and physical therapist to work as a team to provide optimal interventions for Alan and his family.

### Alan in Play Therapy

At his first visit, Alan refused to walk to the playroom. He sat on a chair in the waiting room, biting his fingernails, looking up and down at the therapist. Sensing his feelings of anxiety, the therapist asked Alan's mother to accompany him to the playroom. He agreed with this plan, and, after some continued resistance, he was able to enter the playroom and allowed his mother to return to the waiting area.

During this initial session, Alan found the Lego building blocks and sat with his back to the therapist working to break apart the blocks that were connected together. He did not respond to the therapist's reflections, rather he repeated questions throughout the session such as "Where is my mom?" and "Is it time to go yet?" Each time he asked these questions, the therapist answered the questions and reflected his feelings by saying, "Your mom is in the waiting room. She will be waiting for you when the playtime is over" and "It feels different to be in this new place. You don't know me very well. Our playtime will be over in ten minutes." Although his questions were answered and his feelings reflected, Alan continued to ask the same questions throughout the session, and when the session was over, he ran out of the playroom to embrace his mother.

Although Alan touched many of the toys in the playroom during the first four sessions, he did not engage in play. He spent most of these sessions looking at the floor or choosing one particular toy to examine, such as a truck or a hospital playset. Alan continued to ask questions throughout the initial sessions such as "What is this?", " How much longer do I stay here?" and "What should I do next?" Each time he asked these questions, the therapist returned the responsibility and control to Alan by saying, "You can choose how to spend your time here" and " In here, that can be whatever you would like it to be." Alan never responded to these comments by the therapist. Instead, he would turn from the toy he was examining and look away, unsure of how to react.

During the sixth session, Alan entered the playroom independently and began constructing a house with a set of wooden blocks. He communicated to the therapist, "This is a house for people to live." This was the first session in which Alan created something in the playroom. His continuing level of anxiety was reflected in questions such as "When is it time to go?" but these questions were significantly less frequent, and he seemed to be reassured by the therapist's words as he nodded after each response. Alan constructed a simple house and began to take blocks out of it one by one, while he attempted to keep the house from falling down. He engaged in this activity for the duration of the session.

In the next three sessions, Alan continued to initiate constructive play activities. During these sessions, Alan began to make more decisions about what and how he would play. In one session, he chose to construct a hospital room with a nurse and a hospital bed. In another session, he chose to stack toy trucks on top of one another, as he attempted to build a "tower." It seemed that Alan was beginning to understand that the playroom was a place where he could safely explore, experiment, and create.

## Testing the Relationship

The next several sessions were characterized by consistent limit testing. At the beginning of the ninth session, Alan refused to enter the playroom and sat with his head under a chair in the waiting room. The therapist elected to stay in the waiting room and reflected Alan's feelings by saying "You don't want to go today," and " You would like to be out here with your Mom." Alan responded by yelling "Yeah!" at each reflection, but he did not move from his place under the chair. Sensing the importance of Alan's need to feel in control of his world, the therapist set the limit, but provided Alan with some choices by saying, "Alan, I can see that you need some time before we go to the playroom. You may choose to go in two minutes or three minutes. It is up to you." Alan did not respond. He sat in silence. The therapist said, "I'll wait for you to make your decision. You can let me know if you need two minutes or three minutes out here before we go to the playroom." After some time, Alan yelled, "THREE!" The therapist responded, "OK, you have decided you need three minutes out here. I will walk down the hall and come back in three minutes. Then it will be time to go to the playroom." When the therapist returned, Alan was sitting on the edge of the chair, and he was able to go to the playroom. During this session, Alan did not test the limits, but made frequent contact with the therapist. He conducted his play activities facing the therapist for the first time. Although he continued to look at the floor throughout most of the session, he maintained eye contact when he spoke to the play therapist.

When the therapist met Alan for the tenth session, Alan said, "Can we play in your office today?" Seeing this as significant movement toward controlling his environment, the therapist agreed. In the therapist's office, there was a small box of toys representative of the same categories of toys as the larger playroom. Alan explored all of these toys and the entire space of the office. He appeared open both physically and emotionally to this environment. Alan chose to paint with the finger paints, an activity he had never engaged in during previous sessions. He delighted in showing the therapist his "messy hands" and giggled while he created a painting soaked with paint. Alan also found that he was accepted by the therapist even when some paint accidentally splattered on the office chairs. When the therapist responded by saying, "Sometimes accidents happen," he was jubilant as he repeated this phrase over and over during the session while he painted. "Sometimes accidents happen! Sometimes accidents happen! Sometimes accidents happen!" It seemed that Alan responded to this smaller office setting by exerting his control, choice, and mastery over this environment. The therapist continued to provide Alan with the choice to have their play session in the larger playroom, but Alan continued to prefer the small group of toys in the therapist's office. It seemed that the larger playroom was overwhelming for him, and the smaller room provided an increased level of safety for him.

During the eleventh through eighteenth sessions, it appeared as though Alan's behavior had regressed, as the anxiety that was present during the first play therapy sessions returned. Alan asked repetitive questions and he did not seem to respond to the therapist's answers. The therapist learned that Alan's sister had been hospitalized following a suicide attempt. Although Alan returned to asking questions, his questions pertained to the current family situation such as, "When will my sister come home?" and "Where is my sister?" The therapist responded by reflecting his feelings of loss by saying, "You really miss her" and "It is confusing that she is not at home." For the first time, Alan began responding to these reflections by making small grunting sounds of acknowledgment. His play activities increased in complexity and centered around themes of mastery and control. Alan drew more pictures and identified solutions to difficult situations in the play session. When the Play-Doh was stuck to the jar, he said, "Hey, I'll get it out with this!" as he grabbed a pencil. In response to this movement toward self-direction, the therapist responded by saying, "You figured out a way to do that!" thus affirming his self-responsibility.

## Integrating a Sense of Control

Alan's progress in play therapy is even more significant when viewed in the context of the dynamics in his family. During the last three months in therapy, Alan's stepfather left home and returned three times. The family was not able to pay household bills, and Alan's mother asked friends and family to assist them financially. Alan's mother was extremely distressed during this time and sought individual therapy on the recommendation of Alan's doctors and therapists.

Alan, however, continued to progress in play therapy. His play was characterized by a sense of freedom, self-direction, and confidence. During the nineteenth session, he began talking with the therapist in a conversational manner while he played. He responded verbally to the therapist's reflections and seemed to internalize these reflections. Alan's internalization of self-responsibility was evident in his selection of craft items and his decision to paint a picture. While he painted a picture of a person, he said, "There was a big fight at my house last night." The therapist responded, "Someone got into a fight and it was scary." Alan responded, "Yeah, Jack and another man were real mad. They yelled." The therapist continued to respond to Alan's feelings while he told this story. This was the first time Alan was able to communicate verbally and to integrate the therapist's responses. During this session, Alan continued to paint pictures of family members as he talked.

In the final six sessions, Alan continued to choose toys that he could manipulate and control with ease. He built skyscrapers, smashed Play-Doh, and painted pictures of trees, boats, and helicopters. In the twenty-fourth session, Alan invented a game to play with the therapist and took the lead as he explained the rules of the game. There was a striking difference in the ease with which he directed activity in this session and the anxiety he expressed in the first few sessions. Alan delighted in teaching the game, changing the rules at will, and making jokes when the therapist misunderstood the rules.

At the final parent consult, Alan's mother expressed her confusion about why Alan's behavior had not deteriorated due to the recent family struggles. "He seems to understand what is happening, but it doesn't seem to have affected him. He is doing well at home and at school." When the therapist explained that Alan found a sense of control over his world in play therapy, she began to understand. Tearfully, she said, "I wish I had something I could control. I feel so helpless when things are like this. I'm so happy he can now withstand this." In addition, Alan's behavior at school had improved significantly, as he was able to comply with the teacher's directives, and his mother reported that he had not been physically aggressive at home in several months.

## FILIAL THERAPY

It was recommended that Alan's mother attend filial therapy training, to strengthen the relationship between Alan and his mother. Alan's mother attended six of eight group filial therapy sessions. Although she did not complete the filial therapy group, the therapist was able to schedule parent consultations to present the remainder of the filial training material.

The filial sessions were scheduled during the last phase of play therapy with Alan so that he could begin to transfer his play sessions to the home. Filial training was explained to Alan as: "I am going to teach your Mom how to play with you at home kinda like you and I play here." Alan was enthusiastic, and his mother was able to easily understand the concepts of filial therapy. Although it was difficult for her to give control of the play sessions to Alan, she began to trust him as the guide during their special playtimes. She expressed her amazement at Alan's sense of freedom and creativity in the play sessions and began to view him as a capable, imaginative, and confident young boy. During the final two months of therapy, Alan attended play therapy twice a month, frequently inviting his mother to join the play sessions. In these meetings, the therapist was able to continue to coach Alan's mother in the concepts of filial therapy, and finally to terminate Alan's individual sessions.

# DISCUSSION

## The Play Therapy Relationship

The approach to Alan's play therapy was based on the significance of a therapeutic relationship characterized by emotional acceptance, warmth, and consistency. In play therapy, Alan experienced a relationship that accepted his feelings, both negative and positive, and was consistent over time. Alan learned about this relationship in a variety of ways. First, the play therapist identified and reflected Alan's feelings in an accepting manner. Second, Alan tested the limits of the relationship to learn that he would be accepted regardless of his behavior. Also, in testing limits, Alan learned that there were consistent limits in the relationship, and this provided him with a sense of security. In contrast, the limits in his home environment changed frequently and were extremely rigid. Alan did not have the opportunity at home to learn to set his own limits. Although she intended to protect him, Alan's mother controlled all of Alan's activities, therefore discouraging his own sense of direction and control.

## Loss of Control and Need For Mastery

During the initial phase of therapy, it seemed that Alan had forgotten how to play. Studies have shown that children who experience a sense of helplessness over time, such as children with chronic illness, may develop a "playless" quality (Bolig et al., 1986). During Alan's lifetime, he experienced a mother who made most decisions for him, doctors who asked him to "sit still" for medical procedures, and physical therapists who asked him to move his body in ways that were often painful and uncomfortable. Alan rarely experienced a sense of control in his own life. As a result, he began to exert control in negative ways, by refusing to wear his braces or hitting and kicking his physical therapist. At the beginning of play therapy, Alan experienced high levels of anxiety characterized by his difficulty in coping with his life. Over time, however, Alan began to experience his own potential for mastery and he began to exercise his control in appropriate ways.

Children who receive ongoing medical care often feel helpless or anxious about their body due to physical restrictions, intrusive procedures, or external manipulation by doctors. As recommended by D'Antonio (1984), these children "should be provided with play opportunities in which they can achieve mastery or work through conflicts." During his play sessions, Alan's play centered around the theme of mastery and control. He chose toys that he could manipulate and master, such as the building blocks. Alan also sought toys that provided him with the freedom to express himself creatively, such as the finger paints and the craft items. It is interesting to note that Alan was not particularly interested in the medical toys during play therapy. In this case, it was not necessary for him to address the specific issues that may have caused his sense of helplessness, but to work through and conquer those feelings through activities where he was able to experience expertise and control of his environment. The child-centered approach to play therapy trusts this inner direction of the child.

Alan was no longer aggressive, but cooperative both at school and in the medical setting. Alan's mother reported that he complied with his daily routine, and she began utilizing a more effective approach to setting limits at home. As Wall (1987) stated, "the change from passive to active is the healing aspect of many play activities and it leaves the player better able to withstand being passive again, when necessary" (p. 3). Through play therapy, Alan learned that he could control himself and his life events, therefore, he was better able to cope with the inconsistencies of his home environment. In the last stage of therapy, the filial therapy play sessions at home did provide one area of consistency and predictability for Alan at home while strengthening the relationship with his mother by providing a safe play environment characterized by freedom within appropriate limits.

## THE CASE OF ROBERT

Robert, age 8, was seen in play therapy at a summer camp for children diagnosed with insulin-dependent diabetes mellitus. Type I or insulin-dependent diabetes mellitus (IDDM) is a chronic disorder caused by a lack of insulin secretion from the pancreas. Medical treatment for children with IDDM is aimed at the maintenance of normal or near normal blood glucose levels, with prevention of hypoglycemia (excessively low blood sugar) or hyperglycemia (excessively high blood sugar). Although it is impossible to replicate the highly sensitive insulin release mechanisms in a normal pancreas, the treatment objective for persons with IDDM is to emulate this process by regulating the factors that effect blood glucose levels including insulin levels through daily injections, exercise, stress management, and diet. For young children, this daily management is most often controlled by the parent, and the summer camp experience allows the child to experience independence while learning about their diabetes in a recreational environment. In addition, children learn that they are "not alone" as they form relationships with other children diagnosed with IDDM.

Robert's parents expressed interest in the play therapy program when they arrived at camp. They described him as a "delightful" boy with no major areas of difficulty, but they felt play therapy might prevent problems as he approached his preteen years. Robert's father reported that they were not concerned with Robert's adjustment to his diabetes as "he is fine with all that," but that they were concerned about his inability to accept "constructive criticism" from them and comply with their family rules. They explained that Robert was normally a quiet child, but that he had recently become "manipulative" when they asked him to finish his daily chores or homework. They stated that they hoped play therapy would prevent the perpetuation of this behavior. When asked if he had difficulty complying with his diabetic routine of insulin injections and dietary restrictions, they both answered "Oh no, he knows how important that is and it doesn't bother him at all."

Robert was seen for twelve daily play therapy sessions while at summer camp. As this was not a conventional setting for therapy, it is important to describe the environment and the implications of the intensive play therapy structure. The play therapist lived on the camp grounds and participated in camp activities such as mealtime, campfires, and sports events. This seemed to encourage Robert to interact with the therapist outside of the play session as well as in the playroom.

In addition to their contact in the playroom and on the camp grounds, the therapist frequently saw Robert at the camp infirmary, as he waited to be seen by the medical staff. The staff informed the therapist that Robert frequently complained of stomach aches and headaches, which they attributed to anxiety. They added that Robert expressed some reservations about being alone at camp without his parents, and they assumed that his complaints were physical manifestations of his anxiety and adjustment to a new environment and new caretakers.

The playroom was a small room on the camp grounds that was easily accessible to the other areas of camp, allowing Robert and the therapist to go to and from the playroom without disrupting Robert's other daily activities. The playroom consisted of an assortment of toys based on those identified by Landreth (1991) including a dollhouse, doll family, dishes, assorted plastic food items, toy telephone, sandbox, soldiers, dart gun, rope, toy handcuffs, various games, art supplies, building blocks, and assorted animals (aggressive and nurturing). Additionally, there was a hospital playset including figures of nurses, doctors and medical equipment, and a complete medical kit with the addition of specific items utilized by children with IDDM (syringes and glucometer for testing blood sugar).

## The Battles Begin

Robert appeared comfortable in the playroom during the first session, as he quietly explored the different toys and sat down next to the sandbox facing the therapist. During the majority of his play therapy sessions, Robert was primarily non-verbal, but expressed himself fully through the content of his play.

Robert's silence did not feel uncomfortable to the therapist, but instead it felt as if there was an implicit understanding between them. Robert immersed himself in his play during the first three sessions, as he created detailed scenarios and stories. He created a battle scene in the sandbox, as he carefully placed the soldiers on hills and in valleys he made in the sand. The therapist communicated her understanding of his play by reflecting, "You are putting those right where you want them" and "You know just how you want that to be." Each time Robert nodded slightly and remained focused on his play activity. At the end of these sessions, Robert would conduct a violent battle between the soldiers, with loud sound effects of shooting guns and stabbing, "killing" all the soldiers he had worked so hard to set up carefully. At the end of the second play therapy session, the following exchange occurred between Robert and the play therapist:

Robert: "Does your stomach hurt when you have anxiousness?"

Therapist: "Sounds like someone told you that feeling nervous can make your stomach hurt."

Robert: "No. They said when I feel anxiousness—like I want to do something real bad."

Therapist: "Oh. That didn't make much sense to you."

Robert: "Yeah, what does anxiousness mean?"

Therapist: "You already said one thing that it means, that you want something real bad or you are waiting for something to happen. It can also mean that you feel nervous or worried inside."

Robert: (*his face brightened as he clearly understood*) "Oh! OK I'm ready to go now."

During the fourth session, Robert set up a similar battle scene as in the previous sessions, but with one significant difference. On the left side of the sandbox, he meticulously arranged all of the soldiers. On the right side of the box, he set up all the plastic food items, such as slices of pizza, scoops of ice cream and French fries. Again, he conducted an elaborate battle scene between the food and the soldiers with loud gunfire and fights between the soldiers and the food. During this battle, Robert included the play therapist by narrating the scene, "Die, pizza, die!" and "Mr. Ice Cream, you're gonna get it now!" The therapist reflected, "They are really fighting hard!" and "Mr. Ice Cream is really gonna get it!"

## A Hospital Scene

During his fifth and sixth play therapy sessions, Robert began to explore the hospital playset with figures of nurses, doctors, patients, and hospital equipment. He carefully set up the nurses and patients facing one another, and he armed the nurses with plastic crutches. These crutches became guns as he waged a violent battle between the medical personnel and the patients. As the war continued, the therapist noticed that the nurses would be shot by the patient but would "come back to life," as Robert stated. The therapist reflected, "Boy, it's hard to get them all." In a voice filled with a sense of hopelessness, Robert replied, "Yeah, they just keep coming back." In the silence that followed, Robert completed the battle by shooting and "killing" all of the figures.

During the seventh session, Robert continued to play with the hospital playset, although the end of his battle scene was quite different. As the nurses, doctors and patients fought with guns, knives, and other weapons he created, one patient stood outside the group and shot the figures with great skill. The therapist commented, "Wow. He is really getting them." Robert replied, "Yeah. He is all powerful. He can do anything he wants to them." In the end, the "powerful" figure won the war, and Robert shifted his play toward the medical kit and began to examine the therapist's eyes, ears, and pretended to perform a blood sugar test on her.

### The War is Over

During Robert's final sessions in the playroom, he did not recreate the elaborate battle scene as he had in previous sessions. Although he played with the soldiers at times, he lost interest quickly, and moved on to other projects. Robert painted pictures, played with the doll house family, and brought his Star Wars figures to the playroom to educate the therapist about his favorite characters in Star Wars. In the final session, the therapist reminded him that it was their last time together in the playroom. Robert asked many questions about this saying, "Why don't I get to come anymore?" and "Where will you be when I go home?" The therapist reflected his feelings by saying, "You really like coming here" and provided the information he requested by answering, "I am going home, too, but I will always remember our time in the playroom together." Robert smiled.

## DISCUSSION

Although Robert's time in the playroom was short, his play behaviors had great significance. Robert's case provides insight into the meaning of children's play and the natural ability children have to express their inner conflicts through play. It is clear that although Robert's parents did not view his behavior as related to his medical condition, Robert had significant feelings about doctors, nurses, food, and medical care. It seemed that Robert struggled with the "battle" between his medical requirements and his inner feelings. Children with IDDM are frequently not able to choose when and how much to eat, when to take insulin injections, or when to visit the doctor. In Robert's case, feelings of anger and sadness arose from these experiences. Although Robert's feelings were typical for any child or adult coping with a chronic medical disorder, it was important for Robert to be able to express his feelings in a developmentally appropriate manner within an environment of safety and trust.

Robert seemed to benefit from his play therapy experience in several ways. First, he was able to express the negative feelings he had toward his diabetes and his medical routine in a safe and acceptable manner. It was preferable that he express his anger toward his dietary restrictions, for example, in play rather than by refusing to eat when it is necessary for him to do so. Second, play therapy was a developmentally appropriate means of communication and expression for Robert. Often, children who are diagnosed with chronic illness are forced into the adult world of hospitals, medicine, painful medical procedures, and life-threatening diagnoses. Many of these children begin to communicate in an adult manner, while they lack the cognitive capacity to fully understand the complex issues of living with chronic illness. In the playroom, Robert was able to express himself fully in the language that came most naturally to him, the language of play. Finally, Robert benefited from being able to express these feelings in an accepting and nurturing environment, promoting self-acceptance and self-understanding. This allowed him to develop an increased understanding and sense of control over his own emotions, preventing future negative expressions of these feelings.

## REFERENCES

Acord, L. T. (1980). One five-year-old boy's use of play. *Maternal Child Nursing Journal, 9,* 29–35.

Adams, M. A. (1976). A hospital play program: Helping children with serious illness. *American Journal of Orthopsychiatry, 46,* 416–424.

Axline, V. M. (1969). *Play therapy.* New York: Ballantine Books.

Barton, P. H. (1962). Play as a tool of nursing. *Nursing Outlook, 10,* 162–164.

Bentley, J. (1975). Psychotherapeutic treatment of a boy with eczema and asthma. *The Journal of Asthma Research, 12,* 207–214.

Billington, G. (1972). Play program reduces children's anxiety, speeds recoveries. *Modern Hospital, 118*(4), 90–92.

Bolig, R., Fernie, D., & Klein, E. (1986). Unstructured play in hospital settings: An internal locus of control rationale. *Children's Health Care, 15*(2), 101–107.

Cassell, S. (1965). Effect of brief puppet therapy upon the emotional responses of children undergoing cardiac catheterization. *Journal of Consulting Psychology, 29*(1), 1–8.

Clatworthy, S. (1981). Therapeutic play: Effects on hospitalized children. *Journal of Association for Care of Children's Health, 9*(4),108–113.

Cooper, S. E., & Blitz, J. T. (1985). A therapeutic play group for hospitalized children with cancer. *Journal of Psychosocial Oncology, 3,* 23–37.

Daniel, C. A., Rae, W. A., Sanner, J. H., Upchurch, J., & Worchel, F. F. (1989). The psychosocial impact of play on hospitalized children. *Journal of Pediatric Psychology, 14,* 617–627.

D'Antonio, I. J. (1984). Therapeutic use of play in hospitals. *Nursing Clinics of North America, 19,* 351–359.

Ellerton, M. L., Caty, S., & Richie, J. A. (1985). Helping young children master intrusive procedures through play. *Children's Health Care, 13,* 167–173.

Erikson, E. H. (1963). *Childhood and society.* New York: Norton.

Garot, P. A., (1986). Therapeutic play: Work of both child and nurse. *Journal of Pediatric Nursing, 1,* 111–115.

Glazer-Waldman, H. R., Zimmerman, J. E.,

Landreth, G. L., & Norton, D. (1992). Filial therapy: An intervention for parents of children with chronic illness. *International Journal of Play Therapy, 1,* 31–42.

Hobbs, N., Perrin, J. M., & Ireys, H. T. (1985). *Chronically ill children and their families.* San Francisco: Jossey-Bass.

Koocher, G. P., & O'Malley, J. E. (1981). *The damocles syndrome: Psychosocial consequences of surviving childhood cancer.* New York: McGraw-Hill.

Landreth, G. L. (1991). *Play therapy: The art of the relationship.* Muncie, IN: Accelerated Development.

Perrin, J. M. (1985). Introduction. In N. Hobbs & J. M. Perrin (Eds.), *Issues in the care of children with chronic illness* (pp. 1–10). San Francisco: Jossey-Bass.

Piaget, J. (1962). *Play, dreams, and imitation in childhood.* London: Norton.

Tew, K. L. (1997). *The efficacy of filial therapy with families with chronically ill children.* Unpublished doctoral dissertation, University of North Texas.

Wall, A. D. (1987). A brief review of the use of therapeutic play in the treatment of pediatric cancer patients. *Association for Play Therapy Newsletter, 6,* 1–4.

Zilliacus, K., & Enberg, S. (1980). Play therapy in the pediatric outpatient department. *Paediatrician, 9,* 224–230.

*18*

# Play Therapy
# with Traumatized Children
## *A Crisis Response*

### PAMELA WEBB

P sychological trauma refers to a typically unexpected, extremely stressful external event or happening that is usually atypical in the life experiences of the child and is distressing to the point of being overwhelming, causing an inability to cope. According to Eth and Pynoos (1985), psychic trauma oc-curs "when an individual is exposed to an overwhelming event resulting in helplessness in the face of intolerable danger, anxiety, and instinctual arousal" (p. 38). Characteristic symptoms involve (a) reexperiencing the traumatic event, such as nightmares and play reenactments; (b) avoidance of stimuli or situa-tions associated with the event or that remind the individual of the trauma; (c) numbing of general responsiveness; and (d) elevated arousal, such as hypervigilance, irritability, or difficulty sleeping (American Psychiatric Associa-tion, 1994).

Based on years of observations of child victims of trauma, Terr (1991) iden-tified four characteristics that children exhibit following exposure to a trau-matic event: (a) recurrent and intrusive, distressing visual recollections of the event; (b) repetitive behaviors, such as repeated reenactment of the distressing episode during play or through behavioral idiosyncrasies; (c) trauma-specific fears, such as fear of mundane things (food, noise) or avoidance of stimuli asso-ciated with the trauma; and (d) changed attitudes about people, aspects of life, and the future. Terr reported that repetitions are experienced by the child in their dreams, play, reenactment, and repeated visualizations. The child's attitu-dinal change seems to be based on the belief that more traumas are bound to happen, and that life must be endured, not cherished. Eth and Pynoos (1985) stated that "children's early responses to psychic trauma generally involve deleterious effects on cognition (including memory, school performance, and learning), affect, interpersonal relations, impulse control and behavior, vegetative function, and the formation of symptoms" (p. 41).

## MEDIATING VARIABLES

The effects of trauma may be mediated by such factors as how quickly the child receives help following the traumatic event and the child's own internal protective factors of self-esteem, self-confidence, problem solving skills, the child's belief in his own ability to deal with change, and the child's emotional support system. Terr (1990) pointed out that putting off treatment for trauma is about the worst thing one can do. Trauma does not ordinarily get "better" by itself. It burrows down further and further under the child's defenses and coping strategies. Suppression, displacement, overgeneralization, identification with the aggressor, splitting, passive-into-active, undoing, and self-anesthesia take over. The trauma may actually come to "look" better after all these coping and defense mechanisms go into operation. But the trauma will continue to affect the child's character, dreams, feelings about sex, trust, and attitudes about the future. (Terr, 1990, p. 293)

Children's responses to trauma are different from adult responses. An observer might look out of a window and see a child riding her bike or playing only hours after a terrifying incident, while adults, having experienced the same event, are sitting on their couch in the living room sobbing and talking about what has happened. Looking at the child, the adult might be led to think, "Hey, the kid is out there playing and having a good time. She's okay! Look, she's already forgotten about it. Better leave well enough alone. After all, we don't want to inflict further pain on her by talking about it. She's been through enough already." Such commonly held attitudes might keep adults from making it safe and okay for children to reenact the event, tell what they experienced, and ask their important questions. Quick therapeutic intervention is critical for children who have experienced trauma in order to minimize the effects of the distressing event and to prevent long-term psychological disturbance.

## UBIQUITOUS FEAR AND PAIN

In relating to children with trauma-specific fears, encouraging them to ask questions and responding to them with appropriate honesty is crucial to easing some of their fears. After the lingering illness and death of a child, I was asked by school officials to make a comforting place in the school library with my books and toys, in order to help the classmates of the deceased student. A slow stream of children visited me throughout the day. Some needed a place to cry or talk.

Others wanted to play and experience that close attention that play therapy creates. Two memorable boys had questions that were bothering them, and they needed answers. One boy, who had been unable to attend the highly publicized spaghetti dinner that the school had conducted to raise funds to defray the classmate's medical costs, came to me wringing his hands and with tears in his eyes, he questioned, "If I had come to the spaghetti dinner would he [his classmate] have lived?" The second boy had concerns about his own health. He wondered if poison ivy had caused the classmate's cancer. The previous summer the worried boy had gotten into poison ivy, experienced a resultant rash, and was worried now about contracting cancer from that contact. These questions point out the very specific fears that can develop in traumatized children.

There are two general categories of childhood trauma as identified by Terr (1990): (a) children suffering from Type I traumas, a single, sudden, and unexpected stressor, and (b) children suffering from Type II traumas, resulting from repeated or long-standing ordeals. Although the characteristic changes that occur in children as a result of these traumas differ somewhat, the treatment is similar (Terr, 1990, 1991). Most play therapists have a caseload of children with Type II trauma and appropriately assist those children with ongoing, or several-session, therapy. Crisis response is different. This chapter focuses on Type I trauma in children.

## MELDING PRINCIPLES OF PLAY THERAPY WITH CRISIS RESPONSE

Play therapy is the recommended therapeutic medium because play is the child's natural means of expression and play enables the child to distance from the traumatic events through the use of symbolic materials. Thus, play provides the needed safety for children to express and explore their innermost feelings. The natural reaction of children is to reenact or play out the traumatic experience in an unconscious effort to comprehend, overcome, develop a sense of control, or assimilate the experience.

Play serves to protect the child who has limited ego strength by providing the child with the opportunity to work through external difficulties without having to identify and label the painful incident as his own. This process allows children to work through extremely traumatic events without being further challenged to communicate these confusing events to adults (Terr, 1990). Play also allows the child to begin to work through issues at a slower pace, revealing the personal aspect of the play at a later time. By establishing a therapeutic environment in a slow and controlled manner, the child can begin to feel respected and understood, thereby dealing with threatening feelings and moving toward internal health (Axline, 1969).

According to Terr (1990), "Children show a healthy tendency to cope with external difficulties and inner feelings through play. Post-traumatic play, however pathological it is, can be effectively used therapeutically. It is, in fact, the most potent way to effect internal changes in young, traumatized children" (p. 299). Schaefer (1994) asserted that "In marked contrast with the sense of helplessness children experience during a disaster, play affords them a strong sense of power and control. The child towers over the play materials and determines what and how to play during the therapy session. Eventually, this competing response (power) helps overcome the child's feelings of insecurity and vulnerability" (p. 309).

Using play therapy in response to crisis situations may require some departures from what play therapists might normally do under ideal conditions, such as allowing the process of play therapy to unfold within the child's own time frame, and to do so at a slower pace, undirected by the therapist. When a therapist is called to the site of an emergency, whether a crime or a natural disaster, the physical conditions under which the therapist meets with the child may demand great flexibility. Under such conditions, toys and materials may be limited to what the therapist is able to carry, or to what authorities allow to be brought to the site of the incident. Time available for helping is another factor that may be drastically limited. In dealing with traumatized children at the site of a critical incident, a therapist must simply take what is available, which may be a onetime 30-minute session. With such a small window of opportunity, the degree of direction provided by the therapist during the session may also become another area begging flexibility on the part of the therapist. When the window of opportunity opens, the therapist jumps through it quickly and adapts to what is given, because it won't be open for long.

## OKLAHOMA CITY: AN OPPORTUNITY TO SERVE

At about nine o'clock on the morning of April 19, 1995, a bomb ripped through the Alfred P. Murrah Federal Building in downtown Oklahoma City. Our nation watched on television as the shocking drama of death and destruction unfolded. Interviews with survivors and live coverage of rescue efforts dominated the media. I, like most of the world, watched and listened intently to news shows, hoping for good tidings of people found alive and safe in the rubble of the partially destroyed building.

Six days after the explosion, April 25, 1995, I was presented with the opportunity to test my belief in using play therapy in a crisis response situation as part of a National Organization of Victim's Assistance (NOVA) team. I was one of three school counselors who had cross-trained with an emergency response team connected with the Austin, Texas Police Department's Victim's Services, called to go to Oklahoma City in response to the bombing. Our part of the NOVA team mission was to go into the Oklahoma City schools to help students and faculties handle the effects of the disaster. On short notice, we were asked to leave very quickly. We were allowed only two small carry-on bags, so that we could be mobile and flexible.

## The Toys in the Bag

One of my bags was my portable play therapy kit, which contained the following:

- Lone Ranger type mask
- doll family
- toy gun
- doll furniture
- rubber knife
- multicolored pipe cleaners
- toy shark
- paper (newsprint)
- toy alligator
- crayons
- baby doll
- transparent tape
- baby blanket
- scissors (plastic, blunt tip)
- nursing bottle (plastic)
- long, cotton shoe strings (2)
- plastic car
- Koosh ball
- plastic airplane
- spoons, cups, and plates (2 each)
- Gumby figure
- nondescript, blue, big-mouthed figure
- Swat team figures (6)
- telephone
- hand-crocheted, finger puppets (5)
- exotic-looking bracelets (2)
- medical kit

## Getting Started

On April 26, 1995, we spent the day working through mountains of red tape and bureaucratic delays. Our group assembled at the educational administration building of the Oklahoma City public schools. We were told that the Assistant Superintendent would assign us to schools that he felt had the greatest needs. Some of the schools were geographically close to the blast while others were deeply affected because of the number of relatives and close friends who were victims of the bombing.

On April 27, we were finally dispatched to the schools. I was assigned to a small, elementary school that had been close to the bomb site. It was located near the downtown area in a very low socioeconomic region of town referred to as "the flats." A driver from the administration building drove me through the impoverished neighborhood and dropped me off at the front steps of the school. Built in 1929, the building had a relatively small population of two hundred students. The principal told me that the adults in the building were handling everything "just fine." He wanted me to concentrate my attention on the children in the school and took me to a small room on the second floor of the building, which was to serve as my work site. He opened the door, ushered me inside, and said, "Do your stuff." Under such conditions, one cannot expect or wait for further instruction or attention; rather, one must simply forge ahead as if it were but another routine day.

When I realized that I was alone, I took a deep breath and sized up my surroundings. The room was a small one at one end of a hallway. I cleared a place on the floor by moving furniture around and stowing loose materials away in the filing cabinets. I left my bag of toys sitting on the cleaned-off table and walked down the halls to introduce myself to the staff and find out how I could be of help in this school.

Another crisis counselor met me in the hall and told me there were some needs in a classroom that time constraints would not allow her to attend. She asked me to check them out. I followed her lead and went outside to the portable building that housed the indicated class. I called the teacher to the classroom door to introduce myself. She immediately began to cry as we talked. She told me that on the day of the bombing the explosion had knocked her out of her chair and onto the floor with such force that her keys had flown out of her pocket. She cried some more and told me how she had known in the first instant that the sound she had heard was a bomb. She had traveled to Israel the year before and a bomb had exploded near a restaurant where she had been eating. After listening to her for awhile, I asked to see the students from her class who she thought needed some help.

## A Group of Grieving Girls

The teacher gave me the names of four girls who were experiencing stomachaches and overwhelming feelings of sadness. The teacher called the girls over and introduced them to me. I told the teacher that I would check on her later, and I led the four 11 and 12-year-old girls up to the makeshift playroom. I told the girls that they could play with any of the toys. They chose to draw pictures. We sat around the table and I tracked their progress as they drew and colored their pictures. The girls talked to each other and to me as they drew. Two of the girls had lost a mutual relative in the blast. Their 23-year-old cousin had worked in one of the offices in the Federal Building. The girls had attended her funeral the day before. They told me about the sadness in their whole family.

Another girl in the group had lost an aunt and a cousin in the explosion. This girl said that she felt like "a cracked face." The fourth girl was very quiet. She had not lost a relative in the bombing, but she quietly cried and told us that her mother had been watching the television "all the time" ever since the blast.

The girl stated that both she and her mother were having bad dreams at night. At that moment I couldn't help but realize the power of television to spread and/or compound the problem of trauma in children. Due to the intense and ongoing nature of the media coverage, not only did the bombing traumatize those directly affected by it, but also those who watched it in living color from the comfort of their living rooms, and who watched their parents become un- done by the carnage as coverage inundated every waking moment. Adults and children alike were "caught up" in the experience, in some cases, as much as if they had been on the scene.

We talked about grief as they colored their pictures, which depicted hearts and flowers around drawings of the victims whom they were mourning. I gave them some information about what they might expect to feel in the coming weeks and months. Each of the girls shared with the others what she was doing to "make things better." As our time ran out, I summarized the excellent coping strategies the girls had shared. When they left the room, one girl asked if she could come back to see me later.

I went to the teacher's lounge and met more of the faculty. The teachers gave me the names of students in distress and the best time to meet with them. A schedule was worked out for the afternoon.

## Lunch with the Custodian

Around noon, I went to the cafeteria and asked the custodian if he would join me for lunch. We got our trays and sat down together. As we ate lunch, he told me about himself. He was a military veteran who had taken up custodial work when he retired. He felt as if what was going on in Oklahoma City was like a war. He told me that violence was an everyday occurrence in this neighbor- hood. The kids were used to it. The bomb blast was just bigger than the usual stuff. One can often get a clearer picture of life in a school by spending time with the custodian.

## Reenactment in Play: The Story of Randall and Kim

After lunch, I began to work through the schedule I had planned for the rest of the afternoon. I started with two 7-year-old children for whom their teacher had expressed great concern. After we arrived at the playroom, Randall asked permission to touch the toys, even though I had given both children the you- may-play-with-any-of-the-toys-in-most-of-the-ways-you-want speech. Randall was quiet and stiff. He did not talk freely or interact with me at first, and he moved his body in a jerky, mechanical way. Kim more than made up for the Randall's quietness by filling the air with continual talk. While Randall stood in uncertainty considering the toys, Kim jumped right in and picked up toys. She chose the shark, the alligator, the gun, and the knife. With each of these toys, she acted out violent play toward me. Although she never touched me, she shot at me, stabbed at me, and made the alligator and shark growl at me and attack me.

While the noisy and ferocious attack was ensuing, Randall hesitantly sat down at the table, chose paper and crayons, and began to draw a picture. As I verbally tracked his actions, he gave me a shy little smile. Kim halted her assault on me and began to focus on the alligator. She examined it thoroughly. Then she gathered five crocheted finger puppets into her play space, and one by one she began to stuff the puppets down into the mouth and hollow body of the alligator. She labored diligently at this task while Randall told me about his picture. He was going to draw a picture of the building downtown before it got hurt. He worked very slowly and carefully at his art.

After stuffing all five of the puppets down the throat of the alligator, Kim began yelling in a distressed tone, "Oh, no! They are down there and I can't get them out! Oh, how can I get them? I will have to try, but I don't think I can." Randall stopped drawing and joined me in watching the dramatic play. Kim struggled and continued to make similar comments while she spread the alligator's mouth apart and dug her fingers down the throat of the toy. "I don't think I can get Greenie out! Oh, dear. I will keep trying!" When she got the first puppet out of the alligator's mouth she smiled and gently laid it on the table and took care to arrange it in just the way she wanted. Kim said, as she patted the puppet, "I got him out and he is alive. He is not hurt." Kim went through the same process for each of the four remaining puppets. She yelled, struggled, and doubted her efforts as she dug her little fingers down into the throat of the toy alligator, working hard to retrieve each puppet. Finally, she succeeded in arranging all five finger puppets in a neat row on the tabletop. Then she said, "I got them out. I got them all out, and they are safe and not hurt [big sigh]."

Kim looked up at Randall and me as if she were aware of us for the first time since she began her struggle. She had been so engrossed in her play that she had forgotten about us. I had been so mesmerized by what she was doing that I had remained silent throughout the drama. I knew that she had been reenacting the rescue efforts that were going on at the site of the Federal Building, and I wished that I had responded with my awareness of her as she played and replayed.

Randall went back to his drawing without comment, and Kim began to repeat the alligator and puppet drama again. She repeated the drama exactly as she had played it before, except that this time I tracked her play transcribed below.

Kim: Ugh. Hmm. (*making noises while struggling to stuff finger puppets into the mouth and hollow body of the alligator*)

Therapist: You're putting those in there just the way you want them.

Kim: Mmm. Ooof. Oooh. (*continuing to make straining noises while stuffing the rest of the finger puppets down the alligator's mouth*)

Therapist: You worked really hard to get all of those in there.

Kim: Yep. (*looking down the mouth of the alligator*) Oh, no! They are down there and I can't get them out! What am I going to do? (*an exaggerated look of horror on her face*)

Therapist: You are scared for them and don't know what to do.

Kim: Oh, dear! How can I get them? I will have to try to get them, but I don't think I can.

Therapist: You are going to try and you're just not sure . . .

Kim: I've got to get Greenie out! Oh, no! I don't think I can do it. I will try hard. Oh! (*digging her fingers into the mouth of the alligator*)

Therapist: You're trying hard to get Greenie out of there.

Kim: (*nodding and moving closer to me*) Greenie is just about out! I got him and he is alive! He's okay!

Therapist: You are so happy that you rescued Greenie. You worked hard to get him out.

Kim: (*nodding and smiling as she placed the puppet on the table and patted it with her hand*)

Therapist: It feels good to you that Greenie is okay.

Kim: (*turning back to the alligator's mouth*) Oh, no! Whitey is still down there! I have to get him out. I don't know if I can do it. What am I going to do? Oh, dear!

Therapist: Now you are scared about Whitey. You're wondering how to get him out.

Kim: (*leaning toward me*) I don't know if I can get Whitey out but I will try hard. I will keep trying. Oh, my!

Therapist: You are not going to stop trying to get Whitey out of there.

Kim: I can't . . . Oh, no! (*frowning and digging her fingers into the alligator's mouth*) Wait! Here he is. I got him! I got Whitey! He's out and he's okay. Yea! He's not hurt!

Therapist: You rescued Whitey! Yea!

Kim: He's safe. (*smiling and holding the puppet in her hand for me to see*)

Therapist: That feels "soooo" good to you.

Kim: (*looking at me and nodding*)

This dramatic play continued as Kim struggled and succeeded in rescuing all five of the finger puppets from the alligator. I named the feelings she exhibited and gave verbal language to her scene. She seemed to be very aware of me during this second rescue operation. She leaned toward me and played in closer proximity to my body. When she finished, she patted the row of safe and happy puppets.

Kim: There. (*sighing*) I got them all out. I did it! I was afraid that I couldn't get them, but I did. They are all safe. Nobody got hurt. (*a satisfied look on her face*)

Therapist: You worked hard to get them out, like they are doing downtown. You are so glad that they are safe.

Kim: (*nodding, then looking over at Randall's picture*)

Note: This situation illustrates the power of tracking the play and giving words to the message the child is communicating. Only when the therapist correctly reflects back to the child what the therapist understands the message to be at that moment, will the child feel heard. When a child's message is received and accepted in this manner, whether through words, play, or art, the repetitive reenactment of the trauma can begin to cease and resolution can begin to occur. The monotonous, long-lasting post-traumatic play to which Terr (1990) refers can then begin to find its rest.

Randall had finished his carefully produced drawing and was holding it up for us to see. He explained that it was a picture of the Federal Building with all of its lights on, the windows intact, and in good shape. He pointed out the pretty, blue sky that he had created, and in front of the building, he had drawn a perfect sidewalk, without holes. He seemed pleased with his picture. Both children, given the chance, had revisited the recent, tragic incident and had been able to create a new and different ending.

Kim looked at the picture that Randall had presented to us and announced that her mommy did not know that "people got hurt and damaged." Her mommy did not know "that a building got broke." Her mommy did not know that people "got 'squished' and hurt and would dream about it." And, her mommy did not know that people "got all cut with glass" and died, but Kim knew it. I remarked that she certainly knew a lot. She replied, "Yep. I go to school."

In the time that remained before my next appointment, I went back to the classroom in the portable building to check on the distressed teacher I had talked with earlier. She stepped out of her classroom to talk with me again. She cried and said that she was having difficulty with her thinking processes. She expressed hope that she could hold on until the end of the school year for the sake of the children.

### Mysteries Unresolved: Dramatic Play with Chad

Next on my appointment list was Chad, whose teacher had expressed concern for his emotional well being. He had demonstrated feelings of extremely poor self-esteem during the entire school year, and since the bombing had made many negative comments about himself and all aspects of his life. I introduced myself to nine-year-old Chad and walked with him to the playroom. He impressed me immediately as being an extremely bright and verbal child. As we entered the room, he stated without any prompting, "I know why that building got bombed. These people just got jealous of us 'cuz we got more money. So, they blew us up." (He included himself in the group of "blown up" people.)

Chad sat right down and began to play. After examining all of the toys, he picked out characters and dove into dramatic play. Chad used almost all of the toys in playing out various scenes filled with action, and he used a wide range of voices for his different characters. In all of the scenes he played out, the shark was the designated "good guy." The shark won every battle and was the hero of several adventures. Chad told me that he was the shark. He performed a puppet show with three of the finger puppets, which he named "Grape," "Apple," and "Mitten." Toward the end of our time together, Chad confided to me that the baby doll was really his mother. He then played several scenes with the baby doll respresenting his mother. The "Mama" character shot the toy gun all over the room until she became tired and had to go to bed. "Mama" put the gun under the bed while she slept, "so she could be safe." In the final part of the story line, the shark picked up the gun and "accidentally" shot the "Mama" character. Chad explained at length about how the shark did not know about guns and how the shooting was really an accident. Far too soon our time was gone.

## An Empathic Response: The Story of Kara

The next child that I went to see had come to her teacher's attention during a class discussion the day before. During the discussion, Kara had expressed her wish that she had died in the bombing. The teacher stated that Kara was very intelligent and was normally a happy child. Since the bombing, Kara had acted quite sad, and the statement she had made in class had alarmed the teacher.

I met eleven-year-old Kara, and we walked back to the playroom. The expression on her face, indeed, appeared sad. She immediately and openly talked about the bombing, without any prompting. She told me that she was sad about the deaths that had occurred from the bomb, and that she was the only person in her classroom who felt as sadly. She thought that all the other children in her class should feel such sadness that they should wish that they had died too. Just to check it out, I asked her if she wanted to be dead or gone. She responded with a shocked look and said, "Of course not! Who would wish to be dead?" She explained further that people should feel "so sad" that they should wish to be with those people who died, and to know what it was like for them. I began to understand that she was trying to describe her feelings of empathy with the victims and the survivors, and was possibly dealing with some survivor guilt. She wanted others around her to feel as deeply as she did. I talked with her about grief and the grief process until our time was over. After we walked back to her classroom, I commended her teacher for picking up important cues, and shared with her my view concerning the child's own struggle with strong feelings of empathy. The teacher appeared relieved and grateful.

## Wrapping Up

School was over for the day. As the teachers were freed from their duties, they flocked to me. They overwhelmed me with stories and names of more children to add to my list. The list now included 25 additional children for me to see the following day. Before I left the building, I remembered the teacher who had cried with me earlier in the day. I returned to her portable classroom to see her one more time. She smiled and expressed hope for her students and her community. This time there were no tears.

## LESSONS CLOSER TO HOME

### Back to Austin: The Power of Grief Unresolved

The day after a popular middle school teacher in Austin died, I was called to respond to the needs of grieving students, along with other crisis counselors. We were positioned in the school library while an announcement went out over the public address system, telling teachers and students that counselors were available for anyone struggling with emotional upset. We were unprepared for the response to the announcement.

In addition to the students who were sad and upset over the loss of the teacher (mainly those who had been behavior problems in her class and were feeling sorry for giving her trouble), we had a wave of Hispanic girls who were grieving the loss of Selena. Selena, a Hispanic singer-superstar, had been murdered three or four months previously by an employee and fan. The death of Selena, a one-of-a-kind role model for young Hispanic girls, Selena's death had been a tremendous shock and loss for her fans and had not been dealt with by helping professionals in these children's lives. We were surprised and somewhat caught off guard by the number of students and the intensity of their emotional responses. As the girls trailed into the library, crying and feeling very sad, we decided to allow them the opportunity to express themselves in various ways.

A few of the girls wanted to talk about their sadness and loss. Most of them wanted to do something and were at a loss to know how to express themselves. We quickly rounded up some art supplies and spread them out around the school library. They eagerly chose to draw a picture, make a poster or mural, design a card, or write a letter. Some girls worked in groups and others worked alone. Most of them wanted to explain their creation when they were satisfied that it was finished. Their art became the vehicles of expression.

The experience of spending the day with a library full of emotional middle school girls reminded me of the power of unresolved grief and how it can be resurrected by a current event. Whether the triggering event is somewhat similar or not, a powerful emotional response may unexpectedly manifest. I think that we were experiencing the effects of contagion that day. Among seasoned school crisis responders there is an unwritten warning concerning "tidal wave" emotional hysteria that can sweep through girls in a middle school setting.

## Helping Adults Help Children: Dealing with Death

The second event that taught me an important element of crisis response involving children happened at an elementary school after the death of the school's principal. The very beloved principal had died after a short battle with cancer just twenty-four hours prior to our team coming to the campus. Our team was setting up early in the day to be available to children with emotional needs, when a call came to the office with the news that a third grade class was in need of immediate assistance. I very quickly made my way to the classroom, unaware of the nature of the situation.

When I reached the classroom door, the teacher quickly met me and pulled me into the room. She was crying and unable to talk. Several of the children were crying out loud and some were walking around the room holding their faces in their hands and sobbing. I turned to the teacher and told her that I would stay with her and help as long as she needed me. I asked her to talk to the children and direct them to engage in some kind of activity, which would allow her to tell me what had happened. She quickly complied with my request. All but two of the children busied themselves with the activity. One girl continued to cry quietly at her desk, a boy sat with his head laid down on the desk.

The teacher related to me that she had just finished reading the announcement of the death of the principal when a boy named Joe raised his hand and asked, "Am I going to die now too?" The teacher realized that this was a student who had been diagnosed with cancer and had been undergoing treatment for the disease. She had been struck speechless by the question and had started to cry uncontrollably. Then, of course, some of her students began to cry while Joe buried his face in his arms folded on his desk. Feeling completely helpless in the situation, the teacher had called the office for backup assistance. After obtaining information concerning Joe's current health condition, I asked the teacher if she was up to handling her class if I moved him to another location to talk with me. She said that she could do that if I would come back later and talk to the whole class about the situation. We made a deal.

I approached Joe, who still had not moved from his head-down position at his desk. I squatted low beside him and quietly told him my name and asked his permission to speak with him. After a few, long moments he raised his head, averted his face, and nodded his response to my question. We found a quiet place to be together where he was able to talk about his fears, express his pain, and ask his questions. Joe was like a fountain just overflowing with pent-up thoughts and feelings. As the word flow slowed and his body relaxed, he asked if he could go back to class and continue his school day. He was feeling much better and did not want to miss Physical Education class. Joe smiled and waved at me as he hopped back to his class.

I spent the next few hours talking with Joe's teacher, his class, and his parents. I had called Joe's parents immediately after my time with him. They became upset and angry that I had talked with him. They came to school and complained to the assistant principal. They did not want anyone at the school talking to their son about death or cancer. They did not want him to hear about the death of the principal. They considered us irresponsible for announcing the death of the principal to the class. After making their concerns known in the office, I was asked to conference with the angry parents.

When I sat down to talk with Joe's mother and father, it was immediately apparent that they were far more afraid than angry. Their child had developed cancer and that terrified them. They told me that they did not allow anyone in their home to talk about cancer. They felt that children were unable to handle "that kind" of information or conversation. A couple of times when Joe had asked questions about his disease or treatment, they had told him not to talk about it. I spent most of the morning talking with and teaching Joe's parents and teacher the importance of allowing him to express his feelings and thoughts through words, play, art, and any other way that he chose.

The lesson that was driven home to me in dealing with this specific crisis response was that an important and large part of working with traumatized children is helping the adult caretakers learn how to help their children. It is a mistake to assume that parents, teachers, and other caring adults know what is helpful to children after a traumatizing event. And sometimes, even if the adult has the knowledge of how to help a child, emotionally they may not be able to respond to a child's needs, especially if the adult is also traumatized by the event.

# CONCLUSION

Children will play. Even in the days after a major trauma has affected their lives, they will play. Through their play the important processes of telling their experiences and defusing powerful emotions can occur. Whether a young child is attended to immediately or in the weeks and months following a critical event, play therapy is the most effective approach to trauma resolution at this developmental level.

# REFERENCES

American Psychiatric Association. (1994). *Diagnostic and statistical manual of mental disorders* (4th ed.). Washington, DC: Author.

Axline, V. (1969). *Play therapy*. New York: Ballantine.

Eth, S., & Pynoos, R. (Eds.). (1985) *Post-traumatic stress disorders in children*. Washington, DC: American Psychiatric Press.

Schaefer, C. (1994). Play therapy for psychic trauma in children. In K. O'Connor & C. Schaefer (Eds.), *Handbook of play therapy: Vol. 2* (pp. 297–318). New York: Wiley.

Terr, L. C. (1990). *Too scared to cry*. New York: Harper & Row.

Terr, L. C. (1991). Childhood traumas: An outline and overview. *American Journal of Psychiatry, 148*, 10–20.

# 19

# Play Therapy with Selective Mute Children

## PHYLLIS POST

*J*oshua stood in the middle of the playroom without moving or speaking. It was his first day in play therapy. His hands were clasped behind his back. He stared straight ahead. He did not look at the room or at any of the toys. His face showed a warm expression. He smiled. At times, he laughed. Forty-five minutes later, he returned to his fifth grade classroom, without having spoken a word or looked at anything in the playroom. As early as the second grade, Joshua would decide with whom he would talk. During the fourth grade, he talked in a limited way with several students, but he did not speak to teachers. This year, one month into the fifth grade, he had not spoken to a single person in the school.

Joshua was a 10½-year-old selective mute. Because the American Psychiatric Association (1994) changed the name of this disorder from "elective" to "selective" mute, both terms will be used when citing the literature.

## DEFINITION AND CHARACTERISTICS OF SELECTIVE MUTISM

Children who are selective mutes choose to remain silent in certain key social situations, such as school, in spite of their ability to comprehend language and speak (Black & Uhde, 1992; Cook, 1997; Hesselman, 1983; Knell, 1993; Landreth, Homeyer, Glover, & Sweeney, 1996). Tramer (1934) first coined the term "elective mute" when he described children "who spoke with only a small group of intimates in specific situations, the most common of which was the child's home" (as cited in Kolvin & Fundudis, 1981, p. 219).

The speech development of selective mutes is usually normal; however, as these children enter more social situations, they stop speaking in certain selected settings (Kolvin & Fundudis, 1981). For the majority of mute children, the problem becomes apparent when they enter school and refuse to speak to classmates and teachers (Cook, 1997). The difficulty for these children is that their silence can create significant educational problems, such as interfering with the ability of teachers to evaluate their reading skills. In addition, their limited interaction with peers can adversely affect their social and emotional development.

### Incidence

The incidence of selective mutism is rare. Many cases of selective mutism are unknown until children enter school. Brown and Lloyd (1975) report that 7.2 children out of 1,000 do not speak in school at the age of five. Fewer than one percent of individuals seen in mental health settings are diagnosed as selective mutes (APA, 1994). Because many of these young children begin speaking during their first few years of school, the prevalence of selective mutism decreases with age (Cook, 1997).

### Characteristics of Selective Mute Children

The characteristics of selective mute children have been widely studied. They have been described as the following: excessively shy (APA, 1994; Black & Uhde, 1992; Cook, 1997; Knell, 1993; Powell & Dalley, 1995), fearful of social embarrassment (APA, 1994), anxious (Afnan & Carr, 1989; Cook, 1997; Jackson, 1950; Kolvin & Fundudis, 1981; Weininger, 1987), socially isolated (APA, 1994; Black & Uhde, 1992;), clinging, negative (APA, 1994), prone to temper tantrums (APA, 1994), oppositional (APA, 1994; Krohn, Weckstein, & Wright, 1992; Landreth et al., 1996), defiant (Knell, 1993; Landreth et al., 1996), moody (Landreth et al., 1996), aggressive (Landreth et al., 1996), stubborn (Black & Uhde, 1992; Chetnik, 1973; Kolvin & Fundudis, 1982; Landreth et al., 1996), strong willed (Landreth et al., 1996), distrustful (Landreth et al., 1996), submissive (Kolvin & Fundudis, 1982), and exhibiting a high occurrence of enuresis (Barlow, Strother, & Landreth, 1986; Bozigar & Hansen, 1984; Kolvin & Fundudis, 1982).

In families with selective mute children, the mothers and children often have a close, overly dependent relationship, as indicated physically by clinging to and hiding behind their mothers (Hesselman, 1983; Kolvin & Fundudis, 1982). By contrast, the fathers have been described as passive, indifferent, and stern. The families are often socially isolated. One or both parents have been characterized as shy and reserved, providing children an example of silence (Hesselman, 1983).

With such a broad list of characteristics, the question becomes whether selective mutism is a distinct children's problem. To address this question, Wilkins (1985) compared the personalities, characteristics, and attitudes of children diagnosed as elective mutes with children diagnosed as emotionally disturbed.

The results indicated no difference between the two categories of children in terms of shyness, temper tantrums, overdependence, enuresis, or mothers' shyness or aggressiveness. However, the elective mute children were more anxious, depressed, and manipulative; their mothers were more overprotective and "spoiling." These findings suggest that selective mutism is a separate condition, which can be distinguished from other emotional problems experienced by children.

While selective mutism is usually first observed between the ages of 3.7 and 14-years, the onset for most children is before or during their preschool years (Cook, 1997). The average age for intervention is between six and eight (Wright, Holmes, Cuccaro, & Leonhardt, 1994).

Although opinions differ about the prognosis of therapy for selective mute children, researchers agree that intervention should occur as early as possible (Cook, 1997; Hesselman, 1983; Porjes, 1992). Early intervention not only prevents children from developing academic problems, but also prevents them from developing social problems resulting from not interacting with other children. Kolvin and Fundudis (1981) suggested that after the age of ten children are likely to be "resistant to intervention" (Kolvin & Fundudis, 1981; Labbe & Williamson, 1984), and spontaneous remission is unlikely.

## COUNSELING APPROACHES

Counselors have found no standard approach for helping selective mute children. Most research depicts single case studies with varying degrees of success (Cook, 1997). The variety of counseling approaches that have been used include: psychodynamic (Harris, 1996), family therapy (Afnan & Carr, 1989; Wright et al., 1994), behavior therapy (Black & Uhde, 1992; Harris, 1996), behavior therapy combined with family therapy, learning theory (Porjes, 1992), group therapy (Bozigar & Hansen, 1984), play therapy (Barlow et al., 1986), and psychopharmacology (Black & Uhde, 1992; Golwyn & Weinstock, 1990; Harris, 1996; Wright et al., 1994).
Emphasizing the importance of respecting the child and the child's dignity, Hultquist (1995) stated

> no matter what treatment approach professionals choose, concern [for the child] must be maintained and integrated into all aspects of the therapy. . . . There is more involved with these children than simple silence, and there is a need for more than behavioral interventions. Family therapy and play therapy seem to be logical alternatives or additions—family therapy due to the presence of family problems in many researcher's reports and play therapy because it provides young children with the means of communicating nonverbally. (pp. 8–9)

The greatest difficulty in counseling with selective mute children is "establishing a relationship with a child who is both silent and refrains from all other forms of expression" (Hesselman, 1983, p. 305). A counselor depending solely on verbal communication is likely to have a problem developing a relationship with the child (Barlow et al., 1986). Child-centered play therapy is an appropriate therapeutic approach with selective mute children. The child is in charge of the process; therefore, children having high needs for control, which many selective mute children do, have an opportunity to work through those issues by assuming responsibility and making decisions for themselves in the playroom. The counselor can demonstrate understanding and acceptance of the child's nonverbal communications in the playroom (Axline, 1947; Ginott, 1961; Landreth, 1991). In addition, the counselor communicates acceptance to the child whether the child is verbal or nonverbal. Undoubtedly, child-centered play therapists believe that they can help children whether the children talk or not (Barlow, Strother, & Landreth, 1985).

Two follow-up studies have been conducted to determine changes in children who were selectively mute. Brown and Lloyd (1975) studied 6,072 children entering kindergarten. Fifty-eight percent were speaking eight weeks after kindergarten started; twelve months later, ninety percent were speaking. In a five and ten-year follow-up study of twenty-four elective mute children, Kolvin and Fundudis (1981) found that after five years, 11 of 24 of the children had improved. Most of the improvement occurred before the child was ten years old. At the time of the ten-year follow-up, only one more child was found to have improved. Based on their findings from the follow-up study, the authors concluded that elective mutism "proved to be a rather intractable condition" (p. 232).

A number of research studies have addressed selective mutism among older children. The issues for these children become more complicated, because mutism becomes increasingly problematic as the normal social needs of older children grow (Joseph, 1999). While selective mute individuals may appear passive; in truth, they are working extremely hard not to speak or express themselves (Hesselman, 1983).

## CASE STUDY

### Description of Joshua

Joshua, a bi-racial fifth grader, had been a self-imposed mute at school for three years when I met him. He lived with both parents. His mother was white; his father, African-American. He identified with the African-American culture. Joshua was an only child, and he had one stepbrother from his father's earlier marriage. Both of his parents were high school graduates.

Joshua was described by his mother as "unruly" during preschool. Because he had severe temper tantrums at preschool, he was placed in a special child development center. A review of Joshua's cumulative folder indicated that he was in the normal range of intelligence and that he had been diagnosed with a behavioral/emotional handicap (BEH). He was placed in a special BEH classroom during kindergarten and first grade. As early as second grade, Joshua would decide with whom he would talk. During the fourth grade, he talked in a limited way with other students, but not with teachers. This year, during the fifth grade, he did not talk with teachers or other students. In addition, he did not speak in public. For example, he had never ordered food at a restaurant. His talking outside of his home was becoming progressively more restricted. Even at home, his mother reported that if Joshua were "in trouble," he would not speak to his parents.

Joshua's mother described him as secretive. In her view, privacy, trust, and his race were issues with which he struggled. She said he was angry and often unresponsive to directions. According to Joshua's teacher, he was quiet, he kept to himself, and he did his schoolwork well. Both his mother and teachers reported that he often withdrew and sulked.

Joshua's selective mutism was atypical. At 10 ½ years, he was older than most children who are mute. Additionally, the mutism had become progressively more pronounced with time. Descriptions of Joshua implied he wanted to control his own behavior and often the behavior of those around him with his choice to be silent. Considering Joshua's issues from a person-centered perspective (Rogers, 1951), I suspected that he was dealing with a great deal of incongruence between who he was (not speaking and therefore not developing relationships with peers) and who he wanted to be (speaking and developing social relationships).

## Indications for Using Child-Centered Play Therapy with Joshua

The literature indicates that the prognosis for selective mute children older than ten years of age is poor and that mutism is seen as resistant to treatment (Kolvin & Fundudis, 1981; Labbe & Williamson, 1984). I recognized that I could not develop a relationship with Joshua if I depended upon his speaking. So I entered the relationship accepting that speaking was entirely under Joshua's control and that I would have to relate to him in a way that would encourage his own desire to talk. Child-centered play therapy seemed the most hopeful approach for this to happen. Using this approach, there would be no pressure for Joshua to speak. I hoped that my acceptance of Joshua's feelings and behaviors, including his silence, could free him to have the courage to speak.

## Counseling Goals

My counseling goals with Joshua were to make emotional contact with him; maintain an "unwavering belief in his capacity for growth and self-direction" (Landreth & Sweeney, 1997, p. 29); create an environment in which he felt safe, accepted, and understood; return responsibility to him; and encourage his independence and decision making. As Ginott (1961) stated, I wanted to convey not only understanding, but "acceptance of the child and faith in his capacity to more forward under his own steam" (p. 85). I wanted to recognize Joshua as a person worthy of respect, not as a "selective mute."

The goals for Joshua were to help him resolve the incongruence of his ability to speak and his decision to be silent in school and help him develop social skills with peers that would be more satisfying for him.

The goals for working with Joshua's parents were to maintain a collaborative relationship to provide them support in raising a child that had special challenges, insight about Joshua, and information about effective parenting skills. Close collaboration with teachers was also critical in working with Joshua. His teachers were encouraged not to "force" Joshua to speak.

### Playroom and Materials

The playroom was in a mobile unit behind an inner-city elementary school. The room was 10 feet by 10 feet square, had small windows with bars across them, and contained shelving, tables, chairs, and a chalkboard. To encourage a wide range of expressions, toys were selected according to the three categories described by Landreth (1991): real-life toys (e.g., doll family, dollhouse, nursing bottle, dishes, car, airplane, cash register), acting-out or aggressive release toys (e.g., handcuffs, several types of toy guns, toy soldiers, rubber knife), and creative or emotional release toys (e.g., play-doh, popsicle sticks, sand, water, art supplies).

## SESSION HIGHLIGHTS

Significant interactions and happenings in this case are described. In addition, I have included my personal reactions.

### Introduction

Joshua transferred to the school as a fifth grader. His father brought him on the first day, registered him at the office, and left. No one was told that Joshua was mute. His teacher noticed that he did not speak. While his cumulative folder indicated that he had received counseling in the first grade, there had been no intervention since that time. Perhaps that is because Joshua was quiet, completed his work on time, and performed well. Joshua's mutism was brought to the attention of the school counselor. I worked in this school one day each week as a play therapist. Joshua was referred to me in mid-September.

### Session 1: Joshua (September 17)

The day I met Joshua, he stood in the middle of the playroom without moving or speaking. His hands were clasped behind his back. He stared straight ahead. He did not look at the room or toys. His face showed a warm expression. He smiled. At times, he snickered. In an effort to demonstrate understanding and acceptance, I responded to him frequently with "You feel comfortable standing quietly," "You do not want to check out the toys here," "You feel uncomfortable," and "You're not sure what to do here." After forty-five minutes, I walked him back to his classroom.

**Consultation with Teacher (September 19).**   Later that week, I consulted with Joshua's teacher. She reported that he had written a report on Harlem and the ghetto. In his journal, he had written about getting a gang together. She reported that Joshua did the work required in the classroom, that he liked structure, and that she thought that he would talk in the classroom when he felt more comfortable.

**My Reactions.**   Joshua's interest in writing about gangs, a group that maintains strong member identity, did not seem unusual. Speaking children this age are expanding their social interests from their homes into the wider community of their school. Since Joshua was not a member of any groups at school or in his neighborhood, I was not surprised that he was writing about gangs.

## Session 2: Joshua (October 1)

Joshua did not speak any words. Again, as in session 1, he stood like a statue in the middle of the room. In an attempt to build trust and not have secrets about him, I told Joshua what I knew about him: that he did not talk at school, that he did talk at home, and that I had heard about some problems he had in kindergarten and first grade. As I spoke, Joshua stared at me and snickered. I returned eye contact, trying to make my eye contact warm. My goal was to be there "with" him, to demonstrate to him my acceptance and respect. After a few minutes, he no longer looked at me. I responded to his feelings of comfort and discomfort. I also said, "In here, you may choose what to do."

**My Reactions.**   By this time, I had already had several consultations with Joshua's mother. Her concern and empathy for Joshua were enormous and her willingness to participate in any way was strong. Therefore, in addition to individual play therapy, I decided to try a strategy described by Richburg and Cobia (1994) and Ratner (1995) involving another family member, his mother, in counseling sessions. The goal of these conjoint sessions was to learn about Joshua's life from his mother's perspective and to respond empathically to both Joshua and his mother. I planned to include Joshua in the interactions and restate to him what was said by his mother through reflective statements, such as, "You must have felt angry when that happened" or "You look sad as your mother speaks of that." I would not push him to speak. Also, this approach would provide emotional support for Joshua's mother. She was pleased to meet with Joshua and me for these sessions.

## Session 3: Joshua and His Mother (October 1)

During this joint session, Joshua's mother described Joshua's experiences during preschool and early elementary school. She spoke of his temper tantrums at school, relating that these tantrums did not happen at home. In addition, she described his pattern of speaking in his home and neighborhood.

I responded empathically, directing my responses to both Joshua and his mother with responses such as, "It sounds like you [Joshua] had such a hard time in preschool" and "You must have felt so bad about what was happening with Joshua" (to his mother).

### Session 4: Joshua (October 8)

Joshua entered the playroom and immediately sat down in a chair beside me. He seemed much more comfortable than in the earlier sessions. He looked for items in the pocket of his vest and took a coin off the zipper of his vest. At one point, he leaned over and looked at the floor, completely blocking me out. I tried to be warm, attentive, and responsive. During this session, he did not stare at me.

### Session 5: Joshua and His Mother (October 8)

We met for forty-five minutes. Joshua's mother addressed her concerns and feelings about Joshua. I responded empathically to both Joshua and his mother. His mother spoke about his temper tantrums in preschool and about how the teachers responded to this behavior in severe ways. I responded, "Joshua, you must have felt terrible when you were treated so harshly during your preschool." His mother reassured him.

As his mother spoke, Joshua responded to her in a "mumbling" way that I could not understand. She could understand what he said. He indicated that he did not like his preschool teacher. This surprised his mother, because she had always believed that he did like her. When his mother spoke about his being bi-racial, he communicated to her his feelings of shame. His mother told him how much she wanted to have him and how sorry she was that this is so hard for him. She told him that he was bright and could do whatever he wanted to do and how hard it must be not to speak.

**Consultation with School Counselor: (October 9).** The school counselor reported that Joshua spoke three times in class today.

### Session 6: Joshua (October 15)

Overall, Joshua seemed comfortable and at ease. His eye contact was relaxed, not glaring. I re-stated to Joshua that what he did with me would always be private, even from his mother and teachers. I thought that it was important to continuously emphasize confidentiality in this relationship to build a trusting relationship. Joshua listened attentively.

Joshua was silent. Again, he showed no interest in any of the toys in the playroom. He zipped his jacket to the top and put his mouth and lower part of his face in the jacket. I said, "It looks like you're hiding from me." He looked out the window. He snickered a few times, and I responded, "You're feeling uncomfortable."

## Session 7: Joshua and His Mother (October 15)

During this session, the mother continued to focus on events that occurred in his preschool. Again, she described the beginning of severe temper tantrums that were not occurring at home. I had a strong sense that something significant had happened during preschool. I said, "I wonder if something very uncomfortable happened to you during this time." He indicated that it had. At that time, I wondered aloud, whether Joshua would like to tell his mother, so I asked him. He indicated that he would, but not in my presence. I left the room, so that Joshua and his mother could speak privately. When I returned, Joshua's mother told me, with Joshua's permission, that one of the times when he wet his pants in preschool, the teacher pulled his pants down and spanked him with a stick in front of the class. His mother said that this information explained why Joshua was uncomfortable going to the bathroom at school, even to this day. I responded to Joshua's feelings of betrayal and anger. His mother expressed her own anger and dismay about what had happened to Joshua. After expressing her feelings about the experience to Joshua, his mother asked him if he was ready to start speaking at school. He nodded that he was.

**My Reactions.**   I thought about the research on selective mutism that says that many children who are mute also have a problem with enuresis. It seems that the humiliation Joshua experienced when his teacher spanked him had an appalling impact on him. This incident seemed to be a catalyst for aggressive behavior in preschool and first grade. Then, Joshua withdrew into silence.

## Session 8: Joshua (October 22)

During this session, Joshua seemed unhappy, withdrawn. He sat. He did not speak.

**Consultation with Teacher: (October 22).**   The teacher told me that she was putting more pressure on Joshua to talk in the classroom. While I empathized with the stress she was feeling in the classroom, I discouraged her from entering into a power struggle with Joshua.

**Telephone Call (October 22).**   Later that day Joshua's mother called and said she was unable to attend the conjoint session that was scheduled for later that afternoon. When I went to tell Joshua, I found him at a table in the lunchroom with two other boys. He smiled warmly at me when I approached him. They told me to "make him talk." I responded that I could not, that he would decide about his talking.

## Session 9: Joshua (November 5)

When I arrived to get Joshua from his classroom, he was running errands for his teacher. During the session, he did not speak. At times, he appeared relaxed, and at times, he laughed, almost hysterically. I responded frequently to his feelings of both comfort and discomfort.

**My Reactions.** I thought that Joshua felt both comfortable with me and uncomfortable. So I responded to both, wondering what these changes meant. Joshua's laughter reminded me of Amy, reported by Barlow et al. (1986), who was "often inappropriate, in the sense of periodic bursts of hostility or lengthy laughter" (p. 48).

## Session 10: Joshua (November 12)

Before our session, Joshua said to me, "I'm going to the office." In the playroom Joshua did not speak or interact with any of the toys. He looked at the floor. I responded to how he appeared to be feeling—sad, uncomfortable. Joshua looked like he wanted to hide from me.

**Consultation (November 12).** In a consultation, Landreth (1999) suggested inviting a friend to a play session to "free the child to become involved with the play materials. . . . This might be the beginning of a social relationship which he desperately needs."

## Session 11: Joshua (November 19)

As Joshua left his classroom to come to the playroom with me, he spoke to another student. The child who was in the playroom before Joshua had put toy coins in the play-doh. When Joshua came to the playroom, I asked him if he would help me get the coins out of the play-doh. Joshua happily helped me. Then he continued to play with the play-doh for the remainder of the session.

First, Joshua made a figure of a human. The figure had detailed eyes and mouth. I responded, "It looks angry." He shook his head indicating "no." I said, "It looks sad." Again, he shook his head indicating "no." I said, "It looks surprised." He nodded indicating "yes." Then he changed the mouth to a smile, and I said, "It looks happy." He nodded again. The second figure he made was of a head with long pointed ears and nose. The third figure looked like a gargoyle—a figure with arms crossed, sitting cross-legged, with wings. Again, the face was detailed with what looked to me like a sad mouth. When I commented about the sad look, he changed the mouth again—this time to having no mouth. He made a shape that appeared to be a baby. He placed the baby in the arms of the figure. I responded that it looked safe in the arms of the figure. He nodded and then wrapped the wings around the small shape.

**My Reactions.** Joshua shared some of his world with me by interacting—for the first time—with materials in the playroom. I was touched by the figures Joshua made with the play-doh. He seemed to want me to know how the first figure felt, for he "corrected" my responses to the figure's feelings. Considering that Joshua was a selective mute, it was intriguing that he focused on transforming the mouth of the figure. And the last figure had no mouth.

### Session 12: Joshua and His Mother (November 19)

Joshua's mother spoke with me for a moment before we went to get Joshua for a joint session. She said, "It was absolutely incredible." She told me that Joshua was ordering food at fast food restaurants for her—going up to get her more coffee—for the first time in his life. She was amazed and thrilled. She attributed his talking to the session we had together when he described the spanking. She thought that was a clear turning point for Joshua.

In our joint session, Joshua spoke to his mother in a clear, distinct voice in my presence. They had a normal conversation. While he never directed any of his responses to me, he did speak openly in front of me for the first time.

**My Reactions.** The counseling with Joshua was making a difference. His mother reported such dramatic changes. Although little change was evident in the playroom, Joshua was changing outside of the playroom.

**Call from School (November 21).** The school counselor called and reported to me that Joshua had called two people, including a teacher, "m——f—— crackers." They asked me to join them in a consultation with his mother.

### Session 13: Joshua (November 26)

Joshua did not speak or use any materials. At times he laughed and stretched. I spoke with him for about one minute at the beginning of the session. I told him that I had heard that he had called one of his teacher's a name. I told him that I felt concerned that he might feel angry and lonely keeping everything inside. Joshua looked at me, warmly, while I spoke, but he only responded by making a gesture with his head indicating that he had not called the teacher a name.

### Session 14: Joshua and His Mother (November 26)

Joshua, his mother, and I met briefly with Joshua to tell him about the previous meeting. He spoke distinctly and understandably in my presence, denying that he had cursed at the teacher.

**My Reactions.** The purpose of our meeting was to continue building trust with Joshua by showing him we would not keep "secrets" from him.

### Session 15: Joshua (December 3)

When I went to get Joshua from his classroom, another student asked if he could come to play with Joshua. I told him I would talk with Joshua about it. When we got to the playroom, I asked Joshua if he would like to have another child join him sometime, and he said, "Fine."

Joshua played with play-doh voluntarily. He made three figures. The first one appeared to be a dinosaur. He worked on the second with his hands under the table. I wondered if he was intentionally preventing me from seeing what he was doing. He laughed a lot while he was making it and looked at my face frequently. To show my understanding, I responded with the statements, "You're working hard on that," "You know just how to make what you want," and "You're having fun." I made no attempt to look at what he was making or ask him to share it with me. I wanted to show acceptance of what he was doing. When he was finished, he threw what he had made on the table. It appeared to be male genitals. I responded with a calm tone, "You wonder if I'm surprised and upset." I was not. Then he created what appeared to be a bird on a stand. He changed the bird to a human looking face, with wings. He made what looked like a witch's hat for the figure.

**My Reactions.**   My thought about the phallic figure was that Joshua was testing me to see if I would censor what he chose to do in the playroom. I did not. I accepted what he did. I was interested that he, again, created a human looking face with wings. This was the second time he had created such a figure.

### Session 16: Joshua (January 14)

Joshua seemed pleased to see me. He indicated that his mother was going to come for a session later that day. Joshua voluntarily straightened the playroom. This was the first time he had examined any of the toys. He sorted figures in the sand. Then he returned to his usual position in the chair beside me, and sat silently. I asked if he would like to help me soften up some new play-doh. He did. He looked very sad.

**Consultation with Teacher (January 14).**   When I went to consult with his teacher this afternoon, Joshua was standing in front of her desk. She was waiting for him to speak before she would let him leave the room. Finally, she let him leave without speaking.

### Session 17: Joshua and His Mother (January 14)

Joshua did not speak in front of me. His mother appeared agitated. She expressed frustration about Joshua not talking. When we discussed what happened with his teacher earlier that day, she stated that drawing attention to him is not productive, because he wants that control. I responded to her feelings of impatience and disappointment.

## Session 18: Joshua (January 21)

Joshua did not talk. He sat. He seemed pensive. As I walked him back to his classroom, he did not walk beside me. He stayed a little ahead of me.

## Session 19: Joshua (January 28)

I talked with Joshua about bringing a friend with him to the playroom the next session. He indicated with a nod that he was interested. I asked him which friend he would like to invite to the playroom. He said, "Robert."

**My Reactions.**    In addition to my consultation with Landreth, the literature offers several examples of the positive outcomes of joining selective mute children with other children in therapy (Barlow et al., 1986; Bozigar & Hansen, 1984; Jackson, 1950). Group counseling helped these children work through their mutism by enabling them to develop trusting relationships with their peers in a therapeutic setting.

## Session 20: Joshua and Robert (February 4)

On the way to the playroom with Robert, Joshua laughed a lot. It seemed to be an uncomfortable laugh. Robert's play was extremely active. He immediately started playing with a gun. Then he started creating scenes with the puppet family. Joshua initially sat in his usual chair. Then he stood up and examined the toys. He played with the large gun and the nurf gun. Robert developed a story with the puppets: it was a family that he was robbing and shooting. He said that they weren't dead. They went to the hospital. On several occasions, members of the family shot him (Robert), and he acted like he was dying. Robert engaged in a lot of sexual play. The father and mother puppets were kissing constantly and seemed to have sex several times. Robert kept looking at Joshua to see his reaction. Robert then hung the father with the handcuffs. Joshua saved the father. Then Joshua gave the father a gun. Robert talked about how the children would have to be in a foster home, because the mother was killed. Robert pretended to have a TV interview. He took the microphone up to Joshua for a reaction to the "incident." Joshua did not speak. In a kind voice, Robert said, "Joshua won't talk about it."

Later in the session, Joshua arrested Robert. He put handcuffs on him and took him to sit in a chair. Robert willingly allowed this play to occur. He did not seem to mind being cuffed or "taken in."

Joshua did not talk at all during this session, but he laughed a lot and played. I tracked both of them during their play and responded to how they seemed to feel (happy, involved, and sad) and how the figures in the play felt (afraid, scared, and happy).

**My Reactions.**    This was the first time Joshua had ever played with toys other than play-doh. He seemed to focus on the guns. I thought that Joshua was watching

Robert—almost as if to see how to play. One time, Robert accidentally touched Joshua, and Joshua seemed extremely uncomfortable. He quickly backed away.

Joshua selected a peer with a high level of activity and active talking, unlike himself. Joshua seemed to know just what he needed to help him change.

### Session 21: Joshua and Robert (February 12)

I saw Joshua on my way to pick him up, so he went with me to get Robert. I said I didn't know where Robert was. Joshua said, "He's in classroom 5." I showed no surprise at his use of words and wondered if he would speak in the playroom. We found Robert. The trailer was locked, so I asked them to go to the office to get the key. When they returned, Joshua and Robert were talking loudly with each other. Again I showed no surprise that he was speaking. Joshua ran up to me with the key.

When they entered the playroom, Joshua immediately started exploring the toys. Robert started drawing on the blackboard. Joshua was very interested in what Robert was doing. It appeared that Robert drew something obscene on the side of the blackboard that I could not see. Joshua started laughing loudly. I responded, "You are having fun," and "It feels good being together." Both boys got involved in drawing on the blackboard. They wrote math problems and the words "Malcolm X." Robert started playing in the sand. Joshua played with the gun. Robert was the doctor and used the stethoscope, blood pressure, and thermometer on Joshua. Joshua seemed comfortable and pleased.

Joshua communicated throughout the session with noises, play and gestures, but again, no words were spoken in the playroom. I responded frequently to their activities and feelings.

### Session 22: Joshua and Robert (February 25)

On the way to the playroom, Joshua told me that he and Robert had planned to get together that weekend. Joshua talked a lot in the playroom, more than Robert did. He led the play. He played with soldiers. He engaged in two battles. He won one. Robert won one. Joshua talked about killing Hitler and being in a gang. Robert talked about not using drugs, about hurting his knee when he was five, and about other friends.

**My Reactions.**    For the first time, Joshua spoke in the play therapy session. The two boys played well together. They were cooperative and compromised well. Joshua behaved like a typical fifth grader.

### Joshua and His Father (March 26)

Joshua's father took Joshua and Robert to the circus. Joshua spoke. They found Jimmy, a person from the school who had taken a group of children to the circus, and talked with him for awhile.

## Session 23: Joshua and Robert (March 4)

In the playroom Joshua and Robert started playing basketball. The play was rough and active. Most of the toys were knocked off the shelves. Both boys said they wanted to go outside and play basketball, and I responded with "I know you want to go outside, but we need to spend our time in the playroom. You can play basketball outside during your PE time."

At one point Robert was about to pick up some toys that were knocked over when Joshua was throwing the ball. Joshua said, "Pick those up. You're my slave." Robert stopped at that moment and did not pick up the toys. I responded to Robert, "That remark made you feel bad." A few minutes later, Robert left the playroom. Joshua then sat in a chair and did not say anything. I said, "I wonder if we should go and see Robert. You might want to talk to him." Joshua wanted to do that. We went to see Robert. Joshua said, "You're mad at me?" Pointing at me, Robert said "No, I'm mad at her, because it was hot in there [the playroom] and I wanted to go play basketball." At the end of the conversation, I told Robert that I'd see him next week. He said "No, you will not."

**My Reactions.**   Joshua was clearly dominant in this session. He was more verbal and more aggressive than Robert. My reaction was that Joshua desperately wanted to have a relationship with Robert and that he was learning how to do that. I believe that Joshua recognized that Robert was uncomfortable with his interactions with him. With regard to his remark about Robert being his slave, I believe that this reflected his issues about power in his newly developing relationship. His sincere apology to Robert showed me the strength of his interest in developing this friendship. He had not had experience interacting with children his own age. My hope was that we would have more sessions together, so that Joshua could have more experience interacting with a peer in the play therapy environment. Robert's threat that he would not come back to the playroom indicated to me that he was more comfortable directing his anger at me than at Joshua. He, too, wanted to protect this growing relationship.

## Consultation with Joshua, His Mother, and His Father (March 4)

Joshua seemed upset to see his father at the session. He did not speak. He stormed out of the playroom. He held the door closed. He came in one time and then stormed back out again.

Joshua refused to get into his parents' car at the end of the session. He ran from the school. The school counselor saw him as she was driving home. She stopped. As she was talking to him, he walked away. She motioned for nearby police to come. Three policemen surrounded him. After a few minutes, he got in the car with his parents, though he did not want to.

His mother reported that on the way home, Joshua's only words were that he was "going to beat up Robert."

**My Reactions.**   I was surprised by Joshua's strong negative reaction to seeing his father at a counseling session, since he knew his father was coming. However, of all the events of that afternoon, I was particularly struck that Joshua's summary of the day was that he wanted to beat up Robert. His relationship with Robert, and how that relationship was developing, was the most critical issue on his mind.

Joshua's behavior was intriguing, also, in light of the research about selective mutes. First, his reaction to his father probably reflected a stronger, more trusting bond with his mother. Also, his behavior reflects Cook's (1997) idea that wanting to run away among selective mutes "continues to emerge in new situations and with new people" (p. 97). On this day, Joshua was faced with several new situations—conflict with Robert, his father joining the counseling session, contact with police. And, he ran away.

### Telephone Call from Joshua's Mother (March 6)

Two days later, Joshua's mother called me, in tears, from their home. The police were there, at that time, talking with Joshua. She told me that Joshua tried to leave the house, and she had physically restrained him. He then kicked in the back door, "tore up" the back room, and threw a lot of things around. She was distraught. I called her back an hour later and spoke with Joshua's father. Joshua and I had a brief conversation on the phone. He spoke a little and told me that he was OK.

**My Reactions.**   While I was saddened to hear of Joshua's aggressive behavior, I was not surprised. The literature on selective mute children offers numerous examples of children who express great anger at school and in their family as they begin to speak (Barlow et al., 1986; Bozigar & Hansen, 1984). I tried to support Joshua and his parents.

### Session 24: Joshua and Robert (March 12)

I asked Joshua and Robert if they wanted to see me separately or together. Both said "Together." At the arranged time, they were waiting for me in a hallway, and Joshua was speaking loudly with both Robert and other students.

During the session, both boys talked with each other and with me freely. Joshua both responded to my interactions with him directly, and he initiated talking to me. Joshua and Robert were both animated and happy. The content of the session was about an R-rated movie that they both liked. As they talked, Robert was running his fingers through the sand, and Joshua was sitting on the table beside him. They were chatting with each other. Robert started playing with the mother and father dolls. The mother was sitting on the father's lap. Then Robert started playing with the dishes. He said he was cooking grits. Joshua commented about his "playing house." Robert did not seem bothered, and continued with his play.

When the session was over, neither boy wanted to leave the session. I responded by saying, "I know you don't want to leave the playroom, but our time is up for today." They were enjoying their time together and resisted returning to their respective classrooms. The process of ending the session took about fifteen minutes.

**Call from School Social Worker (March 13).** A social worker from the school called and reported that Joshua was "talking like crazy with other children" today at school. Also, he went to a school talent show last night and was talking there.

**My Reactions.** My work was done.

## SUMMARY

The dominant themes addressed in play therapy were control and anger. During my relationship with Joshua, I looked for the right combination of therapeutic interventions. In addition to individual play therapy and group play therapy, I also counseled with Joshua and his mother. Thus, over the course of six-and-one-half months, I conducted thirteen individual child-centered play therapy sessions with Joshua, five group sessions with Joshua and Robert, and six sessions with Joshua and his mother. In addition to these counseling sessions, I consulted with Joshua's mother, the school counselor, the teacher, and the school social worker regularly.

### Follow-up

In a conversation with Joshua's mother two and a half years after our last contact, she reported that Joshua was talking in school and in other situations and that he was doing well with his schoolwork. There had been no relapses in his speaking.

## CONCLUSIONS

While child-centered play therapy is an ideal approach for working with selective mute children, actually being with a totally inactive, silent child for forty-five minutes was difficult. I needed to remind myself frequently of Ginott's (1961) advice that the "therapist should not show or feel impatience. He should not persist in trying to inspire activity by offering suggestions or examples. He should not attempt to select the activities or set the pace of the child's play session" (p. 85).

I tried to establish and maintain a close collaboration with teachers. At times, that was difficult. Teachers who did not fully understand the goals and methods of play therapy felt that Joshua did not "deserve" to play and that he was "pulling the wool over my eyes." I understood that this was a reflection of the frustration they experienced teaching a child who refused to speak in the classroom.

Joshua began to speak in many social situations, including school, and he developed a social relationship with a child in his classroom. In addressing the issue of learning social skills in play therapy, Barlow et al. (1985) state, "They learn how to stand up for themselves, share toys, fight with words, and express their feelings toward other children. Realistic social skills are developed as the children become more aware of their interpersonal effect on other children" (p. 355). Joshua demonstrated this in his work with Robert. It was most apparent during the session in which Joshua called Robert his slave. He looked extremely remorseful and immediately made an effort to re-establish their relationship. Joshua was learning about friendship.

For Joshua, beginning to speak was a process, not a single event. After one and a half months of individual play therapy sessions and joint sessions with Joshua and his mother, he began to speak in settings where he had never spoken before, such as in restaurants. Therefore, as suggested by Barlow et al. (1986) and others (Black & Uhde, 1992; Chetnik, 1973), success should be measured both in and out of the playroom when counseling with selective mute children.

Inviting a peer into the playroom was the unmistakable catalyst for Joshua both to speak during counseling and to become involved with the materials in the playroom. Before Robert joined the therapy, Joshua had only played with the play-doh. When Robert joined Joshua, Joshua immediately became active in the playroom. His verbalizations progressively increased, and during their last sessions, Joshua and Robert interacted like typical fifth grade boys. I believe that this counseling experience enabled Joshua to develop a social relationship. Following these counseling sessions, Joshua reportedly "talked like crazy" with other children at school and sought out a friend for a conversation at the circus.

Joshua had been a cooperative, "easy" student for many years. Although he did not speak, he bothered no one, did his schoolwork, and performed well. When Joshua did begin to speak at school, he talked about gangs and he cursed others, expressing, at times, a great amount of anger. In addition, he expressed his anger more aggressively at home. While the literature warns us that when selective mute children begin to talk, they sometimes express anger (Barlow et al., 1986; Bozigar & Hansen, 1984; Richburg & Cobia, 1994), it was frightening when it happened, especially for those people who had so much invested in helping him. It was surprising to discover what this formerly "calm" child held inside. As a result, some people doubted the efficacy of the counseling, because the result was such an angry and defiant child. Play therapists need to remember, and to help others understand, that for "older" children to maintain mutism is extremely difficult, and many unresolved and angry feelings may emerge when the child chooses to speak. Through understanding, and perhaps anticipating anger when they finally speak, play therapists can better help these children as they emerge from their mutism.

Selective mutism is a difficult and puzzling problem. The reasons that children become mute—and how to help them—are unclear. This case demonstrates the powerful impact of child-centered play therapy on a 10½ -year-old boy. Joshua was able to use the play therapy relationship to address the incongruence between his desire to speak and his desire to exert control in most social settings by not speaking. Through his involvement in therapy, Joshua felt accepted enough, safe enough, and empowered enough to allow his voice to be heard.

## REFERENCES

Afnan, S., & Carr, A. (1989). Interdisciplinary treatment of a case of elective mutism. *British Journal of Occupational Therapy, 52,* 61-66.

American Psychiatric Association. (1994). *Diagnostic and statistical manual of mental disorders* (4th ed.). Washington, DC: Author.

Axline, V. M. (1947). *Play therapy.* Boston: Houghton Mifflin.

Barlow, K., Strother, J., & Landreth, G. (1985). Child-centered play therapy: Nancy from baldness to curls. *The School Counselor, 32,* 347–356.

Barlow, K., Strother, J., & Landreth, G. (1986). Sibling group play therapy: An effective alternative with an elective mute child. *The School Counselor, 34,* 44–50.

Black, B., & Uhde, T. W. (1992). Elective mutism as a variant of social phobia. *Journal of the American Academy of Child and Adolescent Psychiatry, 31,* 1090–1094.

Bozigar, J. A., & Hansen, R. A. (1984). Group treatment for elective mute children. *Social Work, 29,* 478-498.

Brown, B. J., & Lloyd, M. (1975). A controlled study of children not speaking at school. *Journal of the Association of Workers for Maladjusted Children, 3,* 49–63.

Chetnik, M. (1973). Amy: The intensive treatment of an elective mute. *Journal of the American Academy of Child Psychiatry, 12,* 482–498.

Cook, J. (1997). Play therapy for selective mutism. In H. F. Kaduson & D. M. Cangelosi (Eds.), *The playing cure: Individualized play therapy for specific childhood problems* (pp. 83–115). Northvale, NJ: Jason Aronson, Inc.

Ginott, H. M. (1961). *Group psychotherapy with children.* New York: McGraw-Hill.

Golwyn, H. D., & Weinstock, R. C. (1990). Phenelzine treatment of elective mutism: A case report. *Journal of Clinical Psychiatry, 51,* 384–385.

Harris, H. F. (1996). Elective mutism: A tutorial. *Language, Speech, and Hearing Services in Schools, 27,* 10–15.

Hesselman, S. (1983). Elective mutism in children: 1877–1981. *Paedopsychiatrica, 45,* 297–310.

Hultquist, A. (1995). Selective mutism: Causes and intervention. *Journal of Emotional and Behavioral Disorders, 3,* 100–108.

Jackson, L. (1950). "Non-speaking" children. *British Journal of Medical Psychology, 23,* 87–100.

Joseph, P. R. (1999). Selective mutism: The child who doesn't speak at school. *Pediatrics, 104,* 308–310.

Knell, S. M. (1993). Cognitive-behavioral play therapy with children with speech and language problems. In S. Knell (Ed.), *Cognitive-behavioral play therapy* (pp. 143–170). Northvale, NJ: Jason Aronson, Inc.

Kolvin, I., & Fundudis, T. (1981). Elective mute children: Psychological development and background factors. *Annual Progress in Child Psychiatry and Child Development, 22,* 219-232.

Krohn, D. D., Weckstein, S. M., & Wright, H. L. (1992). A study of the effectiveness of a specific treatment for elective mutism. *Journal of the American Academy of Child and Adolescent Psychiatry, 31,* 711–718.

Labbe, E. E., & Williamson, D. A. (1984). Behavioral treatment of elective mutism. *Clinical Psychological Review, 4,* 273–292.

Landreth, G. L. (1991). *Play therapy: The art of the relationship*. Muncie, IN: Accelerated Development, Inc.

Landreth, G. L. (1999). Personal communication, November 12.

Landreth, G. L., & Sweeney, D. S. (1997). Child-centered play therapy. In K. O'Connor & L. M. Braverman (Eds.), *Play therapy theory and practice: A comparative presentation* (pp. 17–45). Baltimore: Brooks Publishing Co.

Landreth, G. L., Homeyer, L. E., Glover, G., & Sweeney, D. S. (1996). *Play therapy interventions with children's problems*. Northvale, NJ: Jason Aronson, Inc.

Porjes, M. D. (1992). Intervention with the selectively mute child. *Psychology in the Schools, 29,* 367–376.

Powell, S., & Dalley, M. (1995). When to intervene in selective mutism: The multimodal treatment of a case of persistent elective mutism. *Psychology in the School, 32,* 114–123.

Ratner, J. (1995). A young woman chooses to be mute. In M. A. Blotzer & R. Ruth (Eds.), *Sometimes you just want to feel like a human being: Case studies of empowering psychotherapy with people with disabilities* (pp. 135–149). Baltimore: Brooks Publishing Co.

Richburg, M. L., & Cobia, D. C. (1994). Using behavioral techniques to treat elective mutism: A case study. *Elementary School Guidance and Counseling, 28,* 214–220.

Rogers, C. R. (1951). *Client-centered therapy*. Boston: Houghton Mifflin.

Weininger, O. (1987). Electively mute children: A therapeutic approach. *The Journal of the Melanie Klein Society, 5,* 25–42.

Wilkins, L. (1995). A comparison of elective mutism and emotional disorders in children. *British Journal of Psychiatry, 146,* 198–203.

Wright, H. H., Holmes, G. R., Cuccaro., M. L., & Leonhardt, T. V. (1994). A guided bibliography of the selective mutism (elective mutism) literature. *Psychological Reports, 74,* 995–1007.

# 20

# Play Therapy with Dissociative Identity Disorder Clients with Child Alters

JEFFREY W. KLEIN
GARRY L. LANDRETH

According to Putnam (1989), child alters were one of the two principle types of alter personalities reported in the literature over the last century and a half. He also concluded that child alters are one of the two principle types seen in multiple personality disorder (MPD) clients today (current *Diagnostic and Statistical Manual of Mental Disorders* (DSM-IV) references are Dissociative Identity Disorder, DID). Often these child alters have many of the same difficulties expressing themselves verbally that children have. Therefore, these child alters could derive much of the same benefit from play therapy that children do. Children with emotional disturbances can best be treated using play therapy, since children have difficulty responding to traditional verbal therapies used by adults. Play is a natural expression for children and is acted out effortlessly. Therefore, expressions of the child alter of the adult client will more readily be facilitated.

## OVERVIEW OF DID

### Definitions

Dissociative identity disorder (DID) is the most severe of the dissociative disorders (DD). The DSM-IV (American Psychiatric Association, 1994) defines this

From "Play Therapy with Multiple Personality Disorder Clients," by Jeffrey Klein and Garry Landreth. In *International Journal of Play Therapy*, 2(1), pp. 1–14. Copyright 1993. Reprinted with permission.

disorder as 1) the existence within the person of two or more distinct personality states; that each has a relatively enduring pattern of perceiving, relating to, and thinking about the environment and self; and 2) at least two of these personality states recurrently take full executive control of the person's behavior. It is also important to note that the age of onset is almost invariably childhood, but does not typically come to attention until much later. Literature supports the contention of childhood onset (Kluft, 1985; Braun, 1986; Putnam, 1989). In nearly all cases the predisposing factors are abuse—often sexual abuse—or other severe trauma in childhood. Kluft (1984) proposed a four-factor theory of causality of DID in which he described the kinds of traumatic events that overwhelm a child's defenses and contribute to the development of DID in children: sexual abuse, extreme physical abuse, abandonment, neglect, psychological abuse, loss or death of significant others, witnessing a murder, an accident or carnage of war, receiving serious death threats, cultural dislocation, a bitter divorce situation, or being treated as if the child is the opposite gender. The DSM-IV also states that the disorder is not nearly as rare as once thought to be. In a study of epidemiology of MPD (DID) and DD, Ross (1991) reported the prevalence in the general population to be in the range of about one percent. The prevalence in clinical populations is even higher. Ross concluded that MPD (DID) and DD are as common as anxiety and affective disorders.

The following definitions/descriptions are commonly used in reference to individuals with DID (Braun, 1986):

**Personality**–an entity that has: 1) a consistent and ongoing set of response patterns to given stimuli, 2) a significant confluent history, 3) a range of available emotions, and 4) a range of intensity and affect for processes with their concomitant physiological responses, separated by repression barriers from other personalities.

**Host Personality**–the personality that has executive control of the body the greatest percentage of time during a given age period.

**Alter**–any personality or fragment other than the host personality.

**Original Personality**–the entity that developed first after birth and split off or remained separate from the flow of the rest of the thought processes.

**Two-way amnesia**–the state in which one personality or fragment does not know of the existence of another personality or fragment, and vice versa.

**One-way Amnesia**–the state in which personality A does not know anything about personality B, but B knows everything about A.

**Co-consciousness**–the state of being aware of the thoughts or consciousness of another personality. It may be unidirectional or bi-directional.

**Integration**–the process of bringing together the separate thought processes (personalities or fragments) and maintaining them as one.

**Switching**–going back and forth between already existing personalities or fragments.

Although the etiology of DID is complex, the disorder can be thought of as an extreme defense against extreme abuse. Children are often subjected to sadistic sexual abuse (Goodwin, 1985) and many children are subjected to satanic ritual abuse (SRA) involving satanic rituals, murder, rape, incest, impregnation, abortions, cannibalism, dismemberment, and other atrocities (Friesen, 1991). As one comes to understand the severity of the trauma involved, it is easier to understand the nature of DID.

## PLAY THERAPY RATIONALE

There are many reasons for using play therapy with children and many of these same reasons apply to working with child alters of adults with DID, or even with some of their adult alters. One of the primary reasons for using play therapy with children is that a nonverbal approach is more suited to the child's developmental level. Thus, it is often thought that play is for children and talk is for adults. However, when working with adults with DID, a more productive approach may be that suggested by Coggin and Coggin (1979). They consider play and talk as two ends of a continuum rather than a dichotomy. For each individual there is an optimal balance of talk and play. Play is a child's nonverbal way of expressing deep levels of affect. Talk is one way of getting a "handle" on the feeling. The verbal handle makes it possible to recapture, recall, communicate, and process experiences. Thus, play and talk are both important components of therapy.

The following general therapeutic objectives suggested by Landreth (1991, p. 80) as being appropriate for children in play therapy would seem also to have applicability to adults with DID.

Play therapy can help the child to:

1. develop a more positive self-concept,
2. assume greater self-responsibility,
3. become more self-directing,
4. become more self-accepting,
5. become more self-reliant,
6. engage in self determined decision making,
7. experience a feeling of control,
8. become sensitive to the process of coping,
9. develop an internal source of evaluation, and
10. become more trusting of self.

While these are general objectives for working with children, they all have applicability to adults with DID, not only for working with the child alters, but also with many of the fragment personalities.

For adults with DID, fragment personalities are often created to perform very specific functions and have a very narrow range of experience. They are usually present in very select circumstances and for very short periods of time. Fragment personalities may be present during the spontaneous abreactions often seen with DID clients. These fragments seem to have a relatively primitive state of ego development with undifferentiated affective and cognitive states. Since these alters' presentation often has a childlike quality, the above objectives are pertinent to these fragment personalities, especially the objectives of experiencing a feeling of control, engaging in decision making, and learning the coping process. The therapist may facilitate these objectives by giving the alter fragment choices. Choice making is a natural part of the play therapy process and begins with the initial first few minutes in the playroom when the individual is presented with the opportunity to decide which toy to play with first. The fragment personalities' repertoire of life experiences may never have included making a choice, thus a choice may be a totally new experience. As the presenting alter learns to make decisions and experiences an internal locus of control, the alter may feel less compelled to act in a repetitive, scripted-like manner. The alter is then ready to increase the existing behavioral repertoire.

Abreaction is an important issue with most DID clients. Release play therapy (Levy, 1982) was developed to help children abreact the anxiety associated with traumatic events. When children are unsuccessful in their attempts to deal with anxiety, the resulting tension produces disturbances in behavior. Through an acting out process, release play therapy helps the child release the anxiety that the child was unable to express fully in the original situation. Feelings that are unexpressed produce symptomatic behavior. The more the child acts out the feelings, the more the feelings are released. Once this process has occurred to a sufficient degree, the symptoms will be alleviated (Levy, 1982). Since DID is characterized as a post-traumatic dissociative disorder (Braun & Sachs, 1985; Braun, 1990), all of the procedures described by Levy can be readily adopted for use with DID patients. Mann and McDermott (1983) also describe ways play therapy can be used with children who have been abused. Their goal is to help the child master the multiple stressors that accompany abuse and to correct or prevent disturbances of psychosocial development. They indicated that the following problems associated with abuse can be addressed through play therapy: 1) fear of assault or abandonment leading to depression and anxiety, 2) defective object relations, and 3) difficulty achieving separation and autonomy. These are issues that many individuals with DID continue to struggle with in their adulthood.

# DID PLAY THERAPY

## Memory Retrieval

One of the primary features of DID is amnesia. Recovery of memories is considered essential to treatment. Memories are stored within the personality system, and retain much of their traumatic affect because the memories are not integrated with other non-traumatic experiences. Normally, the other non-traumatic experiences would serve to mitigate and dissipate the intensity of the traumatic experiences. The continued presence of the intense traumatic material tends to perpetuate dissociation. Therefore, the memories must be brought forth into consciousness and processed in order for treatment to progress (Waldschmidt, Graham-Costain, & Gould, 1991).

It is estimated that ninety-five to ninety-eight percent of individuals with DID have a history of child abuse (Braun, 1990). It should not be surprising, then, that most of the traumatic memories are retained by child alters. Often the alter has been threatened by the abuser "not to tell" about the abuse (Oke & Kanigsberg, 1991). In cases of SRA, the person may have witnessed murders, so the threat must seem very real and powerful. However, through play the alter is able to "show" the abuse, instead of "telling." This will seem much safer at first. Frye (1991) has also found that sand play is a safe, non-threatening way to release secrets that often involve intense feelings of guilt and shame. She sees nonverbal therapy as an effective way to tap into encapsulated memories and bridge the gap between the client's inner and outer worlds.

A second advantage of a nonverbal approach is that traumatic material can safely be projected onto fantasy characters in play. Displacing this material onto dolls or puppets is much less anxiety provoking than accepting it as an experience of self (Waldschmidt et al., 1991). Since one of the primary objectives of the play therapist is to establish the playroom as a safe place, the expression of traumatic material is facilitated.

## Mastery

After traumatic material has been surfaced, the client can obtain a sense of mastery over the material (Graham-Costain & Gould , 1990; Frye, 1990; Sweig, 1990). During the experiences of abuse, the child usually feels helpless. There is a loss of personal power and control as "bad things" are done to the child. Through play, the client can decide how the plot unfolds and how the story will end. Equally significant, through play the client can punish the perpetrator.

In a recent experience, an adult client went to the playroom and a five or six-year-old alter presented. She went to the sand tray, drew a pentacle in the sand, and then made a circle around the pentacle. She then placed two figures within the circle. She identified one as herself, and the other as her abuser. She then placed other figures around the circle and stated that they were holding hands, forming an unbroken circle from which she could not escape. She then proceeded to enact a scenario in which the abuser did "bad things" to her. After playing out the trauma, she changed the scene. She removed the figures that were holding hands outside the circle, and then had a toy bulldozer erase the pentacle and circle in the sand. When she had finished she said, "The circle is broken." She had changed the play from being helpless and captured within a circle that could not be broken, to play in which the circle was broken. Through this kind of play, clients can slowly reclaim their personal power.

## Emotional Release

The therapeutic process with DID clients requires not only retrieving the content of lost memories, but also working through the emotional affect associated with these memories. When working with DID clients, Putnam (1989) considers abreaction to be inevitable, and valuable when handled therapeutically. Childhood victims of trauma tend to spontaneously engage in post-traumatic play (Gil, 1991) and post-traumatic reenactments of traumatic material (Terr, 1990). Spontaneous abreactions in DID clients are intrusive recall experiences that take the form of flashbacks and dreams. These spontaneous abreactions tend to be uncontrolled and largely out of awareness, often resulting in regressed or psychotic like behaviors. These spontaneous uncontrolled abreactions experienced outside the therapeutic relationship typically do not provide emotional relief. Release play therapy (Levy, 1982) or structured play therapy (Hambidge, 1982) is one approach to accomplishing therapeutic abreaction.

The process of release play therapy is facilitated by including toys in the playroom that could be used to symbolically represent objects that are typically associated with SRA. Some examples are candies, a dagger, crosses, hoods, masks, robes, tombstones, pentagrams, a marble table, demons, devils, etc. These toys could be miniatures that are placed in the sandbox, or dolls and puppets that the clients could role play with while acting out scenarios from rituals. Often the individual is the best source of information regarding the specific items necessary to act out a specific event. All such items may not be necessary since a variety of nondescript toys that can be used symbolically will always be available in the playroom.

The client may spontaneously act out traumatic scenarios, or the therapist may structure the situation by giving the client a selected "plot." With successive enactments of the scenarios, the affect is reported to lessen (Levy, 1982). Eventually a point is reached where affect is minimal. Periods of free play may be interspersed with periods of structured play. When a particular scenario has been played out to its end point, either free play may follow or new structured situations may be introduced (Hambidge, 1982).

Traditional release play therapy does not make use of interpretations or cognitive restructuring. The therapist does not attempt to become involved in the play nor to induce insights. It is considered sufficient for the child to simply abreact the feelings associated with the traumatic events (Levy, 1982).

## Mapping

When working with DID clients, it is important to gather a history of each personality or alter. Braun (1986) stated that at least the following five things should be learned: 1) who—the name for addressing the alter in the future; 2) when—the genesis of the alter and when it has executive control; 3) why—why did the alter first appear and why is it present now; 4) where—where was the patient when the alter first appeared and where the alter fits into the system of personalities; and 5) what—the function of each alter and how he or she aids the system as a whole.

One technique for gathering, organizing, and understanding this data is mapping. Typically, the map is charted or drawn on paper. The playroom, however, offers other possibilities for mapping. One possibility is the sand tray. The client could use a procedure similar to the Lowenfeld World Technique (Lowenfeld, 1950). Other sand tray procedures have since been formulated (C. G. Jung Institute of San Francisco, 1981), and have been specifically applied to work with DID patients by Sachs (1990), Frye (1990), and Sweig (1990, 1991). One of the advantages of mapping in sand instead of on paper is the third dimension. Since personality systems often involve "layers" of alters, three dimensions allow for easier graphic representation of different layers of alters and relationships between alters and systems of alters. In addition to the figures and objects normally used in sand tray techniques, special objects or figures can be added to facilitate mapping for each individual patient. Of course, mapping represents only one possible use of the sand tray for work with DID clients.

Another possibility for mapping in the playroom is the use of clay. Although clay is usually a standard item in the playroom, if used for mapping purposes, a larger than usual quantity may be needed. One client constructed a map of her system made of clay built on top of a serving tray. This made for easy transport of the map to and from therapy sessions. The client had constructed mountains, trees, and other scenery all surrounded by a tall wall with a gate. Tunnels had been dug into the mountains of clay. During a therapy session, the client described to her therapist how certain child alters were being held captive deep within the tunnels in the mountain. By observing the clay map of her system, it was much easier to comprehend the internal situation she was attempting to describe. If the description of her internal system had been verbal, or even just two dimensional on paper, it would have been more difficult to understand some of the nuances of her system. This "playing out" was freeing to the client and she and her therapist were able to use this information as a constructive part of the therapeutic process. Eventually, after some struggle, they were able to retrieve a part of the core personality that had been lost since childhood.

## Increasing Cooperation and Communication among Alters

Alters need to learn both to communicate and cooperate with each other in order for therapy to progress and for full integration to occur. There may be alters that have one way amnesia, and unidirectional co-consciousness with other alters. For example, one child alter may watch and listen and be aware of the activities of other alters, but never send messages or initiate communication with the other alters. Within the safe environment of the playroom, the child may decide to present to the other alters and, possibly, the therapist.

The alters may not be aware of all the other alters within the system. The therapy process becomes a process that is similar to "getting acquainted" with someone new. Often certain alters may despise other alters within the system. Certain alters may have functions that are diametrically opposed to the functions of other alters. There also may be alters that engage in behaviors that are dangerous or even lethal to the body. Yet all the alters must learn to live in and share one body. Obviously, integration is no easy task.

Play, art, and sand therapies offer a way to facilitate communication, cooperation, and acceptance among the alters (Oke & Kanigsberg, 1991; Steckler & Torem, 1991; Sweig, 1990, 1991). Alters may be present and engage in some type of artwork or play activity without ever announcing their presence. In this way, the alters are able to share their memories and experiences. Later, the host personality may not even remember the activity. Therefore, it is important for the therapist to make records of the activity including the name of the alter, if known, the date, and other pertinent details. Artwork can be labeled with this data. Polaroid snapshots of sand tray creations are a useful way to preserve this information, as is videotaping. In this way the various memories can be shared with other alters within the system. When alters observe the creation done by other alters with whom they are not co-conscious, there are often strong emotional reactions. Again, this process is facilitated when the various alters perceive the playroom as a safe place to be.

## Sublimation of Anger

The sublimation of anger is often an important part of the process of play therapy with children. This is equally true in working with DID patients. One can only imagine the depths of the rage that must burn within these victims who have been violated in the most terrible of ways. Play activities are one way in which this intense affect may begin to be ventilated and dissipated. Frye (1991) and Sweig (1990, 1991) have found sand play conductive to the sublimation of anger. The playroom should also include a bop bag, dart guns, and other toys that will allow for expressions of anger. This issue is one in which play offers unique advantages over verbal techniques. Physical activities allow for kinetic dissipation of energy and the playroom provides safe objects onto which anger may be displaced. Anger that has been repressed can be safely expressed with full force through the process of symbolic play since what is being expressed and the recipient of the expression are characters and expressions in a play story. This initial symbolic release seems to be essential in most cases to the process of being able to express such feelings more directly at a later date.

## Accept Each Alter

When working with DID clients, it is important to establish a positive, therapeutic relationship with each alter. Other writers (Friesen, 1991) have also emphasized the importance of accepting each alter. Conveying a sense of warmth, acceptance, and unconditional positive regard can be particularly challenging with certain "malevolent" alters (Steckler & Torem, 1991). Often, certain alters have been created to express anger or rage, or have been given suicidal or homicidal functions. Perhaps, however, these are the personalities most in need of acceptance and positive regard. They have often experienced rejection, discounting, or minimization of their feelings, not only by others in the world, but often by other alters within their own system. Yet, they all have served some function within the system and deserve credit for having performed their function. Experience has shown that these "malevolent" alters can often become powerful allies in the process of integration.

In keeping with these principles of acceptance, it seems most logical to allow child alters to play when they present. Play is often the easiest way to establish rapport with children because play is the most natural thing children do. Often, DID clients state that they were never allowed nor learned how to play. These deprived child alters should be afforded the opportunity to experience the normal play activities of childhood. By this it is not meant that they should play so that memories can be retrieved or for other "therapeutic" reasons (although therapy is still very important). Rather, they should be able just to play for the experience of play. To play is the essence of joy for children and this hope of joy should be extended to all the child alters who were not able to experience it in their chronological childhood, but for whom it is perhaps not too late.

## SUMMARY

It is easy to envision a scenario in which much of the therapy with an DID client could be conducted within the environs of the playroom. Any alter that so wished could present and make use of the materials within the playroom. Alters that wished to only talk could certainly do so, since there is nothing in the playroom that prohibits verbal interactions. Meeting in the playroom would give an implicit message that it is permissible for child alters to come forth and have time for their work. It may be that alters can more easily work through their issues prior to integration, although it can certainly be addressed after integration also.

Although the focus of this chapter has been on the perspective of working with the child alters of adult patients, the concepts would generally apply to working with children who are diagnosed as DID. There is an obvious and increasing interest in this area across the helping professions. McMahon and Fagan (1993) described play therapy with sixty children diagnosed with DID. At the 1992 International Conference on Multiple Personality/Dissociative States (DID) there were at least eight papers presented that dealt specifically with childhood DID.

# REFERENCES

American Psychiatric Association. (1994). *Diagnostic and statistical manual of mental disorders* (4th ed.). Washington, DC: Author.

Braun, B .G. (1986). Issues in the psychotherapy of multiple personality disorder. In B. G. Braun (Ed.), *Treatment of multiple personality disorder* (pp. 3–28). Washington, DC: American Psychiatric Press.

Braun, B. G. (1990). Multiple personality disorder: An overview. *The American Journal of Occupational Therapy, 44*(1), pp. 971–976.

Braun, B. G., & Sachs, R. S. (1985). The development of multiple personality disorder: Predisposing, precipitating and perpetuating factors. In R. P. Kluft (Ed.), *Childhood antecedents of multiple personality* (pp. 38–64). Washington, DC: American Psychiatric Press.

C. G. Jung Institute of San Francisco. (1981). *Sandplay studies: Origins, theory and practice.* San Francisco: Author.

Coggin, J. E., & Coggin, E. B. (1979). When adult therapists work with children: Differential treatment considerations. *Professional Psychology, 10*(3), 330–337.

Friesen, J. G. (1991). *Uncovering the mystery of MPD.* San Bernadino, CA: Heres Life Publishers.

Frye, B. (1990). Art and multiple personality disorder: An expressive framework for occupational therapy. *The American Journal of Occupational Therapy , 44*(11), 1013–1022.

Frye, B. (1991). Mastery in miniature: The use of the sand tray as an expressive modality. In B. G. Braun (Ed.), *Dissociative Disorders: Proceedings of the 8th International Conference on Multiple Personality/Dissociative States* (p. 35). Chicago: Rush University.

Gil, E. (1991). *The healing power of play: Working with abused children.* New York: Guilford Press.

Goodwin, J. (1985). Credibility problems in multiple personality disorder patients and abused children. In R. P. Kluft (Ed.), *Childhood antecedents of multiple personality* (pp. 2–16). Washington, DC: American Psychiatric Press.

Graham-Costain, V., & Gould, C. (1990). The use of play therapy with child and adult survivors of ritual abuse. In B. G. Braun (Ed.), *Dissociative Disorders: Proceedings of the 7th International Conference on Multiple Personality / Dissociative States* (p. 130). Chicago: Rush University.

Hambridge, G. (1982). Structured play therapy. In G. L. Landreth (Ed.), *Play Therapy: Dynamics of the process of counseling with children* (pp. 105–119). Springfield, IL: Thomas.

Kluft, R. P. (1984). Multiple personality in childhood. *Psychiatric Clinics of North America, 7*, 121–134.

Kluft, R. P. (1985). Childhood multiple personality disorder: Predictors, clinical findings, and treatment results. In R. P. Kluft (Ed.), *Childhood antecedents of multiple personality* (pp. 167–196). Washington, DC: American Psychiatric Press.

Landreth, G. (1991). *Play therapy: The art of the relationship.* Muncie, IN: Accelerated Development Press.

Levy, D. (1982). Trends in therapy. Release therapy. In G. L. Landreth (Ed.), *Play therapy: Dynamics of the process of counseling with children* (pp. 92–104). Springfield, IL: Thomas.

Lowenfeld, M. (1950). The nature and use of the Lowenfeld world technique in work with children and adults. *Journal of Psychology, 30*, 325–331.

Mann, E., & McDermott, J. J. (1983). Play therapy for victims of child abuse and neglect. In C. Schaefer & K. O'Connor (Eds.), *Handbook of play therapy* (pp. 283–307). New York : John Wiley & Sons.

McMahon, P. P., & Fagan, J. (1993). Play therapy with children with multiple personality disorder. In R. P. Kluft and C. G. Fine (Eds.). *Clinical perspectives on multiple personality disorder* (pp. 253–276). Washington, DC: American Psychiatric Press.

Oke, S., & Kanigsberg, E. (1991). Occupational therapy in the treatment of individuals with multiple personality disorder. *Canadian Journal of Occupational Therapy, 58*(5), 234–240.

Putnam, F. (1989). *Diagnosis and treatment of multiple personality disorder.* New York: Guilford Press.

Ross, C. (1991). Epidemiology of multiple personality disorder and dissociation. *Psychiatric Clinics of North America, 14*(3), 502–515.

Sachs, R. (1990). The sand tray technique in the treatment of patients with dissociative disorders: Recommendations for occupational therapists. *The American Journal of Occupational Therapy, 44*(1), 1045–1047.

Steckler, J. T., & Torem, M. S. (1991). The successful integration of malevolent alter ego states: Transcendence versus transformation: Art anticipates life. In B. G. Braun (Ed.), *Dissociative Disorders: Proceedings of the 8th International Conference on Multiple Personality/Dissociative States* (p. 64). Chicago: Rush University.

Sweig, T. (1990). The clinical underworld and play with survivors of trauma. In B. G. Braun (Ed.), *Dissociative Disorders: Proceedings of the 7th International Conference on Multiple Personality/Dissociative States* (p. 91). Chicago: Rush University.

Sweig, T. (1991). The persistence of memory: Sand play with multiple personality and dissociation. In B. G. Braun (Ed.), *Dissociative Disorders: Proceedings of the 8th International Conference on Multiple Personality/Dissociative States* (p. 36). Chicago: Rush University.

Terr, L. (1990). *Too scared to cry: Psychic trauma in childhood.* New York: Basic Books.

Waldschmidt, C., Graham-Costain, V., & Gould, C. (1991). *Memory association in play therapy with children with multiple personality disorder.* Paper presented at the 8th International Conference on Multiple Personality/Dissociative States, Chicago: Rush University.

# 21

# Play Therapy
# with the Elderly

## PAT LEDYARD HAYNES

According to Myers (1989) the fastest growing population in the United States is the group of individuals over 65 years of age. As the number of older persons increases, so does the need to provide mental health services for this population.

This chapter describes the use of play therapy with the elderly as a modality for therapeutic change. Therapists have an obligation to themselves, as well as to their adult clients, to understand the adults' experiences of aging before appropriate involvement in therapy can take place (Myers & Schwiebert, 1996; Toseland, 1995). Although older adults share many of the same psychological and physiological concerns, gerontologists warn practitioners not to generalize characteristics to all older adults but to accept each person as an individual with needs to be met (Myers, Loesch, & Sweeney, 1991; Toseland, 1995).

## GERIATRIC CONCERNS

A review of the literature revealed numerous concerns of older adults. Havighurst (1972) listed six developmental tasks to be accomplished in old age: (a) adjusting to decreasing physical strength and health, (b) adjusting to retirement and reduced income, (c) adjusting to the death of a spouse, (d) establishing an explicit affiliation with one's age group, (e) adjusting and adapting social roles in a flexible way, and (f) establishing satisfactory physical living arrangements. Pulvino and Colangelo (1980) pointed out major concerns of the elderly such as (a) death of friends, (b) singular affiliation within an age group of elders, (c) caring for an aged body, (d) making new friends, (e) treating grown children as adults, and (f) facing one's own mortality and death.

Corey and Corey (1996) stated that loneliness, fear, and hopelessness were frequently evident with this population. Corey (1990) suggested that the elderly experience isolation along with feelings of being unproductive, unneeded, and unwanted by society. Link (1997) listed the following issues facing the elderly: (a) coping with loss, (b) decline in independence, (c) depression, (d) anxiety, (e) lack of relatedness, (f) varying degrees of cognitive functioning, (g) suffering from thought disorders, (h) memory deficits, and (i) other limitations to communication or understanding. Myers (1989) described those over the age of 76 as being considered the "old-old," who suffer from decreased overall functioning and having health problems. Knight (1996) stated that older adults suffer from depression, anxiety disorders, isolation, grief, anger, sexual concerns, and somatic complaints.

Lawson and Hughes (1980) listed additional barriers encountered by the elderly: (a) reduced or insufficient income, (b) lack of transportation, (c) inadequate or substandard housing, (d) crime victimization, (e) inadequate food and poor nutrition, (f) movement to a home against one's will, (g) idleness, (h) apathy, and (i) indifference to their problems on the part of the public and, sometimes, their own families.

In view of the wide range of geriatric concerns, the challenge seems to be to discover innovative ways in which to reach this population to help them adjust to their environment with greater life satisfaction. For this reason, a closer examination of how play therapy might be used with a diverse population such as the elderly will be explored.

## DEFINITION OF PLAY THERAPY

Landreth (1991) defined play therapy as

> A dynamic interpersonal relationship between a child and a therapist trained in play therapy procedures who provides selected play materials and facilitates the development of a safe relationship for the child to fully express and explore self (feelings, thoughts, experiences, and behaviors) through the child's natural medium of communication, play. (p. 14)

The play therapist creates a safe environment in which children feel free to express the way they feel with the aid of play materials. The cognitive development of children limits their ability to express verbally how they feel. Since play is their natural medium of expression, children are able to demonstrate through play their strongest emotions in a way that is safe and instrumental in facilitating a solution or developing coping strategies that further growth and development. According to Landreth and Sweeney (1997), the play therapist's objective is "to relate to the child in ways that will release the child's inner directional, constructive, forward-moving, creative, self-healing power" (p. 17).

Play therapy was defined by the International Association of Play Therapy (API) as "the systematic use of a theoretical model to establish an interpersonal process wherein trained play therapists use the therapeutic powers of play to help clients prevent or resolve psychosocial difficulties and achieve optimal growth and development" (APT, 1999, p. 7). With this definition, play therapy can be expanded from children to other populations, such as adults and the elderly.

Even though there is limited research about the use of play therapy with adults, Landreth (1991) stated that there was a growing interest. He further acknowledged that "through play the adult has a conversation with self that is a very personal experience because direct involvement is called for" (Landreth, 1991, p. 36).

Frey (1994) listed adult clients for whom play therapy would be an especially effective treatment modality. Among those included are adults who are resistant to therapy and those who are verbally deficient in their ability to describe a problem. According to Frey (1994) play therapy with adults can be used to (a) diagnose, (b) break through the defense of clients, (c) help clients who find it difficult to verbalize their concerns, (d) relieve tension, and (e) transcend communication barriers.

## PLAY THERAPY WITH THE ELDERLY

Considering the varying degrees of cognitive functioning and limitations to communication that the elderly so often experience, play therapy seems to be an approach that would indeed be worth exploring. Elderly individuals who have difficulty expressing their feelings may find play therapy to be a modality in which no words are necessary. Play therapy may also serve as a springboard to help facilitate the resistant elderly to gain access to emotions, thoughts, or experiences so often concealed. In addition, play therapy can provide an atmosphere and environment in which the elderly feel they are accepted and understood in a time of their life when they are faced with extreme psychological and physiological concerns. In using play therapy, the therapist would typically look for various outcome results, such as (a) decreased depression, (b) less isolation, (c) increased cognitive responses, and (d) an overall increase in life satisfaction.

## NURSING HOME PLAY THERAPY PROJECT

The therapists in this project were enrolled in a master's program, where they were trained in child-centered play therapy, having taken Basic Play Therapy and Advanced Play Therapy. They received individual supervision each week for the play therapy sessions conducted in the nursing home. These sessions were audiotaped or videotaped for supervision purposes. All of the therapists had at least one year's experience working with children using child-centered play therapy.

The nursing home residents who participated in this project were selected by the director and social worker of the nursing home. The residents selected were those individuals who were perceived to have the greatest need of therapy, residents who would consent to therapy, and whose families would agree to the therapy. Some of the residents selected were confined to their beds or wheelchairs, one was totally blind, another had a low IQ, and some were cognitively impaired. Two of the residents were dropped after several sessions when it was determined they were not appropriate for this type of therapy. The remaining clients all appeared to show some improvement following the outcome of therapy.

The therapists and their supervisor met the nursing home staff and families of the residents prior to the beginning sessions. At this time, they discussed how the sessions would be conducted, addressed any questions, and obtained written consent for the sessions. There were ten female and three male participants ranging in ages from 59 years to 89 years. Three of the therapists had three resident participants in play therapy, while the fourth therapist had four resident participants.

The therapists met with their clients for 45-minute individual play therapy sessions once or twice a week for six to ten sessions. Portable play therapy kits were set up in an activity/dining room or transported to the patients' rooms. Toys were selected that could be used to express a wide range of feelings and toys that could be used to explore real-life experiences, such as a medical kit. Landreth (1991) listed the minimal requirements of toys for conducting a play therapy session and that could be easily transported in a tote bag. This kit would include crayons, paper, baby bottles, dolls, dart gun, toy soldiers, play dishes, cars and trucks, balls, telephones, and a doll family, to name a few.

## INTRODUCTION TO CASE STUDIES

The following case studies were the author's clients. Most of the sessions were conducted in an activity room where the toys were displayed on a physical therapy table around a mat designed as a small town. The table was easily accessed by a wheelchair, and the toys could be comfortably reached. Landreth (1991) suggested a dollhouse, a portable sand tray, paints, and BoBo would be facilitative materials for adults, so these materials were included. An additional category of reminiscent objects included: a small wooden jewelry chest that contained men's and women's jewelry, Christmas ornaments, cards, ribbons, bows, a camera, old framed baby pictures, and a number of other items that could be used by nursing home residents to represent something about themselves. If the client was confined to bed or elected not to go to the activity room, the session for that week was held in the client's room or where the client specified. If clients preferred to have a session in which they talked, that was acknowledged and the session was conducted in that manner.

# CASE STUDIES

## Buffalo Bill

Bill was eighty-five years old and had been in the nursing home for over a year. He isolated himself from the other patients as much as possible. On his good days, he sat in his wheelchair in front of his television, leaving his room only to go to the cafeteria to eat. Some days he refused to get out of bed, and stared at the television hour after hour. Bill had two sons and three grandchildren who visited infrequently, leaving him with little contact with the outside world. He had owned a farm, which he had sold before moving into the nursing home. He made no mention of his spouse.

When I arrived for my first session with Bill, I found him in bed. I introduced myself and told Bill that I was a play therapist and would like for him to see my toys. He listened intently to me and was probably thinking, "What the hell!" as I informed him about my work with children. I told him I would appreciate his help in studying how toys could be used to work with other populations. He replied, "I'll need to think about that! I do remember now talking to Janice, the social worker, about something to do with playing with toys." He seemed hesitant about participating but shook my hand and told me, "You can call me Buffalo Bill. Do you remember him?"

I responded, "Sure, I watched Buffalo Bill. He was one of my favorites! Bill, I can tell you are a bit hesitant to play with the toys, but I would love to get to know you better and hope that you will consider it."

Bill was in his wheelchair when I arrived for our next session. When I asked him if he wanted to go to the activity room with me, he said with fear in his eyes, "I really must think about that."

"You seem to be worried about doing something that appears different to you," I replied.

With a nurse aide's encouragement, Bill agreed to go to the activity room with me. He told the aide, "I just might stay awhile. This looks mighty interesting after all!" When he surveyed the table with the toys displayed, he remarked, "Wow, you have a lot of stuff here! I have never seen so much stuff. I have three children. One girl in kindergarten and two boys ages 7 and 8."

I replied, "You are surprised. It makes you think of your children." He did not touch anything, but continued to wheel his chair around the table slowly taking in the display of toys. I tracked Bill by saying, "You are just looking at everything, not sure what you want to do." When I took him back to his room, he smiled and remarked as he shook my hand, "I'll see you next week. You come back, you hear?" The ice had been broken, and Bill was at least showing interest in working with me.

When I arrived for the third session Bill was waiting in his wheelchair, but again was fearful of going to the activity room with me. With the assistance of the aide once again, he agreed to go. He picked a bat and ball and immediately directed me to pitch it to him. "You know what you want to do, and you would like for me to throw the ball so you can hit it," I commented. After many attempts in which he missed the ball, he spotted the football and involved me in playing catch. He began to talk about his sons and how he had played ball with them when they were children. "You are remembering times you played with your sons. It brings back pleasant memories. You seem really pleased about that!" This session, he smiled and laughed easily. He showed greater awareness as he talked about his children and details of his past. Before I left, I told Bill I would be out of town the following week.

When I arrived at his room two weeks later, Bill spoke loudly, "Where in the hell have you been?"

"You're upset with me for not coming last week," I replied. He had forgotten that I had told him I would be out of town for a week. Still a little angry with me, he said he did not think he wanted to go to the activity room this time. With the aide's persuasion, he did go. He found the bat and ball and played with very little enthusiasm. He spotted a rubber-band gun and remarked, "I had one of these when I was a kid." He had me line up some wooden people for target shooting. "You know exactly what you want to do," I tracked. His hands were crippled with arthritis, and without my assistance he could not load the rubber band on the gun. With great precision and accuracy, Bill aimed at the wooden people, showing great pleasure as they dropped. The rest of the session he aimed and shot as he talked about how he had hunted squirrels and then barbecued or fried them when he got home. "This really brings back some memories," he told me.

"You really enjoyed yourself!" I replied. Bill was actively playing and reminiscing.

When I walked into his room for our fifth session, Bill once again showed fear in his eyes. I visited with him for a few minutes before he said, "Well, let's go!"

"You're ready this week," I replied.

He found a Nerf dart gun, and aimed and hit the wooden people with a great deal of accuracy. Bill laughed and expressed alternating emotions from excitement to disappointment when he hit or missed. I tracked his expressions as he continued to shoot. When I commented that he appeared to be getting tired, he said, "No, let's do it some more!"

"You would like to stay awhile longer. You have found something you really enjoy doing," I replied. On the way back to his room, I told him I would see him the next week. He responded by saying, "If you can remember to come!" "You're still a little angry with me for not coming last week," I commented. I assured him I would come back. That afternoon when I passed his room, I noticed Bill slumped over in his wheelchair. Seemingly, he had only been really awake during the time he was in the activity room in our session.

When I arrived for our sixth session, Bill was in bed. He said, "I'm resting, but I'm glad you came to see me." I asked him to tell me about his week. He said, "I played football with my son. I'm not sure which one of us won. Pat, I'm not sure about next week."

"Bill, you seemed worried about something," I responded.

He replied, "I just don't feel so good." Bill called me by my name this week for the first time. He appeared frail and despondent.

For the seventh session Bill was in the hall sitting in his wheelchair visiting with others in the hall. He said, "I don't want to go anywhere today."

"Would you like for me to join you here?" I questioned.

"Sure, why not!" he replied. So I sat in a chair next to him and listened. He told me, "I worked all week with my sons. We picked cotton and corn all week. Hell, I get more sunshine than anyone!" He was quite animated and smiled frequently. Bill had finally ventured into the hall to socialize with other patients. Before I left, I told Bill that our last session would be the following week.

During my sessions with Bill, there were times when he appeared to forget who I was, how old his children were, and even how old he was. He isolated himself from the other residents. Our sessions appeared to help him to move out of himself and join the other residents. As our sessions progressed, Bill began to show less fear and showed he trusted me as well as those in the nursing home. By playing with the toys, Bill was able to relax and feel at ease. He began to reminisce about doing things in the past and sharing with me details of his life. He appeared less depressive and more cognitively alert. It was a big step for Bill to want to be in the hall with the other residents and socialize. He became more aware of his surroundings.

## Valentine Queen

Hannah was eighty-two years old. She moved into the nursing home the same time her brother did when he had a severe stroke and they could no longer care for one another. Hannah never married and had lived with her brother in their family home since childhood. She was the oldest of twelve children and extremely devoted to her brother. Hannah was quite social with an optimistic outlook, but terribly distressed about her brother. Hannah had always been active in her church and had deep spiritual values. She had close contact with her family and still spent holidays with them. Hannah was quite active and walked daily down the halls of the nursing home for exercise and visited while encouraging others.

When I arrived at the nursing home for my first session with Hannah, I went to her room in search of her. I found her bed made with a large doll perched on a pillow. I asked at the nurse's station where I might find Hannah. "Go look in the lobby," the nurse replied. "You will see a whole group of ladies there. Ask which one is the new Valentine Queen."

Hannah looked up from the quiet group with a smile on her face when I questioned, "Which one of you is the new Valentine Queen?" She said, "I am!"

I introduced myself and invited her to come talk with me. I explained to her about play therapy, my work with children, and my attempt to further explore the use of toys with other populations. She was resistant at first. She questioned, "What do you do? You play with toys? You want me to play with toys, too? Why would I want to do that?"

I asked her to tell me about her family. She described her family with great detail. By the time our session was over, she said, "Honey, I would love to play with your toys. We don't do anything on Saturday except watch movies, and I don't want to do that." She smiled with warmth in her eyes and held my hand as I told her I would see her the next week at the same time.

The second session was Hannah's first in the activity room with the toys. She picked up almost every toy and remarked about each one as she turned it over in her hands. She seemed to especially enjoy the dolls and the hand puppets, talking to them while she kissed each one. When she discovered the Christmas box, she recalled many Christmases past, telling me about how her family had spent these special times together. "That really brings back wonderful times you have spent with your family," I remarked.

Hannah disclosed to me that the social worker had talked to her. She sadly told me, "The social worker wants me to tell my brother that it is okay for him to go. She thinks that my brother is suffering and won't die because he lives just for me."

"That really upsets you," I commented.

"It sure does! But, now, every time I go to his room, I tell him how nice it will be in heaven where he can walk and talk like he used to do," she replied. She told me, also, that the week before she had gone to his room with a friend, and she just went to pieces.

"You are really distressed. It is hard for you to accept that the brother you love so dearly is so very ill and may not be with you much longer," I commented. She was struggling with the pain she felt concerning the near death of her brother.

During our third session, Hannah played with the dolls. She picked one up several times, kissing it and remarking how cute it was. She talked about her brother and another conversation she had had with the social worker about telling her brother good-bye. Hannah talked about the illnesses she had during her life, including colon and breast cancer, triple-bypass surgery, and a hysterectomy. "I'm so glad I'm still here!" she exclaimed.

"Even though there is so much pain, you are glad you are still here to be with the ones you love," I remarked.

During the previous week she talked about the death of a 99-year-old woman who had lived in the nursing home. She said, "Others told me I should be happy she was going to a special place where there was no more pain. But, it was hard for me to feel any happiness because I miss her."

"You think you should feel happy, but you are really sad," I replied as her tears began to fall.

She shared with me pictures of being crowned Valentine Queen. "That was a wonderful day for you. You really looked happy," I responded to her picture. She gave me a hug before I left.

When I arrived for our fourth session, I found Hannah in her room. She said, "Oh, honey, I forgot you were coming. I don't feel so good today. It's indigestion or something." I stayed in her room this session. She talked about her week and her concerns for her brother. She also talked about her plans for Easter Sunday. She described with great detail how her family had a reunion each year at Easter, where at least one hundred relatives gathered at their home place. She had gone to a wedding the week before and wanted me to know all about it. As our session came to a close, she said, "You know, I feel better now." She smiled and remarked, "You are what I needed. I don't hurt any more. I don't want to get down. Others on my floor who get down, they have to move to the other side, where the sick ones live." As I was leaving, Hannah said, "Honey, I love you. I'll see you next week." I saw her later that afternoon dressed and in the lobby with her friends.

For the fifth session, Hannah was waiting for me at the nurse's station. She talked all the way to the activity room, which was some distance from her room. She had gotten new dentures the week before and was very proud of them even though they did not fit very well. I had brought a doll with me this session that was similar to one she had in her room. She held it close the whole session and at one point she said, "My brother gave me my doll like this one." The doll seemed to help her reflect about eventful times she had shared with her brother. As we were returning to her room, she said, "Can we go visit my brother? I want you to meet him."

We walked the long hallway to her brother's room. As she approached his bed, her brother smiled, but he did not speak. Tears came to her eyes while we were there, and she told me how upset it made her to see him hurting. As I put my arms around her shoulders, I commented softly, "You love him very much."

After spending some time in her brother's room, I walked her back to her room. She expressed her gratitude to me for going with her to her brother's room. I told her, "I can see how much you love your brother, and how it hurts you to see him in such pain. I'm glad that you can share this with me." I told her I would return the next Saturday. She said, "You are such a good friend to me." She gave me a hug and reminded me she would be out of town with her family for Easter.

Hannah was in her brother's room for the sixth session. One of her sisters was there also. They told me all about their family. Her brother was alert and smiled while playing an arm game with her sister. Hannah remarked that her teeth were bothering her so she was not wearing them. She complained to her sister about getting them fixed. She was feeling good about her brother's health this week. She seemed to think that he was improving and did not want to believe he would die soon.

The seventh and final session, I found Hannah in bed. Her brother had died during the week. Her brother's death was extremely upsetting to her, and she wanted to talk about him. She also told me that she had not been feeling well.

I visited Hannah twice after our sessions had ended. She was still struggling with the loss of her brother, but was joining the activities with the other residents once again. She appeared to have aged and was withdrawn. However, each time she saw me, she would smile with warmth in her eyes.

The play therapy sessions appeared to be beneficial to Hannah because it was a time when she was free to express her feelings in an environment where she was being heard. It was a time when she felt that she did not have to pretend to be optimistic. When Hannah played with the toys, she expressed her deepest feelings until she became apprehensive. She then reverted back to a place where her comfortable level existed. The death of Hannah's brother during this time was an especially difficult time for her. Her play therapy sessions became a time when she was able to hold onto memories that were so important to her.

## Martha

Martha was fifty-eight years old with an IQ of 70. Her brother had been her principal caretaker. After his death the previous year, she had moved into the nursing home. She lacked social skills and isolated herself from the other residents. Her sister-in-law, nieces, and nephew visited with her often.

Martha readily agreed to walk to the activity room during our first session. She walked very slowly, and when we passed other residents, she boldly announced, "I'm going to play with the toys!" She picked up every toy and identified it. When she found the "diamond" ring she let me know she really liked it. She placed it on her hand and raised it high in the air as if to admire it. She remarked, "I wear a size 9. It's just my style." She gestured to me that she wanted to keep the ring. "You really like that. It will be there next week when I return," I commented. When we returned to her room, she showed me her room and played her keyboard. She said, "I took lessons for many years when I was a child."

"You are really pleased and enjoy playing for me," I commented. She gave me her phone number and said, "I'll see you next week."

Martha was waiting outside her door for me when I arrived for our second session. She said, "I was afraid you weren't coming."

"You were really looking forward to our session," I replied. She wanted to hold my hand as we walked to the activity room. She remarked as she took a seat, "I'm ready." She noticed that the jewelry box was open this week. She had struggled last week to open it. She took out each item and placed it on the table. She neatly placed all of the items back in the box just as she had found them. She mentioned the ring that she liked, but left it in the box this time.

During this session she drew me a picture. The picture consisted of a square, which she called a house. In front of the box, she shaded a green space, which she named the yard. She drew a boy by copying a wooden boy doll on the table. She named him Edward, after her nephew. As she drew, Martha talked about her house and the things she and Edward used to do together. On our way back to her room, she wanted to hold my hand once again. I told her I would be back in two weeks. She said, "Pat, I trust you."

For the third session, I found Martha in front of the nurse's station eating popcorn. She was getting out of her room and spending time with the other residents. Before our sessions began, Martha was not socializing and came out of her room only for planned activities and meals. She held my hand all the way to the activity room. She said, "My neighbor moved, and I will miss her. She moved to the other end. She is sick." On our way back from our session, she wanted to find her former neighbor. When we did locate her, the other resident did not recognize Martha. "It's okay, Gladys," she told her. She stopped to talk to several others on the way back to her room.

For the fourth session, Martha was in her room. She wanted to show me a dress she had purchased to wear to church. Her niece was coming on Sunday to take her there. The trip to the activity room was a slow walk during which she wanted to stop and talk to residents along the way. When we got to the activity room, she played with the jewelry box for most of the session. She took every item out, named it, and then placed it back in the box when finished. She said, "I'm going to miss you when you move away. You are a nice lady."

I commented, "You are thinking about our times together. You're a little sad." She talked about her trip to a restaurant and how much fun she had. She played with the music sticks, tapping them in rhythm. She showed me how much she enjoyed music and instructed me on how to play the sticks. When she found a musical recorder, she recalled the titles as she played the tunes. When it was time to leave the activity room, she said, "Do we have to go?"

"You're disappointed that it is time to leave," I remarked.

The fifth session was a celebration of Martha's birthday. I brought her a flower and a videotape of a TV movie. We walked through the courtyard, and she recalled her house in the country. When we passed the piano in the dining room, I asked her if she would like to play. She sat down and asked me, "What would you like to hear?" When residents walked by, she was a bit embarrassed, but smiled and continued to play. This became something she wanted to do each week on the way to our sessions. In the play therapy area, the jewelry box was the first thing she looked at again. Spotting a dart gun, she began shooting and laughing as the dart flew around the room. "What a birthday!" she exclaimed.

"This was a special day for you. You are really happy," I replied.

The piano was the first on the agenda for the sixth session. She was so proud of being able to play. Whenever people came into the room, she smiled and spoke to them. She swayed to the music as the sounds filled the room. During our session in the activity room, she inspected the jewelry box once again, finding the "diamond" ring. She remarked, "It can't be real. I have some diamonds, but mine are real."

"You know it isn't real, but you can pretend," I replied.

When we returned to her room, she stopped to tell several residents that she had played the piano. They did not know she could play. She danced and smiled brightly as she talked with them. She reached out to hold my hand as we walked slowly to her room.

When I arrived for our seventh session, Martha's niece was in the room. I stayed in the room with them. She told her niece, as she smiled mischievously, "I play with toy snakes." She then went on to tell several snake stories. She held my hand the whole time I was there. I told her before I left that we had only one more session.

At our last session, Martha wanted to talk about Hannah's brother dying. From there, she began talking about the death of her brother. Previously, the social worker had told me that Martha would not talk about her brother. Even this time, when she became uncomfortable, Martha abruptly changed the subject to a safe area where she did not hurt so badly. She told me that she was planning a trip home to play her piano. Before I left, she expressed how much she enjoyed our sessions and how much she loved me.

During our sessions, Martha began to socialize with the other residents and was less isolated. Her self-esteem was boosted as she found others enjoyed her music and cared about her. During our play therapy sessions, Martha showed me that she was feeling more at ease by her easy smile and her relaxed body language. She learned to trust me and herself, thereby freeing emotions that had been repressed for many years. She talked about the death of her brother and other painful experiences. Her adjustment at the nursing home improved as she was able to take a more active part in the activities.

## CONCLUSIONS AND LIMITATIONS

The therapist, a social worker, staff members, and the elderly participants reported a number of benefits resulting from play therapy with the residents of the nursing home. Clients became more active, less isolated, and more appropriate in their social interactions. Clients who had hesitated to leave their rooms began to join others in the halls and participated in the social activities. Reduced forgetfulness and increased mental sharpness were reported. Residents who previously did not remember appointments or their therapist's name now responded differently by being prepared for their appointments and calling the therapist by her name. Depression appeared to decrease and there seemed to be an increase in self-esteem. Participants appeared to be happier and less withdrawn. Clients showed interest in attempting to resolve issues, such as loss of loved ones, isolation, lack of control over life situations, loneliness, and fears. These clients were now able to talk about issues they had once thought they had to keep to themselves, thereby finding solutions and discovering others ways of doing things.

Although the therapists found play therapy with this population to be beneficial, there were limitations to this project. Few references were found in the literature that mentioned using play therapy with the elderly; therefore, little information was available to draw on for direction in this project. Some of the clients were not able to participate due to extreme health concerns and were forced to drop out of the project. Coordination with the staff and administrators of the nursing home and the therapists could have been better organized. The therapists found play therapy difficult to sustain because of the variations in the setting, schedules, and in the daily functioning of the client population. By not having a permanent therapy room, confidentiality between client and therapist could not be guaranteed. This could have become a substantial problem and certainly limited the therapeutic process.

Suggestions for future work using play therapy with the elderly include (a) therapists being more involved in the selection of clients, including more awareness of their medical and family history, (b) more feedback from family and staff members, (c) continuing education for staff and families, and (d) a permanent therapy room with materials set up and privacy guaranteed.

## REFERENCES

Association for Play Therapy, Inc. (1999, March). *Copy Editor, 18*(1), 7.

Corey, G. (1990). *Theory and practice of group counseling* (3rd ed.). Pacific Grove, CA: Brooks/Cole.

Corey, M. S., & Corey, G. (1996). *Groups: Process and practice* (5th ed.). Pacific Grove, CA: Brooks/Cole.

Frey, D. E. (1994). The use of play therapy with adults. In K. J. O'Connor & C. E. Schaeffer (Eds.), *Handbook of play therapy: Vol. 2. Advances and innovations* (pp. 189–205). New York: John Wiley & Sons.

Havighurst, R. J. (1972). *Developmental tasks and education*. New York: David McKay.

Knight, B. G. (1996). *Psychotherapy with older adults* (2nd ed.). Thousand Oaks, CA: Sage.

Landreth, G. L. (1991). *Play therapy: The art of the relationship*. Muncie, IN: Accelerated Development.

Landreth, G. L., & Sweeney, D. S. (1997). Child-centered play therapy. In K. J. O'Connor & L. M. Braverman (Eds.), *Play therapy: Theory and practice a comparative presentation* (pp. 17–45). New York: John Wiley & Sons.

Lawson, G., & Hughes, B. (1980). Some considerations for the training of counselors who work with the elderly. *Counseling and Values, 24*(3), 204–208.

Link, A. L. (1997). *Group work with elders: 50 therapeutic exercises for reminiscence, validation and remotivation*. Sarasota, FL: Professional Resource Press.

Myers, J. (1989). *Adult children and aging parents*. Alexandria, VA: American Association of Counseling and Development.

Myers, J. E., & Schwiebert, V. L. (1996). *Competencies for gerontological counseling*. Alexandria, VA: American Counseling Association.

Myers, J., Loesch, L. D., & Sweeney, T. J. (1991). Trends in gerontological counselor preparation. *Counselor Education and Supervision, 30*, 194–204.

Pulvino, C. J., & Colangelo, N. (1980). Counseling the elderly: A developmental perspective. *Counseling and Values, 24*(3), 130–147.

Toseland, R. W. (1995). *Group work with the elderly and family caregivers*. New York: Springer.

# 22

# Have Toys—Will Travel

## A Traveling Play Therapist in the School Setting

BRENDA NIEL
GARRY L. LANDRETH

*T*he large number of mental health professionals requesting registered status through the International Association for Play Therapy evidences the growing, widespread acceptance of play therapy. With an understanding of play as "the natural and comfortable medium of expression for children" (Landreth, 1983, pp. 200–201), it is only natural to take this form of therapeutic intervention to the one place where children spend the majority of their time, the schools.

## RATIONALE FOR PLAY THERAPY
## IN THE SCHOOL SETTING

As early as 1947, Axline (1947) suggested teaching the principles of play therapy to teachers, which if applied to classroom relationships, might make the process of education more effective. Since that time, numerous articles have been written supporting elementary school counselors' use of play therapy as a component of their counseling programs (Bishop, 1971; Ross, 1972, Landreth, 1977, 1983, 1987, 1991). Play therapy in the schools, as an adjunct to current counseling programs, is a logical extension of this therapeutic dimension.

The primary reason for taking play therapy to the elementary school setting is the ultimate benefit this intervention brings to all aspects of the child's life. The counselor meets the child in the child's familiar school environment, at a time which best suits the child's schedule. No other setting allows the counselor such accessibility to the child as well as to all of the important individuals in the child's life.

According to Landreth (1993), "Child-centered play therapy can be used effectively by elementary school counselors to aid change and growth in a variety of developmental problem areas experienced by children" (p. 28). Fortunately, many school counselors are aware of the benefits of play therapy. Unfortunately, they do not always have enough time in their busy schedules to allow individual thirty-minute blocks of time for the many children needing this specialized help. Some may not have had training in play therapy. A viable solution to this problem could be a trained play therapist that is completing a university internship in the schools or a play therapist in private practice that becomes a traveling play therapist serving several elementary schools. The following account is one play therapist's experience as a traveling play therapist.

## FIRST THINGS FIRST: HOW TO GET STARTED

The play therapist devised a plan of action to get the play therapy program started. A local university professor helped in that he set up the introduction of the play therapist and the identified school district's Director of Guidance. A letter from the play therapist was sent to the director briefly describing the plan.

The director of guidance reported she would be happy to present the plan to her elementary school counselors. Surprisingly, more counselors signed up for assistance than could be served. Their ready acceptance of the plan communicated important information. The counselors needed specialized help for their children and they weren't threatened to receive it. Since the counselors accepted play therapy as a modality for that help, play therapy would more likely be accepted with enthusiasm from the faculty.

## TIPS FOR IMPLEMENTING A PLAY THERAPY PROGRAM

1. Meet the counseling coordinator, present the rationale for play therapy and how a play therapy program works. Describe how play therapy is done, what can be accomplished, and the possible areas in school buildings that might be utilized to conduct the play therapy sessions. Ask for support in presenting the program to the principal and teachers in each school.
2. Present the program to the principal. Set up a time for a teacher in-service meeting to explain the play therapy program and describe children who should be referred.
3. Conduct in-service meeting with teachers.

4. Followup in-service meeting with written information.
5. Meet with teachers as quickly as possible after referrals are made.
6. Stay in contact with teachers. Visit classes, the lunchroom, and the playground.
7. Place responsibility on parents to call for a conference to discuss child's progress.

## TIPS FOR TEACHER IN-SERVICE MEETING

1. Define play therapy, give objectives, discuss what children learn in play therapy (see Landreth, 1991, p. 81).
2. Present general criteria for referral for play therapy: children who are withdrawn, socially isolated, physically or sexually abused, aggressive or acting out, experiencing divorce, lacking self-control, selective mute, traumatized, highly anxious or restricted, chronically ill, etc.
3. Describe the process of referral and forms needed (e.g., a teacher contacts a play therapist about a child of concern or writes a note giving a time for a conference to discuss concerns about a child. The child's class schedule is discussed. Decision is made as to best day and time to come to play therapy. Discuss process of informing parents. Either the teacher will talk with parents, without going into great detail, about her desire to refer the child, or the play therapist can initiate parent contact. Either way, the play therapist follows up by talking with the parents in detail about the play therapy process and obtaining written parent permission (if required by the school system)).
4. Be sure to cover the following: Never tell the child that he/she will be able to do "anything" he/she wants with the toys. Never send a child to play therapy as punishment for a behavior. Remind teachers that the specific things that the child says and does in the play time are confidential between the child and the play therapist. Teachers will receive general information about the child and suggested ways they can help the child (e.g., Robert seems to need a lot of encouragement. David seems to have a poor self-concept.) Suggest play therapy books to read such as *Dibs* by Virginia Axline. Provide a schedule of times you will be in their school. Inform teachers that a form will be sent to the parents with your telephone number and times for conferences to discuss the play therapy process.

## ORGANIZATION OF THE DETAILS

A placement involving three days and three elementary schools was determined to be feasible. The amount of time spent in each school was determined by need. It was agreed that the sessions would take place for one school semester.

Identification of the students most in need in each school was determined through meetings with the school counselors, teachers, and their principals. Teachers were consulted prior to the beginning of the sessions in an attempt to enlist their help as an important part of the team of professionals assembled on behalf of the children in need. In many cases, the classroom teacher had been the primary source of identification to the other school personnel, and the teacher was well aware of the child's need for therapeutic intervention. The teachers were consulted concerning the best times for the sessions and were given the details as to when the children would be absent from their classes to attend play therapy sessions.

Permission slips had to be signed by the children's parents before any therapeutic intervention could begin in some schools. This permission slip and a brochure designed to answer parents' questions about play therapy were sent to the students' homes.

In two of the schools, permission slips were sent only after the school counselor called parents and explained in detail what was being offered to their children. One hundred percent of these parents returned signed permission slips. In the other school where the needs were much more diverse and the numbers of students needing help were much greater, the counselor decided to send permission slips to thirty parents without initial introduction. Although this was not a preferred method because the parents were presented with very little personalized information, 95% of the parents receiving permission slips returned them signed. This response points to a tremendous acceptability rate of play therapy on the part of parents.

## A PLACE FOR THE PLAY SESSIONS

In two of the schools, the counselors shared their office with the play therapist on days the counselors were scheduled to be in the classrooms. In the third school, permission was given to conduct play therapy sessions in a storage/work room. This setting required a simple shifting of stored materials to create a small area of floor space for the play sessions. All three settings assured privacy to the greatest extent possible in a school setting.

A preliminary meeting with school personnel to inform them of the needs of the therapist and children being served, and the location where the play therapy sessions would be held helped to avoid interruptions. A "Play Session in Progress" sign hung on the door signaled the room was occupied. Children in schools adapt remarkably to their surroundings, and do not seem to be disturbed when an occasional misplaced person happens to knock on the door or proceed inside unannounced.

## TOYS: WHAT TO INCLUDE
## AND HOW TO TRANSPORT THEM

Toys recommended by Landreth (1991) for a Tote Bag Playroom were selected as well as a few additional items that seemed to elicit responses in unique ways. The equipment included:

Play-doh (1 can)
plastic place mat to play with play-doh
crayons (several, not necessarily new)
water colors
markers
paper (newsprint and/or construction)
blunt scissors
nursing bottle (small, plastic)
pacifier
rubber knife
dart gun
family of small, bendable dolls: White, Black, & Hispanic mother, father, sister, brother, and baby
animal family with at least three siblings and a mother/father representation
plastic dishes
toy soldiers
small plastic car
Lone Ranger type mask
tinkertoys (Take design suggestions out of the box to allow the child freedom to make creations of their own.)
large laminated floor plan of house, which folds easily
dollhouse furniture (kitchen, bedroom, and bathroom)
doctor kit
play money
telephone
piece of rope 3 to 5-ft.
inflatable punching bag
ring toss game
box of Band-Aids (have only 3 or 4 in kit at a time)
tape (transparent and masking)
snake
alligator
handcuffs
pipe Cleaners
a container for water (small pitcher type with lid, used for paints)
hand puppets (variety including animals and people)
Rubbermaid tub with lid, filled with rice to substitute for sand

Clackers (A 3 ft. plastic dowel with animal head at the end. Mouth can open and shut when operated by child. These can be purchased at aquariums, amusement parks, etc. This was the one item, which elicited the greatest number of responses from every age child.)

Unfortunately, the bag soon became a large toy box, which could no longer be carried. A large, colorful, plastic Rubbermaid trunk was purchased and a luggage carrier provided the portability needed.

The way the toys were arranged for sessions depended on the available space in the room. From the smallest to the most spacious rooms, the children were able to make full use of the toys and had the freedom to play with them at will due to the selected nature of the contents of the trunk. The trunk was always open and inviting to the children as they entered the room. Many times some of the toys were displayed on the floor surrounding the trunk.

## ORGANIZING THE PLAY THERAPY PROGRAM

It was decided that the play therapist would see each child for one thirty-minute session each week. In the case of a trauma or crisis situation the therapist could easily modify that schedule to see the child twice in one day, usually a morning and an afternoon session. Having the child and the therapist in the same location for the entire school day allowed this possibility and would not have been as easily accomplished in a private office setting.

The play therapist went to the child's classroom at the allotted time and walked the child to the designated play session area. After the session the play therapist walked the child back to the classroom to ensure a safe and timely return to school activities. Sessions were scheduled every forty-five minutes, which allowed the play therapist fifteen minutes to return the child to class, prepare the play area, and write notes before the next session.

Most of the children were seen in individual play therapy sessions. Occasionally, group play therapy sessions were conducted. The maximum number of children in a group consisted of three students due to the space limitations of the session areas. Groups consisted of siblings, or children with similar therapeutic issues. The need to be exposed to successful relationship dynamics was the driving force in determining group construction. Group play therapy was found to be a very helpful intervention with children after they had been in individual play therapy sessions and were ready to use their new relationship skills in a safe and monitored environment.

## THE CHILDREN

During the four months in the schools, the play therapist carried a caseload of thirty children. Their presenting problems ranged from the most severe—suicidal tendencies, parental abuse, sexual abuse, divorce, and coping with the murder of a district classmate—to situations that needed preventative therapy—birth of siblings, developmental delays, death of grandparents, stress of relocation, and mild sleep disorders.

## THE PARENTS

The school counselors communicated with the parents of the children, and the play therapist was also available to meet personally with the parents or to talk with them on the phone. The parents were extremely cooperative, non-threatened, and willing to listen and learn about their children. They respected their children's rights to confidentiality and were gratified to learn about themes of behavior and ways to better address those needs. As an example, the play therapist who helps parents understand the dynamics of a child's emotional needs can help them to become more accepting of their children. An important and helpful intervention can take place when a parent and a play therapist work together to discuss general behaviors observed in the playroom and in the child's environment. The specifics of a child's play is not revealed.

## THE TEACHERS

Without exception, the children's teachers displayed a tremendous sensitivity to the needs of the troubled children with whom they worked. However, in many cases the teachers had reached the limit of their ability to effect change with these children. They were frustrated and felt defeated. Knowing they had a play therapist working with their students brought comfort and relief. The play therapist's ability to present themes of behavior to the teachers in an effort to help them better understand the dynamics of the children's situations, helped tremendously. A typical theme of behavior displayed in the playroom that can relate to the classroom is the need for organization. Children who neatly line up toys, baby dolls, play house food etc., display a need for order. In the classroom this can translate to providing that student with an organized space to do their work. Most importantly, as a result of feedback from the play therapist, the teachers were able to see the children in a different, more understanding way and thus, a more nurturing environment was available to the child at school.

The play therapist tried to be very sensitive in scheduling children's play sessions to avoid the disruption of crucial classroom activities. The teachers were willing to talk with the play therapist to determine which activities could more easily be missed, such as physical education, recess, story time, art, etc. Since the play sessions were generally held one time each week, missing an activity did not jeopardize the child's educational experience. Most teachers were willing to send their children to a play therapy session at any time, and were willing to help the children make up work missed in an effort to assure the student received the therapeutic help needed.

# WHAT WAS LEARNED

Due to the specialized training of the play therapist, the therapist was recognized and accepted as a professional in the school building. However, it was important to understand that all the rules and courtesies expected of parents, teachers, and other professionals in the building also applied to the play therapist. Signing in and out of the building, alerting the office of any changes in schedule, and following general safety rules (dismissal, fire drills, etc.,) had to be adhered to by the play therapist. Becoming familiar with these policies helped to make a more successful and welcoming experience in the schools for the therapist.

The most frustrating situations experienced by the play therapist were the results of the actual time it took to get the program started before sessions could begin (due to the all important ground work that was laid) and the eventual termination of the sessions (due to the school semester coming to an end). Although the children were prepared for their therapy sessions to end, several children were not finished with their work. This dilemma was echoed in the statement of a third grade girl, "But, who will really listen to me when you are gone?"

As a result of contact with parents, regular and specialized teachers, the school nurse, and in many cases, siblings, the play therapist was more adequately prepared to assess the nature of the children's presenting problems and could be more accurate in writing diagnostic notes and determining goals of behavior.

Understanding the shy and submissive behavior exhibited by a first grade boy and his anxious third grade sister became more clear as the play therapist talked with the school nurse, school counselor, and mother about the dynamics in the children's home. The school nurse confirmed that the mother and father lived together in what appeared to be a physically safe environment for the children and no unusual illnesses had been noted. The school counselor explained the children were from bi-racial parents and had extended family cultural issues with which to cope. The mother readily came in for a conference with the play therapist and added that the father who lived in the home was often absent due to alcoholism. The ability to readily access this much information in such a short time can be very beneficial to the therapy process.

One of the many advantages to working with the children in their school environment over the traditional therapist office somewhere in town was the ability to work with the children on their time schedule. Most play therapy sessions in an office setting during the school year must begin after school hours. This means that by the time the children arrive to an office they have already spent an entire day working at school and are often tired. Also, this time slot competes with all of their other after school activities, including homework. And, there are only so many time slots available in the afternoons after school. An active full-time therapy practice cannot always accommodate all the children needing to be served in the after school hours.

Limit setting in the schools can and should be accomplished as it is in any other therapeutic setting. Safety is always a priority. Paints and sand have to be used according to the actual setting that is made available for the sessions. It may be necessary to use water colors instead of tempera paints and rice in place of sand for easy cleanup. A dust buster is helpful at the end of the day for quick clean ups.

Children have an incredible ability to know when they have worked through a problem situation. Basically, when they are no longer troubled by the problem that brought them to counseling, they again become preoccupied with the business of childhood. In the schools, when children reach these plateaus, it is easy to send them back to class while keeping close watch over their progress. True to the developmental nature of counseling, if problems present again, the children can easily be called back into play therapy.

## HOW THE CHILDREN CHANGED

The experiences for the children were as diverse as their presenting problems. Reports from school personnel and families indicated each child derived benefits from the play therapy relationship.

- A first grader overcame her fears of bedtime and coming to school by drawing pictures of her home, bedroom, and school room. In describing these pictures to the therapist and having the therapist reflect back to her the positive messages described she became more familiar with her new school environment and realized that she had nothing to fear about going to school.
- A second grader walked in, sat down, and discussed the details surrounding his need to report his dad for an abusive situation. He did not engage in any play behaviors even though the toys were clearly available to him. After four play therapy sessions in which the child sat at the table talking with the play therapist, the child's immediate needs had been satisfied and his concerns shifted to returning to the classroom.
- A third grader unburdened himself of the perceived horrible knowledge that his mom had been involved in an affair and what that meant to his family. He was able to play through this trauma with the use of puppetry and thus gained a greater and less fearful understanding of the dynamics in his family.
- A first grade boy and his third grade sister began to understand the dynamics of living in a bi-racial home where one parent was alcoholic. The boy enjoyed playing self-esteem building games, which were tailored to his age group. The sister engaged in various themes and types of play relating to her role in the family as the oldest and most responsible sibling. For her, the play sessions were a release from that perceived burden.
- A third grade girl with signs of sexual identity confusion experienced

complete acceptance for who she was and thus began to accept herself. She played catch with the therapist as aggressively as the setting would allow and to her heart's content. She found acceptance within the playroom that she was seeking elsewhere but could not attain.

Fortunately, the play therapist was able to work with most of the children for at least twelve to fifteen weeks. Additionally, the play therapist stayed at one school as a volunteer for the next semester. This enabled work to continue with several children for an entire school year. It was with one of these children that the most change was experienced.

Chad, a seven-year-old, second grader presented with few social skills, was prone to getting into fights, and had few friends. His mother was at home full time and was very involved with and concerned for Chad's social, academic, and emotional development.

Chad entered his first play therapy session ready to play and explore. He immediately became immersed in play and offered few verbalizations. The classic good versus evil theme was apparent from the first session. Chad took on the role of the monster (shark) trapping the children (baby seals) and manipulating them at will. He would lock them up and leave them in the dollhouse when he returned to class. Chad was also attempting to manipulate his own friendships in much the same way. His bossy behaviors with other children caused him to have few, if any friendships.

By the third session, Chad was able to verbalize that the shark "really just wants someone to play with." This child was longing for companionship, and continued to ask for them in inappropriate ways. Through his play, he was beginning to at least be aware of the ineffectiveness of the "shark's" ways.

During the sixth session, Chad was still playing out a good versus evil theme. He branched out, however, into the play area and began to incorporate the dollhouse into his play. At the end of this session, the three seals and their mother were left in the play house safe from all harm with no monsters in sight.

During the seventh session, Chad added an element of play that continued to be a part of his play for the next month. An elaborate fort was constructed that served to enhance his good versus evil theme. Soldiers (people) were included in his play for the first time. However, by the end of the battle that ensued, the only survivors were the seals.

The weekly repetitious and tedious building of the fort and the systematic destruction of the soldiers resulted in the play therapist feeling frustrated with her inability to help Chad move on, because she thought he was "stuck." Consultation with a professor who taught play therapy resulted in the play therapist realizing she was the one who was "stuck." Children will reveal their needs through their play. It is the job of the play therapist to read and understand what the children are communicating.

Chad not only was communicating his need to be understood through his play with the play therapist, he was screaming his need all over the school. He had lapsed into what were described as primal, infantile screams during his P.E.

class. The play therapist realized that this behavior made sense. Chad was screaming his needs every Tuesday in play therapy and he hadn't been understood. He
had also begun generalizing his play behavior outside the playroom by building
elaborate forts with desks in the classroom.

During the tenth session, the play therapist became more active in reflecting by naming and identifying the struggles Chad was acting out in his play.
Accurately naming the fear Chad was experiencing when the soldiers threatened the seals elicited relief from him. His smiles of recognition when a struggle
was correctly identified helped the play therapist know she was on the right
track. Finally, after adequately reflecting the content of Chad's play, the bad guy
(whom it was suspected was Chad) stayed behind to protect the children. This
signaled the first survivor of the play scenes other than the seals. Three other
bad guys then approached the house where the seals where hiding. When the
children answered the door, they gave the bad guy directions (wipe your feet,
etc.) and invited him in. The former bad guy (Chad) had helped the seals set up
rules to protect themselves. Chad finally allowed himself, in the safety of the
playroom, to be a part of what he was desperately striving for in his relationships with other children in his school setting. His need to be acknowledged,
needed, and included by his classmates was symbolically acted out by being
accepted by the seals in the play setting.

This session was the beginning of a tremendous change for Chad. Although
he experienced a few minor setbacks in the classroom, the fortress play diminished and became instead a preserve for animals that he directed. By the twelfth
session, the animals were learning to protect each other and they were beginning to develop skills to work out their conflicts. These skills were being taught
by the seals. Chad stated, "When they don't work together well, they just haven't
picked up the other's scent yet." He was aware he still had much to learn about
how to be a friend and was actively working on this concept.

When the play therapist went to the classroom to get Chad for his thirteenth session, she noticed Chad's face was red from an accident in P.E. One
child was comforting him and the offending child was aiding and apologizing to
Chad. During this session Chad engaged in play with the slinky, ping pong balls
and balloons for the first time. On the way back to class, the play therapist
remarked to Chad how she had noticed him with at least three friends today,
similar to the seals in the playroom. He replied, "Yea, I was thinking about that
in the play room," and added, "When I had the seals in a blimp (balloon) today,
maybe they were me and Ryan and Kevin."

From this point on, any attempts Chad made at building preserves, etc.,
soon gave way to spontaneous play. The structures became very disorganized.
He chose instead to blow up balloons with his "goodness" inside them. In the
seventeenth session, Chad was given the choice to include another child in his
play, which he readily accepted. He asked if he could include another child
from his class who "also seemed to have problems." He stated, "This is a place
where you can go to get away from all that goes on out there," and "I think my
friend needs your help."

# REFERENCES

Axline, V. (1947) *Play therapy*. Boston: Houghton-Mifflin.

Bishop, J. (1971). Play therapy in the schools. *Alberta Counselor, 2,* 41–44.

Landreth, G. (1977). Play therapy is for public schools. *Texas Personnel and Guidance Journal,* 5(1), 61–63.

Landreth, G. (1983). Play therapy in elementary school settings. In C. Schaefer & K. O'Connor (Eds.), *Handbook of play therapy* (pp. 200–212). New York: John Wiley & Sons.

Landreth, G. (1987). Play therapy: Facilitative use of child's play in elementary school counseling. Counseling with expressive arts [Special issue] . *Elementary School Guidance and Counseling, 21*(4), 253–261.

Landreth, G. (1991). *Play therapy: The art of the relationship*. Muncie, IN: Accelerated development, Inc.

Landreth, G. (1993). Child-centered play therapy. *Elementary School Guidance and Counseling, 28,* 17–29.

Ross, J. (1972). Play therapy in the school. *Guidlines, 9,* 17–23.

# Index